Foundations, Principles, and Techniques of Online Teaching

Foundations, Principles, and Techniques of Online Teaching

EDITORS

Tricia M. Mikolon
University of the Cumberlands, Kentucky

Tammy Hatfield
University of the Cumberlands, Kentucky

SAN DIEGO

Bassim Hamadeh, CEO and Publisher
Amy Smith, Senior Project Editor
Christian Berk, Production Editor
Emely Villavicencio, Senior Graphic Designer
Stephanie Kohl, Licensing Coordinator
Natalie Piccotti, Director of Marketing
Kassie Graves, Vice President of Editorial
Jamie Giganti, Director of Academic Publishing

Copyright © 2022 by Cognella, Inc. All rights reserved. No part of this publication may be reprinted, reproduced, transmitted, or utilized in any form or by any electronic, mechanical, or other means, now known or hereafter invented, including photocopying, microfilming, and recording, or in any information retrieval system without the written permission of Cognella, Inc. For inquiries regarding permissions, translations, foreign rights, audio rights, and any other forms of reproduction, please contact the Cognella Licensing Department at rights@cognella.com.

Trademark Notice: Product or corporate names may be trademarks or registered trademarks and are used only for identification and explanation without intent to infringe.

Cover Images:
Copyright © 2019 iStockphoto LP/DrAfter123.
Copyright © 2020 iStockphoto LP/FANDSrabutan.
Copyright © 2020 iStockphoto LP/sorbetto.

Printed in the United States of America.

BRIEF CONTENTS

Preface   xvii
Acknowledgments   xxiii

PART I   Foundational Considerations   1

CHAPTER 1   Preparing to Teach Online   3

CHAPTER 2   Online Pedagogy   19

CHAPTER 3   Diversity and Inclusion in the Online Classroom   47

CHAPTER 4   Fostering Student Success Online   61

PART II   Instructional Design   81

CHAPTER 5   Online Course Design   83

CHAPTER 6   Accessibility in the Online Classroom for Student Success   95

CHAPTER 7   Developing an Online Syllabus   109

PART III   Online Teaching from Primary to Post-Secondary   153

CHAPTER 8   Online Teaching and Learning in Primary Education   155

CHAPTER 9   Online Teaching and Learning in Secondary Education   167

CHAPTER 10   Online Teaching and Learning in Post-Secondary Education   181

PART IV   Legal, Ethical, and Other Administrative Considerations   197

CHAPTER 11   Legal and Ethical Issues in Online Education   199

CHAPTER 12   Administration of Online Teaching   215

Glossary   227
Index   237
About the Editors   245
About the Contributors   247

DETAILED CONTENTS

Preface   xvii
Tammy Hatfield, PsyD, and Tricia Mikolon, PhD, CRC, LPC, BC-TMH

Acknowledgments   xxiii

PART I   Foundational Considerations   1

CHAPTER ONE
Preparing to Teach Online   3

Kristin Page, PhD, LMHC, NCC
Tera Rumbaugh Crawford, MEd, LPCA, NCC

Why Online Education?   3
History of Distance Learning   4
Questions to Ask Before Getting Started   4
Considerations   5
   Work Life   5
   Professional Fulfillment   6
   Virtual Classroom   7
   Relationships   9
   The Cost of Teaching Online   10
Setting Up the Home Office and Virtual Classroom   10
   Locating the Right Place   11
   Intangible Factors for the Home Office—Virtual Classroom and Community   11
Mastering Technology for Online Education   11
Preparation for Online Education   12
Developing and Using Support From a Distance   12
Balancing Work and Personal Time in the Remote Environment   13
Mental Health and Wellness in the Remote Environment   13
Chapter Summary   15
Online Resources   15
References   16

CHAPTER TWO

Online Pedagogy   19

Tammy Hatfield, PsyD

Portia Allie-Turco, LMHC, NCC

Sarah E. Johansson, MEd, NCC

Melissa Brennan, MA, LPC

Defining Pedagogy   19
Traditional Pedagogical Frameworks   20
    Traditional Pedagogy   20
    Andragogy   20
Online Pedagogical Frameworks   21
    Heutagogy   21
    E-Pedagogy   22
Toward Inclusive Pedagogical Frameworks   23
    Decolonialization as an Aim of Inclusive Pedagogy   24
    Critical Pedagogy   25
    Intersectional, Black Feminist, and Feminist Pedagogy   28
    Liberatory Pedagogy   29
    Culturally Responsive Pedagogy   30
    Culturally Sustaining Pedagogy   31
Trauma-Informed Pedagogy   32
    Trauma's Impact on The Brain   32
    Trauma-Informed Pedagogy in Practice   33
    Educator Self-Care   35
Common Factors: Effective Teaching Strategies Across Pedagogies   35
    Building Community   36
    Connecting Lived Experience and Classroom Content   37
    Centering Students and Co-Creating Knowledge   38
    Self-Involvement of the Educator   38
Chapter Summary   39
Online Resources   39
References   41

CHAPTER THREE

Diversity and Inclusion in the Online Classroom   47

Alcia A. Freeman PhD, LPC, NCC

Tiffany Darby PhD, LPCC-S (OH), PSC (OH), LPC (PA), LPCC-S (KY)

Background   47
    Diversity, Equity, and Inclusion in Online Learning   48

Multicultural   49
   Identifying Multicultural Concerns   49
Critical Cross-Cultural Education   53
Other Considerations   55
The Importance of Intersectionality   55
   Universal Design for Online Learning   56
Chapter Summary   56
Online Resources   57
References   57

CHAPTER FOUR

Fostering Student Success Online   61

Tricia M. Mikolon, PhD, CRC, LPC, BC-TMH
Debra Perez, MA, LPCC, SCPG
Diedre Leigh Wade, LPCC-S, LPCC-S

Classroom Management   62
   Online Classroom Management in Primary School   63
   Online Classroom Management in Secondary School   64
   Online Classroom Management in Postsecondary Education   64
Supporting Success Through Structure   64
   Rules and Policies   65
   Communicating Expectations   65
   Holding Students Accountable   65
   Why Structure Is Important   66
   Providing Structure Online   66
Communication in and out of Class   67
   Communication in Primary School   68
   Communication in Secondary School   68
   Communication in Postsecondary Education   68
Building a Sense of Connectedness and Community   69
   Building Community Online   70
   Building a Sense of Connectedness and Community in Primary School   71
   Building a Sense of Connectedness and Community in Secondary School   71
   Building a Sense of Connectedness and Community in Postsecondary Education   72
Assessment   73
   Why Assessment Is Important   73
   Completing Assessment Online   74
Remediation   75
   Remediation in Primary School   76
   Remediation in Secondary School   76
   Remediation in Postsecondary Education   77

Chapter Summary 78
Online Resources 78
References 78

PART II Instructional Design 81

CHAPTER FIVE

Online Course Design 83

Tara Koger, MA

Historical Overview 84
    Making Science of Understanding Online Learning 84
    Development of the Online Learning Environment 85
Why Use Your School's System? 86
    Learning to Use the LMS 86
Online Learning Environments vs. Storage Closets 87
    Good and Bad Practices 88
    Mindfully Adding Course Content 90
    The Case Against Documents 90
Chapter Summary 92
Online Resources 92
References 93

CHAPTER SIX

Accessibility in the Online Classroom for Student Success 95

Megan Fogel, MLT

Unique Challenges 95
    Vision Differences 96
    Hearing Differences 96
    Mobility Differences 96
    Cognitive Differences 96
    Other Differences 97
Proactive Approach 97
    Higher Ed Context 97
    K–12 Context 98
Accessibility and Universal Design for Learning 98
    Multiple Means of Representation 99
    Multiple Means of Expression 99
    Multiple Means of Engagement 100
    Assistive Technology 100

Accessibility Best Practices   101
    Course Pages   102
    Documents   102
    Websites   103
    Hyperlinks   104
    Alt Text   104
    Captions   105
    Recap   105
    Getting Started   106
  Chapter Summary   106
  Online Resources   107
  References   107

CHAPTER SEVEN

Developing an Online Syllabus   109

Tricia M. Mikolon, PhD, CRC, LPC, BC-TMH

Brooke Murphy, MS, LPC, NCC, CCTP

  Overview of Syllabi Use and Importance   110
    Importance to Instructor   110
    Importance to Student   111
    Fundamental Components of the Syllabus   111
    Multicultural/Ethical and Social Justice Considerations Regarding Syllabi   117
  Example of Rubrics   118
  Syllabus Outline   123
  Example Syllabus   124
  Chapter Summary   149
  Online Resources   149
  References   150
    Credits   151

PART III   Online Teaching from Primary to Post-Secondary   153

CHAPTER EIGHT

Online Teaching and Learning in Primary Education   155

Jason Creekmore, EdD

  History of Online Learning in Primary Education   156
  Assisting Students with Technology   157
    Clear Learning Targets   157

Tutorials and Instructional Videos   157
   Managing Time   157
   Managing Materials   158
   The Virtual Classroom Environment   158
Student Engagement   158
   Creating a Virtual Classroom   159
   Scavenger Hunts   159
   Learning Stations via Breakout Rooms   159
   Guided Notes   159
Communication   160
   Make Videos Personable   160
   Create Recordings   160
   Limit the Length of Recordings   160
Assessment   161
   Quizzes   161
   Essays and Open-Ended Responses   161
   Drag and Drop   162
   Polling   162
Remediation   162
   Direct Instruction   162
   Chunking Work   163
   Learning Styles   163
   Self-Assessment   163
Chapter Summary   164
Online Resources   164
References   165

CHAPTER NINE

Online Teaching and Learning in Secondary Education   167

Shannon Deaton, EdD

Context of Technology and Online Learning   167
Assisting Students with Technology   168
   Identification   168
   Training   169
Student Engagement   169
   Energy Shifts   169
   Student Response Groups   170
   Random Selection   171

2-Minute Response   173
  Flipped Classroom   174
Communication   174
  Visuals   175
  Learner Feedback   175
  Screensharing Best Practices   176
Assessment   176
  Polling   176
Differentiation and Extension   177
Chapter Summary   179
Online Resources   179
References   180
  Credits   180

CHAPTER TEN

Online Teaching and Learning in Post-Secondary Education   181

Adrienne Sarise Baggs, PhD

Laura N. Moore, MEd, NBCC, LPC

Evolution of Distance Education and Online Learning   181
  Correspondence Learning Utilizing the Postal Service   182
  Audio and Visual Media Learning Utilizing the Radio and Television   182
  Online Learning Through Use of the Internet   183
  Definitions   184
Relationship, Connection, and Communication in Online Learning   185
  Relationship and Connection   185
  Communication in Online Learning   186
  Online Engagement Framework   187
Creating the Online Classroom   189
  Course Policies and Procedures   190
  Weekly Announcement Hub   190
  Weekly Module Folders   190
  Informal Chatroom   191
  University/College Resources   191
Mastering Technology in Online Learning in Higher Education   192
Chapter Summary   193
Online Resources   193
References   193
  Credits   195

PART IV Legal, Ethical, and Other Administrative Considerations — 197

CHAPTER ELEVEN

Legal and Ethical Issues in Online Education — 199

Gary L. Patton, PhD

Principles of Ethics   200
   Autonomy   200
   Beneficence   200
   Nonmaleficence   200
   Justice   200
   Fidelity   200
Moral Distress   201
Ethical Decision-Making Model   201
   Federal Regulations   202
   Family Educational Rights and Privacy Act (FERPA)   202
   Health Care Portability and Accountability Act (HIPAA)   202
   Health Information Technology for Economic and Clinical Health Act (HITECH)   203
   Clery Act   203
   Title IX   203
   Privileged Communication   203
   Mandated Reporting/Duty to Warn   204
   Preventing Violations of HIPAA/HITECH   205
Gatekeeping   206
   Decision-Making Capacity   207
Syllabus   209
Vicarious Liability   209
Boundaries in Online Education   210
Social Media   212
National Council for State Authorization Reciprocity Agreements (NC-SARA)   212
Chapter Summary   213
Online Resources   213
References   213

CHAPTER TWELVE
Administration of Online Teaching 215

Matthew Lyons, PhD
Marina Bunch, MA, LMHC

Leadership Matters   216
    Transformational Leadership   217
    Authentic Leadership   217
Building the Team—Faculty and Staff   218
    Recruiting and Retention   218
    Faculty and Staff Training and Engagement   219
    Faculty and Staff Connection   219
    Evaluation   220
Student Engagement and Support Services   221
    Support Services   222
Legal and Ethical Considerations   222
    Information Security   222
    Student Safety and Crisis Management   223
Special Consideration for Clinical Programs   223
Chapter Summary   224
Online Resources   224
References   225

Glossary   227
Index   237
About the Editors   245
About the Contributors   247

PREFACE

Tammy Hatfield, PsyD, and Tricia Mikolon, PhD, CRC, LPC, BC-TMH

Introduction

With rapidly evolving advances in technology and the growth of online platforms for education, the way in which instructors work has shifted. Changes in the format of education have brought about changes in the skills necessary for instructors, administrators, and students (Roddy et al., 2017). Online education, with its increased flexibility and adaptability, has challenged the conventional means of delivering educational materials as well as an instructor's capability to connect with a diverse group of students in their classrooms (Bailey et al., 2014; Bates, 2005; Brown, 1997, 2011; Johnson, 2015; Roddy et al., 2017). These advantages, coupled with current environmental concerns, have increased the number of students exploring online education as a safe and practical option by which they may meet their education goals and needs. While institutions of higher education have been developing and implementing online, blended, and hybrid course work for some time, the global impact of the COVID-19 pandemic resulted in rapid shifts to online instruction and education from primary to postsecondary levels and beyond.

Our current reality in 2021 has highlighted the need for educators, across grade levels and institutions, to be trained in online teaching. Online teachers for grades K–12 must have the skills to create an effective learning environment and implement creative and productive learning strategies to assist students in managing technology while simultaneously ensuring engagement and active participation in classes and exercises (Shattuck & Bruch, 2018). The authors stress the responsibilities of online teachers encompass the need for clear expectations of students as well as prompt, consistent feedback to students but additionally the responsibility to role model "legal, ethical, and safe behaviors related to technology use" (p. 4). Awareness of diversity in the classroom and competency in online assessments equal to that of the traditional classroom must be considerations of all teachers while guiding class and assisting students with remediation. Finally, to ensure student success, online teachers need to provide professional interaction with parents, community members and colleagues (Shattuck & Bruch, 2018).

In the context of higher education, Baldwin and Ching (2019) summarize standards for providing effective online instruction to include providing clear course objectives and related polices to students while preparing an easily navigated platform that allows for both ease of communication throughout the course but also the enhancement of the learning process. Effective online instructors couple their basic teaching skills with clear communication of course expectations and assignments through the use of rubrics outlining the grading procedure for transparency aligned with course objectives, an understanding of the applicable technology, open communication with students and consistent constructive feedback (Baldwin & Ching, 2019; Roddy et al., 2017). Instructors also need to ensure students are aware of support available to them and accommodations for inclusion by providing them with links to those services (Baldwin & Ching, 2019). Researchers found that students place great value on the quality of instruction and clarity of course expectations and requirements when feeling satisfied with their learning experience regardless of the platform it is presented on (Bailey et al., 2014).

Goals for the Text

The impact of COVID-19 resulted in rapid and significant shifts to online education and subsequently highlighted the need for training and development in online teaching at all levels of education, from primary school through doctoral training. During the 2019–2020 school year, teachers, professors, administrators, and students were forced to hurriedly develop and transition to the online classroom while many had no training or experience providing online instruction, and preferred face-to-face instruction.

Regarding training, traditional teaching preparatory and graduate programs preparing future professors typically focus on traditional methods of instruction with little attention toward preparing competent online instructors. Having taught in both traditional and online formats as professors, we understand and recognize that transitioning from traditional to online teaching requires preparation, mindset shifts, pedagogical shifts, and shifts in instructional approaches.

With traditional training having a lack of focus in the online arena and with limited resources available to assist educators in developing the knowledge base and skills necessary for successfully making the transition to online instruction, we believe there is a need for a textbook that may be used in training programs that are preparing instructors at all levels of education and as a resource for instructor self-development. Our goal is to provide a resource that prepares educators to teach online through foundational knowledge and practical skill development resources. We believe that our *Foundations, Principles, and Techniques of Online Instruction* textbook will serve as a timely response to the need for this type of resource to prepare our future teachers and to support our current instructors and educators who are pursuing excellence in online teaching.

Conceptualizing Online Teaching

A historical perspective of online teaching is limited in the research. The coupling of education and technology has brought about dramatic increases in the number of students from primary school through higher education who attend classes in the online format (Allen & Seaman, 2017; Borup & Evmenova, 2019; Gemin & Pape, 2017). COVID-19 expedited this transition exponentially, impacting students and teachers on a global level. Suddenly, teachers were mandated to teach on a format that many had little training or experience in.

Historically, teachers, having learned in the face-to-face classroom, often approach teaching in the same manner, although this does not necessarily transition well to online learning (Banas & Velez-Solic, 2013; Cox & Prestridge, 2020; Ellis & Hafner, 2003; Schmidt et al., 2016). As teachers transition from the traditional to the online classroom, they challenge their own perceptions of teaching in this format and need to acquire modifications to their instructional design to ensure success of their students (Baran, 2011; Cox & Prestridge, 2020; Kilgour et al., 2019; Rodrigues et al., 2019). Additionally, they are left to manage the range of emotions they may experience related to their transition to online teaching and the loss they may feel regarding the easily accessible sense of community often found in traditional classrooms and settings (Hatfield et al., 2020). Perry and Steck (2019) explored the instructional factors of

(a) faculty enthusiasm for ODL teaching; (b) instructor-student interaction; (c) promoting student collaboration; (d) requiring active student participation; (e) use of a variety of instructional techniques; (f) timely instructor communication and feedback; and (g) providing clear criteria for assessment of student performance (p. 97)

and found that as instructors teach online, they prioritize the promotion of both active learning and student engagement and become more comfortable with how they incorporate their teaching style into the online format. This study highlights the need for faculty to be diligent in their delivery of quality instruction, thereby increasing the likelihood that students will take an active role in their education. It also brings awareness to the notion that online teaching style may develop as a result of trial-and-error as instructors may lack training in online pedagogy or translating their on-ground pedagogies to the online environment.

Specific training and education in online instruction is necessary, but unfortunately to date has been lacking, often defaulting to teachers learning from their online instructors, not all of whom have been trained specifically in this format (Borup & Evmenova, 2019; Cox & Prestridge, 2020; Meyer & Murrell, 2014; Norton & Hathaway, 2015). This may lead to teachers using skills that were modeled by their instructors but not necessarily those that are evidence based to provide the best results for students (Borup & Evmenova, 2019; Meyer & Murrell, 2014; Norton & Hathaway, 2015). The prior lack of education for teachers to instruct online has helped spur the writing of this book. As current events mandate more and more teachers to function in the online format, we wanted to provide a resource supporting their transition and assisting in ensuring student success at all levels of education.

Striving for Inclusivity in Online Teaching

As editors of this textbook, we are supportive of inclusive instructional approaches that are culturally responsive, culturally sustaining, antiracist, and liberatory. We want to provide information about educational best practices that recognize and highly value the cultural background, personal identities, and various lived experiences of students. We understand that because of the positions in which each student is socially located, they have diverse experiences when entering the classroom. We recognize that historical educational practices have silenced many students and that we must intentionally advocate for inclusivity in training efforts and the practice of online teaching. Without intentional focus on inclusion of perspectives and ways of being across cultures, we realize that educational practices may be harmful to historically marginalized and oppressed groups.

In support of this effort, we have requested that chapter authors include evidence-based multicultural and socially just perspectives into their work. In addition to weaving diverse perspectives within each chapter, we included a chapter that specifically focuses on antiracist educational strategies in the online environment. It is our hope that this textbook will serve as a resource that honors and draws attention to the importance of the lived experience of individuals in the classroom and beyond.

Organization of the Textbook

Part I: Foundational Considerations

This section is designed to provide foundational guidance to current online instructors and to those who are considering teaching online. In this part, readers will find a series of chapters that help them understand and prepare for the experience of being an online instructor. The first chapter in this part will outline research based [experiences] and personal experiences of online instructors and will overview topics such as how one decides to pursue or accept an online teaching position, the challenges and rewards online instructors face, and practical considerations such as setting up your home office and maintaining connection with others. Other chapters will focus on pedagogical best practices for the online setting; diversity, inclusion, and antiracist practice in the online setting; and practical strategies for fostering student success in the online setting. Additionally, this segment should leave the reader with an understanding of the skills and personal qualities good online instructors possess and who may or may not be a good fit for online teaching.

Part II: Instructional Design

In this part, readers will be provided an overview of standards and best practices in online course design. Topics include setting up the online classroom, making the classroom accessible for all students, building assessment into course design, and developing an online syllabus.

Part III: Online Teaching From Primary to Postsecondary

This portion of the text will overview online teaching theory and practices from primary through postsecondary education. Chapters will focus on aspects of online education that are unique to each specific level of education while also providing best practices and tips for online instructors. At each educational level, topics such as building community, student engagement, assisting students with technology, using technology to promote student learning, communication, assessment, and remediation will be overviewed.

Part IV: Legal, Ethical, and Other Administrative Considerations

This final section is designed to provide administrators, across various educational levels, with information relevant to the administration of online education. Specific topics will include hiring and accountability practices, ethics and online teaching, and legal considerations in online teaching.

Skill-Building Resources

Across chapters, readers will find resources that are developed to assist in online teaching skill development. These helpful resources are labeled as follows.

Teaching Skills and Modification/Adaption Summaries: As applicable, summaries will be provided at the end of each chapter, reviewing basic teaching skills and noting modifications necessary to successfully adapt them to the needs of the online instructor, students, and administrators. Within this part, authors will also address accessibility, inclusivity, assessment, communication, remediation, and course policies.

Online resources: Each chapter will provide list of online resources to supplement the learning and worksheets provided.

Summary

The need for specialized training for teachers on the online format has become painfully evident in recent times. The mass transition to online teaching brought on by COVID-19 further highlights the need as many teachers from primary schools to postgraduate institutions were suddenly moved to a format few had experience with as students and even fewer as instructors. This textbook responds to these needs while providing additional guidance to teachers on foundational considerations, inclusivity, tailoring instructional design to the online format, and building success for students and teachers from primary school through secondary to postsecondary classes. Administrative and legal/ethical issues are also provided, rounding out an inclusive textbook for all teachers on all levels who are entering or already teaching on the online platform. This textbook will provide you with a firm foundation upon which to build your online teaching career.

References

Allen, I. E., & Seaman, J. (2017). *Digital learning compass: Distance education enrollment report 2017*. Babson Survey Research Group. http://onlinelearningsurvey.com/reports/digtiallearningcompassenrollment2017.pdf

Bailey, M., Ifenthaler, D., Gosper, M., & Kretzschmar, M. (2014). Factors influencing tertiary students' choice of study mode. In B. Hegarty, J. McDonald, & S.-K. Loke (Eds.), *Rhetoric and reality: Critical perspectives on educational technology* (pp. 251–261). Ascilite. https://www.ascilite.org/conferences/dunedin2014/files/fullpapers/211-Bailey.pdf

Baldwin, S., & Ching, Y. (2019). Online course design: A review of the canvas course evaluation checklist. *International Review of Research in Open and Distributed Learning*, 20(30), 268–282. https://doi.org/10.19173/irrodl.v20i3.4283

Banas, J. R., & Velez-Solic, A. (2013). Designing effective online instructor training and professional development. In J. Keengwe, & L. Kyei-Blankson (Eds.), *Virtual mentoring for teachers: Online professional development practices* (pp. 1–25). IGI Global.

Baran, E. (2011). *The transformation of online teaching practice: Tracing successful online teaching in higher education* [Doctoral dissertation, Iowa State University]. ProQuest Dissertations & Theses Global.

Bates, A. W. (2005). *Technology, e-Learning and Distance Education*. Routledge.

Borup, J., & Evmenova, A. S. (2019). The effectiveness of professional development in overcoming obstacles to effective online instruction in a college of education. *Online Learning*, 23(2), 1–20. https://doi.org/10.24059/olj.v23i2.1468

Brown, A. (1997). Designing for learning: What are the essential features of an effective online course? *Australian Journal of Educational Technology*, 13(2), 115–126. https://doi.org/10.14742/ajet.1926

Brown, V. (2011). Changing demographics of online courses. *US-China Educational Review*, 8(4), 460–467.

Cox, D., & Prestridge, S. (2020). Understanding fully online teaching in vocational education. *Research and Practice in Technology Enhanced Learning*, 15(1), 1–22. https://doi.org/10.1186/s41039-020-00138-4

Ellis, T. J., & Hafner, W. (2003). Engineering an online course: Applying the "secrets" of computer programming to course development. *British Journal of Educational Technology*, 34(5), 639–650. https://doi.org/10.1046/j.0007-1013.2003.00356.x

Gemin, B., & Pape, L. (2017). *Keeping pace with K–12 online learning 2016*. Evergreen Education Group. http://files.eric.ed.gov/fulltext/ED576762.pdf

Hatfield, T., Freeman, A., & Page, K. (2020). *Counselor educator wellness in online teaching* [Manuscript submitted for publication].

Johnson, G. M. (2015). On-campus and fully-online university students: Comparing demographics, digital technology use and learning characteristics. *Journal of University Teaching and Learning Practice*, 12(1), Article 4. https://files.eric.ed.gov/fulltext/EJ1054620.pdf

Kilgour, P., Reynaud, D., Northcote, M., McLoughlin, C., & Gosselin, K.P. (2019) Threshold concepts about online pedagogy for novice online teachers in higher education. *Higher Education Research and Development*, 38(7), 1417–1431. https://doi.org/10.1080/07294360.2018.1450360

Meyer, K. A., & Murrell, V. S. (2014). A national study of training content and activities for faculty development for online teaching. *Journal of Asynchronous Learning Networks*, 18(1), 3–18. https://files.eric.ed.gov/fulltext/EJ1030527.pdf

Norton, P., & Hathaway, D. (2015). Teachers' online experience: Is there a covert curriculum in online professional development? *Journal of Technology and Teacher Education*, 23(4), 509–533.

Perry, D., & Steck, A. (2019). Changes in faculty perceptions about online instruction: Comparison of faculty groups from 2002 and 2016. *Journal of Online Education*, 16(2), 96–110. https://files.eric.ed.gov/fulltext/EJ1223933.pdf

Roddy, C., Amiet, D. L., Chung, J., Holt, C., Shaw, L., McKenzie, S., Garivaldis, F., Lodge, J. M., & Mundy, M. E. (2017). Applying best practice online learning, teaching, and support to intensive online environments: An integrative review. *Frontier Education*, 2(59). https://doi.org/10.3389/feduc.2017.00059

Rodrigues, H., Almeida, F., Figueiredo, V., & Lopes, S. L. (2019). Tracking e-learning through published papers: A systematic review. *Computers and Education*, 136, 87–98. https://doi.org/10.1016/j.compedu.2019.03.007

Schmidt, S., Tschida, C., & Hodge, E. M. (2016). How faculty learn to teach online: What administrators need to know. *Online Journal of Distance Learning Administration*, 19(1). http://www.westga.edu/~distance/ojdla/spring191/schmidt_tschida_hodge191.html

Shattuck, K., & Burch, B. (2018). National standards for quality online teaching (K–12) literature review. *Quality Matters*. https://distance-educator.com/national-standards-for-quality-online-teaching-k-12-literature-review/

ACKNOWLEDGMENTS

The editors would like to acknowledge the contributing authors as leaders in their field and thank them for their time and dedication to this project. We are amazed by your enthusiasm for your topics and passion to guide future instructors in online teaching. Thank you for making this process so enjoyable. We are both thankful and grateful for the feedback from our reviewers: Susan Weaver, EdD., Sarah Littlebear, PhD, LPC, and Melinda Mays, PhD. And of course, we are appreciative of Kassie Graves, Amy Smith, Christian Berk and the entire Cognella team for all their hard work and guidance in bringing our vision to a reality.

Tricia M. Mikolon Acknowledgement

I would like to thank my parents Emil and Patricia and my nephew E. J. Mikolon for always believing in me and encouraging me to achieve my dreams. Your love and support kept me moving through this process. Thank you to Amy Talipski, Sherri Howe, and Jason Smith, and my in-laws James and Darlene Hanson for always being there for me. Tammy Hatfield, my co-editor, I truly appreciated all your enthusiasm, feedback, and hard work on this project. I couldn't ask for a better working partner. And finally, I'd like to thank my husband, Frank A. Levai, Jr., for always encouraging and loving me. Your support is always, and throughout this project was, as amazing as you are.

Tammy Hatfield Acknowledgement

The inspiration for this book began with a conversation with Matthew Lyons, PhD. Dr. Lyons and I were chatting at a professional development conference a few years ago and he presented the idea that we might someday collaborate on a book about online teaching. Because of the vast amount of experience and expertise faculty at our institution have in teaching online, it seemed like a great idea! A couple of years passed while we were busy focusing on other prioritized projects and then, in 2020, a world-wide pandemic forced a major transition to online education across all levels of education. At that point, the reality of the widespread and immediate need for this type of book could not be questioned. In late Spring, 2020, I was chatting with Dr. Mikolon about another project and tossed out the idea of creating this book. She was immediately on-board and did the work of reaching out to our publishing company. I am so grateful to Dr. Lyons for originating the idea and while Dr. Lyons was not able to join as an editor for the book he inspired, he did contribute by serving as lead author on our final chapter. Thanks Dr. Lyons!

I would like to give a big "shout out" to Dr. Mikolon who has been an amazing partner to work with on this project. Your ability to be steadfast and goal oriented helped keep us on track with meeting goals and deadlines. I could always count on you to be there when something needed to happen quickly. I look forward to working with you on another project.

Thanks to all of my family (Vannie, David, Stacey, Rhonda, Kevin, Colton, Tanner, Makena, Dylan, and Hassina) for their support and for providing entertaining distractions when needed during this process.

To my life partner and husband, Diddah Sidi Abdellah, thank for your unrelenting support and patience while I worked on this project. Thank you for being excited about it when I needed the encouragement. Thank you for always being there and listening when I needed it. I am grateful that you were understanding of the time I lost with you while writing and editing this book. You are the most patient, kind, and loving man I have ever known. I am so grateful to share my life with you.

PART I
Foundational Considerations

CHAPTER ONE

Preparing to Teach Online

Kristin Page, PhD, LMHC, NCC
Tera Rumbaugh Crawford, MEd, LPCA, NCC

Why Online Education?

With the advent of new technology, the process of educating students has always evolved. From the stylus to the pen, abacus to the calculator, innovation has always shaped the inculcation of knowledge to students. Today is no different with online education. As a result, many educational institutions have implemented online education to further serve their students. There are myriad reasons why this has occurred. From increasing institutional profit to providing access to underserved populations, or due to external factors regulating face-to-face instruction, the fecundity of online instruction cannot be denied. It was, is, and will continue to be the focus of distance education for the foreseeable future. As such, educators must adapt to this innovation, and therefore, for better or worse, educators must come to terms with it.

From a practical perspective, the implementation of online education will, by definition, limit the ability of educators to offer face-to-face instruction with their students, the modus operandi for traditional pedagogical structure for both K–12 and higher education. Fortunately, this challenge is no longer a problem as technology, such as high-speed internet, video streaming, and online educational platforms, provides the necessary tools to educate students from a distance. If utilized correctly, educators can still deliver an outstanding learning environment for their students outside the face-to-face classroom setting.

As external factors are generally the catalyst for innovation, educators are generally passive participants who must adapt to their pedagogical circumstances. Online education is no exception. As such, regardless of the impetus for the transition to online teaching, educators must be prepared for this mode of instruction. While online teaching enables educators to provide this essential service effectively, the transition itself can be difficult for instructors who have always taught using traditional methods. As with most change, the transition to online teaching may seem overwhelming. The purpose for this chapter is to assist the educator in overcoming concerns or anxiety regarding the move to online instruction. To this end, this chapter summarizes the history of distance learning and the considerations for implementing this new paradigm of online education. The chapter then offers recommendations for setting up a home office, grasping new technology, understanding the preparation for an online course, and maintaining health and wellness for the online educator.

History of Distance Learning

Distance learning is defined as a method of education that occurs while the student and educator are in different geographical locations. Distance learning has existed since the 1700s, with the **correspondence school model** being the original version of distance education (Harting & Erthal, 2005). This form of distance education would be referred to as asynchronous. **Asynchronous learning** takes place when the educator's instruction and the student's participant do not occur at the same time. The development of a reliable postal service, created by the U.S. Second Continental Congress in 1795, made the correspondence school model possible. To execute this form of distance education, educators would provide instruction and feedback by mailing lessons back and forth with the student. In 1873, Eliot Ticknor opened the first correspondence school in the United States. Many of the first students in Eliot Ticknor's school were young women who were confined to their homes due to family obligations (MacKenzie & Christensen, 1971).

Oxford and Cambridge were among the first major universities to see the value in correspondence education (Harting & Erthal, 2005). Following their lead, educational institutions in the United States followed suit. By the late 1800s, distance education programs were established by Illinois Wesleyan and Correspondence University in New York. William Rainey Harper, the father of modern correspondence education, established a correspondence program at the University of Chicago in 1891 (Harting & Erthal, 2005). Distance education was further accelerated in 1914 by the Cooperative Agricultural Extension Act (Harting & Erthal, 2005). With each new program, additional innovations to the method and process of distance education continued to improve.

As technology and mailing services advanced, distance education continued to evolve and grow within the United States. In the 1920s, educators began utilizing educational broadcasting on the radio to deliver information to students (Simonson, 2019). Televisions then opened up a whole new world of opportunities for distance education. For example, in the 1950s, 17 programs began utilizing television as an instructional medium (Harting & Erthal, 2005). This innovation became the mustard seed for all future educational television shows that are still enjoyed today.

In the 1970s, microwave networks were utilized in distance education for the first time (Harting & Erthal, 2005). This structure permitted students to become an active part of the distance educational classroom. A microwave network is a communication system of radio waves in the microwave frequency that travels quickly for a greater distance between two fixed locations. In the 1980s, the Adult Learning Service made television college credit courses available to distance students for the first time (Harting & Erthal, 2005). By the late 1980s, fiber-optic communication systems revolutionized distance education again by allowing for two-way audio and video communications between student and instructor (Simonson, 2019). This structure allowed distance education to become a **synchronous learning** environment for the first time. A synchronous learning environment occurs when the educator's instruction and the student's participation take place simultaneously. With this innovation, distance education in the 1990s really started to develop into the juggernaut everyone knows today, utilizing computers, internet, and digital video (Harting & Erthal, 2005). Today, students frequently experience a hybrid form of instruction referred to as a **blended learning environment**. This takes place when some of the instruction occurs synchronously and other activities are completed in an asynchronous method. With this short historical background, educators can now enter online teaching knowing that distance education is efficacious with a long pedagogical history.

Questions to Ask Before Getting Started

- Do I have the necessary credentials to teach online at my desired institution?
- Do I have the necessary technology skills? If not, am I prepared to attend trainings to develop those skills?

- Will my desired institution's salary fit my lifestyle?
- Will I be comfortable working at home?
- How do I feel about online education? Is the online setting equal to the in-person setting? (Please see Table 1.1: Pros and Cons of Online Teaching)
- Is my home internet and technology sufficient for teaching online?
- Am I willing to proactively find ways to make connections with other educators?

Considerations

Work Life

With the advent of email, cell phones, and video chatting, our understanding of working in the traditional way (nine-to-five business day at the office) is now outdated and, as result, has been discarded as technology continues to advance. Accordingly, the work life of an educator has also changed drastically as more and more schools implement technology and transition to online education. With the implementation of online learning, the rigid schedules of the past no longer apply to educators. This is a serious attraction for many educators as the flexibility, simplicity, and convenience draw many individuals into the realm of online teaching. For instance, online educators have more flexibility and control over creating their own schedules. Unsurprisingly, this autonomous structure is very appealing for educators with young children (Bennett & Lockyer, 2004; Teaching Nomad, 2018). In addition, some online educational institutions offer both part-time and full-time teaching positions. This two-tiered structure permits educators to select career paths tailored to their unique circumstances. Furthermore, online teaching may be more streamlined for the educator because there are certain programs which provide premade videos, premade assignments, and instant grading features (Teaching Nomad, 2018). As such, online teaching offers both flexibility and simplicity for the educator. Online teaching also adds the convenience and comfort of teaching from home, forever removing the dreaded commute to and from work. In times of health epidemics, it also provides educators with additional personal safety.

As there are two sides to every coin, online teaching is not a panacea for all educators. As with any work structure, there are positive and negative attributes with online education, as summarized in Table 1.1. While the rigid structure of traditional teaching fades away with online education, the battle with personal discipline and time management begins. When teaching for an online educational program, many educators find it hard to turn off the switch at the end of the workday. If the educator does not work for a company that streamlines all the material, online teaching generally requires more time for preparation than traditional face-to-face teaching (Ley, 2009). Educators must also adjust to doing all teaching tasks online (Adams, 2009). Under this new paradigm, a great deal of time will be spent communicating with students, responding to noncontent-related issues, and helping students manage the course (Ley, 2009). It must also be noted that employers at online educational institutions can set up their own expectation of how an educator's workday is spent. Rarely is the online educator given carte blanche over their courses. This fact must be a consideration for any aspiring online educator. From the business side, online teaching contracts may include certain requirements, including, but not limited to, the number of weekly hours required for responding to students, a set schedule for meeting with students, and mandatory interaction time with other online faculty. Note that there will always also be pressure for online educators to be present for students and faculty. This may be become a burden for someone who seeks flexibility and simplicity. Many online students also expect instantaneous responses and feedback from their instructor. While this would generally be easy in the traditional classroom setting, it can become very time consuming in an online class structure. More information on how to manage communication with students in the online setting can be found in Chapter 4.

Technology, and its application and use, is the bane of many online educators. As such, many online educators have a love-hate relationship with it. While online education would not exist without technology, it can and does become a serious obstacle for an online educator. For instance, when utilizing an online platform, inevitable glitches and internet issues may overwhelm online educators. Online educators must therefore quickly develop skills to master relevant technology (Keengwe & Kidd, 2010; Rehfuss et al., 2015; Wasik et al., 2019). Technology skills include troubleshooting in the platform used, altering computer settings, and problem solving student issues remotely. If those skills are not developed, educators are left to rely on their institution's technical support for assistance. Many times, this support arrangement can be frustrating and stressful. To remedy this issue, there is a constant pressure on online educators to master the ever-changing world of technology.

Professional Fulfillment

An educator's quest for professional fulfillment never ends. Professional fulfillment may be obtained through feelings of satisfaction, meaningfulness, and professional self-efficacy (Trockel et al., 2018). For example, many educators require a constant challenge to feel satisfied. Others need to know that they are making a difference with their students. Online educators are no different. In any event, online educators must actively seek out professional fulfillment because of they are removed from traditional educational settings.

The internet is one way for online educators to actively seek out professional fulfillment. The internet's global reach continues to expand every day, making it possible for online educators to connect with students throughout the world. This offers many new opportunities for education that never existed before. For instance, online education and the cost savings involved can provide education to traditionally disadvantaged groups (Fulgham & Shaughnessy, 2010). It also allows students who are unable to attend courses on a traditional campus the opportunity to receive education opportunities previously denied based on distance, inflexibility, and unaffordability (Wasik et al., 2019). Taken together, online teaching enables an educator to make an impact on many students in various geographical locations. The online setting is therefore one of the few classrooms where a large class size might be a positive, as an increase in student access is the most frequently reported benefit of a larger class size (Lowenthal et al., 2019). This opportunity offers online educators an unlimited potential to inculcate knowledge to others.

The opportunity for career growth may also be an important part of professional fulfillment. As discussed above, online teaching is the future of education. It should be no surprise that higher education institutions have increased the number of staff associated with online learning (Bennett & Lockyer, 2004). Universities continue to see a strong demand for online courses (Wasik et al., 2019). In fall 2018, 34.7% of postsecondary students enrolled in distance education course (National Center for Education Statistics, 2018a). That is an increase from 25.5% in fall 2012 (National Center for Education Statistics, 2018a). Obtaining skills to teach in an online setting will therefore prepare educators to thrive in a growing field.

The online setting can also give educators a sense of job security during difficult times. For example, thousands of educators were forced out of their classroom and pushed onto a remote platform during the 2020 COVID-19 pandemic (Kaden, 2020). Educators were then able to educate students from the comfort and safety of their own homes. As such, this pandemic event may have catalyzed a structural shift that will change education forever (Kaden, 2020).

Location is also a factor for the growth of online education. In the past, many educators have declined job opportunities that require relocation due to family commitments, responsibilities, or an aversion to relocation. Online teaching allows educators to acquire positions that are not available in their immediate area. Since an individual may work from anywhere in the world, there are now limitless online educational opportunities for instructors (Teaching Nomad, 2018).

Practically speaking, educators have always been said to "wear many hats." Online education expands this statement in many ways. For some, this can be the constant challenge that they long for in their career. For others, this can be overwhelming. Online teaching encompasses the role of the educator, administrator, troubleshooter, and co-learner (Hauck & Stickler, 2006). According to Goodyear et al. (2001), online educators have eight roles in the digital classroom:

- Process facilitator
- Advisor-counselor
- Assessor
- Researcher
- Content facilitator
- Technologist
- Designer
- Manager-administrator

While expansive, the different roles of an online educator are not limited to this description. They must also execute the traditional duties of an instructor. From content instruction to mentoring students, an online educator must wear many hats in the instructor role. This is an important consideration for any online education position.

One important consideration for pursuing online education is its reputation in the business and educational world. Today, online teaching continues to suffer from stigmatization and bias. Research has shown that there are still negative perceptions of online education (Faulk, 2011; Grossman & Johnson, 2016). Historically, individuals and organizations perceived online education as not equivalent to traditional face-to-face instruction (Burt et al., 2011; Hall et al., 2010; Jones & Karper, 2000). Many employers view online education on a résumé as inadequate (Grossman & Johnson, 2016). Fortunately, this antiquated view is beginning to dissipate. Research now shows that opinions are changing regarding the benefits of **online education** vis-a-vis traditional education (Applegate, 2019). As online education becomes more ubiquitous, it is likely this historical stigma will disappear.

TABLE 1.1 Pros and Cons of Online Teaching

PROS	CONS
- Flexibility - No commute to work - Reaching more students - More job possibilities without relocation - Possibility of small class size - Meaningful relationship with students - More intentional relationships with co-workers - Save money on normal work expenses	- Struggles with time management - Technology issues - Extra responsibilities - Stigma of online education - Possibility of large class size - Requires additional effort for relationships with students and co-workers - Possibly spending more money on internet and utilities - Struggles of work-life balance

Virtual Classroom

Before diving into the online classroom, online educators should become familiar with certain facts. First, what is the size of the average in-person classroom? On average, private schools have a student-teacher ratio between 16.7 to 17.8 students per class (National Center for Education Statistics, 2018b). The class size ranges from 16.3 to 26.2 for public elementary, middle, and high schools

(National Center for Education Statistics, 2018b). Table 1.2 shows that nearly half of university classrooms have 20 students or fewer (Public University Honors, 2019). However, almost 15% of classes have over 50 students. The average class size in a public university honors-only class is 17.54 students (Public University Honors, 2019). This information can be used to make judgements about the virtual classroom size.

TABLE 1.2 The Average on Campus Class Size of Colleges in the United States

NUMBER OF STUDENTS PER CLASS	Fewer than 20	More than 50	Between 20 to 50	Fewer than 50
PERCENTAGE OF CLASSES	49.8%	14.97%	35.14%	84.97%

Source: The average on-campus class size data was adapted from Public University Honors (Public University Honors, 2019).

SMALL CLASS SIZE

Educators may be able to reach more students in a large class, but smaller class sizes are appealing for many reasons. From the perspective of comparison, consider the grading and classroom management for 10 students versus 50 students. Most educators would choose 10 students over 50 students every time. Why? Smaller class sizes are generally described as having easier classroom management (Adams, 2009). The class size for many online educator companies consists of one to three students (Teaching Nomad, 2018). Small class sizes enable online educators to quickly identify their students' strengths and weaknesses when working with a small number of students (Teaching Nomad, 2018). In a 2019 study, which consisted of 10,648 enrollment records, 47% of online classes studied had 10 students or fewer (Lin et al., 2019). That is half the size of the majority of in-person university courses. Small class sizes are therefore one of the great benefits of online education as online educators are generally able to give individualized attention to their students. Moreover, this structure also permits online educators to tailor their classes for their students' unique abilities.

LARGE CLASS SIZE

Unfortunately, not every online educator is graced with the opportunity to teach a small class. In a study of online courses at universities, professors reported the following class size information: 43% reported 16, 21% reported 50–74, 14% reported 75–99, 14% reported 100–149, and 8% reported 150+ (Lowenthal et al., 2019). While the efficacy of large online class sizes is an open question, they do appear rare in the online setting. Only 8% of professors in the previously mentioned study drew the short straw and were doomed to teaching 150+ students. It is promising, however, that almost half of the professors taught class sizes of 16 or fewer students. Research shows that online professors of large classes identified interaction, grading, and lack of time as their leading challenges (Lowenthal et al., 2019).

DELIVERY METHOD

As educators shift to the online paradigm, they will have to reevaluate their historical conceptions, attitudes, and beliefs about teaching (Baran & Correia, 2014; Bennett & Lockyer, 2004). The online educator will have to dedicate their time to "meaning making" rather than merely content transmission (Bennett & Lockyer, 2004; Salmon, 2011). In this environment, online educators must identify their students' learning styles and then plan how to meet those various learning styles within the online setting. This can be done through course design, assignments creation, and providing a variety of class participation options (Wasik et al., 2019).

Online classes are delivered synchronously or asynchronously, or by a combination of both. Research has found that there is no significant difference between different delivery options on students' outcomes (Beyth-Marom et al., 2005; Russell, 1999). Research has shown, however, that class size is very important when students are engaging in synchronous discussions (Haynie, 2014). Facilitating an in-person discussion of 50 or more students via video chat can be extremely difficult. By comparison, class size matters less for students who are enrolled in asynchronous courses that utilize readings, prerecorded lectures, and discussion boards (Haynie, 2014). Some universities utilize instructional assistants to help facilitate asynchronous classrooms with a large class size. Due to the impersonal nature of this **modality**, an asynchronous course will likely be the most difficult for developing meaningful relationships with students.

Relationships

Relationships are imperative for education—not only for the student, but for the educator as well. First, effective online educators must labor to facilitate a strong sense of community. Since they are now teaching at a distance, they cannot rely on traditional methods of support and interaction. A strong sense of community enables them to maintain close relationships with students, faculty, administration, and staff. On both a personal and professional level, it provides them with support and feedback relating to their courses and teaching efficacy. It prevents isolation and improves their accountability for their role as online educator. This is explored in more detail in Chapter 4.

STUDENT RELATIONSHIPS

Authentic and supportive relationships are necessary to create a positive classroom environment (Gregory et al., 2014). Building relationships with students can benefit the students emotionally and academically. Research has shown that student-educator relationships help decrease challenging behaviors in students (Yassine et al., 2020). Relationship building can also reduce racial inequalities in out-of-school suspension (Anyon et al., 2018).

Strategies used to build relationships in the traditional classroom setting can be used in distance education as well. Positive interactions with caregivers can help build relationships when teaching minors (Anyon et al., 2018). Other relationship-building strategies include checking in with students, learning about their lives, identifying common interests, and other nonacademic discussions (Anyon et al., 2018). All these strategies may be implemented with distance learning. Emailing, calling, and video chatting all allow for individual contact to occur and close relationships to be established between educator and student (Adams, 2009). As discussed above, distance education also has the advantage of smaller class sizes. Smaller class sizes facilitate true one-on-one interactions between student and educator. This further enables the education process by letting the educator know each student on a personal level (Teaching Nomad, 2018).

There are many opportunities and methods for educators to establish (and build) an engaging community in their online classrooms (Wasik et al., 2019). The most important component is communication. Communication needs to occur on two levels—teacher-student and peer to peer (Wasik et al., 2019). Certain forms of communication foster community better than others. Potentially useful examples of communication include praising students, enthusiastic greetings, sharing stories, and student-led discussions involving their point of view (Plante & Asselin, 2014).

When people think back to the educator who impacted their life the most, they often recall their relationship. Teaching online still allows for those personal connections to be established. Even with the personal connections, some educators still miss the traditional face-to-face interactions. Sometimes, educators may feel like they are not really teaching because they spend more time preparing materials, assessing, communicating, and providing feedback (Bennett & Lockyer, 2004). To remedy this feeling, greater thought must be utilized to create meaningful interactions in distance education. Close relationships with students are possible; they just require intentional planning. Fostering a sense of community is explored further in Chapter 4.

PROFESSIONAL RELATIONSHIPS

Outside the historical structure of brick-and-mortar education, educators must seek outside support, both personal and technological, when teaching online. Isolation and doubt can become problems. To remedy these issues, educators should participate in any formal opportunities for community, support, and continuing education (Major, 2015). Major suggests the following focusing on the following areas: (1) engaging in self-study to further refine their online teaching skills; (2) participating in opportunities for socialization; (3) developing a personal learning network (defined as a group of people who can assist learning by identifying opportunities, answering questions, and being a center of knowledge and experience); (4) learning from the experience of teaching peers; (5) studying research to develop knowledge; (6) keeping up with technology; and (7) developing a strong relationship with technical support employees.

The Cost of Teaching Online

Like many things in the world, the feasibility and practicality online education generally boils down to money. So how much money is really saved by working from home? The average person in any career can save up to $4,000 a year by working remotely (Pelta, 2020). The cost of a professional wardrobe can be significantly reduced (Pelta, 2020). A dress shirt, polo, or blouse with yoga pants or athletic shorts can become the new dress code if the camera angle is only from the waist up; just be careful not to stand up in front of the camera. Working from home also reduces the cost of commuting, gas, and car maintenance (Pelta, 2020). Online educators can spend less on classroom supplies, lunches, and possibly childcare (Pelta, 2020). While online educators may save money in some areas, they might find themselves spending more on utilities, faster internet packages, and materials not provided by their employers. There are also nonmonetary costs to online teaching. Online teaching can be extremely costly in time, energy, and imagination (Fulgham & Shaughnessy, 2010).

Teaching online may save educators some money, but how much money does this new career pay? According the U.S. Bureau of Labor Statistics (2020), pre-kindergarten through high school educators' salaries range from $34,650 to $67,060. Postsecondary educators net $90,970 on average, but this varies based on focus area (U.S. Bureau of Labor Statistics, 2020). Educators' income in the online setting varies based on focus area, level of education and experience, and employer (Get Educated, 2020). On average, online college instructors make $1,000–$3,000 per course (Get Educated, 2020). Educators are often paid based on the number of students taught in some online teaching organizations (Get Educated, 2020). Depending on the circumstances, educators may or may not make a comfortable living working online. This outcome is generally a function of the educator's experience, education, and institution.

Setting Up the Home Office and Virtual Classroom

When teaching online, the use of online platforms, software programs, and other multimedia can enhance the student learning process. When used appropriately, it helps students learn better

(Fulgham & Shaughnessy, 2010). While exciting, utilizing the new technology for learning can be overwhelming for educators used to in-person learning paradigms as teaching online is a "constitutively different way of offering instruction" (Major, 2015, p. 8).

Upon accepting an online teaching position, the next step for the online educator will be setting up their home office. Setting up a home office for online instruction is foundational for pedagogical success. Here are a few basic recommendations:

Locating the Right Place

Before starting, you must find a place to teach. This should be a specific place, preferably a room, that you dedicate to this task. Table 1.3 summarizes the important factors that should be considered when selecting a space for your home office.

TABLE 1.3 Setting Up a Home Office

FACTORS	WHY IMPORTANT
• Lighting	A well-lit room is required for video
• Sound	A quiet room away from noise
• Office equipment	Comfortable chair, desk Computer with camera and microphone
• Teaching materials	Textbook, lesson plans, other aids
• Technology	Software, internet, online platform

Intangible Factors for the Home Office—Virtual Classroom and Community

When learning online, a student's traditional sense of community formed by sharing a time, place, space, and experience is lost (Major, 2015). This is a critical issue that educators must overcome when setting up their home office and, in essence, establishing their virtual classroom and community. As such, when setting up your home office you must establish an environment that serves as a place for your students to thrive. This environment will serve as the cornerstone of the student's online education. It will also provide students a sense of belonging and facilitate their acquisition of knowledge. Developing a sense of connection and community is further explored in Chapter 4.

Mastering Technology for Online Education

Online teaching is very different from face-to-face classrooms. Educators must understand and adapt to this reality. To be successful, they must use technology and be prepared to utilize available online platforms to deliver knowledge to their students. As mentioned above, this means online educators may have to take on other roles such as technology guru, facilitator, et cetera, and anticipate student needs and challenges in a different way than face-to-face instruction (Bryans-Bongey & Graziano, 2016). However, this does not mean the educator must discard prior methods of teaching; on the contrary, the educator must supplement their traditional teaching methodologies and skills within the online classroom. When implementing online teaching, the use of technology is essential, and therefore it becomes the largest area of concern for the educator (Fulgham & Shaughnessy, 2010). Educators must familiarize themselves with computer hardware (camera, microphone, speakers), settings (lighting and noise levels), and their online platforms.

First, educators must be able to master basic use of the computer hardware and online platform. They must know how to set up their camera, speakers, and microphone for effective use. If other demonstrative aids, programs, or simulations are utilized, educators must know how to incorporate them within their online platform. They must also ensure proper lighting and noise level are maintained during each educational session. Lastly, educators must balance their use of technology with effective teaching methods, as their goal is to provide their students with the best education experience possible (Fulgham & Shaughnessy, 2010).

Preparation for Online Education

A serious concern for educators who are new to online teaching is the amount of time it requires to teach online (Bryans-Bongey & Graziano, 2016). Joseph Cavanaugh (2005) studied the time required to prepare and teach a traditional course and same course taught online. He concluded that teaching online requires significantly more time than an in-person class. He found that the time spent on preparation depended on three factors: (a) the number of students, (b) the time spent online for the class, and (c) time demands outside of class. The time spent on preparation is therefore a function of whether the educator is developing the content alone, how many classes and students the educator is responsible for, and how much time the educator devotes to facilitating the class through discussion boards, emails, advising, and tutoring (Bryans-Bongey & Graziano, 2016). As such, these factors will depend on the unique circumstances of each educator.

Practically speaking, the structure and modality, be it asynchronous or synchronous, of the course itself will determine the educator's preparation time. Depending on the modality utilized, there are several options when it comes to selecting and using the online platform for your class. The modality utilized will affect the classroom setting and influence the preparation of the educator. For example, online environments that are synchronous are not as time flexible, but they enable the educator to interact with the students and permit dialogue during each live session. This interactive structure enables a less structured environment and, therefore, may lessen the preparation time for the educator.

Likewise, an asynchronous classroom gives the educator more flexibility to prepare and record sessions on their personal schedule. It also provides students with the same flexibility to attend sessions. This modality, however, does not enable face-to-face interaction and, therefore, it will likely require more preparation because of its impersonal delivery. This likely means more communication via discussion boards, emails, and phone calls outside of teaching time. As such, the modality utilized by the educator will likely dictate the type of preparation required.

Developing and Using Support From a Distance

As the majority of educators have been trained to teach in traditional face-to-face environments, they have been accustomed to brick-and-mortar locations, in-person teaching, faculty lounges, and personal interactions with students, colleagues, administrators, and support staff. The transition to distance learning is a substantial change, which will likely require a large readjustment for all teaching faculty. It is therefore essential to establish clear guidelines related to student participation and support; what participation is required for the online community; and how educators and students will receive technical support for the computer hardware, software, and online platforms.

Balancing Work and Personal Time in the Remote Environment

Another major factor for being a successful online educator is learning how to balance work with their personal life. One key factor is by increasing productivity and managing the workload so that time will be devoted to teaching, guiding, and interacting with students (Martin & Martin, 2015). To prevent being time constrained and overwhelmed, educators must be organized, disciplined, flexible, and able to balance work with their personal life. This is very important because online educators may feel they need to work and be available at all times. As such, Martin and Martin (2015, p. 154) state "it is essential for the educator to set boundaries by managing student expectations through explicit communication about policies" such as email responses, assignment feedback, and availability for nonwritten communication outside the class.

Notwithstanding these expectations, educators must be cognizant of the time requirements necessary to administer an online course. Research has shown that approximately 152 hours will be needed to prepare and administer an online course for first-time instructors (Conceicao & Lehman, 2011). To manage this commitment, educators should undertake the following procedures:

1. Prioritize their time and workload
2. Become proficient with technology
3. Utilize time management
4. Limit their work time for set times
5. Establish schedule for checking emails and student communication
6. Maintain personal time during the week

At the end of the day, daily discipline will assist educators to maintain their work and personal lives. Establishing these procedures will keep educators organized, efficient, and effective. It will also help them to save time and relieve stress.

Mental Health and Wellness in the Remote Environment

Teaching can be a stressful profession regardless of the setting. High levels of stress can cause educators to perform poorly, be unsatisfied with their jobs, and search for other careers (Pennsylvania State University, 2016). Educator stress comes from constantly adapting to new job requirements and lacking resources, training opportunities, respect, and autonomy (Layton, 2015). Mental and physical wellness needs to be a priority for online educators. There are resources available and actions that educators can take to promote their wellbeing. Information on the role of administration in faculty wellness can be found in Chapter 12.

An American Federation of Teachers survey report shows that 80% of educators often feel physically and mentally exhausted after work (Layton, 2015). At least in the traditional setting the educator could leave the building at the end of the day and attempt to switch off from work mode. Online educators can struggle with work-life balance. The constant emails and communication can allow work to seep into the educator's personal life. The online setting can be demanding and time consuming, and make the educator feel as if they are on call 24/7 (Adams, 2009). On top of a demanding career, parenting and working in the same space can be another blow to an educator's sanity. It could be helpful for online educators to have a space dedicated to work. The separate space can allow educators to physically and mentally disconnect from work.

Everyone, regardless of their career, must devote time to self-care. This could be exercising, reading a book, or just taking some quiet time alone. Online educators need to find what is the healthiest option for their wellbeing. One of the main sources of stress for educators is low social-emotional competence (Pennsylvania State University, 2016). Social-emotional competence is the ability to regulate and understand one's emotions and understand others' emotions to effectively interact with them (Alzahrani et al., 2019). Mindfulness and stress management programs could be helpful for educators who need intervention strategies to deal with their stress and emotions. These intervention programs can improve overall health and reduce anxiety and depression (Pennsylvania State University, 2016).

Educators need to dedicate time to promoting self-esteem and opportunities for emotional sharing (Won Hur & Brush, 2009). Educator communities can act as support groups to promote professional and personal wellness. A support group of individuals dealing with similar issues can be beneficial to online educators (Won Hur & Brush, 2009). New educators can join mentoring programs to work with experienced educators. Mentoring programs can improve educator satisfaction and increase student achievement (Pennsylvania State University, 2016).

If educators do not want to focus on their wellness for themselves, they should at least do it for their students' sake. Research has shown that increased educator stress and depression produce environments that lead to poor academic performance, increased behavioral problems, and lower levels of social adjustment in students (Pennsylvania State University, 2016). Instructors need to take the steps to deal with their stress and learn preventative strategies before the stress occurs. Educators' and students' wellness will be protected by taking these steps.

This is especially true for educators working within online learning environments—namely, remote workers may suffer from mental health and wellness problems. First, loneliness and isolation are some of the most common problems with remote working (Larson et al., 2020). In such solitary environments, educators will likely miss their social interaction with students, colleagues, and administrators. Loneliness and isolation are especially hard on extroverts, who lose the personal interaction on which they thrive. Such lack of personal interaction may lead to depression and anxiety or cause additional mental health issues (Brzozowski, 2019). It is therefore imperative for online educators to focus on connectivity and relationships with other individuals both inside and outside the virtual classroom.

Maintaining healthy habits is also a problem for remote workers. While it would seem that remote workers have more free time to exercise and maintain healthy lifestyle habits because they don't have to commute or get dressed up, studies show, paradoxically, this is not the case for most remote workers (Brzozowski, 2019). For instance, when teaching remotely, an educator may not be moving around as much during the workday as they used to by walking from the parking lot, moving around campus, and moving around the classroom. They may lose access to their institutions' exercise facilities and develop unhealthy eating habits, as they may lack access to the healthy food options at their worksite. They are also likely to become sedentary, less efficient, and unproductive as they fail to take breaks throughout the day.

Taken together, the change to a new solitary, sedentary lifestyle that may accompany teaching from home may be unhealthy. It is therefore important for online educators to focus on their wellness, remain organized and disciplined during the workday, incorporate exercise in daily life, and maintain healthy eating habits. Ignoring these concerns places the online educator at peril.

Chapter Summary

As the phenomenon of online teaching continues to expand, educators must adapt to the changing educational environment around them. While exciting, the transition to online education may be difficult for those who have always taught using traditional methods. While it might seem overwhelming, there are many tools to navigate this new educational frontier. First, by understanding the history of distance education, educators can see that innovation in distance learning is the norm and, therefore, it should not be feared. Next, educators should ponder the considerations involved with online education, the positives and negatives associated with this structure, and the changes expected when transitioning to this form of educational environment. With this knowledge in hand, educators are then empowered to make informed decisions regarding their individual career field. If educators elect to take the plunge, or are forced to do so by their educational institution, they may utilize the recommendations offered above for setting up their home office, grasping new technology involved with online education, understanding the preparation required for teaching online courses, and maintaining a healthy lifestyle. Regardless of the reason for moving to online instruction, online educators can now take advantage of this form of distance learning to pursue fulfilling careers.

Online Resources

7 Steps for Preparing to Teach Online

A list of helpful tips to assist instructors for teaching online: https://elearningindustry.com/7-tips-prepare-for-teaching-online

Cornell University, Center for Teaching Innovation: Preparing to Teach Online

Contains a self-assessment for faculty: https://teaching.cornell.edu/resource/preparing-teach-online

Inside Higher Ed: Peer Advice for Instructors Teaching Online for the First Time

Guidance for instructors teaching online for the first time: https://www.insidehighered.com/digital-learning/article/2017/11/15/peer-advice-instructors-teaching-online-first-time

North Carolina State University, College of Science: Tips From Faculty for Quickly Preparing to Teach Online

Contains tips to assist faculty in switching over from traditional to online teaching: https://sciences.ncsu.edu/news/tips-from-faculty-for-quickly-preparing-to-teach-online/

PBS: Bring the World to Your Classroom

Provides various educational resources from PBS for teachers to use in their classrooms: https://wvia.pbslearningmedia.org/?gclid=CjwKCAiA_Kz-BRAJEiwAhJNY73EOoe3cIf4jMw7YkcoCk4AUNpYAfbwoPES9oL-HqXdGN8SiVVpKAhoCCJ4QAvD_BwE#.X8vDMGhKg2w

Teach for America: 7 Tips for Being a Great Virtual Teacher

Tips to assist teachers online: https://www.teachforamerica.org/stories/7-tips-for-being-a-great-virtual-teacher

We Are Teachers: 350+ Amazing Online Learning Resources

Online resources for teachers in pre–K through postsecondary: https://www.weareteachers.com/free-online-learning-resources/

References

Adams, C. (2009). Is teaching online right for you? As more of your peers enter the virtual classroom, we take a look at the pros and cons. *Instructor, 118*(6), 41–43.

Alzahrani, M., Alharbi, M., & Alodwani, A. (2019). The effect of social-emotional competence on children academic achievement and behavioral development. *International Education Studies, 12*(12), 141–149. https://doi.org/10.5539/ies.v12n12p141

Anyon, Y., Atteberry-Ash, B., Yang, J., Pauline, M., Wiley, K., Cash, D., Downing, B., Greer, E., & Pisciotta, L. (2018). "It's all about the relationships": Educators' rationales and strategies for building connections with students to prevent exclusionary school discipline outcomes. *Children and Schools, 40*(4), 221–230. https://doi.org/10.1093/cs/cdy017

Applegate, C. (2019). Interviewing principals to obtain their perceptions of certified teaching candidates with a degree from an online teaching program. *International Journal on E-Learning, 18*(2), 129–145.

Baran, E., & Correia, A. (2014). A professional development framework for online teaching. *Tech Trends, 58*(5), 96–102. https://doi.org/10.1007/s11528-014-0791-0

Bennett, S., & Lockyer, L. (2004). Becoming an online teacher: Adapting to a changed environment for teaching and learning in higher education. *Educational Media International, 41*(3), 231–248. https://doi.org/10.1080/09523980410001680842

Beyth-Marom, R., Saporta, K., & Caspi, A. (2005). Synchronous vs. asynchronous tutorials: Factors affecting students' preferences and choices. *Journal of Research on Technology in Education, 37*(3), 245–262. https://doi.org/10.1080/15391523.2005.10782436

Bryans-Bongey, S., & Graziano, K. J. (2016). *Online teaching in K–12: Models, methods, and best practices for teachers and administrators*. Information Today.

Brzozowski, C. (2019). Out of sight, out of their minds. *Workforce, 98*(5). https://www.workforce.com/news/remote-employees-out-of-sight-out-of-their-minds

Burt, I., Gonzalez, T., Swank, J., Ascher, D. L., & Cunningham, L. (2011). Addressing the technology gap in counselor education: Identification of characteristics in students that affect learning in college classrooms. *Journal of Counselor Preparation and Supervision, 3*(1), 18–33. https://doi.org/10.7729/31.1023

Cavanaugh, J. (2005). Teaching online—A time comparison. *Online Journal of Distance Learning Administration, 8*(1). https://www.westga.edu/~distance/ojdla/spring81/cavanaugh81.htm

Conceicao, S., & Lehman, R. (2011). *Managing online instructor workload: Strategies for finding balance and success*. Jossey-Bass.

Faulk, N. (2011). Perceptions of Arizona and New Mexico public school superintendents regarding online teacher education courses. *Review of Higher Education and Self-Learning, 3*(11), 79–85.

Fulgham, S., & Shaughnessy, M. F. (2010). *Pedagogical models the discipline of online teaching*. Nova Science.

Get Educated. (2020). *How to become an online teacher*. https://www.geteducated.com/career-center/detail/online-instructor-post-secondary/

Goodyear, P., Salmon, G., Spector, M., Steeples, C., & Tickner, S. (2001). Competencies of online teaching: A special report. *Educational Technology Research and Development, 49*(1), 65–72.

Gregory, A., Bell, J., & Pollock, M. (2016). How educators can eradicate disparities in school discipline: Issues in intervention. In R. J. Skiba, K. Mediratta, & M. K. Rausch (Eds.), *Inequality in school discipline: Research and practice to reduce disparities* (pp. 39–58). Palgrave MacMillan.

Grossman, A. M., & Johnson, L. R. (2016). Employer perceptions of online accounting degrees. *Issues in Accounting Education, 31*(1), 91–109. https://doi.org/10.2308/iace-51229

Hall, B. S., Nielsen, R. C., Nelson, J. R., & Buchholz, C. E. (2010). A humanistic framework for distance education. *Journal of Humanistic Counseling, Education, and Development, 49*(1), 45–57.https://doi.org/10.1002/j.2161-1939.2010.tb00086.x

Harting, K., & Erthal, M. J. (2005). History of distance learning. *Information Technology, Learning, and Performance Journal, 23*(1), 35–44.

Hauck, M., & Stickler, U. (2006). What does it take to teach online? *CALICO Journal, 23*(3), 463–475.

Haynie, D. (2014) *Experts say class size can matter for online students*. U.S. News. https://www.usnews.com/education/online-education/articles/2014/09/26/experts-say-class-size-can-matter-for-online-students

Jones, K. D., & Karper, C. (2000). How to develop an online course in counseling techniques. *Journal of Technology in Counseling, 1*(2), 1–7. https://www.researchgate.net/publication/234714293_How_To_Develop_an_Online_Course_in_Counseling_Techniques

Kaden, U. (2020). COVID-19 school closure-related changes to the professional life of a K–12 teacher. *Education Sciences, 10*(6), 165. https://doi.org/10.3390/educsci10060165

Keengwe, J., & Kidd, T. (2010). Towards best practices in online learning and teaching in higher education. *Journal of Online Learning and Teaching, 6*(2), 533–541.

Kilian, C. (1997). Why teach online. *Educom Review, 32*(4), 31–34.

Larson, B. Z., Vroman, S. R., & Makarius, E. E. (2020, March). *A guide to managing your (newly) remote workers*. Harvard Business Review. https://hbr.org/2020/03/a-guide-to-managing-your-newly-remote-workers

Layton, L. (2015, May). *Is the classroom a stressful place? Thousands of teachers say yes*. The Washington Post. https://www.washingtonpost.com/local/education/is-the-classroom-a-stressful-place-thousands-of-teachers-say-yes/2015/05/12/829f56d8-f81b-11e4-9030-b4732caefe81_story.html

Ley, K. (2009). *Time management tips for online instructors*. Faculty Focus. https://www.facultyfocus.com/articles/online-education/time-management-tips-for-online-instructors/

Lin, C. H., Kwon, J. B., & Zhang, Y. (2019). Online self-paced high-school class size and student achievement. *Educational Technology Research and Development, 67*(2), 317–336. https://doi.org/10.1007/s11423-018-9614-x

Lowenthal, P. R., Nyland, R., Jung, E., Dunlap, J. C., & Kepka, J. (2019). Does class size matter? An exploration into faculty perceptions of teaching high-enrollment online courses. *American Journal of Distance Education, 33*(3), 152–168. https://doi.org/10.1080/08923647.2019.1610262

MacKenzie, O., & Christensen, E. L. (1971). *The changing world of correspondence study: International readings*. Pennsylvania State University Press.

Major, C. H. (2015). *Teaching online: A guide to theory, research, and practice*. Johns Hopkins University Press.

Martin, M., & Martin, D. (2015). *Online teaching in education, health, and human services: Helping faculty transition to online instruction and providing tools for attaining instructional excellence*. Charles C. Thomas.

National Center for Education Statistics. (2018a). *Percent of students enrolled in distance education courses*. https://nces.ed.gov/ipeds/TrendGenerator/app/answer/2/42

National Center for Education Statistics. (2018b). *2017–2018 National teacher and principal survey tables*. https://nces.ed.gov/surveys/ntps/tables_list.asp

Pelta, R. (2020). *6 ways working from home will save you $4,000 or more annually*. FlexJobs. https://www.flexjobs.com/blog/post/does-working-remotely-save-you-money/

Pennsylvania State University. (2016) *Teacher stress and health: Effects on teacher, student, and schools* [Issue brief]. https://review.prevention.psu.edu/uploads/files/rwjf430428-TeacherStress.pdf

Plante, K., & Asselin, M. E. (2014). Best practices for creating social presence and caring behaviors online. *Nursing Education Perspectives, 35*(4), 219–223.

Public University Honors. (2019). *Estimated class sizes: More than 90 national universities*. https://publicuniversityhonors.com/2015/10/20/estimated-class-sizes-more-than-90-national-universities/

Rehfuss, M. C., Kirk-Jenkins, A., & Milliken, T. (2015). Students' experiences with different course delivery modalities: On campus, online, and satellite. *Journal of Human Services, 35*(1), 28–38.

Russell, T. E. (1999). *No significant difference phenomenon as reported in 355 research reports, summaries and papers: A comparative research annotated bibliography on technology for distance education*. North Carolina State University.

Salmon, G. (2011). *E-moderating: The key to teaching and learning online* (3rd ed.). Routledge.

Simonson, M. (2019). *Distance education: Definition and glossary of terms* (4th ed.). Information Age.

Teaching Nomad. (2018). *Pros and cons of teaching online*. https://www.teachingnomad.com/discover-more/nomad-blog/item/373-pros-cons-teaching-online

Trockel, M., Bohman, B., Lesure, E., Hamidi, M., Welle, D., Roberts, L., & Shanafelt, T. (2018). A brief instrument to assess both burnout and professional fulfillment in physicians: Reliability and validity, including correlation with self-reported medical errors, in a sample of resident and practicing physicians. *Academic Psychiatry, 42*(1), 11–24. https://doi.org/10.1007/s40596-017-0849-3

U.S. Bureau of Labor Statistics. (2020). *May 2019 national occupational employment and wage estimates: United States*. https://www.bls.gov/oes/current/oes_nat.htm#25-0000

Wasik, S. Z., Barrow, J. C., Royal, C., Brooks, R. M., Scott-Dames, L. S., Corry, L., & Bird, C. (2019). Online counselor education: Creative approaches and best practices in online learning environments. *Research on Education and Psychology, 3*(1), 43–52.

Won Hur, J., & Brush, T. A. (2009). Teacher participation in online communities. *Journal of Research on Technology in Education, 41*(3), 279–303. htpps://doi.org/10.1080/15391523.2009.10782532

Yassine, J., Tipton, F. L. A., & Katic, B. (2020). Building student-teacher relationships and improving behavior-management for classroom teachers. *Support for Learning, 35*(3), 389–407. https://doi.org/10.1111/1467-9604.12317

CHAPTER TWO

Online Pedagogy

Tammy Hatfield, PsyD
Portia Allie-Turco, LMHC, NCC
Sarah E. Johansson, MEd, NCC
Melissa Brennan, MA, LPC

Defining Pedagogy

Pedagogy is a term used to describe one's approach to teaching. Pedagogy is a combination of theory and practice, as it includes what teachers do with students in the classroom as well as the theoretical rationale for the approach. Historically, pedagogy has been referred to as a teaching approach for children wherein the learner is dependent upon the instructor to impart content knowledge. There is some debate in the scholarly literature about the use and/or misuse of the term *pedagogy* being applied with frequency to specific types or frameworks of teaching practice. Some teaching frameworks, in an act of dismantling oppressive practices that place educators as imparters of knowledge and students as passive recipients, reclaim the term *pedagogy* in naming their teaching framework. In this chapter, pedagogy is defined as the theoretical framework from which one approaches the practice of teaching.

While some graduate programs prepare their doctoral students to engage in teaching through the study of various theories of pedagogy and learning, other graduate programs offer no instruction or training in pedagogy. When training is offered, it is often focused on face-to-face teaching and not connected to the online classroom (Anderson et al., 2011). One recent study found that only 15.2% of teachers training in the education field had studied online pedagogy (Cox & Prestridge, 2020). Given the increasing presence of online education, there is a need for universities to offer training in online pedagogy to faculty and to train their graduate students to teach online (Kebritchi et al., 2017). With the many approaches to pedagogy that are found in scholarly literature, and the lack of training in online pedagogy, selecting an approach can be challenging. Approaches to teaching are situated in educational philosophy and further grounded in general philosophical world views. One's **ontological** and **epistemological** positions can lead to choosing pedagogies that are most consistent with one's world views. Ultimately, there is no single pedagogical perspective that can universally apply to all people and all classroom situations. Some pedagogies, however, are more inclusive than others, and a theoretical foundation paves the pathway to the practice of teaching. Without theory to guide, educators may get lost, so to speak, in what feels like a never-ending sea of discrete techniques and strategies that can be used in the classroom. Educators may use many of the same techniques or strategies for different purposes, depending on their conceptions of good teaching (González, 2012) and the context of their specific pedagogy. When teachers know, conceptually, what their aims are and how their goals are accomplished, they can choose from a variety of techniques that can be altered or used as defined to fit the educators' specific aim.

The experiences of educators in transitioning to online learning during COVID-19 point to the need for a well-developed pedagogical framework for online teaching. For those who were not already teaching in an online format, the rapid shift, along with the reality of the global pandemic, was a source of anxiety and stress. Many were inundated with materials and resources related to various strategies to use for online teaching. The added workload of sorting through all of those sources of information while trying to move classes online, learn new technology, and stay safe during the pandemic was likely overwhelming. And, educators report that their workload is a major factor preventing them from enacting teaching practices that they would consider beneficial to students (Cox & Prestridge, 2020). Additionally, some may have found that each new email shared a new teaching strategy that may or not may have been contradictory to the strategy that popped into the inbox 5 minutes prior, thus leaving the educator with uncertainty about which practices are actually helpful to students. While it was probably helpful intent that drove the dissemination of resources so quickly, it was not practical to sift through so much information and accomplish the task of moving classes online. Having pedagogical theory to guide one's practice can significantly simplify this process and perhaps lead to improved quality of teaching. Kember and Kwan (2000) assert that fundamental changes to the quality of teaching and learning are unlikely to happen without changes to lecturers' conception of teaching. Several traditional and contemporary pedagogical frameworks will be discussed in this chapter. While theoretical frameworks for pedagogies in the online setting are sparse in scholarly literature, self-determined learning, or heutagogy, which is discussed below, has frequently been applied to online settings (Agonács & Matos, 2019) and other models of online pedagogy (Serdyukov, 2015; Nickols, 2011) will be reviewed as this chapter unfolds.

Traditional Pedagogical Frameworks

Traditional Pedagogy

The term *pedagogy* is credited to Greek origins in 1623 (Merriam-Webster, n.d.). The Greek word "paidagogos" means a slave who led boys to school, taught them manners, and provided tutoring (Merriam-Webster, n.d.). The origins of the term are rooted in the slave society of ancient Greece and, over time, the word "pedagogue" came to mean "teacher." Over the next few centuries, pedagogy was put into practice in monastery schools in Europe and eventually spread to elementary schools in the 18th and 19th centuries (Akyildiz, 2019). When educational psychology emerged as a science, psychologists started to study the impact of teaching on children's behavior and this further informed the development of pedagogy (Knowles, 1970). Traditional pedagogy, according to Akyildiz (2019), may be a preferable approach to education with children. In this approach the learner is dependent on the educator, and the content and structure of learning is provided and organized by the educator. This approach to teaching is teacher centered versus learner centered (Akyildiz, 2019).

Andragogy

Prior to Knowles (1970), adult learners were taught according to the same learning theories and principles that were originally developed for children (Hase & Kenyon, 2001). Knowles (1970) introduced **andragogy** as the study of adult learning. He reasoned that adults learn by different methods than children, therefore instruction for adults should not be formed by the same pedagogical principles as child learning. Knowles (1970; 1984) outlined five assumptions of andragogy distinguishing the unique qualities of adult learners. These assumptions state that adults are self-directed in their learning, bring rich life experiences with them through the learning process, are intrinsically motivated, are ready to learn if they have sought out education, and learn best from problem-based learning that is applicable to their lives (Blondy, 2007; Halupa, 2015; Knowles, 1970, 1984). Due to these key differences in the learning needs of adults, Knowles encouraged a shift in educational methodology to focus on learner-centered techniques rather than highly structured methods prescribed by the educator (Halupa, 2015; Knowles, 1970, 1984). In learner-centered education, the planning and implementation of instruction depends of the learner's individual needs rather than employing a one-size-fits-all approach to instruction.

Andragogy shifts much of the responsibilities of the learning process to the learner rather than the educator. Learners are expected to establish appropriate learning conditions, goals, and objectives for themselves, determining how their own learning needs will be met (Akyildiz, 2019). This empowerment of students is important, as it gives learners the opportunity to engage more actively in their own learning process. However, further innovation toward a completely learner-directed approach is still necessary to truly meet the needs of diverse 21st-century learners (Akyildiz, 2019).

Online Pedagogical Frameworks

Heutagogy

Heutagogy is viewed as an "extension to andragogy and has also been referred to as a potential theory for online and distance education" (Agonács & Matos, 2019, p. 223) and can be described as the study of self-directed learning (Hase & Kenyon, 2001). While andragogy initiated the development of learner-centered education methods, heutagogy goes a step further with the concept of self-directed learning (Halupa, 2015; Hase & Kenyon, 2001). Heutagogy is not only learner centered, but also learner directed, allowing the learner to determine what and how they would like to learn. Both andragogy and heutagogy diverge from traditional pedagogy by considering the learner, not the educator, to be the central individual in the learning process. The learner truly becomes the manager of their own learning in heutagogy. The goal of heutagogy is not only for students to learn content, but also for students to learn how to learn (Blaschke, 2012). Knowing how to learn is a foundational skill that is developed when heutagogy is applied. Educators become guides, simply supplying the resources and support necessary for their students to begin their independent learning journey (Blaschke, 2012; Halupa, 2015; Hase & Kenyon, 2001). The process of learning becomes more important than the content. In heutagogy, there is less educator control and more autonomy for the learner.

Certain instructional methods are more conducive to heutagogical practice than others. Collaborative activities, reflective journaling, or assignments that allow the learner to select the process or platform are suggested (Blaschke, 2012; Halupa, 2015; Hase & Kenyon, 2001). These self-directed learning activities are more likely to increase motivation and engagement in learners, promoting confidence and critical thinking skills (Blaschke, 2012; Hase & Kenyon, 2001). Glassner and Back (2019) studied students' perceptions of being taught from a heutagogical lens in their teacher education course. The students reported higher levels of intrinsic motivation to learn the course content, as well as an increase in skills that can be applied to real world settings and situations following their experiences in the course. Maykut et al. (2019) also examined the heutagogical course experience from the student perspective. Their study highlighted benefits of a heutagogical approach to include strengthened relationships between student and teacher, as well as improved engagement and enjoyment experienced by the students.

Heutagogy has become an increasingly relevant approach to teaching and learning as the use of internet and technology in education continues to rise (Blaschke, 2012; Mulrennan, 2018). Heutagogy has been referred to as a "net-centric" learning approach that provides an appropriate framework for distance learning (Blaschke, 2012; Mulrennan, 2018). The basic tenets of heutagogy, such as autonomy and self-directedness of learners, pair well with technological learning activities (Blaschke, 2012; Mulrennan, 2018). Despite the research supported benefits of a heutogogical approach for current day learners, 39 out of 40 educators surveyed by Akyildiz (2019) had never heard of the term *heutagogy*. Increasing awareness of this emerging and innovative approach to education is clearly needed.

E-Pedagogy

Nickols (2011) and Serdyukov (2015) articulate models of online teaching that they refer to as **e-pedagogy**. The models presented use educational theories of learning such as behavioral theory, cognitive theory, and constructivist theory as a foundation for the pedagogy. These models were developed with a focus on postsecondary educational structures. Serdyukov (2015) argues that there is a need for a pedagogical framework that is specifically developed for the online setting. He asserts that, in the modern world, universities must move beyond producing graduates who have a certain knowledge base and skill set by moving toward sending graduates into the workforce who can produce original ideas and new knowledge (Serdyukov, 2015). Commonly, technology-based education has been led by advances in technology and its application versus sound methodological and pedagogical considerations (Nickols, 2011; Serdyukov, 2015). Educators are frequently presented with new technology, new applications, and new platforms as teaching tools without any consideration of the theoretical framework through which education is conceptualized and, sometimes, without research backing their effectiveness. There is a concern about **technocentrism** or "the subtle tendency to associate interactivity, convenience and engagement through the application of technology with improved education" (Nickols, 2011, p. 323). Technocentrism centers the use of technology and places little emphasis on pedagogical frameworks. This can lead educators to overly rely on implementing the latest technology without focusing on their own self-development in pedagogy (Nickols, 2011; Serdyukov, 2015). While many schools and institutions provide training on new technologies, the question remains about how methods using these technologies fit into pedagogical frameworks. In many ways, it seems a process of trial-and-error and movement to the latest advancement in technology without consideration of how this might impact student learning. Effective online learning must combine sound pedagogy with reliable, easy to use technology (Nickols, 2011).

E-pedagogy views the educator's role as one of both facilitator and mentor (Serdyukov, 2015). The application of this model requires the need for university administrators to support pedagogical development by providing educator training in online pedagogy and ensuring that there are evidence-based protocols to assess and provide feedback to educators. Refer to Chapter 12 for further discussion of how administrators can support online educators.

A third consideration, outlined by Serdyukov (2015), is the importance of communication, collaboration, and socialization in the online environment. Creating opportunities for peer-to-peer and peer-to-educator communication and collaboration, and ensuring that there is quality depth of engagement, can be challenging in the online environment. In asynchronous courses, discussion board posts and other forms of prompted written communication are often used, while synchronous courses include some virtual face-time that allows for pairings and small-group breakouts. Synchronous courses provide additional opportunities for collaboration and socialization when compared to asynchronous courses. Refer to Chapter 4 in this textbook for further discussion and ways to engage students in online education.

While Serdyukov (2015) provides an outline of the components of his model and refers to it as an all-inclusive model, he also stresses the need for a comprehensive theory of online pedagogy that is constantly being modified in response to the changing social and technological world. Nickols (2011) presents five principles related to online teaching:

- The focus should be on the end product of transformational education rather than on which specific technique should be applied in a given situation. In other words, there are multiple pathways to produce transformational education and what matters is that, in the end, students are transformed.
- Being conversational is an aim. This includes engagement with students and ensuring that students understand the educator's thinking about the course and how the learning may occur.
- Keep the subject at the center while bringing students' voices and experiences to the subject.
- Providing feedback and ensuring that students have conceptual understanding is a major focus. It is important that students are able to understand versus recall information.
- Be transformative by creating uncertainty, exploration, and the adoption of new perspectives.

While heutagogy has been applied in the online setting, the frameworks called e-pedagogy need further development. Serdyukov's (2015) model presents some general areas of focus and consideration in online teaching and outlines a way to build a comprehensive theoretical framework, and Nickols (2011) presents five principles to consider when teaching online.

Toward Inclusive Pedagogical Frameworks

While many educators were trained from traditional theoretical perspectives that erased the position of the speaker from analysis and viewed the stance of the educator as neutral or value free, this position, in reality, ensures that one is reproducing the values of the dominant culture and often supports noninclusive ways of being and doing (hooks, 1994; Kendi, 2019). "The hegemonic Eurocentric paradigms that have informed western philosophy and sciences ... assume a universalistic, neutral, objective point of view" (Grosfoguel, 2011, p. 4). These traditional approaches to education "can marginalize rather than include students in the classroom" (Grier-Reed & Williams-Wengerd, 2018, p. 1).

Pedagogy that is culturally inclusive, such as culturally sustaining, liberatory, feminist, intersectional, and critical pedagogies, focus teacher efforts on providing an inclusive classroom for all students and view the classroom as a space that is not value free or neutral. Educators' and students' perspectives and ways of viewing the world cannot be separated from their **social location**. One's social location intersects with systems of oppression and privilege and shapes one's experiences, influences one's world view, limits or expands one's access to resources, and impacts how educators show up in the classroom. Educators will want to understand how their **positionality** is connected to, and cannot be separated from, their work. Reflective practice in developing awareness of how one's worldview and positionality impacts one's practice in education and research is considered a fundamental guideline for promoting equity—for example, in the field of psychology (American Psychological Association, 2019). In addition to educators being socially located into categories such as race, gender, and class, the act of physically or virtually appearing in a classroom space is contextually located in an institution and within social structures in a given time period.

> Online practice, like face-to-face instruction, is situated by the cultural spaces in which lecturers' act. The cultural values and beliefs of professional communities and the informing epistemologies are enacted through the interactions between participants as they engage in, and through, online spaces. (Coker, 2018, p. 140)

The physical presence of the educator, socially located within multiple systems of privilege and oppression, has an impact on what happens in the classroom (Kannen, 2012). Students make presumptions about race, class, gender, and other social categories, based on the perceived social locations of the educator (Kannen, 2012). Students' perceptions and beliefs about the social location of the educator can grant or take away authority and power in the classroom and minimize or exaggerate the message from the educator.

> All bodies that enter into the classroom are consistently engaged in relations of power; therefore, to attempt to remain neutral when in the position of authority ... may not only be impossible, but also antithetical to the project of critical and progressive education. (Kannen, 2012, p. 642)

Decolonialization as an Aim of Inclusive Pedagogy

While there are global discussions about the impact of colonization and colonialism, efforts toward **decolonialization** in academia seem to have recently gained momentum. **Colonization** can be viewed as an event with a start and end date, during which one group of people traveled to another geographical area, conquering and dominating another group of people and then instituting colonialism (Omanga, 2020). **Colonialism** is a complex power structure that shifts power, possession, and resources from indigenous people to those who are invading and conquering (Omanga, 2020). Colonialism sets up colonizer-colonized relationships in which colonized persons are exploited and dominated while purporting to be civilizing them (Omanga, 2020). Colonialism, as a power structure, "invades the mental universe of a people, destabilizing them from what they used to know, into knowing what is brought in by colonialism" (Omanga, 2020, para. 5) and engages in the process of "killing and displacing preexisting knowledges ... killing and displacing the languages of a people and imposing your own" (Omanga, 2020, para. 5) and killing or replacing the culture of a group of people (Omanga, 2020).

Decoloniality is considered "a method and paradigm of restoration and reparation" (William & Mary, n.d., para. 2) that "aspires to restore, elevate, renew, rediscover, and acknowledge and validate the lives, live-experiences, cultural and knowledge of indigenous people, People of Color, and colonized people as well as decenter hetero/cis normativity, gender hierarchies and racial privilege" (William & Mary, n.d., para. 2). In this chapter, the terms *decolonize, decolonizing,* and *decolonization* are consistent with the definition of decoloniality described in the previous paragraph. Therefore, in this chapter, decolonialism, decolonialization, and decolonization can be used interchangeably. They refer to the process of dismantling power hierarchies and oppressive educational practices; promoting inclusive practices and policies; and valuing diverse ways of knowing, being, and doing.

Decolonialization practices and efforts are frequently discussed in academia, and while many academics want to create inclusive classroom space that value the diversity of students' experiences and social realities, strategies for inclusivity can sometimes be elusive. Many of us who are thinking about, writing about, talking about, and putting into practice decolonization efforts were trained in Western, colonialized universities. Doing the self-work to continually examine, unlearn, and relearn is an ongoing process and requires much vigilance and commitment.

In the United States, and particularly at historically white institutions, colonialism is present in educational settings (Battiste, 2013; Gaztambide-Fernández, 2012; hooks, 1994; Zembylas, 2018). **Eurocentric, androcentric,** and **heterocentric** colonial practices place people, based on their social locations, in a hierarchical framework and place knowledge, and acceptable sources in knowledge, in a hierarchy (Sleeter & Bernal, 2004; Vavrus, 2010). The realities, lived experiences, and voices of those who are marginalized and oppressed are often left out of curriculum, and institutional policy is a systemic factor that contributes to the reproduction of colonial values (Vavrus, 2010). Consistent with the practice of educators who use traditional approaches that profess neutrality, many leaders in higher education have adopted a color-blind racial ideology and view themselves as politically neutral administrators (Vavrus, 2010). Additionally, they have the belief that Eurocentric curricula is superior, academic achievement has no connection to oppression and privilege, and that poor students and students of color have knowledge deficits and lack the ability to succeed (Vavrus, 2010).

Critical Pedagogy

Critical pedagogy, which originates from critical theories, addresses the oppressive practices of education. It attempts to offer tools to educators that deepen social theory and lead to increased equality (Tarlau, 2014). Contrary to the traditional approach and value of independent learning, critical pedagogy emphasizes collective learning, with the educator walking along side of their students, working and engaging in dialogue to create new knowledge (Tarlau, 2014). Collective learning emphasizes teaching from a foundation of students' previous knowledge. Students bring their life experiences with them into the classroom, and these experiences serve as a foundation for building knowledge. Individual experiences and perspectives, paired with group learning, lead to learning and development within critical pedagogy (Tarlau, 2014).

The role of educators in critical pedagogy is vital, as they address inequality and racism that silences marginalized groups; examine course texts, assignments, requirements, discussion, and how they may contribute to inequalities; provide a safe environment for conversation about intersectionality, experience, diversity perspectives; and integrate social justice, issues of access, and embrace controversy (Haskins & Singh, 2015). Using a critical framework, educators view students as active co-creators of knowledge (Wang & Torrisi-Steele, 2015) and engage in open dialogue with students about curriculum developments and choice of texts and assignments, and include challenges and achievement of marginalized people in teaching (Thompson, 2014). Students play a crucial role in their own development and learning as well as the direction of the class. Critical pedagogy challenges traditional approaches to learning.

Critical theories acknowledge that "educational systems, the process of knowledge building and knowledge itself can never achieve objectivity, but instead are social constructions deeply rooted in power relations" (Case & Lewis, 2017, p. 130). These power relations are not always visible and are maintained in educational institutions through policy and ways of doing business that are reproductions of colonization (Kendi, 2019). Creating safer spaces, within academia, for Black and Indigenous People of Color (BIPOC) has been thought to contribute to more equitable access (Ali, 2017) and is a goal of critical pedagogy. The term *safe space* has been used to signify a space where people who are marginalized, based on their social locations, can safely work in the educational arena (Ali, 2017). "These spaces and the ability to operate within them connect heavily to accessibility and power, even though these spaces lack a physical manifestation" (Ali, 2017, p. 5).

Critical pedagogy, with its focus on critical thinking, as well as the role of the educator being that of facilitator and co-collaborator, fit well in the online learning environment. Online courses offer countless activities such as forums and discussions that allow the educator to change their role from the traditional leader and holder of the information to one who is on the journey with their students. Student experience and knowledge as the foundation of intellectual growth and development shows the importance of online dialogue. According to Boyd (2016), an online discussion can lead to meaningful dialogue that expands understanding and leads to deeper knowledge and increased connection between participants, ultimately leading to greater critical consciousness.

How technology is being used can impact critical thinking as well. As noted by Wang and Torrisi-Steele (2015), the technology being used in the class is not important, but how the technology is being used is. Critical pedagogy includes exercises and assignments that allow students an opportunity to explore social and cultural contexts, including the online environment (Boyd, 2016). This theoretical framework includes a foundation of inclusive and thought-provoking activities. Within a critical framework, educators working in the online environment must navigate the complexity of online displays of power and silencing of voices (Caruthers & Friend, 2014). These authors argue that social and political influences can reduce the likelihood of students from marginalized groups speaking in the classroom.

At the time of writing this chapter, systemic racism is at the forefront of national conversations, people are protesting for the rights of Black and Brown people, and there is division about what steps should be taken to pave an equitable path forward. It seems that we have become increasingly aware, as a nation, that our public spaces do not provide equal access for all people, and this lack of equal access extends to our educational institutions. It is likely that most of us want to create a safe space in the classroom where all students can learn, grow, and develop. While honoring the herstorical origins of the term *safe space* in critical and womanist ways of viewing the world, the term *brave space* has significance in today's educational settings. **Brave space**, in the classroom, is a space that invites controversy with civility, allows for authentic displays of emotion and processing of intention versus impact, supports personal choice and reflection on the use of challenge, and increases awareness of the different way respectfulness can be demonstrated in dialogue (Arao & Clemens, 2013). Creating this brave space may allow for dialogue about emotionally laden topics, increase participation of all students, and support students in the development critical consciousness.

In the context of a critical framework, Caruthers and Friend (2014) proposed "a **Thirdspace** within the online learning environment, a socially constructed space built from the multiple perceptions, meanings, values, and ideologies of students and instructors" (p. 13). In this thirdspace, there is the use of "new knowledge forms to rethink material and pedagogy" (Caruthers & Friend, 2014, p. 14). The authors define the traditional, face-to-face classroom where transmission of knowledge occurs as "firstspace." "Secondspace" is the term used to describe the online classroom as a space that is covertly designed to transfer knowledge in a traditional model. In contrast, thirdspace is critical pedagogy enacted in the online environment that views educators and students as co-creators of knowledge and promotes shared power between them. Thirdspace is created in the online setting when the educator brings critical pedagogy to the classroom in an effort to reduce power differentials, co-create knowledge, and connect learning with social change (Caruthers & Friend, 2014). The authors suggest that, in this space, critical thinking efforts also focus on the relationship between people and technology and how this impacts learning. While their research focused on the experiences of students in teacher and administrator preparation programs, Caruthers and Friend (2014) noted that online educators, across all disciplines and levels, can take responsibility for utilizing practices that support liberation versus those that are oppressive.

CRITICAL CONSCIOUSNESS DEVELOPMENT

The development of **critical consciousness** is grounded in critical theory and critical approaches to pedagogy. Living in a diverse, multicultural world requires that educators and students develop cultural understanding. The development of critical consciousness is a process wherein one becomes aware of the major and interlocking systems of power and oppression (e.g., racism, sexism, classism, ageism, sizeism) and how they work to promote and sustain oppression and privilege, and develops a level of efficacy in action against oppression (Heberle et al., 2020). Critical consciousness has also been defined as "an individual's capacity to critically reflect and act upon their sociopolitical environment" (Diemer et al., 2006, p. 445). As a result of the development of critical consciousness, one begins to engage in social justice action. This action can take place at the individual, group, community, or systems level. At the individual level, one reflects on sociopolitical realities, deeply questioning and discerning for oneself, although often with others, how and why power relations are structured and maintained, in order to begin the process of radical healing (French et al., 2020). In addition to being able to navigate relationships and dialogue in a diverse world, for individuals who are socially located in multiple systems of oppression, this type of critical self-reflection may result in the reduction of psychological distress caused by systemic oppression. Heberle and colleagues (2020) found that "critical consciousness was associated with a number of adaptive developmental outcomes, including career-related, civic, social-emotional, and academic outcomes—especially for marginalized youth" (p. 525).

Several studies have examined pathways to the development of critical consciousness among educators (Landreman et al., 2007; Paccione, 2000) and students (Heberle et al., 2020; Taylor, 2019). Across these studies, awareness of and self-reflection on one's socio-politico-cultural context and positionality, along with the ability to view and step outside of dominant ways of thinking, is necessary for critical consciousness development. In one phenomenological study inquiring about the development of critical consciousness among educators from prekindergarten to university level, the researcher found that cultural immersion experiences and exposure to diversity in literature and coursework stimulated critical examination of various dominant sociopolitical, economic, and educational systems (Paccione, 2000). These opportunities for critical reflection were viewed as necessary for developing commitment to equity and inclusion (Paccione, 2000). Classroom spaces wherein educators provided a space for participants to openly discuss controversial issues, such as social justice, and encouraged community building were positively associated with the development of critical consciousness among youth (Heberle et al., 2020).

Regarding the process of critical consciousness development, a study examining this development among university educators found that critical consciousness occurred in two phases—awareness raising and moving to critical consciousness (Landreman et al., 2007). The awareness raising phase included four themes:

> (a) exposure to people different from one's own cultural experience; (b) the experience of a critical incident related to these differences; (c) self-reflection on the meaning of cultural differences or an incident; and (d) an "aha moment" or new realization that resulted from reflection. (Landreman et al., 2007, p. 281)

Centering race and racism by focusing on the development of critical consciousness of **anti-Black racism**, Della Mosley and colleagues (2020) found that three process categories emerged: witnessing anti-Black racism, processing anti-Black racism, and acting critically against anti-Black racism. Based on this work, bearing witness to anti-Black racism through lived experiences or the lived experiences of others and experiencing some type of racial trauma is a first step in the development of critical consciousness. In the second step, processing anti-Black racism, critical consciousness is further developed by connecting the historical and systemic roots of oppression to current realities of lived experiences, processing through the range of psychological and social outcomes of anti-Black racism, fostering intersectional growth through awareness of multiple social locations and personal identities, and finding ways to cope with the personal experience of racial trauma. During the third step, reflection and processing result in action to prevent or resist anti-Black racism and racial trauma (Mosley et al., 2020).

Emerging from the work of Mosley and colleagues (2020) is a liberatory process, shared by their Black activist participants, that may be considered across social locations. The steps that these participants shared in developing their own critical consciousness related to anti-Black racism can be applied to other methods of discrimination and oppression (e.g., sexism, heterosexism, sizeism, classism, and ageism). These include storying survival, activism, physical resistance, organizing, teaching, coalition building, modeling/mentoring, scholar activism, and space making (Mosley et al., 2020).

Based on the relevant findings in the scholarly literature mentioned above, critical consciousness development among educators and students can result in decreasing the impact of minority stress and racial trauma. Educators can demonstrate the process of lifelong learning in the area of critical consciousness development and create classroom spaces that encourage this process for students, thereby increasing positive outcomes for marginalized students. Educators will want to be mindful that critical race theory and the development of critical consciousness provides a pathway for teachers and students to develop "the ability to be aware of racial barriers and to use this knowledge as a motivating factor for continued scholastic engagement and achievement" (Chapman-Hilliard & Beasley, 2018, p. 133).

Intersectional, Black Feminist, and Feminist Pedagogy

The first use of the term **intersectionality** in scholarly literature, and the development of intersectionality theory, is credited to Black feminist legal scholar Kimberlé Crenshaw (1989). Crenshaw (1989), using a critical race theoretical lens, asserted that while Black women have experienced discrimination throughout history based on their unique social location, it is only when the intersection of racism and sexism are examined that one can understand the experiences of Black women. Looking at gender and experiences of sexism without focusing on race and experiences of racism cannot explain the experiences of Black women. While this theory was originally conceptualized within critical race theory and applied to the intersection of sexism and racism, intersectionality is now widely used within and outside of critical theories to explain how people are socially located in categories such as gender, race, sexual orientation, ability, and age and how the major systems of oppression (e.g., racism, sexism, classism, ageism) are interconnected and create advantage, privilege, disadvantage, and oppression, based on one's social location. An individual within this framework can simultaneously experience oppression and privilege because they are socially located into multiple categories such as race, gender, and class (Collins, 1990). Therefore, it could be said that no person is always and only privileged and no individual is always and only oppressed (Collins, 1990; Crenshaw, 1989, 1991). It is our social locations and the interlocking systems of power and oppression that create unique lived experiences.

Intersectionality theory is rooted in the work of Black feminists (Collins, 2000; Crenshaw, 1989) and is at the core of **intersectional pedagogy.** In an effort to avoid extracting the work of Black feminists, it is important to recognize these herstorical roots of intersectionality theory. In her 2017 book, Kim Case presented a model of intersectional pedagogy, developed with intersectionality theory as a framework. Her model emphasizes the analysis of "social location with structural and institutional power, deconstructing privilege and implementing social justice action" (Case, 2017, p. 8). She writes that effective intersectional pedagogy acknowledges that intersecting systems of oppression work to influence the lived experiences of persons based on their social location; includes numerous systems of oppression such as racism, sexism, ableism; acknowledges that these systems of power and oppression are often invisible and aims to uncover them; examines privilege; analyzes power; encourages educator self-reflection and student reflection; promotes the dismantling of oppression through social action; places value on the voices of students who experience multiple layers of oppression; and infuses intersectionality across the curriculum (Case, 2017). Intersectional pedagogy, as a framework, is also a feminist pedagogy and provides educators with strategies to examine social structures and processes that create inequity and provide a pathway to equity through social justice efforts and the decolonization of education.

Black feminist pedagogy is an intersectional feminist pedagogical approach that centers race. While Black feminist pedagogy is intersectional, critical, and feminist, there are various feminist perspectives on teaching. Common themes found across feminist pedagogies are knowledge co-creation, community building, centering the experiences and voices of those who have historically been left out of curriculum, and critical self-reflection (Onufer & Rojas, 2019). These themes, along with social justice action, are foundational for feminist pedagogies. When striving to promote inclusion, diversity, and equity, and naming their approach as feminist, educators will want to be prepared for personal reactions from students and colleagues. Feminist writer bell hooks (1994) explained that when increasing diversity and inclusion are discussed, those from social locations with more social power, who have always been centered in educational practices, may feel challenged or reactive to the process of inclusion and decentering of dominant narratives. They may have a variety of strong reactions, devalue the need for equity and inclusion, and feel as if their social group is being removed from the experience (hooks, 1994). With promotion of equity and inclusion as the aim, the development of critical consciousness as a goal can be helpful in assisting students understanding experiences outside of their own.

Intersectional feminist pedagogical frameworks influence educators to think critically about creating their course and interacting with students while also examining the institutions, structures, and social positions that contextualize lectures, discussions, and activities. The authors of this chapter assert that feminist pedagogies, to be inclusive, must be both intersectional and critical. While it could be argued that all feminist approaches are intersectional, some feminist approaches may center gender while others center race. Integrating intersectional and feminist approaches assures that educators work to center the voices and perspectives of all who have been historically left out of the curriculum, while valuing the lived experience of students, co-creating knowledge, and building community in the classroom. In intersectional feminist approaches, and other inclusive approaches to pedagogy, the co-creation of knowledge serves as an act of inclusivity and valuing of diverse ways of knowing. It actually calls for students' and professors' self-involvement in the process of creating knowledge. Combining these strategies is thought to help build engagement in the learning community and help students feel valued.

Liberatory Pedagogy

Liberatory pedagogy perspectives involve the development and emergence of critical consciousness and an emphasis on reflecting upon and changing the social world. Educators are actively involved in creating community wherein students can learn, grow, and share in the knowledge-building process. Traditional pedagogical approaches have often focused on what Freire (1970) referred to as the "banking" concept of education. "In the banking concept of education, knowledge is a gift bestowed by those who consider themselves knowledgeable upon those who they consider to know nothing" (p. 72). Using this approach, educators maintain the status quo and replicate oppressive strategies (Freire, 1970). Following the banking model of education, the roles of the teacher include imparting knowledge, being the subject, disciplining, and choosing content while students are passive learners who are disciplined, adapt to the needs of the teacher, and serve as objects (Freire, 1970; hooks, 1994).

Approaching teaching from a liberatory stance means liberating the oppressed. It means engaging students in an inclusive environment where there is mutual respect and trust, as well as one where the instructor is interested in student well-being (Freire, 2018). Liberatory pedagogy recognizes power relations, thus improving the educational experience for members of oppressed populations (Stanger, 2016). Students are active learners in this space that encourages critical thinking and dialogue, and that challenges existing structures of power, privilege, and oppression (Freire, 2018). Consider the impact of open, honest dialogue that explores students' social locations. The critical conversations that take place within this framework allow students to think differently about themselves and about the world, challenging power structures and social injustice (Dalmage & Martinez, 2020). While liberatory pedagogy and feminist pedagogies have much in common, one point of departure is the focus of liberatory pedagogy on rationalism, valuing thinking, and excluding emotion as a way of knowing (Valle-Ruiz et al., 2015). In contrast, feminist pedagogical approaches recognize the interconnectivity of thought and emotion and value both emotion and thinking as part of lived experience and, therefore, forms of knowledge.

Culturally Responsive Pedagogy

Culturally responsive pedagogy (Gay, 2002; Ladson-Billings, 1995a and 1995b; Villegas & Lucas, 2002) emerged in the late 1990s to challenge a historical struggle against inequality in educational pedagogy for Black and Indigenous People of Color (BIPOC) students. Starting in the 1960s with what was termed **"deficit approaches"** to teaching, it then moved through **difference pedagogies** in the 1970s–1980s. The elementary characteristic of these models was a perception that BIPOC students needed to be reeducated toward dominant-culture, middle-class expectations about secular education.

The perception was that cultural practices imposed limitations to their academic potentialities. Educational policy sought to overcome this by aligning students with what was believed to be enhanced modalities of learning. The goal of these methods was to decrease the achievement gap that was identified in BIPOC students by implying that their societal ways of "being and knowing" were deficient and lacking (Paris & Ball, 2009). Early examples of these approaches include the agenda-driven "Indian schools" that stripped Native American students of their traditional cultural practices and languages (McCarty et al., 2006). What is currently considered mainstream education is directly associated with White, middle-class norms, the purpose being to reeducate students according to these normative standards.

Culturally responsive pedagogy was an educational philosophy conceptualized by Ladson-Billings (1995a) during research on the educational disparities facing racial minority students in the United States. Ladson-Billings (1995a) highlighted the pervasive educational achievement gap associated with the deficits in the mainstream curriculum, which often promoted the marginalization of BIPOC students by promoting colonized education. Ladson-Billings (1995a,) recognized that racial minority students experience inequity in the secular academic setting, and that school is a place where minority students cannot fully be themselves due to the historical and ongoing colonialization of education. BIPOC students continue to score lower on IQ tests due to cultural bias inherent in standardized testing (Ortiz, 2008). They are also underrepresented in "gifted and talented" programs, while overrepresented in special-needs programs (Wright et al., 2017). Public schools are also often racially segregated and poorly resourced (Logan et al., 2012); Black students are pushed out of school due to culturally insensitive discipline measures associated with the school-to-prison pipeline (Welsh & Little, 2018). Culturally responsive pedagogy highlights the influence of culture on thinking and behavior, and stresses that educators adapt teaching to integrate student culture to facilitate optimum learning (Villegas & Lucas, 2002).

Ladson-Billings (1995a) outlines three central tenets of culturally responsive pedagogy. The first emphasizes educator high expectation for student success. The second requires the nurturing of positive cultural identity by promoting provider cultural competence. The final tenet necessitates that educators guide students in developing a critical consciousness that they can use to critique or interrupt current and historical social inequities (Ladson-Billings, 1995a).

HIGH ACADEMIC EXPECTATIONS

Scholars have researched the characteristics of culturally responsive educators who demonstrate high expectations for student achievement. Kleinfeld (1975) coined the phrase **"warm demander"** to describe an educator who demonstrated effective teaching of Native students in Alaskan schools. These teachers created classrooms with explicit rules for conduct and communicated personal warmth toward their students while also setting high standards for educational achievement. Warm demander educators ensure that the educational setting is safe and nurturing for all students. Researchers have also studied similar traits in educators who are successful with African American and Latinx students. These educators, termed *othermothers* by James and Busia (1993), demonstrate kinship qualities in their educational practice. Their instructional support is built on creating a relationship with students that extends beyond the classroom by connecting and learning about students' lives, including their cultures, belief systems, and future goals (Gay, 2002). Evidence indicates that BIPOC students in predominantly White institutions may experience a deficit in opportunities to form relationships with faculty and may have less contact with faculty outside the classroom (Brunsma et al., 2017). These students miss the opportunity for mentorship that comes from a relationship with a senior, more experienced member of a profession, and this is correlated with a drop in retention and graduation (Banks & Dohy, 2019). According to Guiffrida (2005), research of African American and Latinx students shows that faculty who are student centered incorporate the holistic approach to advising that is conceptualized in the philosophy of othermothering. Bernard et al. (2000) refer to this faculty-student relationship as "other-mothering in the academy" and describe faculty who invest time in building a relationship where they mentor, motivate, and advocate to ensure students' academic success and overall well-being.

CULTURAL COMPETENCE

Ladson-Billings (1995b), posits that culturally responsive pedagogy nurtures the development of positive ethnic and cultural identities and does not require that students give up their cultural identity in order to assimilate into mainstream culture. Educators support cultural competence (Gay, 2002) by disrupting colonialized, Eurocentric curricula; incorporating student's cultural knowledge; and establishing relationships between the school and student's communities. This relationship allows community members shared governance over curriculum design and school policy and encourages the school to draw upon the cultural expertise of their students' community.

When the curriculum is reshaped to reflect the identities of students (Gay, 2002), there is representation of various identities and beliefs systems in classroom materials, artwork, books, and other materials from specific cultural groups. Examples of affirming students' identities are frequently researched in the use of language. Language is a representation of culture, and in a racial minority family is closely tied to belief systems and cultural practices (Hakuta, 2011). Second-language students, or African American students who are **"code-switching"**—using a variation from Standard American English—can be supported to engage the curriculum using their preferred language (Hakuta, 2011). According to Ladson-Billings (1995b), culturally responsive educators support the development of critical consciousness (Ladson-Billings, 1995b) by helping students examine the existing power structures in mainstream society. Therefore, students are encouraged to adopt a social justice agenda that includes the sharing of power and the co-construction of class content, process and assessment.

Culturally Sustaining Pedagogy

Paris and Alim (2017) argue that mainstream education continues to perpetuate the forced acculturation of BIPOC students by promoting explicit and implicit policies and practices that undermine the sustainability of their cultures. Culturally sustaining pedagogy expands the conceptualization of culturally responsive pedagogy by highlighting its usefulness in confronting earlier deficit pedagogies. These authors express an urgent need to not only respond but also sustain the cultural and belief systems of BIPOC students in the face of annihilation by embracing, nurturing, and supporting multilingualism and multiculturalism. According to Paris (2012), "culturally sustaining pedagogy seeks to perpetuate and foster—to sustain—linguistic, literate, and cultural pluralism as part of the democratic project of schooling" (p 95). Paris and Alim (2017) provide examples of culturally sustaining pedagogy by highlighting that the United States is a country that is rich with over 300 languages, yet the prevailing school climate discourages the daily use of any language other than American English. Examples of this power imbalance is reflected in the widely researched phenomenon of code-switching (whereby Spanish-speaking and African American students move between their preferred home language to use American English). A culturally sustaining classroom would encourage the use of both languages and support students expressing themselves in their preferred language. Culturally sustaining pedagogy sustains the cultural frame of reference (Paris & Alim, 2017) by designing curricula that celebrates and recognizes the beliefs, historical knowledge, and achievements of BIPOC cultures. Additionally, the framework promotes student self-agency by teaching ways to disrupt the larger sociopolitical influences impacting education such as the historical basis of the achievement gap and nurtures the concept that academic success is attainable (Paris & Alim, 2017). Furthermore, students are encouraged to be co-constructors of a curriculum that is reflective and affirming of their communities (Sleeter, 2014), and to be involved in its implementation and to shape the learning environment conducive to their learning. Culturally affirming practice that is increasingly recognized as sustaining the cultural practices that promote hope and engagement in BIPOC students in the classroom and at school include spoken word (Fisher, 2007), hip-hop (Hill, 2009), and *el teatro campesino* (farm workers theatre) (Pawel, 2009).

Trauma-Informed Pedagogy

Trauma can be understood as any personal or vicarious exposure to abuse, violence, racism, domestic violence, accidents, or natural or man-made disaster that overwhelms an individual's emotional and psychological ability to cope (Herman, 1998). Exposure to trauma or hearing about another's trauma (secondary trauma) significantly increases the risk of mental and other health problems and is associated with negative outcomes for learning due to the physiological changes affecting the brain (van der Kolk, 2014). By the time they reach college, a majority of students report experiencing one or multiple traumatic events (Bruffaerts et al., 2018). With so many students, across all ages, experiencing trauma, it is critical that educators have an understanding of how trauma impacts students' lives and bring an informed awareness of trauma into their pedagogical approach.

Trauma's Impact on The Brain

The human brain is geared for survival; therefore, under real or perceived threat it remains in a hypervigilant state that is on the lookout for danger. This constant vigilance is associated with the neurochemical response referred to as fight-flight-freeze (van der Kolk, 2014). When the environment feels threatening, the brain allocates resources to this survival system, which in turn compromises the areas of the brain associated with executive function such as those linked to comprehension, attention, emotional regulation, and impulse control.

In the last few years, the college campus climate has been increasingly recognized as detrimental to the emotional and psychological well-being of BIPOC students (Wei et al., 2011). While scholars celebrate the increase in enrollment of BIPOC students, most argue that institutions of higher education still promote White Eurocentric educational ideologies that are injurious to racial minority students (Gay, 2000; Ladson-Billings, 1995a and 1995b; Paris & Alim, 2017). These ideologies replace the overt form of racism that is typically associated with the Jim Crow era (Horsford, 2019) and operate in subtle yet equally damaging ways. Termed *color-blind ideology* by Bonilla-Silva (2013), this form of racism assumes that the United States is in a postracial era that is characterized by an end to racism. However, studies show that racism within higher education has not ended and instead has been transformed into a more sinister, less obvious, form through racial microaggressions. Pierce (1970) first proposed the term *racial microaggressions* to describe the routine behavioral and environmental insults and invalidations targeted toward African Americans. Since then, academics such as Sue et al. (2019) have expanded the concept to include other minoritized groups who experience both explicit and implicit acts of discrimination. These daily injuries have a damaging effect on the psyche of BIPOC students (Hardy, 2010) and are experienced as racial trauma.

Racial trauma, also known as "racial battle fatigue" (Smith, 2010), is the cumulative injury experienced by BIPOC individuals as a result of exposure to real or perceived racial discrimination (Carter, 2007; Helms et al., 2010). These experiences threaten physical, psychological, and or emotional well-being (Carter et al., 2013) and are implicated in poor health outcomes and an increase in mental health disorders such as depression, anxiety, and posttraumatic stress (Sibrava et al., 2019). According to Smith (2010), symptoms of racial trauma include increased hypervigilance, guarded suspiciousness, emotional outbursts, flashbacks, numbing, aggression, and nightmares. These microaggressions have negative implications in the educational setting and divert energy away from academics by increasing focus on survival and managing the stress associated with racial assaults (Minikel-Lacocque, 2013). Furthermore, increased vigilance decreases trust in social institutions and in education (Pérez et al., 2015), which impacts the relationship between educators and BIPOC students. Increased sensitivity to threat heightens defensiveness and impairs the ability for abstract thought, thereby limiting the ability to learn or consolidate new information (Franklin, 2019). Trauma also impacts the ability for self-regulation, which increases the potential for emotional outbursts (Smith et al., 2011). This dysregulation has been associated with argumentativeness, disinterest in learning, and increased use of illicit substances as a form of self-soothing (Boynton et al., 2014).

Trauma-Informed Pedagogy in Practice

Trauma-informed pedagogy aims to alleviate the impact of trauma (Carello & Butler, 2015) on learning by acknowledging the role that education institutions can play in providing safety, stability, and support for traumatized students. Lack of knowledge about trauma-informed pedagogy increases the risk of inadvertently retraumatizing students by provoking their symptoms in various ways that compromise safety in the educational environment.

According to Fallot and Harris (2009), five key principles are fundamental to a trauma-informed pedagogy: "safety; trustworthiness; choice; collaboration and empowerment" (pp. 7–12). Trauma-informed pedagogy requires educators learn about the impact on trauma on the brain and on learning. This first step integrates trauma awareness by highlighting how the impairment of executive functioning impacts students' social-emotional development. This knowledge facilitates improved understanding of student behavior that may be challenging or disruptive. According to Dorado et al. (2016), trauma-informed pedagogy acknowledges that traumatized students are at increased risk of failing or dropping out of school; therefore, understanding traumatic stress allows educators to practice empathetic responsiveness and cultural humility, and to establish safe, predictable, and empowering relationships in the classroom. Porche et al. (2011) explained that student behaviors associated with trauma are often mistaken for avoidance, lack of ability, or disengagement. These perceptions often lead to punitive academic discipline measures that can retraumatize students.

TRAUMA-INFORMED STRATEGIES FOR EDUCATORS

Carello and Butler (2015) advocate that educators need to not only understand the impact of trauma in the classroom; they highlight that it is imperative to incorporate pedagogical strategies that minimize the risk of further traumatizing students. Furthermore, these authors maintain that it is crucial for educators to promote the five key strategies of trauma-informed care by learning strategies that can inform curriculum design. Sample strategies include promoting trustworthiness by providing students with a course orientation that clearly articulates course objectives and outcomes and a course syllabus outlining assignments and grading policies, as well as providing grading rubrics for all major assignments. Trauma-informed educators provide strengths-based and timely feedback (Carello & Butler, 2015) on assignments and evaluate course objectives for suitability and appropriateness. Educators are cautioned against presenting material solely to provoke strong reaction from students. When students cannot avoid interacting with difficult course content, educators are advised to develop a warning system to help students anticipate what they may be exposed to (Carello & Butler, 2015). Educators are encouraged to debrief following every encounter with difficult or emotionally charged content and inquire about students' ability to self-regulate and cope with the content.

Trauma-informed educators build positive classroom culture by creating community and fostering positive peer relationships (Carello & Butler, 2015). Teaching strategies such as modeling respectful communication and providing effective feedback can impact these relationships. Students are assisted to evaluate the possible impact of self-disclosure during coursework. Trauma-informed pedagogy recognizes the shared power of decision-making and includes student voices in co-creating the educational experience (Carello & Butler, 2015). In turn, instructors actively solicit the input of students when designing curricula and use course feedback in making the necessary changes. Table 2.1 provides a list of questions for consideration by educators within each core principle of trauma-informed pedagogy.

TABLE 2.1

CORE VALUES	GUIDING QUESTIONS FOR TRAUMA-INFORMED PRACTICE
Safety (physical and emotional)	• Is the classroom environment safe and predictable? • Are there easily accessible exits? • Are directions clear and readily available? • Are signs and other visual materials welcoming, clear, and legible? • Are restrooms easily accessible (e.g., well marked and gender neutral?) • Are faculty and staff welcoming, respectful, and engaging? • Is there emotional support or resources available when needed?
Trustworthiness	• Are there clear explanations and information about policies and procedures? • Are syllabi clear, with specific goals and objectives? • Do syllabi provide rubrics for major assignments? • Are there appropriate personal and professional boundaries?
Choice and control	• Are students informed about their choices and options? • Do students understand their rights and responsibilities? • Are there negative consequences for making different choices? • Do students have choices about attending various meetings or engaging in certain activities or assignments? • Do students choose how contact is made (e.g., by phone or mail to their home or other address)?
Collaboration	• Is student input requested for service planning, goal setting, and the development of program priorities? • Do educators identify tasks that students can collaborate on? • Are there student/educator committees?
Empowerment	• How are students' diverse strengths and skills recognized? • Do educators communicate a sense of realistic optimism about students' capacity to achieve their goals? • How can each class, contact, or service be focused on skill development or enhancement?

Source: Fallot & Harris, 2009; Davidson & Northwest, 2017.

Educator Self-Care

Educator self-care is noted as being a critical component of trauma-informed pedagogy. Fowler (2015) and other researchers (Abenavoli et al., 2013; National Child Traumatic Stress Network, 2016; Sharp & Jennings, 2016) recognized the toll that compassion can have on the emotional well-being of educators and highlight that continual exposure to the trauma narrative and experiences of students can increase educators' vulnerability to the impact of secondary trauma. Secondary traumatic stress leads to physical, emotional, and mental fatigue and diminishes the ability to attend to and engage students (Abenavoli et al., 2013). Educators experiencing vicarious trauma can appear apathetic, cynical, or withdrawn because they have exhausted their ability to show compassion without replenishing their own reserves. Abenavoli et al. (2013) and other researchers such as Bliss (2017) and Sharp and Jennings (2016) have promoted mindfulness-based strategies as an effective way to combat educator burnout and improve emotional well-being. Furthermore, trauma-informed pedagogy highlights the need for educators to attend to and heal their own experiences and histories with trauma in order to better serve trauma-affected students.

Common Factors: Effective Teaching Strategies Across Pedagogies

There are many differences in the aims and goals of online education across primary through postsecondary levels and, therefore, the actual teaching methods used in any given setting and across educators may vary considerably. Individual characteristics of the students as well as sociocultural influences may impact the effectiveness of any given teaching strategy. In this chapter, several pedagogical frameworks and their theoretical concepts have been discussed. Having a guiding framework helps educators know when and how to use and/or modify various teaching strategies in the online environment. While teachers often discuss best practices in teaching, the term *best practices* often leads educators to think that there is an agreed upon consensus about what is best practice (Cato, 2001; Johnson & Cox, 2020; Osborne et al., 2014) and "implies a reductive mentality to online teaching ... instructors and administrators who promote certain practices as best are reducing the teaching enterprise to adhering to a list of activities whose value has not been verified" (Johnson & Cox, 2020, p. 3). Based on their study reviewing articles that discuss best practices in online teaching, Johnson and Cox (2020) report six activities that were consistently described as best practices across the articles they reviewed:

1. Instructors should communicate often with students.
2. Instructors should respond quickly to student questions.
3. Instructors should grade and return assignments/tests quickly.
4. Instructors should maintain a strong "presence" in the virtual classroom.
5. Instructors should have group discussions/activities.
6. Instructors should keep recorded lectures short. (p. 7)

The same researchers assert, however, that the first five of these activities represent good teaching strategies, not necessarily best practices, that have also been applied in face-to-face teaching and that the sixth purported best practice does not have the empirical evidence to support it.

While there is no set of consistently agreed-upon best practices in online teaching (Steele et al., 2019), there are some contextual factors that may make certain strategies more effective, in a given context, than others. For example, the significance of educator presence in the online setting is well-documented in research (Steele et al., 2019), and the relationship between educator and student is critical in promoting student achievement (Dalton, 2018). Both common factors, as well as other strategies supported by scientific research, are outlined below. In addition to these factors, the authors of this chapter assert that applying strategies from a trauma-informed lens is foundational to promote student and educator well-being.

Building Community

While it could be argued that building community is an essential part of any classroom, the role of the educator in intentionally creating a sense of community in the online classroom cannot be understated (Dalton, 2018). Educators may recognize the importance of building relationships with students and facilitating student-to-student relationships; but there is lack of "consensus on which interpersonal interaction strategies best promote effective student learning and satisfaction" (Mehall, 2020, p. 183) and teachers may not be familiar with strategies that encourage peer-to-peer interaction (Paquette, 2016). Mehall (2020) stresses that much of the research that focuses on interaction in the online setting focuses on the number of interactions versus qualitative descriptors of interaction. In his research, Mehall (2020) proposed that purposeful interpersonal interaction can help build community and described it as involving purposeful interpersonal instructional interaction, purposeful social interaction, and supportive interaction. The quality of the social interaction contributes to social presence while the number of social interactions, if there are too many, may detract from quality social presence (Mehall, 2020; Tu & McIsaac, 2002). In 2003, Robyler and Wiencke developed a rubric for assessing interactive qualities of distance courses and this tool that can be used to assess the amount of quality interaction in the online classroom (Mehall, 2020). For further reading, the author cites a body of research supporting the notion that interpersonal interaction, when present, is beneficial for students and when absent, is a barrier for student learning and satisfaction. Additionally, the same source provides a detailed description of behaviors that indicate a high level of purposeful interpersonal interaction. While effective communication and frequent interaction with students has been found to help build a sense of community (Dalton, 2018), increasing the number of interactions without sound educational rationale to support the need can lead to students feeling frustrated and overwhelmed, and may promote disengagement from the classroom (Castano-Munoz et al., 2013; Downing et al., 2007; Mehall, 2020; Northrup et al., 2002).

Inclusive approaches that intentionally reform policy and curriculum can help create learning communities wherein all people may experience a sense of community and belonging. According to the National Committee on Science Education Standards and Assessment (1996) and Dalton (1998), building relationships with students and creating a sense of community is an effective standard practice of teaching. Creating relationships that are safe, predictable, and empowering is an essential practice in trauma-informed pedagogy (Dorado et al., 2018). While educators who have some physical presence in a classroom with students and blend on-ground teaching with online teaching may have an easier time developing relationships, faculty who teach solely online bear a great responsibility for the intentional development of community. Chick and Hassel (2009) recommend two strategies to foster community building utilizing the discussion board tool. The first strategy, called "Ask the Class," involves the development of an online forum wherein students can post questions and receive answers from their peers (Chick & Hassel, 2009, p. 200). The instructor also participates but allows classmates to take the lead in responding. And, when offering a response, the educators offers it in a way to keep the conversation going between peers rather than acting as the expert sharer of knowledge. The second strategy, called "The Hallway," provides "a virtual environment that simulates the hallway on campus where students can talk to each other and us about anything" (Chick & Hassel, 2009, p. 200). To set up this space, instructors create a forum and explain its purpose to students. Educators may want to encourage use of the space by posting creative, or simple, get-to-know-each-other activities. Sharing of inspirational quotes or professional development opportunities could also be posted here. Refer to Chapter 4 for further reading about engaging students in the online classroom.

Connecting Lived Experience and Classroom Content

Borrowing from andragogy, Knowles (1970) argues that adult learners benefit when they can connect real-world experience to what they are learning in the classroom. Across grade levels, the National Committee on Science Education Standards and Assessment (1996) directed teachers to develop knowledge about students' background and experiences so that classroom content can be made relatable to students. Effective instructional strategies include teachers' consideration of local community norms and students' cultural preferences in communication style (Dalton, 1998). The teacher builds relationships with students and connects what they already know with classroom content. Inclusive pedagogical approaches, such as intersectional feminist pedagogy, among others, broaden this notion by stressing that lived experience serves as another way of knowing and should be valued in the classroom. Students and educators bring their own lived experiences into the classroom setting and these experiences can serve as important sources of information related to the content in the course (Case, 2017). Learning while one's experience is central and significant has been a privilege afforded to those with more social power, while oppressed groups are often faced with course content that is not reflective of their life experience (hooks, 1994). "White students experience an education that is harmonious with their self-knowledge, ... students of colour are alienated from theirs" (Leonardo, 2009, p. 94).

Students who are presented with textbooks, materials, authors, examples, and other resources that do not represent their social location or ways of being in the world may fail to connect content to their own lives. For students to learn and engage fully in course content, diversity must by embedded in the curriculum. Integrating diverse perspectives as valid ways of knowing, instead of adding diversity as an afterthought or including diverse perspectives in comparison to dominant cultural experiences, is critical in the endeavor to create an inclusive classroom. Inclusive pedagogical approaches that are relevant to marginalized students are crucial to student growth and feelings of belonging (Odegard & Vereen, 2010).

In support of equity, the classroom must become a space where all students feel responsible to participate and contribute. In additional to the inclusion of diverse readings and voices in the curriculum, educators must be willing to talk about the implications that intersections of racism, classism, sexism, and ableism, among others, have on education and on the lives of students. Educators must be willing to examine their curriculum and the components in which oppression is perpetuated.

Applying the practice of connecting lived experience to the classroom in the online setting can be very similar to face-to-face settings. Some online educators may be from the same local community where students reside and likely have a good understanding of cultural norms and practices in the general geographical region. In this case, educators can focus on learning more about students' individual differences in cultural expressions across social locations and identity and on bringing that lived experience into the classroom. Other online educators, especially those in higher educational settings, may have a virtual classroom of students from different geographical locations and know little about the cultural backgrounds of their students. While this makes it initially challenging to make classroom content relevant to students' daily lives, it is the responsibility of the educator to gain knowledge about students' backgrounds and experiences and find ways to intentionally bring lived experience into the classroom. An intentional strategy for understanding the cultural background and perspectives of students and for building relationships in an online classroom is creating an "About Me" forum as a discussion board assignment (Chick &

Hassel, 2009, p. 199). Chick and Hassel (2009) suggest that students could post information about themselves and include a personal photo or other image that represents who they are. Encouraging other students to read these posts by integrating them into an assignment is also recommend for increasing peer-to-peer interaction.

Centering Students and Co-Creating Knowledge

Student-centered approaches are thought to be necessary for good pedagogical practice in the online setting (Cox & Prestridge, 2020; Dalton, 2018; González, 2013; Sun & Chen, 2016). While pedagogy that is student centered shifts the role of the instructor to facilitator, this does not mean that students should be responsible for teaching themselves (Gordon, 2016). Instead, there is a co-learning process wherein students and teachers are creating knowledge and learning together. Students as co-creators of knowledge is an aspect of pedagogy that is student centered (Kember, 1997), and educators who believe that good teaching involves facilitating learning are more likely to use student-centered approaches than teachers who believe that good teaching involves the transmission of knowledge (Kember & Kwan, 2000). In the online setting, student-centered educators provide students with spaces for collaboration, communication, building knowledge, developing students' understanding and critical thinking, and expanding their worldview (González, 2012; Sobko et al., 2020). Feminist pedagogy provides a lens for recognizing and sharing power in the classroom. Through a feminist pedagogical framework, an educator strives to find various ways to share power and remove, to the extent possible, hierarchy from the classroom. One strategy for enacting this effort could be to implement discussion board postings in a nonhierarchical way. For example, students could participate by writing the discussion board starter posts and be responsible for summarizing the main points across participants. Educators could comment on process rather than content and avoid placing themselves in the role of being the ultimate authority on the topic. Teacher-centered educators provide learning materials that are structured so that students may learn independently (González, 2012). One study of online educators found that teachers who have taken online classes are more likely to engage in student-centered approaches than those who have not (Cox & Prestridge, 2020). Given that COVID-19, in 2020, led to educators both receiving and producing online education, the findings of Cox and Prestridge (2020) could point to the possibility that educators might increasingly use student-centered approaches to teaching.

Self-Involvement of the Educator

Unlike traditional pedagogical perspectives, critical, intersectional, and feminist approaches to pedagogy place an emphasis on the personal responsibility of the educator to be self-involving in the learning process (Case, 2017; hooks, 1994). In contrast to historical narratives that place educators as value free or value neutral, and objective professors of knowledge, educators must be aware of their positionality, values, and social context, and how the sociopolitical environment influences their approach to education. Being self-involving is seen as one way that educators can help connect their own lived experience to classroom content and serve as a model that assists students in bringing their own relevant lived experience as a way of knowing into the classroom. Willingness on the part of the educator to share aspects of their life, relevant to the course and application of content, demonstrate sharing of power with students and, in this way, the educator avoids using coercive power-based strategies with students (hooks, 1994).

Chapter Summary

Pedagogy, or the theory and practice of teaching, has evolved considerably since its inception. Although educators may be exposed to pedagogical frameworks in graduate school, this training is often from the perspective of traditional pedagogical approaches and is focused on face-to-face teaching. Many educators do not receive training in online teaching in their educational institutions, and if they do, the focus may be on the use of technology versus the important role of theory in guiding conceptualization of online teaching. Additionally, approaches that intentionally place value on diversity, equity, and inclusion as integral to the pedagogical framework are rarely taught in graduate programs, and if they are, may be considered in an additive way that seems to suggest they are an afterthought.

In this chapter, both traditional approaches to teaching, such as traditional pedagogy and andragogy, and inclusive approaches to teaching, such as intersectional feminist pedagogy and critical pedagogy, were discussed. Current models of online learning were presented and the need for the development of a comprehensive online pedagogy, as use of online education increases, was noted. While there does not seem to be enough current research with consistent findings to support a set of best practices in online education, there are common factors across pedagogies that are supported by scholarly literature as effective in promoting student engagement and learning. These include community building, connecting lived experiences and classroom content, centering students and co-creating knowledge, and the self-involvement of the educator as teaching strategies that ensure inclusivity of all students.

Online Resources

A Guide to Feminist Pedagogy

An overview of the theory and application of feminist pedagogy from the Vanderbilt Center for Teaching: https://my.vanderbilt.edu/femped/

Back to the Basics: Revisiting the ABCs of Teaching Online Courses

A Faculty Focus article; a list of basic tips for teaching in an online environment: https://www.facultyfocus.com/articles/online-education/back-to-the-basics-revisiting-the-abcs-of-teaching-online-courses/?st=FFdaily;sc=FF200819;utm_term=FF200819&utm_source=ActiveCampaign&utm_medium=email&utm_content=Back+to+the+Basics%3A+Revisiting+the+ABCs+of+Teaching+Online+Courses&utm_campaign=FF200819

Best Practices: Online Pedagogy

A Harvard University guide with a list of tips for online teaching: https://teachremotely.harvard.edu/best-practices

Blended and Online Learning

From the Vanderbilt University Center for Teaching, a guide to developing and facilitating online learning: https://cft.vanderbilt.edu/guides-sub-pages/blended-and-online-learning/

Bloom's Taxonomy

Check out the Vanderbilt University Center for Teaching website for a discussion about the use of Bloom's taxonomy: https://cft.vanderbilt.edu/guides-sub-pages/blooms-taxonomy/

Creating Cultures of Trauma-Informed Care (CCTIC): A Self-Assessment and Planning Protocol

An assessment and planning protocol for implementing trauma-informed care in organizations or agencies can be found at the Anna Institute website: https://www.theannainstitute.org/CCTICSELFASSPP.pdf

Creating Inclusive College Classrooms

University of Michigan, Center for Research on Learning and Training; tips for creating an inclusive college classroom: https://crlt.umich.edu/gsis/p3_1

Decolonizing Your Syllabus

A Loyola University Chicago resource for decolonizing your syllabi: https://www.luc.edu/fcip/coursedesign/decolonizingyoursyllabus/

Developing and Writing a Diversity Statement

This site provides guidance on developing and writing a diversity statement: https://cft.vanderbilt.edu/guides-sub-pages/developing-and-writing-a-diversity-statement/

Engaging in Difficult Dialogues

The Vanderbilt University's Center for Teaching website offers strategies for having difficult and effective conversations: https://cft.vanderbilt.edu/guides-sub-pages/difficult-dialogues/

Flipping the Classroom

If you're interested in learning more about how to "flip" your classroom, check out this resource from Vanderbilt University's Center for Teaching website: https://cft.vanderbilt.edu/guides-sub-pages/flipping-the-classroom/

Inclusive Teaching and Learning Online

Guidance from Columbia University's Center for Teaching and Learning on developing inclusive online teaching: https://ctl.columbia.edu/resources-and-technology/teaching-with-technology/teaching-online/inclusive-teaching/

Increasing Inclusivity in the Classroom

From Vanderbilt University's Center for Teaching, a guide that provides a rationale and strategies for inclusivity in the classroom: https://cft.vanderbilt.edu/guides-sub-pages/increasing-inclusivity-in-the-classroom/

Learning Styles

Check out Vanderbilt University's Center for Teaching website for a brief discussion of the significance of learning styles in the classroom: https://cft.vanderbilt.edu/guides-sub-pages/learning-styles-preferences/

Managing Hot Moments in the Classroom

The Elon University website provides guidance on managing challenging conversations in the classroom: https://www.elon.edu/u/academics/catl/wp-content/uploads/sites/126/2017/04/Managing-Hot-Moments-in-the-Classroom-Harvard_University.pdf

SAMHSA's Concept of Trauma and Guidance for a Trauma-Informed Approach

A Substance Abuse and Mental Health Services Administration document providing guidance for implementing a trauma-informed approach: https://ncsacw.samhsa.gov/userfiles/files/SAMHSA_Trauma.pdf

Strategies and Tips for Successful Online Teaching

A six-part series from SAGE Publications providing strategies and tips for successful online teaching: https://us.sagepub.com/en-us/nam/tips-for-transitioning-to-teaching-online?priorityCode=0B0479&utm_medium=email&utm_content=0B0479&utm_campaign=not%20tracked&utm_term=&em=82381Bebf954345b0a19ab054aa62335a383231c30441e22a66db1340ef4eab6ad&utm_source=adestra

Teaching Race: Pedagogy and Practice

The site below provides guidance on discussing racial justice in the classroom: https://cft.vanderbilt.edu/guides-sub-pages/teaching-race/

Turning Hardships Into Strengths: Advancing Learning During COVID-19

A Faculty Focus article; A professor shares lessons learned while teaching online during COVID-19: https://www.facultyfocus.com/articles/teaching-and-learning/turning-hardships-into-strengths-advancing-learning-during-covid-19/?st=FFWeekly;sc=FFWeekly200807;utm_term=FFWeekly200807&utm_source=ActiveCampaign&utm_medium=email&utm_content=%22Help%21+I+m+Moving+My+Course+Online%21%22+-+Practical+Advice+for+New+Online+Instructors&utm_campaign=FF200807

References

Abenavoli, R. M., Jennings, P. A., Greenberg, M. T., Harris, A. R., & Katz, D. A. (2013). The protective effects of mindfulness against burnout among educators. *Psychology of Education Review, 37*(2), 57–69.

Agonács, N., & Matos, J. F. (2019). Heutagogy and self-determined learning: A review of the published literature on the application and implementation of the theory. *Open Learning: The Journal of Open, Distance and e-Learning, 34*(3), 223–240. https://doi.org/10.1080/02680513.2018.1562329

Akyildiz, S. T. (2019). Do 21st century teachers know about heutagogy or do they still adhere to traditional pedagogy and andragogy? *International Journal of Progressive Education, 15*(6), 151–169. https://doi.org/10.29329/ijpe.2019.215.10

Ali, D. (2017). *Safe spaces and brave spaces: Historical context and recommendations for student affairs professionals* (NASPA Policy and Practice Series 2). NASPA Student Affairs Administrators in Higher Education. https://www.naspa.org/images/uploads/main/Policy_and_Practice_No_2_Safe_Brave_Spaces.pdf

American Psychological Association. (2019). *Race and ethnicity guidelines in psychology: Promoting responsiveness and equity.* https://www.apa.org/about/policy/guidelines-race-ethnicity.pdf

Anderson, D., Imdieke, S., & Standerford, N. S. (2011). Feedback please: Studying self in the online classroom. *International Journal of Instruction, 4*(1), 3–15.

Arao, B., & Clemens, K. (2013). From safe spaces to brave spaces: A new way to dialogue around diversity and social justice. In L. Landreman (Ed.), *The art of effective facilitation: Reflections from social justice educators* (pp. 135–150). Stylus.

Banks, T., & Dohy, J. (2019). Mitigating barriers to persistence: A review of efforts to improve retention and graduation rates for students of color in higher education. *Higher Educations Studies, 9*(1), 118–131. https://doi.org/10.5539/hes.v9n1p118

Barrington, A. J., & Shakespeare-Finch, J. (2013). Working with refugee survivors of torture and trauma: An opportunity for vicarious post-traumatic growth. *Counselling Psychology Quarterly, 26*(1), 89–105. https://doi.org/10.1080/09515070.2012.727553

Battiste, M. (2013). *Decolonizing education: Nourishing the learning spirit.* Purich.

Bernard, C., Thomas Bernard, W., Ekpo, C., Enang, J., Joseph, B., & Wane, N. (2000). "She who learns teaches": Othermothering in the academy. *Journal of the Association for Research on Mothering, 2*(2), 66–84.

Blaschke, L. M. (2012). Heutagogy and lifelong learning: A review of heutagogical practice and self-determined learning. *International Review of Research in Open and Distributed Learning, 13*(1), 56–71.

Bliss, S. A. (2017). Exploring Shunyata (emptiness) and the cultivation of mindfulness practices: Educators finding their zero-point balance. *Childhood Education, 93*(2), 114–118.

Blondy, L. C. (2007). Evaluation and application of andragogical assumptions to the adult online learning environment. *Journal of Interactive Online Learning, 6*(2), 116–130.

Bonilla-Silva, E. (2013). *Racism without racists: Color-blind racism and the persistence of racial inequality in America* (4th ed.). Rowman and Littlefield.

Boyd, D. (2016). What would Paulo Freire think of Blackboard: Critical pedagogy in an age of online learning. *International Journal of Critical Pedagogy, 7*(1), 165–186.

Boynton, M. H., O'Hara, R. E., Covault, J., Scott, D., & Tennen, H. (2014). A mediational model of racial discrimination and alcohol-related problems among African American college students. *Journal of Studies on Alcohol and Drugs*, 75(2), 228–234. https://doi.org/10.15288/jsad.2014.75.228

Bruffaerts, R., Mortier, P., Kiekens, G., Auerbach, R. P., Cuijpers, P., Demyttenaere, K., Green, J. G., Nock, M. K., & Kessler, R. C. (2018). Mental health problems in college freshmen: Prevalence and academic functioning. *Journal of Affective Disorders*, 225, 97–103.

Brunsma, D. L., Embrick, D. G., & Shin, J. (2017). Graduate students of color: Race, racism, and mentoring in the white waters of academia. *Sociology of Race and Ethnicity*, 3(1), 1–13.

Carello, J., & Butler, L. D. (2015). Practicing what we teach: Trauma-informed educational practice. *Journal of Teaching in Social Work*, 35(3), 262–278.

Carter, R. T. (2007). Racism and psychological emotional injury: Recognizing and assessing race-based traumatic stress. *Counseling Psychologist*, 35, 13–105. http://dx.doi.org/10.1177/0011000006292033

Carter, R. T., Mazzula, S., Victoria, R., Vazquez, R., & Hall, S. (2013). Initial development of the Race-Based Traumatic Stress Symptom Scale: Assessing the emotional impact of racism. *Psychological Trauma: Theory, Research, Practice, and Policy*, 5(1), 1–9. https://doi.org/10.1037/a0025911

Caruthers, L., & Friend, J. (2014). Critical pedagogy in online environments as thirdspace: A narrative analysis of voices of candidates in educational preparatory programs. *Educational Studies*, 50(1), 8–35. https://doi.org/10.1080/00131946.2013.866953

Case, K. (2017). Toward an intersectional pedagogy model. In K. A. Case (Ed.), *Intersectional pedagogy: Complicating identity and social justice* (pp. 1–24). Routledge.

Case, K., & Lewis, M. (2017). Teaching intersectional pedagogy in racially diverse settings. In K. A. Case (Ed.), *Intersectional pedagogy: Complicating identity and social justice* (pp. 130–146). Routledge.

Castano-Munoz, J., Sancho-Vinuesa, T., & Duart, J. M. (2013). Online interaction in higher education: Is there evidence of diminishing returns? *International Review of Research in Open and Distance Learning*, 14(5), 240–257. http://files.eric.ed.gov/fulltext/EJ1017547.pdf

Cato, P. (2001, February). *Best practices: What does that imply?* (Excerpt). Society for the Preservation of Natural History Collections Newsletter. https://spnhc.org/wpcontent/uploads/2018/11/cato_BP.pdf

Chapman-Hilliard, C., & Beasley, S. (2018). It's like power to move: Black students psychosocial experiences in Black studies courses as a predominately White institution. *Journal of Multicultural Counseling and Development*, 46, 129–151.

Chick, N., & Hassel, H. (2009). "Don't hate me because I'm virtual": Feminist pedagogy in the online classroom. *Feminist Teacher*, 19(3), 195–215. https://www.jstor.org/stable/40546100

Coker, H. (2018). Purpose, pedagogy and philosophy: "Being" an online lecturer. *International Review of Research in Open and Distributed Learning*, 19(5), 128–144.

Collins, P. H. (1990). *Black feminist thought: Knowledge, consciousness, and the politics of empowerment*. Routledge.

Cox, D., & Prestridge, S. (2020). Understanding fully online teaching in vocational education. *Research and Practice in Technology Enhanced Learning*, 15(1), 1–22. https://doi.org/10.1186/s41039-020-00138

Crenshaw, K. (1989). Demarginalizing the intersection of race and sex: A Black feminist critique of antidiscrimination doctrine, feminist theory, and antiracist politics. *University of Chicago Legal Forum*, Article 8, 139–167. https://chicagounbound.uchicago.edu/cgi/viewcontent.cgi?article=1052&context=uclf

Crenshaw, K. W. (1991). Mapping the margins: Intersectionality, identity politics, and violence against women of color. *Stanford Law Review*, 43, 1241–1299.

Dalmage, H. M., & Martinez, S. A. (2020). Location, location, location: Liberatory pedagogy in a university classroom. *Sociology of Race and Ethnicity*, 6(1), 123–129.

Dalton, M. H. (2018). Online programs in higher education: Strategies for developing quality courses. *FOCUS on Colleges, Universities and Schools*, 12(1), 1–8.

Dalton, S. S. (1998). Pedagogy matters: Standards for effective teaching practice. *UC Berkeley Research Reports*, 1–47. https://escholarship.org/uc/item/6d75h0fz

Davidson, S., & Northwest, E. (2017). *Trauma-informed practices for postsecondary education: A guide*. Education Northwest. https://educationnorthwest.org/resources/trauma-informed-practices-postsecondary-education-guide

Diemer, M. A., Kauffman, A., Koenig, N., Trahan, E., & Hsieh, C. (2006). Challenging racism, sexism, and social injustice: Support for urban adolescents' critical consciousness development. *Cultural Diversity and Ethnic Minority Psychology*, 12(3), 444–460. https://doi.org/10.1037/1099-9809.12.3.444

Dorado, J., Martinez, M., McArthur, L., & Leibovitz, T. (2016). Healthy environments and response to trauma in schools (HEARTS): A whole-school, multi-level, prevention and intervention program for creating trauma-informed, safe and supportive schools. *School Mental Health*, 8, 163–176.

Downing, K. J., Lam, T., Kwong, T., Downing, W., & Chan, S. (2007). Creating interaction in online learning: A case study. *Research in Learning Technology*, 15(3), 201–215. https://doi.org/10.1080/09687760701673592

Fallot, R. D., & Harris, M. (2009). *Creating cultures of trauma-informed care (CCTIC): A self-assessment and planning protocol*. Community Connections. https://www.theannainstitute.org/CCTICSELFASSPP.pdf

Fisher, M. T. (2007). *Writing in rhythm: Spoken word poetry in urban classrooms*. Teachers College Press.

Fowler, M. (2015). Dealing with compassion fatigue. *Education Digest*, 81(3), 30–35.

Franklin, J. D. (2019). Coping with racial battle fatigue: Differences and similarities for African American and Mexican American college students. *Race Ethnicity and Education*, 22(5), 589–609.

Freire, P. (1970). *Pedagogy of the oppressed* (50th ed.). Bloomsbury.

French, B. H., Lewis, J. A., Mosley, D. V., Adames, H. Y., Chavez-Dueñas, N. Y., Chen, G. A., & Neville, H. A. (2020). Toward a psychological framework of radical healing in communities of color. *Counseling Psychologist, 48*(1), 14–46. https://doi.org/10.1177/0011000019843506

Gay, G. (2002). Preparing for culturally responsive teaching. *Journal of Teacher Education, 53*(2), 106–116.

Gaztambide-Fernandez, R. A. (2012) Decolonization and the pedagogy of solidarity. *Decolonization: Indigeneity, Education, & Society, 1*(1), 41-67.

Glassner, A., & Back, S. (2019). Heutagogy (self-determined learning): New approach to student learning in teacher education. *Journal Plus Education, 24*, 39–44.

González, C. (2012). The relationship between approaches to teaching, approaches to e-teaching and perceptions of the teaching situation in relation to e-learning among higher education teachers. *Instructional Science, 40*(6), 975–998.

González, C. (2013). E-teaching in undergraduate university education and its relationship to approaches to teaching. *Informatics in Education, 23*(2), 92–92.

Gordon, M. (2016). Why should scholars keep coming back to John Dewey? *Educational Philosophy and Theory, 48*(10), 1077–1091. https://doi.org/10.1080/00131857.2016.1150800

Grier-Reed, T., & Williams-Wengerd, A. (2018). Integrating universal design, culturally sustaining practices, and constructivism to advance inclusive pedagogy in the undergraduate classroom. *Education Sciences, 8*(4), Article 167.

Grosfoguel, R. (2011). Decolonizing postcolonial studies and paradigms of political economy: Transmodernity, decolonial thinking, and global coloniality. *Transmodernity: Journal of Peripheral Cultural Production of the Luso-Hispanic World, 1*(1), 1–38 http://escholarship.org/uc/item/21k6t3fq

Guiffrida, D. (2005). Othermothering as a framework for understanding African American students' definitions of student-centered faculty. *The Journal of Higher Education, 76*(6), 701-723.

Hakuta, K. (2011). Educating language minority students and affirming their equal rights: Research and practical perspectives. *Educational Researcher, 40*(4), 163–174.

Halupa, C. M. (2015). *Transformative curriculum design in health sciences education*. IGI Global.

Hardy, K. V. (2013). Healing the hidden wounds of racial trauma. *Reclaiming Children and Youth, 22*(1), 24–28.

Hase, S., & Kenyon, C. (2001). Moving from andragogy to heutagogy: Implications for VET. *Ultibase Articles, 5*, 1–10. https://d1wqtxts1xzle7.cloudfront.net/47350253/Moving_from_andragogy_to_heutagogy_impli20160719-16580-fomhps.pdf?1468932871=&response-content-disposition=inline%3B+filename%3DMoving_from_andragogy_to_heutagogy_impli.pdf&Expires=1611168220&Signature=Xl-oXo5q-BoZmkLSUQmXTYWrQyp4X-uUoF2d1OZ-1JuPXZ5Bgxki-S3wS926eBNQWPeiOuvyKejOidHX-qzi2lBpT4jLWuohgwM7PYyK7oMEMK5kefDao6g3g8ohAUo5pt-sQBnujpqSfRNxux5vQp1dAFkAqrb-8WEhQBD-dU5-Wy3aQ-6V-s2TeikBofjQUPEw95aqF3cyQNmzZnpFTcERlUamC4W9dtjSBw5EvhCbEXWk4ssne4-HzXf2cOz2B-fGqpzWzRubYof-Yn-qMKsbJTK9rIX-aRv4n-nia8qKyPOz8yQH84p6HDNOWfEQ36VSB-BhlpaYVqpvgO5wM-V7iQ__&Key-Pair-Id=APKAJLOHF5GGSLRBV4ZA

Haskins, N. H., & Singh, A. (2015). Critical race theory and counselor education pedagogy: Creating equitable training. *American Counseling Association, 54*, 288–301.

Helms, J. E., Nicolas, G., & Green, C. E. (2010). Racism and ethnoviolence as trauma: Enhancing professional training. *Traumatology, 16*(4), 53-62.

Heberle, A. E., Rapa, L. J., & Farago, F. (2020). Critical consciousness in children and adolescents: A systematic review, critical assessment, and recommendations for future research. *Psychological Bulletin, 146*(6), 525–551. https://doi.org/10.1037/bul0000230.supp

Herman, J. L. (1998). Recovery from psychological trauma. *Psychiatry and Clinical Neurosciences, 52*(Suppl. 1), S98–S103. https://doi:10.1046/j.1440-1819.1998.0520s5S145.x

Hill, M. L. (2009). *Beats, rhymes, and classroom life: Hip-hop pedagogy and the politics of identity*. Teachers College Press.

hooks, b. (1994). *Teaching to transgress: Education as the practice of freedom*. Routledge.

Horsford, S. D. (2019). School integration in the new Jim Crow: Opportunity or oxymoron? *Educational Policy, 33*(1), 257–275.

James, S. M., & Busia, A.P.A. (Eds.). (1993). *Theorizing Black feminisms: The visionary pragmatism of Black women*. Routledge.

Johnson, D., & Cox, J. (2020). The linguistic deception of the phrase best practices: A critical analysis of articles discussing "best" practices in online learning. *Online Journal of Distance Learning Administration, 23*(1), 1–12.

Kannen, V. (2012). "My body speaks to them": Instructor reflections on the complexities of power and social embodiments. *Teaching in Higher Education, 17*(6), 637–648. https://doi.org/10.1080/13562517.2012.658566

Kebritchi, M., Lipschuetz, A., & Santiague, L. (2017). Issues and challenges for teaching successful online courses in higher education: A literature review. *Journal of Educational Technology Systems, 46*(1), 4–29.

Kember, D. (1997). A reconceptualization of the research into university academics' conceptions of teaching. *Learning and Instruction, 8*(3), 255–275.

Kember, D., & Kwan, K. P. (2000). Lecturers' approaches to teaching and their relationship to conceptions of good teaching. *Instructional Science, 28*(5), 469–490.

Kendi, I. X. (2019). *How to be an antiracist*. One World Press.

Kleinfeld, J. (1975). Effective teachers of Eskimo and Indian students. *School Review, 83*, 301–344.

Knowles, M. (1970). *The modern practice of adult education: Andragogy versus pedagogy*. Associated Press.

Knowles, M. (1984). *Andragogy in action*. Jossey-Bass.

Ladson-Billings, G. (1995a). Toward a theory of culturally relevant pedagogy. *American Educational Research Journal*, *32*(3), 465–491.

Ladson-Billings, G. (1995b). Toward a critical race theory of education. *Teachers College Record*, *97*, 47–68.

Landreman, L. M., Rasmussen, C. J., King, P. M., & Xinquan Jiang, C. (2007). A phenomenological study of the development of university educators' critical consciousness. *Journal of College Student Development*, *48*(3), 275–296. https://doi.org/10.1353/csd.2007.0027

Leonardo, Z. (2009). *Race, whiteness, and education*. Routledge.

Logan, J. R., Elisabeta, M., & Sinem, A. (2012). The geography of inequality: Why separate means unequal in American public schools. *Sociology of Education*, *85*(3), 287–301.

Maykut, C., Wild, C., & May, N. (2019). Heutagogy: Enacting caring science practices. *International Journal of Caring Sciences*, *12*(1), 11–17.

McCarty, T. L., Romero, M. E., & Zepeda, O. (2006). Reclaiming the gift: Indigenous youth counter-narratives on native language loss and revitalization. *American Indian Quarterly*, *30*, 28–48.

Mehall, S. (2020). Purposeful interpersonal interaction in online learning: What is it and how is it measured? *Online Learning*, *24*(1), 182–204. https://doi.org/10.24059/olj.v24i1.2002

Merriam-Webster. (n.d.). Pedagogy. In *Merriam-Webster.com dictionary*. Retrieved January 5, 2021, from https://www.merriamwebster.com/dictionary/pedagogy#learn-more

Minikel-Lacocque, J. (2013). Racism, college, and the power of words: Racial microaggressions reconsidered. *American Educational Research Journal*, *50*, 432–465.

Mosley, D. V., Hargons, C. N., Meiller, C., Angyal, B., Wheeler, P., Davis, C., & Stevens-Watkins, D. (2020). Critical consciousness of anti-Black racism: A practical model to prevent and resist racial trauma. *Journal of Counseling Psychology*. Advance online publication. https://doi.org/10.1037/cou0000430

Mulrennan, D. (2018). Mobile social media and the news: Where heutagogy enables journalism education. *Journalism and Mass Communication Educator*, *73*(3), 322–333.

National Child Traumatic Stress Network. (2016). *Secondary traumatic stress: A fact sheet for child-serving professionals*. Secondary Traumatic Stress Committee. https://www.nctsn.org/resources/secondary-traumatic-stress-fact-sheet-child-serving-professionals

National Committee on Science Education Standards and Assessment. (1996). *National Science Education Standards*. National Academy of Sciences. https://doi.org/10.17226/4962

Nickols, M. (2011). Articulating e-pedagogy for education. In J. Barrett (Ed.), *Open learning for an open world: Reflections on open and distance learning and teaching at the Open Polytechnic of New Zealand* (pp. 321–336). Open Polytechnic of New Zealand, Lower Hutt.

Northrup, P., Lee, R., & Burgess, V. (2002). Learner perceptions of online interaction. *Proceedings from 2002 World Conference on Educational Multimedia, Hypermedia and Telecommunications* (pp. 1–7). Association for the Advancement of Computing in Education. http://files.eric.ed.gov/fulltext/ED477075.pdf

Odegard, M. E., & Vereen, L. G. (2010). A grounded theory of how counselor educators integrate social justice into their pedagogy. *Counselor Education and Supervision*, *50*, 130–149.

Omanga, D. (2020, January 14). *Decolonization, decoloniality, and the future of African studies: A conversation with Dr. Sabelo Ndlovu-Gatsheni*. Social Science Research Council. https://items.ssrc.org/from-our-programs/decolonization-decoloniality-and-the-future-of-african-studies-a-conversation-with-dr-sabelo-ndlovu-gatsheni/

Onufer, L., & Rojas, L. M. (2019). *Teaching at PITT: Introduction to feminist pedagogy*. University Times. https://www.utimes.pitt.edu/news/teaching-pitt-8.

Ortiz, S. O. (2008). Best practices in nondiscriminatory assessment. In A. Thomas & J. Grimes (Eds.), *Best practices in school psychology V* (pp. 661–678). National Association of School Psychologists.

Osborne, J., Caruso, G., & Wolfensberger, W. (2014). The concept of "best practice": A brief overview of its meanings, scope, usage, and shortcomings. *International Journal of Disability Development and Education*, *58*, 213–222. https://web.b.ebscohost.com/ehost/pdfviewer/pdfviewer?vid=5&sid=4015a892-4069-438f-b21c-1932dea4dade%40sessionmgr101

Paccione, A. (2000). Developing a commitment to multicultural education. *Teachers College Record*, *102*(6), 980–1005.

Paquette, P. (2016). Instructing the instructors: Training instructors to use social presence cues in online courses. *Journal of Educators Online*, *13*(1), 80–108. http://files.eric.ed.gov/fulltext/EJ1087698.pdf

Paris, D. (2012). Culturally sustaining pedagogy: A needed change in stance, terminology, and practice. *Educational Researcher*, *41*(3), 93–97.

Paris, D., & Alim, H. S. (2017). *Culturally sustaining pedagogies: Teaching and learning for justice in a changing world*. Teacher's College Press.

Paris, D., & Ball, A. (2009). Teacher knowledge in culturally and linguistically complex classrooms: Lessons from the golden age and beyond. In L. M. Morrow, R. Rueda, & D. Lapp (Eds.), *Handbook of research on literacy instruction: Issues of diversity, policy, and equity* (pp. 379–395). Guilford.

Pawel, M. (2009). *The union of their dreams: Power, hope, and struggle in Cesar Chavez's farm worker movement*. Bloomsbury.

Pérez Huber, L., Malagón, M. C., Ramirez, B. R., Camargo Gonzalez, L., Jimenez, A., & Velez, V. N. (2015). *Still falling through the cracks: Revisiting the Latina/o education pipeline*. Los Angeles: Chicano Studies Research Center, University of California, Los Angeles. https://www.chicano.ucla.edu/files/RR19.pdf

Pierce, C. (1970). Offensive mechanisms. In F. B. Barbour (Ed.), *The Black seventies* (pp. 265–282). Porter Sargent.

Porche, M. V., Fortuna, L. R., Lin, J., & Alegria, M. (2011). Childhood trauma and psychiatric disorders as correlates of school dropout in a national sample of young adults. *Child Development, 82*(3), 982–998.

Robyler, M. D., & Wiencke, W. R. (2003). Design and use of a rubric to assess and encourage interactive qualities in distance courses. *American Journal of Distance Education, 17*(2), 77–98.

Serdyukov, P. (2015). Does online education need a special pedagogy? *Journal of Computing and Information Technology, 23*(1), 61–74.

Sharp, J. E., & Jennings, P. A. (2016). Strengthening teacher presence through mindfulness: What educators say about the cultivating awareness and resilience in education (CARE) program. *Mindfulness, 7*(1), 209–218.

Sibrava, N. J., Bjornsson, A. S., Pérez Benítez, A. C. I., Moitra, E., Weisberg, R. B., & Keller, M. B. (2019). Posttraumatic stress disorder in African American and Latinx adults: Clinical course and the role of racial and ethnic discrimination. *American Psychologist, 74*(1), 101–116. http://dx.doi.org/10.1037/amp0000339

Sleeter, C. (2014). Toward teacher education research that informs policy. *Educational Researcher, 43*(3), 146–153. https://doi.org/10.3102%2F0013189X14528752

Sleeter, C., & Bernal, D. (2004). Critical pedagogy, critical race theory, and antiracist education: Their implications for multicultural education. In J. A. Banks & C. M. Banks (Eds.), *Handbook of research on multicultural education* (2nd ed., pp. 240–260). Jossey-Bass.

Smith, T. B., Rodriguez, M. D., & Bernal, G. (2011). Culture. *Journal of Clinical Psychology, 67*, 166–175.

Smith, W. (2010) *The impact of racial trauma on African Americans*. African American Men and Boys Advisory Board. http://www.heinz.org/userfiles/impactofracialtraumaonafricanamericans

Sobko, S., Unadkat, D., Adams, J., & Hull, G. (2020). Learning through collaboration: A networked approach to online pedagogy. *E-Learning and Digital Media, 17*(1), 36–55.

Stanger, C. (2016). From critical education to an embodied pedagogy of hope: Seeking a liberatory praxis with Black, working class girls in the neoliberal 16–19 college. *Studies in Philosophy and Education, 37*, 47–63.

Steele, J., Holbeck, R., & Mandernach, J. (2019). Defining effective online pedagogy. *Journal of Instructional Research, 8*(2), 5–8.

Sue, A. (2019). Disarming Racial Microaggressions: Microintervention Strategies for Targets, White Allies, and Bystanders. *The American Psychologist, 74*(1), 128–142. https://doi.org/10.1037/amp0000296

Sun, A., & Chen, X. (2016). Online education and its effective practice: A research review. *Journal of Information Technology Education: Research, 15*, 157–190.

Tarlau, R. (2014). From a language to a theory of resistance: Critical pedagogy, the limits of "framing" and social change. *Educational Theory, 64*(4), 369–392.

Taylor, K. B. (2019). Exploring the complexities of peer interactions in fostering development toward critical consciousness. *Journal of Diversity in Higher Education*. Advance online publication. https://doi.org/10.1037/dhe0000134

Thompson, F. T. (2014). Effective multicultural instruction: A non-color-blind perspective. *SAGE Open, 4*, 1–5. https://doi.org/10.1177%2F2158244014522070

Tu, C-H., & McIsaac, M. (2002). The relationship of social presence and interaction in online classes. *American Journal of Distance Education, 16*(3), 131–150.

Valle-Ruiz, L., Navarro, K., Mendoza, K., McGrath, A., Galina, B., Chick, N., Brewer, S., & Bostow, R. (2015). *A Guide to Feminist Pedagogy*. Vanderbilt Center for Teaching. https://my.vanderbilt.edu/femped/

van der Kolk, B. (2014). *The body keeps the score*. Viking Press.

Vavrus, M. (2010). Critical multiculturalism and higher education: Resistance and possibilities within teacher education. In S. May and C. E. Sleeter (Eds.), *Critical multiculturalism: Theory and praxis* (pp. 19–31). Routledge.

Villegas, A. M., & Lucas, T. (2002). Preparing culturally responsive teachers. *Journal of Teacher Education, 53*(1), 20–32.

Wang, V. C. X., & Torrisi-Steele, G. (2015). Online teaching, change, and critical theory. *New Horizons in Adult Education and Human Resource Development, 27*(3), 18–26.

Wei, M., Ku, T. Y., & Liao, K. Y. H. (2011). Minority stress and college persistence attitudes among African American, Asian American, and Latino students: Perception of university environment as a mediator. *Cultural Diversity and Ethnic Minority Psychology, 17*(2), 195–203.

Welsh, R. O., & Little, S. (2018). The school discipline dilemma: A comprehensive review of disparities and alternative approaches. *Review of Educational Research, 88*, 752–794.

William and Mary. (n.d.). *Decolonizing humanities project: What is decoloniality?* https://www.wm.edu/sites/dhp/decoloniality/index.php

Wright, B. L., Ford, D. Y., & Young, J. L. (2017). Ignorance or indifference? Seeking excellence and equity for under-represented students of color in gifted education. *Global Education Review, 4*, 45–60.

Zembylas, M. (2018). Reinventing critical pedagogy as decolonizing pedagogy: The education of empathy. *Review of Education, Pedagogy, and Cultural Studies, 40*(5), 404–421. https://doi.org/10.1080/10714413.2019.1570794

CHAPTER THREE

Diversity and Inclusion in the Online Classroom

Alcia A. Freeman PhD, LPC, NCC
Tiffany Darby PhD, LPCC-S (OH), PSC (OH), LPC (PA), LPCC-S (KY)

The culture and climate of the United States of America is changing in complex and dynamic ways. As one of the most diverse countries in the world, America is not beholden to a monolithic culture. America's complicated history with race promotes a climate of unrest that many are attempting to address in various ways. The year 2020 ushered in a pandemic, floods, storms, fires, and the murders of George Floyd, Ahmaud Arbery, and Breonna Taylor. Each traumatic event highlighted the racial, social, economic, and health care inequalities embedded in our society's fabric. As a result, collectively, millions of people had to find new ways to work, learn, shop, and traverse the world. Low-income students, students of color, and first-generation students were disproportionately impacted by the multiple traumatic events of 2020 (Calma, 2020; Liu & Modir, 2020). Accordingly, this chapter aims to provide educators with insight into the superordinate role of **diversity, equity, and inclusion** in online instruction. An overview of diversity, equity, and inclusion in the classroom is discussed. Practical applications and tools for distance educators are provided. Multicultural and social justice considerations are also reviewed.

Background

I, Alcia, sit and type this chapter on diversity, equity, and inclusion (DEI), specific to higher education online classrooms, with a heavy heart and mind. The gravity of this undertaking immobilizes me. What is diversity, equity, and inclusion? As a Black woman who has had to traverse existing in a world where several aspects of my identity push me to the margins, I wonder if "diversity," "equity," and "inclusion" are just words used to help people existing outside of the margin feel better about themselves (Applebaum, 2010). Although I'm thankful for the opportunity, my inclusion in this book is even questionable in this specific chapter. It is complex and complicated. Being a Person of Color, or any marginalized identity, in the academy should not deem you the voice of all things connected to that identity. Yet, as I began a literature review on this subject, I was mindful of who's voice was telling the story. Those addressing DEI rarely reflect the populations on which they speak (Chadderton, 2012; Edwards, 1990; Morrow et al., 2000; Williams & Moore, 2011). The foundation of scholarly practice and academic exchange involves the citation process. Being that citations can empower or disempower the originators of that work, Delgado (1984,

1996) refers to it as a political act (Harris & Patton, 2019). Representation matters (Sathy & Hogan, 2019) and was considered concerning the types of research, articles, journals, and **folx** included in making this chapter. Per Robertson (2018), "folx" is a nonbinary word used to refer to people who exist outside of the gender binary. Robertson emphasized that x is used to "bring in more identities to the conversations, such as womxn, latinx, and alumx" (p. 49), for example. The researcher's and the researched and the educator's and student's positionality and context are significant on identity topics. Thus, I acknowledge that there are elements of my identity that are privileged and oppressed, and places where my identity's various aspects intersect (Crenshaw, 1989, 1991). Therefore, this chapter by no means purports to be the authority on the intricacies that exist within the multiple facets of identity covered. Instead, this chapter aims to offer insight and concepts to consider on the continuous journey toward increasing diversity, equity, and inclusion in an online classroom.

The component of one's identity that is most salient depends on several contextual factors. like time, location, setting, and the people within that setting (Beratan, 2012; Platts & Hoosier, 2020). Therefore, what may be deemed a neutral situation or environment for one may feel like a threat to another (Steele, 2010; Steele & Aronson, 1998). This is particularly true for the classroom (Platts & Hoosier, 2020). As expressed in Chapter 2, colonization and colonialism has left a lasting impact. Historically, fundamental human rights and educational pursuits were withheld from People of Color (POC), particularly African Americans (Harper et al., 2009; Mata, 2018; Yosso et al., 2004), women (Solomon, 1985), the LGBTQ+ community (Graves, 2018), and people living with disabilities (Petit-McClure & Stinson, 2019). Although some strides have been made, the lingering impact of colonialism on education exists in the traditional classroom and has bled over into distance learning (Damary et al., 2017; Smith & Ayers, 2006).

Today, distance learning is synonymous with online education, but this was not always the case. Dating back to the 1890s, institutions of higher education like Pennsylvania State College allowed students to take courses through the mail—hence, the term distance learning (Snow & Coker, 2020). According to Baron and McNeal (2019), the internet's birth in 1970 created a new platform for distance learning, now known as online learning (internet facilitated). The authors state 28% of students in 2015 were taking at least one online course. Phirangee and Malec (2017) note that online course registration rates in higher education are growing faster than traditional brick-and-mortar courses. The coronavirus pandemic further exacerbated this trend. To prevent the spread of the coronavirus, online learning is currently the primary method of instruction throughout the United States (Melnick & Darling-Hammond, 2020). The shift to online learning presented unique challenges in higher education, and it highlighted long-standing operational, social, economic, and psychological inequities (Dorn et al., 2020; Phirangee & Malec, 2017).

Diversity, Equity, and Inclusion in Online Learning

Online learning is often thought of as a social equalizer, inclusive of diversity. However, as previously stated, the inequities that exist in traditional classroom settings can be reproduced in online education (Smith & Ayers, 2006). Since the civil rights movement, colleges and universities have had to address issues surrounding diversity (Gay, 2010, 2018; Harmon, 2012). According to Phillips (2019), "a recent survey of 80 university mission statements revealed that 75 percent mentioned diversity" (p. 3). Shainwald (2020) highlights institutions of higher education need to be ambiguous in their mission and diversity statements when addressing diversity by stating "colleges may list diversity as a goal of their university, but are bound to strict legal restrictions about how they may obtain such a goal and how they may define their success" (p. 27). Within higher education, diversity discussions typically focus on race, ethnicity, gender, disability, nationality, economic status, sexual orientation, and other aspects of a person's identity historically and currently underrepresented at colleges and universities (Shainwald, 2020; Tatum, 2018). As the United States continues to become a more diverse nation, studies have demonstrated that focusing on diversity alone is insufficient to bring systemic change (Roberson, 2006). Diversity research has started to focus on inclusionary practices (Bernstein et al., 2019; Glasener et al., 2019; Roberson, 2006). Clayton-Pedersen and Musil (2009) further demonstrated the importance of diversity, yet it is insufficient without inclusion. They define inclusion as "engagement with diversity in the service of learning and knowledge development, throughout the educational experience and by all members of the campus community" (p. 2). Further, inclusion is the continuous commitment to the recruitment and retention of marginalized populations with varied traits, experiences, and world views (Lotz, 2020; Tienda, 2013).

Equity and social justice have been used interchangeably in the literature (Bernstein et al., 2019; Oztok, 2013; Rodriguez & Morrison, 2019). Along those lines, Bernstein et al. (2019) situate the outcome of diversity and inclusion efforts at the systemic level by calling for the rectification of structural injustices—hence, equity and social justice. For the purposes of this chapter, diversity and equity are defined as stated in Rodriguez (2016):

> Diversity involves the recognition of the visible and invisible physical and social characteristics that make an individual or group of individuals different from one another, and by doing so, celebrating that difference as a source of strength for the community at large (p. 242). Equity refers to the enactment of specific policies and practices that ensure equitable access and opportunities for success for everyone. It is important to differentiate equity from equality ... in order to be equitable, we cannot treat everyone the same. To be equitable, we must treat individuals according to their needs and provide multiple opportunities for success (p. 243).

Inclusion is the "organizational strategies and practices that promote meaningful social and academic interactions among persons and groups who differ in their experiences, their views, and their traits" (Tienda, 2013, p. 1). Through this lens, many of us have failed to live up to our notions of DEI in higher education. The technology platforms upon which online learning occurs broadly reflect Western ideologies, therefore failing to respect and protect pedagogical and cultural diversity (Smith & Ayers, 2006). Acknowledgment of the systemic inequities in higher education must occur in efforts to navigate the DEI tripartite in online learning. Thus, educators must explore the relationship between learning and culture while being mindful of cultural complexities.

Multicultural

Multicultural aspects of online teaching are imperative to consider as our world continues to grow and become inclusive. One of the benefits of teaching online is the ability to encounter a variety of students. Online teaching may reach students across cities, states, and even globally. The design of most online educational environments is for White learners. There is a need for the creation of an online atmosphere that is inclusive of diverse students (Zembylas, 2008). In this chapter, there will be a consideration of the aspects of diverse backgrounds, learning styles, strengths, and barriers when working with varied students, both synchronous and asynchronous.

Identifying Multicultural Concerns

It is essential to consider a variety of aspects regarding culture. The ADDRESSING model (Hays, 2001) is intended to raise cultural awareness and is vital to consider when teaching online. The model addresses 10 main cultural influences that instructors can consider when working with online learners: age and generational influences, disability status (developmental disability), disability status (acquired physical/cognitive/psychological disabilities), religion and spirituality orientation, ethnicity (which may include race), socioeconomic status, sexual orientation, Indigenous heritage, national origin, and gender. The model will serve as a guide in reviewing how some of the cultural aspects impact online learning and instruction.

AGE AND GENERATIONAL INFLUENCERS

The age of the student must be taken into consideration when teaching online. Online learners can be at any age. Some students will have more experience with technology than others. Older students (60+) often feel that they have to negotiate their learning practices and reflect critically on their understanding of social/ethnic/social differences (Zembylas, 2008). Some students who have had courses already and been successful may feel confident in taking new classes (Li et al., 2016). Other students who may have been out of school for a while or have never taken a college course may feel that they need more support in learning the content. Li et al. (2016) suggested, "higher educational institutions may need to use differentiation strategies to satisfy the needs of new and existing online learners" (p. 228).

DISABILITY STATUS

Consideration of people living with physical, developmental, cognitive, and psychological disabilities is required when teaching online. There may be some disabilities that are either hidden, such as deafness or hearing impairment, blind, or the like. There also may be some visual disabilities, including visual impairment or others that may be evident during an asynchronous course. It is essential to be aware of all disabilities so that instructors can taper the course to fit the needs of the learners, which is explored in detail in Chapter 6. Another aspect to keep in mind is the age of the student. Often younger learners and those with special needs may require breaks throughout learning time. Determining the learning audience's needs is an essential element in assessing appropriate breaks during the lecture. Students should have written accommodations filed with the office of disabilities to ensure that all the accommodations needed for the student's success are provided within the course.

RELIGION AND SPIRITUALITY

Considering religious beliefs, including holidays and observances, is imperative when working with students online. Both synchronous and asynchronous courses will include acknowledgment of religious/spiritual beliefs, which often may feel misleading because religion/spirituality can be an undefined space. For example, you may have students who observe a specific religious event and may need to sit in darkness during a synchronous course. If students are required to be visible on the camera, it may be hard to enable them to sit in darkness. It is encouraged to discuss with administration regarding expectations of respecting students' religious/spiritual beliefs. Class time may occur when a student cannot attend for religious reasons (e.g., holidays). Online educators can add statements to their syllabus that specifically addresses religious holiday observance. The statement can read "Excused absences are permitted for illness, religious holidays, or emergencies." According to Fuentes et al. (2020), acknowledging the role colonization plays in the holidays students are given off for breaks (e.g., Christian holidays) and not penalizing students for observing holidays beyond nationally observed holidays is a way to dismantle oppression in higher education.

ETHNICITY (INCLUDING RACE)

It is essential to be aware of specific clothing that some students who attend synchronous classes may wear. For example, in some Muslim cultures, there are hijabs or burkas that students may present within the course. In some African cultures, there are clothing items such as a dashiki or agabada that students may wear during class. Some students who identify as Indian may wear a sari or lehenga. Instructors must be aware of the variety of ethnic clothing that students may wear in class. Awareness will assist in acknowledging who the students are and how they identify. This will help enable students to feel honored and included in the course.

During online courses, students participate in a variety of tasks to assist in their learning of the material. Some activities include online communication such as discussion posts, live chats, blogs and the like, submission of assignments, assigned readings, email, and journaling (Zembylas, 2008). The instructor may use online communication to engage in the facilitation of individual responses to students as well to connect students' content. Instructors are also able to monitor students' interactions with each other, grade items, and interact with students in groups (Zembylas, 2008).

Instructors provide a variety of learning opportunities. One option is to have students complete supplemental readings. A blog is an example of additional reading. A blog is an online journal that usually has a theme and is kept updated with the latest news and trends (Kurubacak, 2008). As with any material, instructors must be cognizant of the idea that there could be discriminatory information in the chosen supplemental reading. As mentioned by Kurubacak (2008), some authors may present **microaggressions** or covert racism. Microaggressions are intentional or unintentional derogatory or harmful slights or insults that target a person or group (Sue et al., 2007). Kurubacak (2008) reviewed the concept of racism in an online world.

Kurubacak (2008) suggested that covert racism in writings is much more dangerous and that it can

> easily influence people's self-concepts (the mental images and perceptions that one has of oneself) and attitudes (people's positive or negative biases, inclinations, feelings, and tendencies that influence their response to situations, activities, and people) as well as their cognitive intimacy (thinking about and responsiveness of other people's sharing values, norms, and ethics). (p. 404)

When selecting textbooks and all readings for a course, the instructor should thoroughly review the resources and determine if the material is inclusive or potentially offensive to the learners. If the material chosen is unknowingly discriminatory, a conversation can take place on intent versus impact and power, privilege, and oppression. Acknowledgement of the impact the material had on the reader and an apology may be in order depending on the context of the situation.

LANGUAGE

Online courses are usually delivered in the language where the school is located. Often in America, we provide courses in the English language even though there may be students whose first language is not English. For students whose first language is not English, it is essential to check with those learners to determine that the text and video content are translated into a language that the learner can understand (Kerr et al., 2018). At the minimum, this demonstrates to the student that you are considering their language and want them to be able to understand the content.

Most institutions do not provide interpreters in different languages, but it is something to consider for all learners. Kerr et al. (2018) suggested "translation can be done by humans, either experts or crowd-sourced, or by machines, and all have their pros and cons in terms of quality and cost-effectiveness" (p. 322). Kerr and colleagues found that most learners appreciated translation services because they felt that the translation was innovative and provided added value.

Online teaching provides the opportunity to minimize thoughts and beliefs. Phrases and colloquialisms are essential to consider with online communication. Often, different cultures may use words that others may not have familiarity with. For example, some students may identify the term *red flag* to mean "warning signs," while others may have a different meaning or no meaning at all.

Human connection and belonging begins with the realization of one's social and cultural acceptance. As educators, the onus is on us to alleviate barriers to connection, as it is directly tied to overall well-being and student performance (Phirangee & Malec, 2017). Human connection can be cultivated through written and spoken word and behaviors. However, colonialism's residual impact permeates every facet of American culture, often unbeknownst to some, and language is not an exception. Culture drives the way people express themselves verbally and nonverbally (including writing). Western customs and norms lay the foundation of American institutions of higher learning, and this includes the online classroom. If students are not acclimated to these customs and norms, they run the risk of being pushed to the margins, and the effects are compounded for those who already possess marginalized identities. Therefore, online faculty can be mindful of verbal and nonverbal communication and what that means for high-context and low-context cultures. Understanding context is key to "lexicon (words of a language), semantics (meaning of words), and syntax (how words and symbols are put together)" (Betts, 2009, para. 4). Fox (2005) discussed that some Black people often communicate with emotion, while some White people may consider the behavior hostile. Both instructors and students can work together and learn to accept all ways of respectful communication.

When there is no face-to-face contact with students, creating videos would be a great way to connect with your students. Some programs offer weekly, or as often as needed, platforms for instructors to post videos with announcements and updates, teach content, and review content for the week. This allows for an option for those learners who may benefit from visual learning.

SOCIOECONOMIC STATUS

There are several aspects to keep in mind regarding socioeconomic status when teaching online. Some students may not be able to afford the internet or have technology in their homes to access the course. Some students may have to use a library or a relative or friend's house to access technology. It is also imperative to provide scenarios of all types of families, not just a nuclear family. Maybe there are two dads, moms, a couple without children, only children, multiple children, adopted children, birth children, foster children, et cetera. The overall make up of a family and internet accessibility plays a role in how students connect to and interact within online spaces in higher education.

SEXUAL ORIENTATION

Existing in a heterosexist society is challenging for lesbian, gay, bisexual, transgender, queer, and other sexually marginalized groups (LGBTQ+) (Flores & Shelly-Moore, 2020). The classroom, be it brick and mortar or virtual, is a microcosm of the greater society at large. As a result, students in the LGBTQ+ community face unique concerns that can compound their stress levels. Flores and Shelly-Moore highlight that the LQBTQ+ community, compared to their counterparts, is three times more likely to experience adverse mental health outcomes, with suicide being the leading cause of death for LGBTQ+ youth. Thus, the discrimination, prejudice, and harassment LGBTQ+ face in hostile college climates (Renn, 2010, 2020; Lange et al., 2019) can heighten psychological distress (Flores & Shelly-Moore, 2020). Adding to the literature on transgender and gender-nonconforming (TGNC) students, Goldberg et al. (2019) stated "within the classroom, trans students may experience threats to their emotional safety in the form of microaggressions" (p. 40). Such experiences, as noted by Goldberg and colleagues, lowered sexually marginalized students' sense of belonging. This can be exacerbated in an online classroom setting. However, there are things that educators can do to thwart feelings of isolation.

For starters, non-LGBTQ+ faculty must educate themselves about the LGBTQ+ community and the issues they face (Guerra et al., 2016). Gaining insight into the heterosexist and cisnormative climate the LGBTQ+ community traverse daily will help educators gain the necessary empathy to build an inclusive online classroom. Guerra and colleagues suggest implementing **safe zone workshops** to promote equity in online learning environments. As an LGBTQ+ ally training initiative, safe zone workshops aim to promote "(1) understanding LGBTQ concepts and developing awareness of biases, (2) understanding LGBT issues and recognizing discrimination and heterosexual privilege, (3) becoming support persons to LGBT individuals, and (4) becoming advocates to create LGBT-affirming campuses: (Guerra et al., 2016, p. 1).

Per Renn (2020), university faculty and staff play a role in creating a positive learning experience for LGBTQ+ students. Renn states this involves creating systemic change through language, actions, and policies based on the information learned from conducting campus audits and process maps. Conducting audits and process mapping involves examining every point of contact a student has with the institution to identify and address practices and policies that result in a disaffirming and unwelcome environment (Renn, 2020). Online faculty can start this process by auditing their classroom and course content. To cultivate a sense of belonging, faculty can add antidiscrimination and inclusion statements and resources to their online classroom platforms (e.g., Blackboard, Google Classrooms) and syllabi to provide social cues that all students are welcome.

GENDER

There are different pronouns besides just he/him or she/her. Although nonbinary conceptions of gender have been used in some cultures for centuries, the United States has traditionally viewed gender as a binary construct. Modern views of gender are nonbinary and fluid and differentiate sex assigned at birth from gender identity and gender expression. Today's students may have a range of gender expressions that could exist on a binary gender spectrum or as nonbinary. Some students may identify as agender. Misgendering someone in the classroom can feel devastating for some students. Educators may be left feeling unsure about how to address gender in the online classroom. A strategy that can be used in synchronous settings is to take a moment at the beginning of class and have students edit their name as it appears on the screen and retype the name they want to be called and their pronouns. Keep in mind that there are a range of pronouns used by students, including she, he, they, zi, and hirs (T. Hatfield, personal communication, September 16, 2020). The Hays (2001) ADDRESSING model is a tool online instructors can use to aid them in exploring various aspects of students' identity and how it impacts their educational experience. We hope that the suggestion provided sparks ideas and inspires educators to continue to find new ways to affirm students' identity and belonging in the academy.

Critical Cross-Cultural Education

Online learning provides a space for both instructors and students to express thoughts and beliefs with limitations. Online, knowledge can be useful to express different emotions, such as racism, nationalism, and prejudice (Zembylas, 2008). Zembylas (2008) discussed three assumptions related to cultural differences and social injustices in online learning:

1. The examination of underlying premises—at individual, institutional, and structural levels; social identity categories (race, gender, ethnicity) often contribute to the perpetuation of racism, nationalism, and social inequalities, and need to be approached critically; and membership in marginalized groups significantly influences an individual's life experiences and beliefs; an empathic understanding is vital to be able to be inclusive of all students.
2. The instructor and students' views are based on their own cultural experiences (Zembylas, 2008). Understanding of your own cultural experiences and biases is vital to keep in mind when teaching online learners. When students are not all from similar backgrounds, they may not always agree with or understand the perspective of the instructor or their peers.
3. Participants expressed that they were shocked by the realization that there is systematic cultivation of "us vs. them" dichotomies (p. 66).

How the course is designed is an essential factor when considering diversity (Li et al., 2016). Providing a few options to how the syllabus, discussion posts, et cetera are designed is essential when considering diverse learners. It would be beneficial to create opportunities for students to review the expectations for the course. In my Online Counseling and Supervision course, I present content in different ways in an effort to assist a variety of learners. For example, creating a table to present the assignments as well as a paragraph format provides a variety of ways for learners to understand assignments. Figure 3.1 is a review of an online graduate-level course, Online Counseling and Supervision, and serves as an example of presenting content in both table and paragraph format.

	Tasks
Assignment	**Description**
Class attendance	**Attendance and active participation in class**: up to *15 points* per week (120 pts total)
Online Counseling or Supervision Advocacy Paper	50 Pts
Online Counseling-Supervision Project	Written Presentation (100 pts)
	Verbal Presentation (100 pts)
	Mock Supervision (50 pts)
	Total of 250 Pts
Possible Total Points	500 Pts

COURSE REQUIREMENTS

Class Attendance and Participation: (120 points; 15 points per class)
Students are expected to attend and participate in all class meetings. Two missed classes will result in earning an automatic "F" in the course.

Discussion Board Assignments: (80 points total; up to 20 points per week)
- Students are required to respond to DB posts during weeks 1, 3, 5, and 7. Each individual post is worth up to 10 points, and a response to a classmate is worth up to 10 points.
- The initial post is due by the day before class at 11:59 PM ET of the assigned week, and respond to at least one classmate is expected by the day of class by 11:59 PM ET of the assigned week.

Online Counseling or Supervision Advocacy Paper (50 points total)
Students will complete a paper on Online Counseling or Supervision Advocacy.

The paper should be 3–5 pages in length. APA formatting will apply, and the paper should demonstrate the professional writing skills necessary for journal or newsletter publication. References (5) are required and should be scholarly, but not included in the page count. A topic may consist of but are not limited to online counseling decreasing barriers for any specific population (physical, psychological, financial barriers), advocating to a State Board for online counseling or supervision, advocating for insurance panels to approve distance counseling or counseling programs to include course work about online counseling services.

Teaching Online Counseling-Supervision Project (250 points total; 50% of final grade)
This is the signature assignment for the course. The Online Counseling-Supervision Project will allow students to demonstrate knowledge, understanding, and skills related to online counseling and supervision in a multidimensional means. Students will be assigned to groups with 3–5 members. Group members will develop a presentation regarding a given chapter in the textbook.

FIGURE 3.1

It is also necessary to provide examples in the course that are inclusive of all learners. For instance, if there are case studies in the course, make sure to include a variety of settings and names so that learners can feel that they are represented throughout the course. For example, including cases where individuals live in a suburb and all have automobiles wouldn't be inclusive of individuals who live in improvised areas and have to use public transportation. It is imperative to include several examples so that learners can connect with the course.

Other Considerations

Sometimes in online courses, there will be familial students including siblings, friends, couples, or the like. Navigating the classroom when there are students in the course who live in the same home can be challenging at times. Instructors must be clear regarding expectations. If it is a synchronous course, it will benefit those students who can have separate devices in separate rooms. If they cannot have separate devices, having rules about who speaks and when will need to be established. Also, expectations regarding having discussions on camera with each other will need to be reviewed. Having expectations for everyone to complete their work may also need to be reviewed for both synchronous and asynchronous courses.

Geographical location is an essential consideration in online learning. Instructors must keep in mind that natural disasters may occur where the student lives. Often, online instructors may not live in the same geographical location as the student. There may be a natural disaster including hurricane, earthquake, or fire or a traumatic event such as a shooting, that may occur where our students reside. Instructors must be willing to accommodate students who may be in a course and experience a natural disaster.

The time zone of both the learners and the instructor must be considered. The program/instructor needs to be clear about what time zone the work will be expected to be completed in. It is imperative to communicate the time zone to learners early in the admission process so that if they live in a different time zone, they can plan accordingly. The instructor needs to state the time zone throughout the syllabus as well as set submission times based on the selected time zone. This will minimize any confusion for those who live in different time zones. Leaners are expected to be aware of any time zone considerations and submit assignments accordingly.

The Importance of Intersectionality

Again, the ADDRESSING model (Hays, 2001) is a useful tool in conceptualizing the various aspects of identity that impact students and educators in an online classroom. However, the model is not intended to serve as a stand-alone tool when tackling the complexities of culture and identity. So far, the various aspects of a person's identity were addressed individually, but it is important to note that identity is not a singular construct. One person may belong to multiple identifiers within the ADDRESSING model. For example, a student can be African American, lesbian, female, and living with disabilities, and each component of the student's identity further marginalizes her, hence a **multiple minority** (Cyrus, 2017). According to Cyrus (2017), the minority stress model has been used to explore the relationship between external and internal stressors experienced by members of the multiple minority community. Intersectionality, coined by legal scholar Kimberle Crenshaw, is grounded in Black feminist and critical race theories (Harris & Patton, 2019). Thus, intersectionality can provide a critical lens through which the systemic inequities that exist along racial, gender, sexuality, ability, educational, and economic lines can be analyzed. Specifically, online educators can use intersectionality to inform their pedagogy to advance "a radical and transformative social justice agenda" (p. 349) in their classroom.

Under the Trump administration, intersectionality has come under attack under the premise that it further perpetuates division and is unpatriotic. In fact, a presidential mandate forced government employees and contractors to remove intersectionality from diversity training altogether and offered no alternative theoretical lens to address the intricacies of a person's identity. Identity salience is real, and depending on the environment or situation, the most salient part of your identity becomes palpable (Steele, 2010). Collectively, we can say with certainty that basic human rights were withheld from Black people and women. Yet the problematic nature of such a statement is only felt by a specific segment of our population that happens to be both Black and a woman. The problem lies in the exclusivity of each construct. Not acknowledging how the various aspects of a person's identity intersect is an assault on that person, as it makes them invisible. This invisibility is dangerous and places them in a position to not be considered in policy and legislation (Mowatt et al., 2013). Intersectionality invites us to acknowledge and embrace our identity's intersectional nature, and that parts of our identity can be oppressed and other parts privileged. It invites everyone to the table to critically examine the ways we can work together toward a more perfect union.

Universal Design for Online Learning

Equally important is the implementation of universal design (Mace et al., 1990) for online learning. Online educators do not have to wait until they receive disability accommodations requisitions to prepare their classrooms. As opposed to reactively providing accommodations for a few students, implementing a universal design will allow instructors to develop a quality design that serves many. Universal design does benefit students living with disabilities; other students also benefit. O'Keefe (2020) used the following example for praxis: "using captioning for videos ensures access for a student who is deaf, however, captions can also benefit nonnative speaking students, students with learning disabilities, or students that are watching the video in a loud environment" (p. 20). See Chapter 6 for more information on this topic.

Chapter Summary

Unlike any year in modern times, 2020 highlighted long-standing inequality in the United States. For some, these inequalities came as a surprise as the dominant discourse was the notion of a postracial American. Yet, for others, the tragic events of 2020, although painful, served as a reminder that many are still waiting for our great nation to live up to her ideals. Depending on one's location in life, the pursuit of happiness (the "American dream") is directly connected to educational attainment. However, the legacy of colonization persists in the academy, whether in-person or virtually. As educators, we have a responsibility to ensure that diversity, equity, and inclusion permeates our teaching philosophy theoretically and practically. Several factors must be taken into consideration when implementing DEI in online classrooms. The complexities of identity cannot be adequately examined without acknowledging the role history plays in forming those identities. By utilizing the ADDRESSING model, intersectionality, and universal design, online educators can provide a welcoming environment where all learners can achieve their highest potential.

Online Resources

Prodigy: 7 Ways to Support Diversity in the Classroom, With Examples

Helpful hints and examples of how to create and support diversity in the classroom for instructors: https://www.prodigygame.com/main-en/blog/diversity-in-the-classroom/#:~:text=Diversity%20in%20the%20classroom%20teaches%20students%20to%20appreciate%20different%20perspectives,the%20rest%20of%20their%20life.

Drexel University, School of Education: The Importance of Diversity and Cultural Awareness in the Classroom

Helpful information for understanding and appreciating diversity and cultural awareness for teachers: https://drexel.edu/soe/resources/student-teaching/advice/importance-of-cultural-diversity-in-classroom/

Edutopia: Preparing for Cultural Diversity: Resources for Teachers

Resources for teachers to prepare for and support cultural diversity in the classroom: https://www.edutopia.org/blog/preparing-cultural-diversity-resources-teachers

GoGuardian: Diversity in K–12 Classrooms

Useful information and considerations for creating and supporting diversity in the K–12 classroom: https://www.goguardian.com/blog/learning/diversity-in-the-classroom/

Scholastic: Teaching Diversity: A Place to Begin

How to help build an appreciation and understanding of diversity in Pre-K, K, and grades 1 and 2: https://www.scholastic.com/teachers/articles/teaching-content/teaching-diversity-place-begin-0/

Excite Education: How to Bring Diversity in the Classroom

Helpful steps and hints on how to foster diversity in the classroom: https://www.excite.com/education/blog/how-to-bring-diversity-in-the-classroom

Kickboard: 5 Ways to Promote Equity and Diversity in the Classroom

Ways to promote equality and diversity: https://www.kickboardforschools.com/blog/post/diversity-equity/5-ways-to-promote-equity-diversity-in-the-classroom/

Teaching Tolerance: Culture in the Classroom

A discussion of celebrating culture in the classroom; includes videos and assists instructors in professional development on the topic: https://www.tolerance.org/professional-development/culture-in-the-classroom

References

Applebaum, B. (2010). *Being White, being good: White complicity, White moral responsibility, and social justice pedagogy.* Lexington Books.

Baron, A., & McNeal, K. (2019). Strategies for teaching online higher education courses with an eye towards retention: Choosing a culturally responsive path. In L. Kyei-Blankson, J. Blankson, & E. Ntuli (Eds.), *Care and Culturally Responsive Pedagogy in Online Settings* (pp. 280–298). IGI Global.

Beratan, G. D. (2012). *Institutional ableism and the politics of inclusive education: An ethnographic study of an inclusive high school* (Order No. 10023021) [Doctoral dissertation, University of London]. ProQuest Dissertations & Theses Global.

Bernstein, R. S., Bulger, M., Salipante, P., & Weisinger, J. Y. (2019). From diversity to inclusion to equity: A theory of generative interactions. *Journal of Business Ethics, 167,* 395–410. https://doi.org/10.1007/s10551-019-04180-1

Betts, K. (2009). Lost in translation: Importance of effective communication in online education. *Online Journal of Distance Learning Administration, 12*(2).

Calma, J. (2020, August 19). *Going remote makes it harder for colleges to reach first-generation students.* The Verge. https://www.theverge.com/21372574/colleges-online-remote-learning-first-generation-students

Chadderton, C. (2012) Problematising the role of the white researcher in social justice research. *Ethnography and Education*, 7(3), 363–380.

Clayton-Pedersen, A. R., & Musil, C. M. (2009). *Making excellence inclusive: A framework for embedding diversity and inclusion into colleges and universities' academic excellence mission.* Association of American Colleges and Universities.

Crenshaw, K. W. (1989). Demarginalizing the intersection of race and sex: A Black feminist critique of antidiscrimination doctrine. *University of Chicago Legal Forum*, 139–168.

Crenshaw, K. W. (1991). Mapping the margins: Intersectionality, identity politics and violence against women of color. *Stanford Law Review*, 43(6), 1241–1299.

Cyrus, K. (2017). Multiple minorities as multiply marginalized: Applying the minority stress theory to LGBTQ people of color. *Journal of Gay and Lesbian Mental Health*, 21(3), 194–202. https://doi.org/10.1080/19359705.2017.1320739

Damary, R., Markova, T., & Pryadilina, N. (2017). Key challenges of on-line education in multi-cultural context. *Procedia-Social and Behavioral Sciences*, 237, 83–89.

Delgado, R. (1984). The imperial scholar: Reflections on a review of civil rights literature. *University of Pennsylvania Law Review*, 132(3), 561–578.

Delgado, R. (1996). The colonial scholar: Do outsider authors replicate the citation practices of the insiders, but in reverse? *Chicago-Kent Law Review*, 71, 969–987.

Dorn, E., Hancock, B., Sarakatsannis, J., & Viruleg, E. (2020). *COVID-19 and student learning in the United States: The hurt could last a lifetime.* McKinsey.

Edwards, R. (1990). Connecting method and epistemology: A white women interviewing black women. *Women's Studies International Forum*, 13(5), 477–490. https://doi.org/10.1016/0277-5395(90)90100-C

Flores, C. A., & Sheely-Moore, A. I. (2020). Relational-cultural theory-based interventions with LGBTQ college students. *Journal of College Counseling*, 23(1), 71–84.

Fox, O. H. (2005). Diversity in online teaching: When culture and online education conflict. *Home Health Care Management and Practice*, 17(4), 342–345.

Fuentes, M. A., Zelaya, D. G., & Madsen, J. W. (2020). Rethinking the course syllabus: Considerations for promoting equity, diversity, and inclusion. *Teaching of Psychology*, 48(1), 69–79. https://doi.org/10.1177/0098628320959979

Gay, G. (2010). Acting on beliefs in teacher education for cultural diversity. *Journal of Teacher Education*, 61(1–2), 143–152. https://doi.org/10.1177%2F0022487109347320

Gay, G. (2018). *Culturally responsive teaching: Theory, research, and practice.* Teachers College Press.

Glasener, K. M., Martell, C. A., & Posselt, J. R. (2019). Framing diversity: Examining the place of race in institutional policy and practice post-affirmative action. *Journal of Diversity in Higher Education*, 12(1), 3–16. https://doi.org/10.1037/dhe0000086

Goldberg, A. E., & Kuvalanka, K. (2019). Transgender graduate students' experiences in higher education: A mixed-methods exploratory study. *Journal of Diversity in Higher Education*, 12(1), 38–51. https://doi.apa.org/doi/10.1037/dhe0000074

Graves, K. (2018) The history of lesbian, gay, bisexual, transgender, queer issues in higher education. In M. B. Paulsen (Ed.), *Higher education: Handbook of theory and research* (Vol. 33, pp. 127–173). Springer. https://doi.org/10.1007/978-3-319-72490-4_4

Guerra, R. C. C., Farrell, S., & Longo, A. (2016). Promoting LGBTQ equality in engineering via online Safe Zone workshops. *Proceedings of the 2016 Frontiers in Education Conference, USA.* Institute of Electrical and Electronics Engineers. https://doi.org/10.1109/FIE.2016.7757731

Harmon, D. A. (2012). Culturally responsive teaching though a historical lens: Will history repeat itself? *Interdisciplinary Journal of Teaching and Learning*, 2(1), 12–22.

Harper, S. R., Patton, L. D., & Wooden, O. S. (2009). Assess and equity for African American students in higher education: A critical race analysis of policy efforts. *Journal of Higher Education*, 80(4), 389–414.

Harris, J. C., & Patton, L. D. (2019). Un/doing intersectionality through higher education research. *Journal of Higher Education*, 90(3), 347–372.

Hays, P. A. (2001). *Addressing cultural complexities in practice: A framework for clinicians and counselors.* American Psychological Association. https://doi.org/10.1037/10411-000

Kerr, R., Merciai, I., and Eradze, M. (2018). Addressing cultural and linguistic diversity in an online learning environment. *Educational Media International*, 55(4), 317–332.

Kurubacak, G. (2008). Online identity: Guidelines for discerning covert racism in blogs. *International Journal on E-Learning*, 7(3), 403–426.

Lange, A. C., Duran, A., & Jackson, R. (2019). The state of LGBT and queer research in higher education revisited: Current academic houses and future possibilities. *Journal of College Student Development*, 60(5), 511–526. https://doi.org/10.1353/csd.2019.0047

Li, N., Marsh, V., & Rienties, B. (2016). Modelling and managing learner satisfaction: Use of learner feedback to enhance blended and online learning experience. *Decision Sciences Journal of Innovative Education*, 14(2), 216–242.

Liu, S. R., & Modir, S. (2020). The outbreak that was always here: Racial trauma in the context of COVID-19 and implications for mental health providers. *Psychological Trauma: Theory, Research, Practice, and Policy*, 12(5), 439–442. http://dx.doi.org/10.1037/tra0000784

Lotz, E. (2020). *Higher Education Consortia: Working Together for Diversity, Equity, and Inclusion* (Doctoral dissertation, Prescott College). https://search.proquest.com/openview/996356ea40d4baf884837fb10703e85d/1?pq-origsite=gscholar&cbl=18750&diss=y

Mace, R. L., Hardie, G. J., Place, J. P., & North Carolina State University. (1990). *Accessible environments: Toward universal design*. Center for Accessible Housing, North Carolina State University.

Mata, C. (2018). *White women in student affairs: Navigating race in a complex work environment* (Order No. 10978393) [Doctoral dissertation, University of California, Los Angeles]. ProQuest Dissertations & Theses Global.

Melnick, H., & Darling-Hammond, L. (2020). *Reopening schools in the context of COVID-19: Health and safety guidelines from other countries* [Policy brief]. Learning Policy Institute. https://files.eric.ed.gov/fulltext/ED606555.pdf

Morrow, G. P., Burris-Kitchen, D., & Der-Karabetian, A. (2000). Assessing campus climate of cultural diversity: A focus on focus groups. *College Student Journal*, 34(4), 589–589.

Mowatt, R. A., French, B. H., & Malebranche, D. A. (2013). Black/female/body hypervisibility and invisibility: A Black feminist augmentation of feminist leisure research. *Journal of Leisure Research*, 45(5), 644–660.

O'Keefe, L., Rafferty, J., Gunder, A., & Vignare, K. (2020). *Delivering high-quality instruction online in response to COVID-19: Faculty playbook*. Every Learner Everywhere. https://www.everylearnereverywhere.org/resources/delivering-high-quality-instruction-online-in-response-to-covid-19/

Oztok, M. (2013). The hidden curriculum of online learning: Discourses of whiteness, social absence, and inequity (Order No. 3666067) [Doctoral dissertation, University of Toronto]. ProQuest Dissertations & Theses Global.

Petit-McClure, S. H., & Stinson, C. (2019). Disrupting dis/abilization: A critical exploration of research methods to combat white supremacy and ableism in education. *Intersections: Critical Issues in Education*, 3(2), 73–90.

Phillips, A. (2019). The quest for diversity in higher education. *Pepperdine Policy Review*, 11(4). https://digitalcommons.pepperdine.edu/ppr/vol11/iss1/4

Phirangee, K., & Malec, A. (2017). Othering in online learning: An examination of social presence, identity, and sense of community. *Distance Education*, 38(2), 160–172. https://doi.org/10.1080/01587919.2017.1322457

Platts, T. K., & Hoosier, K. (2020). Reducing stereotype threat in the classroom. *Inquiry: The Journal of the Virginia Community Colleges*, 23(1), Article 6. https://commons.vccs.edu/inquiry/vol23/iss1/6

Renn, K. A. (2010). LGBT and queer research in higher education: The state and status of the field. *Educational Researcher*, 39(2), 132–141.

Renn, K. A. (2020). Success for LGBT college and university students. In G. Crimmins (Ed.), *Strategies for supporting inclusion and diversity in the academy* (pp. 183–200). Palgrave Macmillan.

Roberson, Q. M. (2006). Disentangling the meanings of diversity and inclusion in organizations. *Group and Organization Management*, 31(2), 212–236. https://doi.org/10.1177/1059601104273064

Robertson, N. (2018). The Power and subjection of liminality and borderlands of non-binary folx. *Gender Forum: An Internet Journal for Gender Studies: Early career researchers VI* [Special issue], 45-59. http://genderforum.org/wp-content/uploads/2018/08/2018_ECRIV_complete.pdf

Rodriguez, A. J. (2016). For whom do we do equity and social justice work? Recasting the discourse about the other to effect transformative change. In N. M. Joseph, C. Haynes, & F. Cobb (Eds.), *Interrogating whiteness and relinquishing power: White faculty's commitment to racial consciousness in STEM classrooms* (pp. 241-252). Peter Lang.

Rodriguez, A. J., & Morrison, D. (2019). Expanding and enacting transformative meanings of equity, diversity and social justice in science education. *Cultural Studies of Science Education*, 14(2), 265–281.

Sathy, V., & Hogan, K. A. (2019, July 22). *Want to reach all of your students? Here's how to make your teaching more inclusive*. Chronicle of Higher Education. https://www.chronicle.com/article/how-to-make-your-teaching-more-inclusive/

Shainwald, E. (2020). Subgroup diversity in higher education: A case study for Asian American recruitment. (Publication No. 1517) [Honors thesis, William & Mary University]. Undergraduate Honors Theses. https://scholarworks.wm.edu/honorstheses/1517

Smith, D. R., & Ayers, D. F. (2006). Culturally responsive pedagogy and online learning: Implications for the globalized community college. *Community College Journal of Research and Practice*, 30(5-6), 401–415.

Snow, W. H., & Coker, J. K. (2020). Distance counselor education: Past, present, future. *Professional Counselor*, 10(1), 40–56.

Solomon, B. M. (1985). *In the company of educated women: A history of women and higher education in America*. Yale University Press.

Steele, C. M. (2010). *Whistling Vivaldi: How stereotypes affect us and what we can do*. W. W. Norton.

Steele, C. M. & Aronson, J. (1998). Stereotype threat and the test performance of academically successful African Americans. In C. Jencks & M. Phillips (Eds.), *The Black-White test score gap*. Brookings Institution Press.

Sue, D. W., Capodilupo, C. M., Torino, G. C., Bucceri, J. M., Holder, A. M. B., Nadal, K. L. & Esquilin, J. M. (2007). Microaggressions in everyday life: Implications for clinical practice. *American Psychologist*, 62(4), 271–286.

Tatum, B. (2018). Identifying inclusive practices on U.S. university campuses that create engagement for diverse populations. (Publication No. 116) [Doctoral Dissertation, Abilene Christian University]. Digital Commons @ ACU. https://digitalcommons.acu.edu/etd/116

Tienda, M. (2013). Diversity ≠ inclusion: Promoting integration in higher education. *Educational Researcher*, 42(9), 467–475.

Williams, A. S., & Moore, S. M. (2011). Universal design of research: Inclusion of persons with disabilities in mainstream biomedical studies. *Science Translational Medicine*, 3(82), 82cm12. https://doi.org/10.1126/scitranslmed.3002133

Yosso, T. J., Parker, L., Solózano, D. G., & Lynn, M. (2004). From Jim Crow to affirmative action and back again: A critical race discussion of racialized rationales and access to higher education. *Review of Research in Education*, 28(1), 1–25.

Zembylas, M. (2008). Engaging with issues of cultural diversity and discrimination through critical emotional reflexivity in online learning. *Adult Education Quarterly*, 59(1), 61–82.

CHAPTER FOUR

Fostering Student Success Online

Tricia M. Mikolon, PhD, CRC, LPC, BC-TMH
Debra Perez, MA, LPCC, SCPG
Diedre Leigh Wade, LPCC-S, LPCC-S

Student success is the goal of all educators regardless of instructional format. Student success is achieved by meeting the student's fundamental needs consistently within an environment that supports learning and growth (National Education Association, 2015). Student success in the online realm is the result of engagement and effective classroom management, supporting success through structure and effective communication, and creating a sense of community (Kuh et al., 2013; Seidman, 2012). These elements combine with effective assessment and feedback to strengthen student learning while providing proactive remediation to assist students who are in need of strengthening specific areas within a subject.

Student success is often viewed through various lenses ranging from sociological, organizational, psychological, cultural, and economic (Kuh et al., 2006). In the mid-1970s, Tinto proposed a sociological perspective in which students go through a process of attrition in their learning, moving through transitions in self-identity as they develop new skills throughout their educational journey (Kuh et al., 2006; Tinto, 1975, 1987, 1993). Organizational views on student success place a great value on the features of the institutions and their impact on student learning (Kuh et al., 2006). These features often align with the credentialing statutes of various programs to include student-to-faculty ratios, administrative influences through policies and procedures, and the mission and social environment of the campus (Berger & Braxton, 1998; Kuh et al., 2006; Pike & Kuh, 2005).

Theorists have suggested specific psychological aspects of students contribute to their educational success. Characteristics such as self-confidence, internal drive, and self-efficacy (Bean & Eaton, 2000), their perception of their ability to learn and be successful (Dweck, 2000), and their relationship to the topic and instructor (Kuh et al., 2006) all contribute to how a student approaches a topic, instructor, and overall course. These things are ever evolving, influenced by the student's past experiences and current events, and may change throughout the duration of a class. Instructors who understand the transitory nature of a student's perspective allow for appropriate adjustments within the structure and expectations of the course. Culturally, each student brings with them a unique combination of values, beliefs, world views, and unfortunately, social injustices in their history. The concept of **habitus**, or the construct through which an individual incorporates their cultural variables to formulate a structure that may enhance or restrict their future success, needs to be a consideration of all instructors (Bourdieu & Passeron, 1977; Kuh et al., 2006). Consideration and exploration of these variables from the student's perspective allows instructors to create effective adaptions, thus fostering success. Finally, appreciating the students' economic responsibility and drive is important in understanding their motivation and relationship to learning (Kuh et al., 2006). Students are multifaceted, and their success requires instructors to consider and address all applicable variables when providing them with an equitable opportunity for learning.

According to the National Education Association (2015), the key elements that encourage student success are providing all students with access to "qualified professionals within a positive learning environment" (p. 9), encouraging active engagement and advocacy for their own learning, viewing themselves as capable learners who value education, and using their new knowledge to form relationships with their educators while preparing themselves for success beyond their educational journey. The effective instructor meets the needs of each student while maintaining a consistent movement through the curriculum, providing a structure to guide them through the material and successfully meet shared standards and goals (National Education Association, 2015). Effective instructors appreciate each unique student, considering the multiple variables that influence the student's perceptions of themselves. Appreciation of each student's aspirations, strengths, values, beliefs, family history and support, prior educational experiences, and need areas is used as a guide for their instruction and means for facilitating student success on the individual level (Kuh et al., 2005). Appreciation of these differences and an understanding of their impact on the student better prepare the instructor to determine necessary interventions to prevent or remediate resulting issues (Kuh et al., 2005).

Classroom Management

Classroom success is the product of good classroom management (Cangelosi, 2013). Iverson (2003) defined classroom management as "the act of supervising relationships, behaviors, and instructional settings and lessons for communities of learners" (p. 4). Proactive classroom management is important for instructors as it contributes to the learning environment and may suppress problems from developing (Stewart, 2008). The instructor's philosophy of classroom management will guide the preparation and execution of the course and management of any issues that develop. Chapter 2 addresses specific pedagogical approaches in detail.

The **syllabus**, as discussed in Chapter 7, provides a foundation upon which classroom management is established. It offers students an introduction to the course, the expectations of their behaviors, policies and procedures, and the means for the assessment of their performance in meeting class objectives. The course schedule, assignment explanations, and associated rubrics assist students in considering time management requirements for successful completion of the course. **Policies and procedures** are necessary to provide structure and are essential to classroom management but need to be presented as guidelines for success rather than punitive directives (Stewart, 2008). The syllabus and its content are best provided to students prior to the start of class for their review and preparation as well as discussed in detail in the first synchronous class together to clarify any requirements and provide a shared understanding of all expectations. In an asynchronous class this may be accomplished by having a discussion board in which students need to identify where certain aspects of the syllabus are located.

The online format brings with it some challenges for students, including the lack of face-to-face contact with their instructor and peers outside of the **synchronous class** time as well as possibly their own varying educational skill sets and experiences (Stewart, 2008). Open communication, the use of discussion boards, and in-class activities help to create a sense of community for students (Berge, 2002). Timely feedback on behaviors and assignments contribute to successful classroom management. Instructors need to embrace inclusion for different learning styles, personality traits, and multicultural variables in their courses. Considerations may include the needs of students with a primary language other than English, and technological abilities and access to various technology such as scanners, printers, and software programs (Stewart, 2008). Considering the unique needs of each student prepares the instructor to incorporate all learning styles and abilities while guiding the class focus toward achieving shared objectives and goals. Effective use of each of these will be discussed in detail as this chapter unfolds.

Problems may develop during the duration of a course, ranging from behavioral issues in class to assignments not being completed. The interventions available for remediation of problems experienced by students requires creativity from the instructor in the online classroom (Stewart, 2008). The discussion of policies and procedures along with their purpose needs to occur throughout the duration of the class both as a reminder and initial remediation. Interventions will depend on the issue present; remediation will be discussed in more detail later in this chapter.

An essential aspect of classroom management is the inclusion of every student. Inclusion involves the mutual respect and understanding of one's own culture and world views, and appreciation for those held by others around them, be it instructor, student, or peer. Instructors need to effectively use classroom management techniques that consider the uniqueness of all students while creating a culturally responsive and caring classroom (Weinstein et al., 2004). Classroom accessibility considerations are explored in detail in Chapter five.

Online Classroom Management in Primary School

Evertson and Emmer (2017) identify that instructors for both face-to-face and online classes need to design their classroom with consideration of the elementary student and their needs. The authors identify common concerns to include choosing and implementing rules and procedures, arranging the physical teaching space, preparing and presenting course materials, addressing student needs, managing student behaviors, and dealing with any problems that may arise, as well as ensuring consistent and effective communication. Choosing rules and procedures for any instructor will involve consideration of the institutional policies as well as the student developmental level. The presentation of classroom rules influences the incorporation of these for the student into their daily classroom interactions. Presenting these in a way in which the students may learn the expectations as well as refer to them is an important consideration for the instructor. This can be accomplished in the online format by taking time at the beginning of each class to review the rules and procedures for the online class with the students. Instructors may achieve this by providing a PowerPoint for the students to review and recite at the beginning of each class as well as posting them in the background of the instructor's teaching space so they are consistently in sight. This also allows for the instructor to readily refer to the rules as a reminder and management technique of any disruptive behaviors which may occur.

The instructor's physical teaching space is also an important consideration, as maintaining an engaging environment while reducing distractions is in itself a skill. Limiting distracting materials and keeping a clean background assists student in developing focusing skills. Posting classroom rules and/or procedures as well as topic-specific materials in the view frame can achieve a focused learning environment for young learners. However, it involves consistent consideration and commitment on behalf of the instructor. This construction of the course materials and instructional plan requires preparation prior to the class meeting time but will assist in minimizing distractions during the lesson.

Addressing student needs as they arise highlights the interactive teaching aspect of the synchronous online classroom. Teaching students how to virtually raise their hand and incorporating question and answer times at the beginning and end of each lesson encourages students to share their concerns in real time, allowing the instructor to provide clarification as needed to guide student learning. The incorporation of regular comprehension checks and appropriate clarification helps to ensure student success and understanding. These concepts are explored in depth in Chapter 8.

Online Classroom Management in Secondary School

The foundational considerations for the elementary classroom remain consistent for the secondary classroom with the modification of incorporating student personal responsibility for their learning and work to a greater degree (Emmer & Evertson, 2012; Emmer et al., 2002). As students mature, it is beneficial to their success to increase their personal responsibility for their assignments and classroom behavior by providing a list of course assignments, increasing their sharing of knowledge via topic-focused discussions, and incorporating the student's application of course rules and procedures in their behavioral management. This may be achieved by increasing the responsibility for learning through completing assigned readings prior to the class discussion, incorporating focused topic discussion times in class and small work groups, and using assignments that reflect student learning such as papers, worksheets, and other application assignments (Weinstein, 2003). Guiding the student through their educational journey to become a self-directed learner is an important aspect of teaching at this level. Supporting this transition through consistent constructive feedback on assignments and behaviors encourages growth and responsibility while ensuring topic-specific learning.

Online Classroom Management in Postsecondary Education

Adult learners bring with them experiences from their educational and employment histories as well as their general life experiences. These experiences need to be appreciated and incorporated as appropriate into their current course of study. Assisting students in finding their personal connection to the topic and an application in their present or future careers will assist students to invest beyond just simply completing assignments to obtain a grade (Eng, 2017; Norman et al., 2010).

Classroom management becomes particularly important at this level of instruction as a student who interrupts, challenges information inappropriately, or incites others may distract other students from the topic as well as cause distaste for the subject for others (Vangelisti et al., 2009). Providing a clear explanation of course policies and procedures to students via the syllabus (explored in detail in Chapter 7) prior to class and referring to this throughout the course as applicable provides students with the framework upon which to build their interactions. Should problems arise, providing instant redirection and feedback in class, as well as follow up via videoconference, is recommended to support the students in understanding their behavioral responsibilities within the course. Sometimes simply listening to the student's frustrations or underlying reasoning is enough to allow them to feel heard, resulting in an improved interaction in future class meetings.

Supporting Success Through Structure

Classroom structure defines the rules, sets up expectations, and provides the overall organization of the classroom. Structure provides students a sense of safety based on the consistency of rules and expectations, and a dependable routine. Students utilize structure to have the space to focus on learning and grow both academically and as individuals. By providing flexible structure that includes students' feelings and perspectives, the teacher increases student autonomy, feelings of capability, and engagement with learning (Cheon et al., 2020). Structure includes lesson planning to effectively manage learning time. Teachers utilize preparation and organization to use learning time effectively, increase learning opportunities, and minimizing administrative tasks. This structure begins with the first interaction with students and continues until the end of the term, semester, or marking period. In the brick-and-mortar classroom, structure also includes physical aspects of the room, such as the layout of student desks and the placement of various working stations throughout the room.

Rules and Policies

Structure begins on the first day of class with general classroom rules and is generated in a collaborative effort between teacher and students. Rules should be clear and fair, with consequences adequately defined. By including the students in rule creation, they are more likely to adhere to and enforce those rules they had input on, making the classroom run more smoothly (Taylor, 2016). Additionally, when students contribute to the rules and consequences of the classroom, they increase their sense of responsibility and develop self-discipline (Marzano & Marzano, 2003). The development of self-discipline takes the burden off of teachers and other adults for policing the student's behavior and places it squarely on the student, where it belongs, helping them to be responsible for their choices, behaviors, and ultimately their education (Marzano & Marzano, 2003). In addition, self-discipline increases autonomy, which leads to the student behaviors being rooted in their own beliefs and sense of correctness rather than being unduly influenced by others (Williams, 2009).

In some instances, especially for secondary and postsecondary students, there will be policies that are dictated by the school or the teacher, such as attendance, tardiness, or assignment submission. In that instance, it is important that the policy is clear and fair and enforced consistently for all students. Additionally, the policy should be explained and discussed during the first meeting to ensure understanding and provide students the opportunity to ask questions and reach clarity.

Communicating Expectations

To further strengthen the structure required in the classroom, the teacher's expectations of the students must be articulated clearly. Students will need to understand exactly what is expected of them to decide if they can meet the requirements and goals. Expectations should be thoroughly discussed with time for students to ask questions and understand the requirements. Assignments will need to be thoroughly explained and the process for submission made clear (Taylor, 2016). Expectations, especially surrounding assignments, should offer choices when possible. Choices provided to students increase internal motivation and lead to students feeling more in control of their learning. Expectations and assignments should make sense, show relevance, allow for meaning making, and help students make connections to importance and future aspirations (Taylor, 2016). Communicating expectations naturally leads to goal setting. Goals need to be set high but attainable for all students, and they will rise to meet those goals and therefore meet expectations. When possible, expectations should be provided in writing as a reference to reflect back on should the need arise.

Holding Students Accountable

Accountability gives credibility to the teacher, their rules, and their expectations. Providing the agreed-upon consequences lets students know that the teacher requires their adherence to the rules and respect of the classroom and their classmates. Accountability needs to be the same for all students and consistent to ensure equality and fairness. It is important that any issues that arise are dealt with immediately to discourage other inappropriate or unacceptable behavior, especially small issues, which can be overlooked but develop into something bigger later.

It is important for teachers to convey respect of the classroom and the students by holding themselves accountable in returning grades and feedback to students in a timely and thorough manner. Additionally, students should be encouraged to provide feedback to the teacher, which can be incorporated to make the classroom a more supportive learning environment and further hold the teacher accountable. Finally, teachers can convey respect by holding each student accountable in a fair and similar manner. Discussing an accountability issue with students should be done in private, when possible, to show respect for students. Educators should include enforcement of rules with a conversation about the reasons behind the behavior, allowing the student to be heard (Taylor, 2016). While the reason will not excuse poor decisions or bad behavior, understanding the situations being faced by the student is important in supporting them as well as building teacher-student relationship (Taylor, 2016).

Why Structure Is Important

By utilizing structure in the classroom, students are free to focus solely on learning, as the daily flow, rules, and expectations have been made clear and are dependable. A lack of structure in the classroom removes the sense of safety and leads to misbehaviors, both of which make the teacher less effective and students less likely to learn or thrive. Structure also strengthens the teacher-student relationship which leads to a greater sense of classroom cohesiveness, reducing misbehavior and increasing achievement (Bergsmann et al., 2013). Flexibility within structure—meaning the ability to evaluate and change when something is not working—is important and allows the teacher to align with students and be an ally with students rather than an adversary (Taylor, 2016). Providing a structure that allows students to make choices and have input into their learning increases internal motivation, self-discipline, and autonomy, all of which lead to more academically successful students.

Providing Structure Online

Providing structure online shares some similarities to the brick-and-mortar classroom. While the teacher cannot control the organization of the room and the setup of desks and learning stations, the teacher can create an online structure within the virtual classroom, beginning with the virtual bulletin board that students see upon entering the class page. A regular and dependable routine can be established virtually, letting students depend on the natural flow of their school day and incorporating time online as well as offline.

PROVIDING STRUCTURE IN PRIMARY SCHOOL

Routines are important at all ages, but especially in the younger grades. While things change online, routines can be established, such as what tasks are completed at the start of the day and what happens to end the day in order to sign off. Additionally, the flow of the day and when topics are addressed can create the routine needed. Younger children require more movement and should not be required to be online without breaks for an entire school day. By incorporating a child's natural curiosity through play and activity, the teacher can encourage learning online rather than hinder it.

Students will be involved in rule creation at differing levels, depending on age. But all students can create basic rules about kindness to classmates, taking turns, and not speaking out and interrupting class. This will be more teacher directed at the younger grades and more teacher influenced in the older grades. Younger students may need more leeway and require more flexibility from the teacher in conveying expectations and explanations of assignments and technology procedures. Teaching students different signals to convey their needs without interrupting class is an option to help students communicate their needs to the teacher without disrupting class structure.

PROVIDING STRUCTURE IN SECONDARY SCHOOL

Routine is important as well at this age, but that routine will require more independent work by students. Students will have greater input into the rules of the virtual classroom, influenced by teacher input to ensure all necessary areas are addressed. Students at this age will greatly benefit from group work, which can be accomplished by breakout rooms. To prevent misbehavior and bullying, chat options should be limited or disabled. A daily agenda should be posted to help students understand the schedule and flow of the day. Developmentally, socialization with peers is important and should be included, as appropriate, in daily schedules. Additionally, students should be encouraged to speak in class, interacting with the teacher, asking questions, and engaging in debates, not just required to sit and listen quietly. Structure in the virtual classroom should incorporate synchronous interaction with asynchronous requirements. Structure in the secondary grades has been shown to lead to greater achievement and higher-level thinking and should be intentionally thought out for best success (Evertson, 2001).

PROVIDING STRUCTURE IN POSTSECONDARY EDUCATION

Structure in higher education online is dictated primarily by the rules of the institution or department and is communicated primarily through the syllabus. College students will still require a thorough discussion of expectations and assignments with the opportunity to ask questions for clarity. Consistency and equality are important at this level to ensure that all students are being held to the same requirements and standards. Explanations of the requirements for attendance, participation, and assignment submission, including the late submission policy, will need to be very clear with little room for questioning or misinterpretation. Structure should incorporate active participation in class to explore the material, whether chat or voice based, as this has been shown to increase work completion and increase final class grades at the college level (Al-Shammari, 2016).

Communication in and out of Class

Communication is fundamental to relational development, capable of both enhancing and spoiling relationships (Brown, 2005; Charles, 2000). Teacher effectiveness is directly impacted by their ability to share information (Brown, 2005); thus, communication is a skill pertinent to student success. Grunert O'Brien et al. (2009) found a positive correlation between student academic success and the amount of information the instructor communicated about the course. Online education mandates regular effective communication between the instructor and students to reduce anxieties associated with technology (Miltiadou, 2001). The importance of effective communication in developing a sense of community for students, an understanding of course expectations and requirements, enhancing higher-order thinking (Sullivan & Clarke, 1991), and providing feedback for areas of improvement and growth cannot be stressed enough.

Communication between student and instructor is necessary regardless of cultural or accessibility concerns. Instructors need to be able to meet a student at their level of understanding and ability, identifying and appreciating communication diversity, and striving to provide accommodations to overcome barriers (Johnson, 1999). This is further explored in Chapter 5.

Communication in Primary School

Effective communication at this level involves both the student and parent/guardian. Communication with students regarding classroom rules and expectations, assignment requirements and due dates, and feedback on behaviors and learning needs to take place in real time during the class session. However, it also requires a follow-up with the child's adult caretaker. In class, communication includes reviewing rules to redirect behaviors, explaining and processing tasks step by step, providing feedback via words, emojis, or other creative measures, and grades. Follow-up communication in the form of emails, class announcements, and videoconferences with the student's parent or guardian allows for a collaborative relationship between instructor, student, school counselor, and the student's home-based support system. This topic is explored in detail in Chapter 8.

Communication in Secondary School

The fundamental communication skills of instructors at the primary school level are simply enhanced and modified to meet the increased maturity and responsibility of the secondary school student. At this level, students will begin to be placed in the liaison role between their instructor and parent/guardian, passing along pertinent information as they progress higher in grade level. This does not absolve the instructor from sharing information via emails, class announcement, and assignment feedback or report cards with parents.

Assignments increasingly make use of the student's verbal and written communication skills. The use of discussion boards, breakout rooms, and classroom discussions of course material will increasingly replace instructor-led explanations or readings. Slowly transitioning a student's responsibility for their own work and behaviors enhances the development of their personal accountability for their learning, furthering their investment in their education and success.

Communication in Postsecondary Education

Instructors need to communicate with students about issues related to confidentiality of peers and clients, if applicable to the course topic (Ko & Rosen, 2001; Smith 2005); course requirements regarding attendance/participation, writing; and submission of assignments, as well as expectations of professionalism (Ko & Rosen, 2001; Palloff & Pratt, 2001; Smith, 2005). An overview of institutional and course policy and procedures, available resources for necessary accommodations, and technical information such as course platform, internet/software requirements, and videoconferencing allow students to prepare prior to the start of the course (Palloff & Pratt, 2001; Smith, 2005). The syllabus, as discussed in Chapter 7, provides the student initial access and introduction to course expectations, assignments, and corresponding rubrics, as well as a valuable reference resource throughout the duration of the class.

Regular contact between instructor and student enhances learning as well as a sense of connectedness to the course. This may be achieved through weekly course announcements reminding students of assigned reading and assignments for the upcoming class time. Use of discussion boards, occasionally viewed as busy work for students, provides an opportunity for students to discuss course-related topics and issues outside of class, mimicking those conversations that would occur prior to class, during breaks, and after class in a face-to-face classroom. Introducing the purpose of discussion boards in this light reinforces their importance in building a sense of community in the online classroom and enhances the students' commitment to discussions and exchange of information with their peers. Classroom discussions, either as an entire class or via breakout rooms, allow students to share their understanding of course materials while discussing its application in their daily lives and reflecting on its importance (Bowman, 2001).

Assignment feedback is yet another form of communication shared between instructors and students. Providing detailed feedback requires additional time from the educator but allows personalized instruction to each student, contributing to their individual understanding and application of the information. Communicating feedback in a timely manner provides structure to the assessment procedures while assisting students in identifying their strengths and incorporating feedback to enhance their areas of need.

Finally, communication via emails and videoconferencing solidifies course communication. For effective advisement, responses to student emails need to be timely and respectful in tone to reinforce the importance of this in professional communication. Providing students with the opportunity to meet via videoconferencing allows personal interaction with the instructor to explore concerns, clarify information, or review assignment feedback. Investment in creating open and effective communication with students can provide a preventative measure against academic struggles and behavioral issues while enhancing student success.

Building a Sense of Connectedness and Community

It is already assumed that building **community** and a feeling of **connectedness** in the classroom is imperative for proper learning and student participation. Educational programs can range anywhere from fully in-person, hybrid, or blended, which includes in-person and online, and fully online programs. Among many other options, online learning management systems, such as Blackboard and Google Classroom, are used by instructors and students to access course materials, discussion boards, and assignments. Fully online learning can be more challenging in building community due to students being located across the country or even the globe. Compared to in-person instruction, students may feel like it takes longer to connect and feel like a community of learners, but it is possible (Vesely et al., 2007). Students may come from vastly different backgrounds, ethnicities, and belief systems. It is the responsibility of the educator to help make the online environment a place where students feel close to one another and to the teacher, despite differences or the miles in between. Sense of community is lost when students only receive isolating assignments and read lecture notes (Ouzts, 2006). Community is developed when students feel satisfied with their learning experience (Ni & Aust, 2008).

Feeling isolated in the academic setting leads to higher dropout rates (Ouzts, 2006; Rovai & Jordan, 2004; Vesely et al., 2007). When students do not feel a connection with their teacher or peers, they feel isolated and burned out and may not view their education as a quality experience (Ouzts, 2006; Rovai & Jordan, 2004). In turn, when students feel connected or feel like they are part of a cohort, they are more likely to finish their programs (Ouzts, 2006). Due to feelings of disconnection or distraction, online programs have a 10%–20% higher dropout rate compared to fully online programs (Rovai, 2002). Swan et al. (2000) found that women might respond more positively to online learning than men. Students 36–45 years of age showed higher levels of satisfaction with online learning, no matter what kind of connection was felt, most likely due to work and home responsibilities and having the opportunity to learn from home (Swan et al., 2000).

Ni and Aust (2008) describe online learning as a form of **pedagogy** rather than a delivery method. They go on to say "pedagogy … connects teachers, learners, course content in a meaningful way … not technology" (p. 478). Learning, collaboration, and interaction should be the focus of online instruction rather than ways to deliver the content (Ni & Aust, 2008; Rovai & Jordan, 2004). Teachers should adopt a pedagogy that promotes a sense of community for their online learners

(Ouzts, 2006). The goal of online pedagogy is learning rooted in a strong connection and community in the classroom, which must be evaluated by the instructor throughout the course. Pedagogy, as it applies to online teaching, is explored in detail in Chapter 2.

According to Ni and Aust (2008), "transactional distance" is the main challenge for distance education (p. 478). Interaction with the instructor and peers is directly correlated to student satisfaction with learning. Swan et al. (2000) found that students who interacted with peers and had a high level of activity within the course also showed greater satisfaction compared to lower activity and less interaction with peers.

Feeling connected consists of students having shared goals, expectations, values for their learning experiences, and focus on the future (Keen, 2020). Teamwork and comradery are part of a meaningful learning experience (Keen, 2020). Knowledge retained by the student is connected to the relationship with the instructor, including how they implement personal examples and information about themselves, the use of humor, and being open to students (Ice et al., 2007).

A positive relationship between the teacher and student is vital for students to feel successful and motivated to do well (Bondy et al., 2007). The classroom can have a sense of community with students encouraged to collaborate with each other and the educator responding to students in a timely fashion with positive and helpful feedback (Ouzts, 2006). The instructor, displaying honesty and integrity by doing what they say they will do, will show students they care and enjoy their position in education. Ni and Aust (2008) discuss the **"guided didactic conversation theory,"** which states the most influential factor in students being motivated to learn is the friendly relationship between the student and teacher (p. 479). When students see positive interactions among their peers with their instructor, they identified this as a standard for the course and tend to interact in the same manner (Vesely et al., 2007). The instructor should focus on keeping students motivated and engaged in the course, or the students might feel isolated (Swan et al., 2000; Vesely et al., 2007).

When students are invested in the course—whether they enjoy the material or see the value for their future—they are also more likely to be invested relationally with peers and their instructor. Taking a course to fill a schedule, seeing no point in the course or having no interest in it, can often lead to students feeling like the course is a waste of their time. Adult learners, compared to students right out of high school, may place less value on this variable as they view every course as contributing to their degree (Ni & Aust, 2008). However, meaningful learning experiences can and must be provided so students invest in the material and in the course/program. The instructor can use a variety of methods to teach content so students can have a vast array of options to learn the material.

Building Community Online

The United Nations has recognized the value in using online learning to bring communities together and to glean understanding of others from different cultures and backgrounds (Hunter & Austin, 2015). Online platforms have shown to be an effective method to get people from various backgrounds together and to learn from one another. Teachers must recognize their own biases and prejudices/ethnocentrism to look at their students in the cultural contexts they come from (Bondy et al., 2007). Any judgment the teacher might make about the student should be looked at through the lens of **"cultural assumptions"** (Bondy et al., 2007, p. 328). Using **"culturally responsive classroom management"** allows teachers to look at students' behaviors in a proper cultural context rather than as disruptive (Bondy et al., 2007, p. 327).

Teachers can exhibit caring behaviors toward students, such as calling them by name and checking in on them outside of class with any concerns. The teacher must make every effort to display unconditional positive regard to students to provide a warm and caring environment. A supportive environment encourages students to be productive and feel safe sharing their ideas and asking questions (Bondy et al., 2007). Students should be comfortable to be themselves and to freely express their ideas.

Building a Sense of Connectedness and Community in Primary School

Primary school students can benefit from the use of learning management systems designed to promote learning and sharing of information with peers. Lui et al. (2020) found that elementary students who used the online program to post assignments and share information with their teacher and peers used peer feedback to be careful with their work, seeing their assignments as required but also as critiqued by their peers. Higher levels of confidence in their academic abilities led to higher levels of learning and assignment completion, according to the authors. Peer participation in online activities led to increased individual participation. However, the student should be evaluated for their ability to understand feedback prior to implementing such a program (Lai et al., 2020).

Elementary school curriculum should be individualized and structured so every child succeeds, fostering a close relationship with the teacher so the child feels secure and connected on a personal level (Bondy et al., 2007). The teacher can use verbal and nonverbal behaviors that the children are familiar with, such as using popular references or certain inflections in their voice. The teacher can model social skills, such as displaying care and respect for students (Bondy et al., 2007), and implement activities that engage the child and the class as a whole, such as singing a song together or through the use of emojis. Encouraging a sense of safety and individuality allows children to share their personalities while still functioning within the structure of the course as discussed previously.

For online learners, having interactive activities, such as sharing their pets or favorite toy, may add to classroom cohesiveness. Scavenger hunts around the house can be used to get the child involved in the activity and to talk with classmates about what they were able to find. Children should be addressed by their name with a warm tone and nonverbal behaviors, such as smiling and nodding when the child is speaking thus displaying "verbal immediacy," which is communication that helps bridge the technology gap between teachers and students (Ni & Aust, 2008, p. 480). Primary school teachers may incorporate fun, interactive activities throughout the class to create interaction among students.

Using age-appropriate online platforms, primary school students can interact and participate in materials to be able to learn outside of the classroom setting. The sharing of classwork pictures and completed homework assignments allows students to share both knowledge and experiences (Lai et al., 2020). The researchers discovered that children are more likely to respond to prompts online when they see the responses of their peers. Feedback from their peers and their teacher led to more participation in the online assignments.

Building a Sense of Connectedness and Community in Secondary School

Teenagers are known for using social media, or "**social sharing**," for nearly every form of communication with their peers (Lai et al., 2020, p. 979). In the learning environment, social media can be utilized by the instructor to get adolescents engaged, not only with the material but with their peers as well (Lai et al., 2020). Secondary school students often share knowledge rather than construct their own about a topic (Lai et al., 2020), such as directing a peer to a topic or page number of study material or by sharing pictures of assignments.

Online teachers of secondary students can develop the relationship with students by sharing information about themselves and showing support and encouragement (Bondy et al., 2007).

Students of this age begin to judge if the teacher is just doing their job or if they have fun and like what they do. The teacher can foster a sense of community by playing games about similarities and differences with the students to form a closeness before diving into learning materials while reinforcing the abilities of each student. Engaging teachers use communication rooted in the culture of the students while providing clear instructions and expectations, which creates a rapport with students (Bondy et al., 2007).

LaBianca (2020) provides several ideas for games that secondary school teachers can play with online students. These games include charades (where the student acts out something and peers try to guess what they are acting out), two truths and a lie (where students try to determine which one is the nontruth about the student), or any type of trivia game using a platform like Kahoot. These games can build rapport and provide interactive ways students can have fun and either get ready for course material or have the course material incorporated into the game, such as using Kahoot.

Teachers can use students' interest in social media to their advantage by getting students active in outside-of-class participation, having them take pictures on their own time to share with classmates during class, or using discussion posts. The internet has many websites that include interactive activities students can participate in on their own. Teachers may also enlist the help of YouTube for students to watch videos about events or topics that pertain to subject matter taught in the classroom.

Building a Sense of Connectedness and Community in Postsecondary Education

Social constructivism is "learning within a social context" rather than just the compilation of knowledge (Ouzts, 2006; Rovai & Jordan, 2004, p. 2). Colleges and universities incorporate this way of learning as it allows students to build on their own knowledge with the help of their peers and instructor (Rovai & Jordan, 2004; Swan et al., 2000). Rather than being the all-knowing sage, instructors help facilitate discussion among students to develop "knowledge building communities" (Swan et al., 2000, p. 380). Interactive activities that encourage critical thinking and problem solving connect students and help lessen feelings of isolation and increase student connection to their discipline of study (Ouzts, 2006). Vesely et al. (2007) identify seven principles that contribute to a good undergraduate experience. These include the professor encouraging participation and contact with each other and with peers, agreement on goals, active learning activities, quick feedback, time to focus on tasks, high expectations of students, and respect for the differences in students and their ways of learning, thus fostering a community of "intellectual growth and self-autonomy" (Rovai & Jordan, 2004, p. 2).

In an asynchronous learning setting, Ice et al. (2007) saw the importance of students needing audio feedback from the instructor rather than just written comments. Students reported higher levels of satisfaction in feedback when their instructors added audio feedback along with the feedback in text form, resulting in the students feeling more connected to their instructor and to the content (Ice et al., 2007). The students reported feeling more cared for, were more invested in learning the materials, and were three times more likely to implement the feedback provided by the instructor when it was also provided in audio form (Ice et al., 2007). Because there is no live interaction in an asynchronous learning environment, text-only feedback can lose the meaning the instructor intended it to have.

For synchronous programs, the instructor should provide a venue for students to communicate about assignments and to have active conversations that facilitate learning. Students can often learn more from discussion in class rather than just from reading a textbook or viewing a PowerPoint presentation. These conversations can also include providing case studies to analyze, sharing personal experiences with students, processing their thoughts about situations, and going through ethical dilemmas. Such conversations can encourage students to conduct more independent research to develop an individual knowledge base about each topic. Instructors can share their screen to go over PowerPoint presentations or show video clips during class. To prevent students from monopolizing the conversation, the instructor can call on individuals for their thoughts about topics or to answer questions. Group projects, debates, and other problem-solving activities ranked high on students' satisfaction with their coursework (Ouzts, 2006).

The use of online discussion boards provides a way for students to communicate and process materials shared by the instructor. Discussion boards should be an integral part of the student's grade and promote sharing of viewpoints among students rather than just busy work the student must complete for a few points (Swan et al., 2000). Students thrive when they participate in threaded discussion boards about topics important to them and to the subject matter, compared to watered-down versions of what they are studying (Ouzts, 2006). Rich discussions provide learning opportunities and increase knowledge base. Group projects outside of class to present in class can connect students on an individual basis but also contribute to feelings of community and unity in learning materials. Such projects encourage interaction outside of the classroom and increase students' accountability to their peers.

Assessment

In order to deliver a sound educational program, educators must be able to assess the level of knowledge gained by students and their capability to perform tasks covered over the course of the class (McAuliffe & Eriksen, 2011). Assessment systems and procedures need to be developed to gather data supporting students' learning within the class meets required standards (McAuliffe & Eriksen, 2011). Assessment is an ongoing process that occurs throughout a class and should not be limited to tests. Robertson and Barber (2017) explain that assessments should be meaningful to the students and beneficial in some way, as well as assist the students to build skills needed in the real world. Boitshwarelo et al. (2017) recommend a blending of multiple forms of assessment to enhance student learning.

Why Assessment Is Important

Assessments provide educators the methods to evaluate their students' learning, progress in the course, and readiness to move on. In addition, well-designed assessments inform teachers what the needs of their students are as well as promote student-centered learning. Assessment in education includes online tests, the use of discussion boards, small-group projects, whole-class discussions, electronic journals, and research papers. They are used to increase student reflections on learning, encourage eagerness for learning and novel experiences, identify potential biases, discuss diversity, develop critical thinking skills, and provide opportunities for experiential learning (McAuliffe & Eriksen, 2011).

McLaughlin and Yan (2017) report that the use of online assessments increased student learning as well as achievement in the classes studied, providing a strong case for the use of online assessments as a measurement of student learning and for reinforcement of required knowledge. Additionally, the researchers reported the use of online assessments showed an increase in students' self-regulating behaviors, also referred to as metacognition, such as student monitoring of their progress, the student's increase in evaluation of themselves, more effective time-management skills, more internal motivation and less external motivation, and more effective goal-setting strategies.

Completing Assessment Online

At the basic content level, online programs can utilize multiple-choice tests that gauge recall of content and provide immediate feedback to the student (McLaughlin & Yan, 2017). This is especially useful in large classrooms, where students can receive feedback quickly and reliably without waiting for the teacher to grade enormous amounts of tests or assignments (Boitshwarelo et al., 2017). Another option for online assessment discussed by McLaughlin and Yan is the one-minute paper, which is a form of journal entry or self-reflection. Students are prompted to share something important learned that week, something they would like to learn, and suggestions for improving the class (McLaughlin & Yan, 2017). This allows the educator to understand what students are learning and the student to gain insight from classmates through peer feedback (McLaughlin & Yan, 2017). Another option proposed by McLaughlin and Yan is an e-portfolio, which is an electronic collection of the student's combined work that shows progress over time. Discussion boards are a final form of assessment recommended by the researchers, allowing students direct application of necessary knowledge while gaining feedback from peers and the teacher and engaging in self-reflection. Furthermore, Robertson and Barber (2017) recommend group work and problem-based learning as additional means of assessment.

ASSESSMENT IN PRIMARY SCHOOL

Assessments in primary school can be formalized or informal. Regardless of the type of class, students are required to take standardized testing that inform teachers what basic knowledge each student has. Additionally, teachers can give formal tests at the end of a certain time block (e.g., semester) or unit, or the school year. Informal assessment is done by the teacher throughout the year and covers everything that the student does in class or turns in as homework. In primary grades, assessment will encompass the homework, packets, or worksheets they are required to complete and submit, observations of interactions and skill demonstration during online classes, and more structured tests like spelling or math. Some of the older students can do more thorough online tests and larger projects that can be written or presented to the class. Chapter 8 explores assessment at this level in more detail.

ASSESSMENT IN SECONDARY SCHOOL

Educators in secondary school can utilize the same assessments used for the primary grades as well. However, students in these grades are older and have more school experience. Developmentally, these students will benefit from group work and collaboration with peers, and the breakout rooms in online platforms will allow students to work together while online. Students can utilize the technology to create presentations that are recorded or given live during an online class. Discussion boards can encourage dialogue between students. Teachers can create game-based assessments to use during an online session. Finally, students can complete research projects encouraging the exploration of credible online sources.

ASSESSMENT IN POSTSECONDARY EDUCATION

In higher education, assessment ensures students are achieving the online classroom standards required of the profession they have chosen. Assessment becomes the main variable in students passing or failing and is typically formal. In the online platform, college students can take tests online. These can be created by the professor to be multiple choice, matching, and/or fill in the blank that the learning management system grades immediately upon submission, providing students instant feedback. Additionally, educators can add essay questions to further explore in-depth learning and higher-level thinking. Discussion boards in postsecondary education can introduce students to the incorporation of research to support their views while simultaneously encouraging dialogue among students on various topics. Small-group projects allow students the opportunity to work as a group utilizing the technology of the online classroom, such as recorded or live presentations. The synchronous online classroom allows for students from any location to engage in class discussions and debates to further explore the material. Students can prepare electronic portfolios or journals of their work. Finally, research papers are key at this level of education and can be completed utilizing the online library and submitted electronically to the professor.

Remediation

At times, students may fall behind academically, even when effective educational techniques are utilized in the classroom. **Remediation** refers to "specific strategies directed toward improving student learning outcomes" (Johnson, 2004, p. 76) and is used to help identify and improve any academic deficits or behaviors that might be viewed as inappropriate. There are two types of remediation. "**Constructivist remediation**" (p. 72) means it is controlled by the teacher, but the student is encouraged to be included in the process and make activities meaningful. Rather than viewing the process as punitive, the student is an active participant in the process to improve their academic functioning, and the focus is increasing student motivation. "**Instructionism remediation**" (p. 72) may be noninteractive and directive (Johnson, 2004), focusing more on the behaviors of the teacher rather than the student. This method could include the teacher lecturing rather than the student interacting directly with the course content. For remediation to be effective, the student must be motivated to do well (James & Folorunso, 2012).

Remediation is sometimes needed for behaviors that are deemed as inappropriate by the teacher. Before implementing a remediation plan, the instructor must first look at the student through the lens of cultural awareness. Goodrich and Shin (2013) talk about the importance of being culturally responsive when addressing needs with students. Students should not be described as "impaired" or "incompetent," due to potential legal issues that can be associated with having a disability (p. 44). The proper term for dealing with less than desired behaviors in the classroom is *problematic* (Goodrich & Shin, 2013, p. 44). Any behavior that is perceived by the educator as problematic must first be viewed in the cultural context of the student (Goodrich & Shin, 2013). Students may be perceived by teachers as acting aggressively, but cultural expression must be evaluated first to see if the student is acting in accordance with their culture (Goodrich & Shin, 2013). The authors go on to say teachers must check their own biases, and for White instructors, European American expectations and values might be a factor in viewing the behavior of students from marginalized populations as problematic.

To implement a behavioral remediation plan, teachers must first check in with themselves to see how they view the student at the "intrapersonal level" (Goodrich & Shin, 2013, p. 46). A teacher who has a good rapport with the student should follow up at the "interpersonal level," in that they talk to the student to see what might be affecting their behavior or performance (Goodrich & Shin, 2013, p. 46). Some teachers or staff members have a stronger rapport with a student compared to other teachers. School administrators should also evaluate the program and the classroom structure to see how they could be affecting the student's behavior or performance (Goodrich & Shin, 2013). Administrators should also evaluate if any patterns are emerging of what they view as problematic behavior in groups of students. This could be patterns in the school or with an educator.

Remediation is important for students to feel confident in their academic abilities and not fall behind in learning competencies (Goodrich & Shin, 2013; Johnson, 2004; Methvin &

Markham, 2015; Schwartz, 2012). Schwartz goes on to say that "remedial education programs will likely be most effective when included as part of a country's overall strategic plan to deliver quality education for all its students" (p. 7). Remediation should not be an afterthought of the core program; rather, it should be assumed that some students will require remedial services to be productive.

Remediation in Primary School

Schwartz (2012) discusses the importance of remediation with children who are academically falling behind, acknowledging that children from disadvantaged populations and lower-income households will more than likely require remedial services. Students from lower-socioeconomic households do not academically perform as well as students from higher-income homes (James & Folorunso, 2012). Parents often seek out tutoring services for help with specific subjects but only if they can afford these services (Schwartz, 2012). It is vital for children to not fall behind academically or they may get discouraged and not care about their school performance (Schwartz, 2012). The **zone of proximal development**, developed by Lev Vygotsky, is the area of learning between what the student can do without help from a teacher and what they require help to comprehend (Mayor, 2005). The author states that students need activities that require the aid of the teacher to be able to learn new ideas. The process of **"internalization"** is learning something apart from one's own thoughts (Mayor, 2005, p. 165). To address students' learning needs, specific educational interventions are provided to help with specific early grade competencies (Schwartz, 2012).

Remediation in reading is often required with primary school students (James & Folorunso, 2012). Time is of the essence when students struggle with reading (Mayor, 2005). Corrective reading is a program geared toward reading remediation (Johnson, 2004). It involves the student looking at the reading material rather than a focus on specific words. Constructionist remediation in primary school includes "compensatory education, direct instruction, corrective teaching, adaptive instruction, diagnostic-prescriptive teaching, and individualized instruction" (Johnson, 2004, p. 76). Some programs can occur during the summer; after regular classes, including staying online longer than their peers; or through the help of peer tutors, family members, or **para teachers**, who are members of the community trained to help students with remedial needs (Schwartz, 2012). Teachers must keep track of activities and textbooks used to accurately assess the reading and writing abilities of their students and how they can continue to practice their skills at home (Mayor, 2005).

Letter writing is a common tool utilized in primary school student remediation (Johnson, 2004). These letters can help the student practice their writing skills, such as writing a letter to Santa or a narrative about themselves. These letters can also be utilized to help the student process a problematic behavior, such as writing a letter to a peer, teacher, or parent about a **problematic behavior** and how they plan to act in the future. Additional information on remediation at this level is provided in Chapter 8.

Remediation in Secondary School

Students who have been behind their peers in secondary school often need remedial assistance before moving on to college courses. Feedback along with immediate remediation produced higher performance scores than just feedback from the teacher alone, resulting in the student beginning to have a different view of themselves and their capabilities (James & Folorunso, 2012). For example, the teacher grades the assignment and gives it back to the student with an immediate offer of remedial help so the student can comprehend what they need to improve. Students who receive remediation while receiving feedback comprehend content better, connecting their understanding of how to correct errors with why these corrections were made, than if they did not receive remedial help (James & Folorunso, 2012).

When too much time has lapsed between receiving the feedback and remedial services, the student has more difficulty in understanding how to improve their academic performance (James & Folorunso, 2012). The authors found that immediate feedback after the student makes an error has the most positive effect on remediation rather than after a final exam. Assessment and other methods of evaluating students' progress provide ways for teachers to be aware of the need for remediation. Proper training in various assessment methods is strongly recommended for all instructors.

Positive reinforcement from the teacher produces more positive results from the student (James & Folorunso, 2012) and may be achieved by the teacher saying, "You are doing better," "Keep up the great work," or "You'll get this, I know you can." Students who receive encouragement and praise show more interest in the subject, while negative feedback results in a feeling of defeat and a desire to give up trying to improve (James & Folorunso, 2012). Students benefit from remediation when they understand the purpose of learning a subject and are active in the learning process (James & Folorunso, 2012). Teachers can work on applying content material to practical matters, such as learning a math skill to help with money management. Wartell (2012) suggests a paradigm shift in remediation for secondary schools to help alleviate the burden of mediation in college, particularly at the community college level.

Remediation in Postsecondary Education

While remedial help is available, as few as 8% of students who participate in remedial programs in college graduate (Methvin & Markham, 2015). In community colleges, more than half of students end up dropping out. Students from minority and low-income groups make up the majority of remedial students (James & Folorunso, 2012; Methvin & Markham, 2015). Educators must view their students through the lens of cultural awareness. This is particularly important with students of marginalized groups, including those with disabilities, students of color, and LGTBQ+ students (Goodrich & Shin, 2013). Faculty must check any biases or prejudice that might hinder their relationship with students. This is especially important for faculty members who are heterosexual, White, and without any disabilities. Goodrich and Shin (2013) explain that the instructor's own culture and world view may influence how they perceive a student. Before a student is viewed as having a problematic behavior, the educator must evaluate if any microaggressions might be at play when determining if their behavior is a problem. Sometimes "expressions of different cultural beliefs" are shown by the student, such as having a louder tone or certain ways of talking in class (Goodrich & Shin, 2013, p. 43). The authors continue to say that before behaviors are viewed as defiant, potential biases must be evaluated by the faculty member. In a study by Houston and Xu (2016), it was found that compared to 35% of White students, 61% of African American students had a remediation plan at the undergraduate level, assuming there might be some bias that had occurred with the faculty member and student.

Assuming proper pedagogy has been offered to the student and cultural biases are in check, a remediation action plan is determined. This could be on a smaller scale with the professor emailing the student if they notice something unusual, such as the student acting differently in class or a sudden drop in their grade. A scheduled meeting could be suggested by the professor to help break down any barriers to the student's success in the course or their program. As already discussed, collaboration with other faculty members or the dean of the program of study ensures that the professor is not acting alone in deciding how to proceed with student remediation.

Chapter Summary

Student success is the result of a combination of classroom management, structure, communication, connectedness, assessment, and remediation. Preparation prior to and consistency during the course by the instructor helps to ensure a foundation upon which students will both learn the knowledge and skills of the course and incorporate it into their personal identity. Each of these elements are perceived differently by students based on their experiences, world view, and personal and cultural variables that combine to make each student unique. Instructors need to consider these elements and incorporate appropriate adaptions to ensure each student gains insight and knowledge while providing a consistent structure that guides all students through the material at a unified pace. Student success is best personalized for each student, and instructors achieve this by fostering a sense of community, managing the classroom, providing consistent structure, and communicating feedback on behaviors and assignments, while providing remediation as needed throughout the duration of the course.

Online Resources

Online Classroom Management: Five Tips for Making the Shift

https://roomtodiscover.com/online-classroom-management/

Zoom Activities to Use With Distance Learning

Lucky Little Learners

https://luckylittlelearners.com/zoom-activities-to-use-with-distance-learning/

References

Al-Shammari, Z. N. (2016). Enhancing higher education student attendance through classroom management. *Cogent Education*, 3(1), Article 1210488. https://doi.org/10.1080/2331186X.2016.1210488

Bean, J. P., & Eaton, S. (2000). A psychological model of college student retention. In J. M. Braxton (Ed.), *Reworking the departure puzzle: New theory and research on college student retention* (pp. 73–89). Vanderbilt University Press.

Berge, Z. L. (2002). Components of the online classroom. *New Directions in Teaching and Learning*, 2000(84), 23–28. https://doi.org/10.1002/tl.843

Berger, J. B., & Braxton, J. M. (1998). Revising Tinto's interactionalist theory of student departure through theory elaboration: Examining the role of organizational attributes in the persistence process. *Research in Higher Education*, 39(2), 103–119.

Bergsmann, E. M., Lüftenegger, M., Jöstl, G., Schrober, B., & Spiel, C. (2013). The role of classroom structure in fostering students' school functioning: A comprehensive and application-oriented approach. *Learning and Individual Differences*, 23, 131–138. https://doi.org/10.1016/j.lindif.2013.05.005

Boitshwarelo, B., Reedy, A.K., & Billany, T. (2017). Envisioning the use of online tests in assessing twenty-first century learning: A literature review. *Research and Practice in Technology Enhanced Learning*, 12, 1-16. doi:10.1186/s41039-017-0055-7

Bondy, E., Ross, D. D., Gallingane, C., & Hambacher, E. (2007). Creating environments of success and resilience: Culturally responsive classroom management and more. *Urban Education*, 42(4), 326–348. https://doi.org/10.1177/0042085907303406

Bourdieu, P., & Passeron, J. C. (1977). *Reproduction in education, society, and culture*. Sage.

Bowman, L. (2001). *Interactions in the online classroom*. ERIC. https://files.eric.ed.gov/fulltext/ED464319.pdf

Brown, D. F. (2005) The significance of congruent communication in effective classroom management. *Clearing House: A Journal of Educational Strategies, Issues and Ideas*, 79(1), 12–15. https://doi.org/10.3200/TCHS.79.1.12-15

Cangelosi, J. S. (2013). *Classroom management strategies: Gaining and maintaining student cooperation*. Wiley.

Charles, C. M. (2000). *The synergetic classroom: Joyful teaching and gentle discipline*. Addison, Wesley, and Longman.

Cheon, S. H., Reeve, J., & Vansteenkiste, M. (2020). When teachers learn how to provide classroom structure in an autonomy-supportive way: Benefits to teachers and their students. *Teaching and Teacher Education*, 90, 1-12. https://doi.org/10.1016/j.tate.2019.103004

Dweck, C. S. (2000). *Self-theories: Their role in motivation, personality, and development*. Psychology Press.

Emmer, E. T., & Evertson, C. M. (2012). *Classroom management for middle and high school teachers* (9th ed.). Pearson.

Emmer, E. T., Evertson, C. M., & Worsham, M. E. (2002). *Classroom management for secondary teachers* (6th ed.). Allyn and Bacon.

Eng, N. (2017). *Teaching college: The ultimate guide to lecturing, presenting, and engaging students.* Author.

Evertson, C. M. (2001). Training teachers in classroom management: An experimental study in secondary school classrooms. *Journal of Educational Research*, 51–58.

Evertson, C. M., & Emmer, E. T. (2017). *Classroom management for elementary teachers* (10th ed.). Pearson.

Goodrich, K. M., & Shin, R. Q. (2013). A culturally responsive intervention for addressing problematic behaviors in counseling students. *Counselor Education and Supervision, 52*(1), 43–55. https://doi.org/10.1002/j.1556-6978.2013.00027.x

Grunert O'Brien, J., Millis, B. J., & Cohen, M. W. (2009). *The course syllabus: A learning-centered approach* (2nd edition). John Wiley and Sons.

Houston, S., & Xu, Y. (2016). The effect of parents' level of education on the need for student remediation in postsecondary mathematics. *College Student Journal, 50*(1), 19–28.

Hunter, B., & Austin, R. (2015, Winter). Building community through online learning in colleges. *College Quarterly, 18*(1). ERIC. https://files.eric.ed.gov/fulltext/EJ1070029.pdf

Ice, P., Curtis, R., Phillips, P., & Wells, J. (2007). Using asynchronous audio feedback to enhance teaching presence and students' sense of community. *Journal of Asynchronous Networks, 11*(2), 3–25. http://dx.doi.org/10.24059/olj.v11i2.1724

Iverson, A. M. (2003). *Building competence in classroom management and discipline* (4th ed.). Merrill.

James, A. O., & Folorunso, A. M. (2012). Effect of feedback and remediation on students' achievement in junior secondary school mathematics. *International Education Studies, 5*(5), 153–162. http://dx.doi.org/10.5539/ies.v5n5p153

Johnson, G. M. (2004). Constructivist remediation: Correction in context. *International Journal of Special Education, 19*(1), 72–88. ERIC. https://files.eric.ed.gov/fulltext/EJ852045.pdf

Johnson, M. B. (1999). *Communication in the classroom.* ERIC. https://files.eric.ed.gov/fulltext/ED436802.pdf

Keen, L. (2020, July). Stories behind the masks: Fayetteville Technical College adapts to the pandemic situation through online education. *Business North Carolina*, 34–35.

Ko, S., & Rosen, S. (2001). *Teaching online: A practical guide.* Houghton Mifflin.

Kuh, G. D., Kinzie, J., Buckley, J. A., Bridges, B. K., & Hayek, J. C. (2006). *What matters to student success: A review of the literature.* National Postsecondary Education Cooperative. https://nces.ed.gov/npec/pdf/Kuh_Team_Report.pdf

Kuh, G. D., Kinzie, J., Schuh, J. H., & Whitt, E. J. (2013). *Student success in college: Creating conditions that matter.* Wiley.

LaBianca, J. (2020, May). 10 fun games to play on Zoom that will amp up your next virtual party. *Good Housekeeping.* https://www.goodhousekeeping.com/life/entertainment/g32098665/best-games-to-play-on-zoom/

Lui, C., Wen, Y., Gao, T., & Lin, C. (2020). Mechanisms of the learning impact of teacher-organized online schoolwork sharing among primary school students. *Journal of Educational Computing Research, 58*(5), 978–1002. https://doi.org/10.1177/0735633119896874

Marzano, R. J., & Marzano, J. S. (2003). *Classroom management that works: Research-based strategies for every teacher.* ASCD.

Mayor, S. (2005). Preservice teachers' developing perspectives on assessment and remediation of struggling readers. *Reading Improvement, 42*(3), 164–178.

McAuliffe, G. & Eriksen, K. (Eds.). (2011). *Handbook of counselor preparation: Constructivist, developmental, and experiential approaches.* Sage Publications, Inc.

McLaughlin, T. & Yan, Z. (2017). Diverse delivery methods and strong psychological benefits: A review of online formative assessment. *Journal of Computer Assisted Learning, 33*, 562–574. doi:10.1111/jcal.12200

Methvin, P., & Markham, P. N. (2015). Turning the page: Addressing the challenge of remediation. *Change: The Magazine of Higher Learning, 47*(4), 50–56. https://doi.org/10.1080/00091383.2015.1060100

Miltiadou, M. (2001). Computer-mediated communication in the online classroom. *International Journal of Educational Telecommunications, 7*(4), 407–419.

National Education Association. (2015). *A new vision for student success: A report from NEA's accountability task force.* http://ftp.arizonaea.org/assets/docs/122096_NEA_V01_LowRes.pdf

Ni, S., & Aust, R. (2008). Examining teacher verbal immediacy and sense of classroom community in online classes. *International Journal on E-Learning, 7*(3), 477–498.

Norman, M. K., Mayer, R. E., Ambrose, S. A., Bridges, M. W., Lovett, M. C., & DiPietro, M. (2010). *How learning works: Seven research-based principles for smart teaching.* Wiley.

Ouzts, K. (2006). Sense of community in online courses. *Quarterly Review of Distance Education, 7*(3), 285–296. https://www.learntechlib.org/p/106764/

Palloff, R. M., & Pratt, K. (2001). *Lessons from the cyberspace classroom: The realities of online teaching.* Jossey-Bass.

Pike, G. R., and Kuh, G. D. (2005). A typology of student engagement for American colleges and universities. *Research in Higher Education, 46*(2), 185–209.

Robertson, L. & Barber, W. (2017). New directions in assessment and evaluation: Authentic assessment in fully online learning communities. *Journal of Education Research, 11*(3), 249–262.

Rovai, A. P. (2002). Development of an instrument to measure classroom community. *Internet and Higher Education, 5*(3), 197–211. https://doi.org/10.1016/S1096-7516(02)00102-1

Rovai, A. P., & Jordan, H. M. (2004). Blended learning and sense of community: A comparative analysis with traditional and fully online graduate courses. *International Review of Research in Open and Distance Learning, 5*(2), 1–13. ERIC. https://eric.ed.gov/?id=EJ853864

Schwartz, A. C. (2012). *Remedial education to accelerate learning for all*. GPE Working Paper Series on Learning (No. 11). https://openknowledge.worldbank.org/handle/10986/26824

Seidman, A. (2012). *College student retention: Formula for student success*. Rowman and Littlefield.

Smith, T. C. (2005). Fifty-one competencies for online instruction. *The Journal of Educators Online, 2*(2), 1-18. http://www.savie.qc.ca/CampusVirtuel/Upload/Fichiers/fifty%20one%20competencies.pdf

Stewart, D. P. (2008). Classroom management in the online environment. *MERLOT Journal of Online Learning and Teaching, 4*(3), 371-374.

Sullivan, P., & Clarke, D. J. (1991). *Communication in the classroom: The importance of good questioning*. Deakin University.

Swan, K., Shea, P., Fredericksen, E., Pickett, A., Pelz, W., & Maher, G. (2000). Building knowledge building communities: Consistency, contact and communication in the virtual classroom. *Journal of Educational Computing Research, 23*(4), 359-383. https://doi.org/10.2190/W4G6-HY52-57P1-PPNE

Taylor, J. C. (2016, February 11). Seven classroom structures that support student relationships. *ACSD Express, 11*(11). http://www.ascd.org/ascd-express/vol11/1111-taylor.aspx

Tinto, V. (1975). Dropout from higher education: A theoretical synthesis of recent research. *Review of Educational Research, 45*, 89-125.

Tinto, V. (1987). *Leaving college: Rethinking the causes and cures of student attrition*. University of Chicago Press.

Tinto, V. (1993). *Leaving college: Rethinking the causes and cures of student attrition* (2nd ed.). University of Chicago Press.

Vangelisti, A. L., Daly, J. A., & Friedrich, G. W. (Eds). (2009). *Teaching communication: Theory, research, and methods* (2nd ed.). Routledge.

Vesely, P., Bloom, L., & Sherlock, J. (2007). Key elements of building online community: Comparing faculty and student perceptions. *MERLOT Journal of Online Learning and Teaching, 3*(3), 234-246. https://jolt.merlot.org/vol3no3/vesely.pdf

Wartell, M. (2012). A New Paradigm for Remediation: MOOCs in Secondary Schools. EDUCAUSE Review. Retrieved from: http://er.educause.edu/articles/2012/11/anewparadigmforremediationmoocsinsecondaryschools.

Weinstein, C. S. (2003). *Secondary classroom management: Lessons from research and practice*. McGraw-Hill.

Weinstein, C. S., Tomlinson-Clarke, S., & Curran, M. (2004). Toward a conception of culturally responsible classroom management. *Journal of Teacher Education, 55*(1), 25-38. https://doi.org/10.1177%2F0022487103259812

Williams, K. C. (2009). *Elementary classroom management: A student-centered approach to leading and learning*. Sage.

PART II
Instructional Design

CHAPTER FIVE

Online Course Design

Tara Koger, MA

Imagine a wooded forest spanning several acres stands before you, and you have been assigned a job to complete. The challenge contains certain objectives. You must do the following:

- Get through the forest efficiently, because your time and energy are limited resources and you have other responsibilities.
- Locate certain items in the forest, each being critical to your ability to meet the expectations held for you.
- Complete tasks with those objects to other people's individual specifications.

Now, imagine that you have no experience doing this and are given no guidance and no map. This will be, undoubtedly, frustrating, and you are bound to fail at that first goal around efficiency, as your time will be spent walking around more than necessary. Further, while you are told what the tasks are, there are no instructions about how to complete them. For instance, one item you are to find is a bag of rocks, and your task is to create a well with them.

But what if you were better prepared to succeed? What if, at the onset of the job

- You were provided an aerial map of the forest showing where all of the items were located.
- You were advised to note that a river ran through the middle of the forest, visible on that map, and that all items in the forest were within roughly 5 minutes walking distance from the river.
- You were provided a two-way radio, instructions on using it, and rules about when and how to ask for help, and what kind of help was okay versus what help would disqualify you.
- You were handed some basic literature about how to complete each task associated with the items you were going to find.

Now, imagine that you had all those tools as well as a gravel path through the woods that visited each area where the items were located. How radically would that shift the dynamic of the work? The path would take you to each area, and you'd waste much less time. You'd have more energy and focus left for completing the tasks, and you would do a better job because you would have instructions. Would you be more confident from the start? Would you be more able to complete the job and tend to your other responsibilities?

When a course is designed well, the learners have a clear path through the woods. They are provided everything they need to do the work effectively, and they can focus their energy on doing the tasks before them. Will they still have to learn and struggle? Try and fail before succeeding? Yes, of course, because they have probably never built a well before. If the tasks in the course are truly measurements of the learning objectives of the course, completing the tasks themselves are adequate trial for the learner and offer the instructor all the knowledge and skill assessment they need.

So how does an instructor set about this work, particularly as it relates to the decisions that must be made in course setup? The field of instructional design has emerged in response to this question, researching how both teachers and learners function in online spaces, how course design choices impact student learning achievement and outcomes, and how instructors can best accommodate the needs of all learners across whatever devices and software they may be using, with consideration of maintaining equity and accessibility.

Historical Overview

Making Science of Understanding Online Learning

For decades, we have been unpacking how best to integrate technology into teaching and learning. In the late 1980s, as early online learning had its birth, there were foundational conversations to examine the impact on participants and what failed or succeeded. As technology advanced, so did the discourse in education about bringing in new tools and requiring students to use them. Key questions have always centered around access and experience: How does each selection or decision impact what students retain? How does it manifest in their performance on assessments? Where do things fail? Where are some students disadvantaged while others benefit?

Since the 1990s, the plethora of tools being used in online education became even more plentiful and diverse, bringing exciting new capabilities for instructors eager to teach creatively. For many, though, the work of selecting, learning, and developing fluency in ever-emerging new technologies has become a daunting category of work unto itself, one they may not have agreed to when they entered the teaching profession. Unaddressed is the reality that people are often teaching because they have subject matter expertise, not because they are interested in or have time to master new technologies and build content and assessments within them.

Thus, instructional design as a subject aims to integrate the functions and validities of learning technology, and determine best practices and make them easier to employee for teachers. Some schools will also have specific staff in the role of instructional designers, who support the implementation of these practices by doing research and making recommendations, building digital templates and assisting in setting them up in courses, and navigating the service gaps that occur between traditional IT desktop support and the school's instructional community.

While many different instructional design theories and practices have been published, many reflect on two models of course design that have influenced those developed thereafter: the ADDIE and backwards design models. The **ADDIE model** has been implemented in education for almost 20 years and provides not a philosophy of teaching but a structure through which one can develop online course-building practices (Peterson, 2003). ADDIE is an acronym for **A**nalyze, **D**esign, **D**evelopment, **I**mplement, and **E**valuate, with this being a circular repeating process (Peterson, 2003). The value of applying the ADDIE model to the work of creating an online course hinges on the instructor's intent to experiment with methods and continually revise approaches in order to discover what is most effective (Peterson, 2003). An overview of the ADDIE model and its iterative instructional design process is provided under the online resources section at the end of this chapter.

Backwards design, on the other hand, is a method of designing course curriculum by first determining key objectives for learners to reach in the course, then choosing instructional methods and forms of assessment. Employing backwards design in curriculum development typically involves three stages:

1. Identify the results desired, primarily what students should know, understand, and be able to demonstrate by the end of the course.
2. Determine what will be as evidence that these results have occurred, focusing on how you will truly measure that the objectives were met via assessments and provide student scores accordingly.
3. Design activities that will make desired results happen or plan what type of content and information must be delivered to students in order for them to succeed, and what modality of delivery will be most effective.

Thus, one could first practice the tenants of backwards design to make all decisions about the course curriculum, then use the ADDIE model to reflect on how well those choices worked and make revisions for an improved experience in the next round of the term or the next employment of the assignment type. Essentially, backwards design offers a strategy for designing your course to succeed, while ADDIE suggests a means of evaluating it afterward.

Development of the Online Learning Environment

The history of **learning management systems** (**LMSs**) may appear to have begun in the late 1990s when the first tools were developed, but the story of the mechanism itself is quite a bit older. In 1723, a professor of shorthand offered an exchange of teaching materials via mail, advertising this opportunity in the *Boston Gazette* (De Salvo, 2002; Nonyongo, 2002). It is unknown exactly how this instructional program worked, whether the recipient students ever submitted work back for critique. However, in 1840, a professor in England, Isaac Pitman, is documented as having created a shorthand course that did require students to receive the material, complete tasks related to Biblical transcription into shorthand, and then mail their work back to Pitman to be assessed (Davis et al., 2009; De Salvo, 2002; Nonyongo, 2002; Threstha, 1997). Thus, correspondence teaching was born a century before the world began to hear about an elusive new technology that took up rooms in laboratories—the computer.

From the first correspondence courses that mailed paper materials, distance education had its next big evolutionary step in the early 20th century with the integration of multimedia teaching: specifically, recorded audio lectures. A few decades later, the 1930s and 1940s would see the creation of the first teaching machines that offered students multiple types of exercises and ways to assess their knowledge, with some being able to compare problems and solutions. Eventually, radio, telephone, television, and recorded audio files would all be integrated into these formats.

And then the internet brought to distance learning the potential for entirely different formats and types of informational organization. Importantly, the web-based modality drastically reduced the temporal and spatial boundaries students and teachers felt with older correspondence models: information and interaction could be live, bringing a different level of cognitive engagement and human presence to the experience. The modern learning management systems were initially designed to analyze data in learner activity, skills, and performance, especially being able to identify gaps. Today, we have sophisticated integrations that allow our LMSs to automate a variety of work, pulling information from across many different systems in order to centralize it to one point of access. The proliferation of teacher-created videos and multimedia and easier embedding has further enriched the LMS environment. And in the last decade, mobile usability has become a priority, with companies building and updating LMSs to ensure that all users can access their course content regardless of device or software used to do so, meaning that a student on a laptop using a browser should see the same information as a student using a mobile app on a smartphone.

The LMS has become the digital hub for the course, enabling group and teacher-student communication, notifications, assignment submission, content publishing, and examination of student comprehension in addition to file storage, secured cloud storage of gradebooks, and digital feedback on student work. The advancements have been fast and robust.

Why Use Your School's System?

Using your school's platform:

- The importance of the learning management system (LMS)
- Why use the LMS provided (FERPA, security, consistency, centralization)
- Locating instructional support resources available to you (from university, vendor, online communities, guides)

Imagine a scenario where the four to five people in leadership positions above you at work communicated their needs and expectations to you in many different ways—some sent email, some printed off paper notes, others stored documents on a cloud that you were expected to look at, some wrote their communications on a physical wall, and others spoke them verbally, either in person, in live streamed videos, or in recorded videos hosted on a website. How challenging would it be for you to stay updated on this information? Further, how difficult would it be to manage your workload in addition to checking all these different locations?

In education, students have many different instructors with varied expectations and practices, and they may change every few months in the case of higher education. Centralizing all course information in one consistent location models the practices we expect in our own work environments: clear communication, minimal confusion, intentional consideration of our labor and time. As instructors, you can best provide this for your students through using your school's LMS—the platform on which you create online learning environments for the courses you teach.

One of the most well-intentioned but faulty approaches to course design can be seen when an instructor sets out on their own to discover exactly which platform they want to use for their course delivery, or they create a website of their own for this purpose. The hope is often to find something that will share content in specific, customizable ways. The effect, however, is unnecessary and burdensome learning experiences for students who now have to navigate additional systems with less protection. Platforms outside of the school-designated LMS do not have the same security measures and reviews and are not supported by the school's IT staff. As a result, they do not comply with the requirements of the Family Educational Rights and Privacy Act, more commonly known as FERPA, the policy that was enacted to ensure student data was protected and parental access was restricted after the child turns 18. See Chapter 11 for more information about FERPA and its implications for educators.

Because each school ensures that its LMS settings are congruent with FERPA requirements, instructors may use the systems to store grades, share grades and performance notes with students, and accept student assignments virtually. The teacher intent on designing their own masterful housing of the course content is centering themselves, thinking primarily about what they will be most satisfied with. The student experience, however, suffers as a consequence.

Learning to Use the LMS

While there are many different LMSs available, there are a handful that are used at most schools: Desire2Learn (D2L)/Brightspace, Canvas, and Blackboard, with Google Classroom following behind them. These systems are the most commonly used, with other smaller systems behind them. One piece that's important to note is that while two schools may use the same LMS, their systems may appear differently or have different functionality within them. Why is that? Because the system administrators at your school must make many specific choices about what to enable or disable, and how to adjust system settings in order to stay compliant with the policies specific to your state and school. Thus, there are two primary types of resources for learning to use your LMS.

VENDOR RESOURCES

The company that built the LMS your school uses has also created guides, often including versions for different users such as students, instructors, and support staff. These guides are tremendously helpful in learning the jargon for the LMS as well as the specific steps to major functions (e.g., posting a syllabus, creating an assignment). Some also include community spaces where users across schools can ask questions and suggest changes they would like to see to the system.

Vendor resources, however, cannot speak to the specifics of your school's instance of the tools. Your school may have a specific way of enrolling new students, an expectation around how things look, or dates that determine your workflow. Thus, it's important to recognize both sources and what they offer.

CUSTOM RESOURCES

The breadth of each's school's **custom resources** is determined by many factors, including how large the school is, how much the governing authorities understand the priorities around learning technology and fund them accordingly, and the overall learning environment needs and values of the institution. However, each school does have a unique instance of the LMS they use, and therefore whatever resources are available should be sought out. These may include workshops, tutorials, templates, or guides and documentation.

Online Learning Environments vs. Storage Closets

One of the most common mistakes we see is faculty who assume that the file storage behavior that is fine on their personal laptop is also appropriate in their teaching. On their desktop, they may have folders full of files with names like "syll_engcomp-spring2019-FINAL.doc," which make perfect sense to them, and they may have files that are relevant but not going to be used soon. All of this is normal. However, when that content is dropped into the LMS, the impact is huge and simultaneously invisible to the instructor, who remains unaffected: the students take on the burden of sorting through someone else's disorganized closet when they should actually be welcomed to an appropriately designed learning environment. And therein rests one key concept: the course site within the LMS is not a cloud storage area, a place to administer exams, or a tool for pushing out announcements. It's an online learning environment, and your students will experience it as such, regardless of how much or little care is put into its creation.

Imagine being invited to a colleague's home for dinner. You arrive and the exterior is nicely maintained with pleasant landscaping choices. When you walk into the home, you do smell some aromatic foods, but your attention goes to the fact that the living room is mostly boxes and randomly scattered furniture pieces. There are boxes continuing throughout the space, and the host jovially announces, "The food is done! I'm so excited for you to try this recipe. It means a lot to me to share it with you and is part of my family's heritage. Go through the boxes and find yourself a plate and some silverware."

In this scenario, you likely feel a few different things:

- Frustration at the work you're being asked to do that normally, and reasonably, your host would have done long before inviting folks over.
- Growing regret at coming, as you struggle to find the things you need, instead opening boxes of sweaters and coats, old photos, and things that do not serve you.
- A little panic about whether you're going to find the plates and silverware at all, and a little anxiety about asking the host to provide more helpful direction or accommodation.

When students enter an online space that has been populated by an instructor "dumping" content, their experience is much the same. They cannot ignore the mess or disorder, or the empty rooms. They experience all of it.

Good and Bad Practices

First, let's consider the difference between the following two approaches:

- Setting up a course
- Designing a course

What is the difference between these two functions, both of which typically take place in the weeks before the semester begins? Both include an instructor making decisions about their course organization and how they will use the tools available. The mindset behind each is different, though. Instructors who initiate this work with the mentality that they will "setup" the course for the term are often aiming to check off the items on a list, written or mental, in which they complete the necessities: getting a syllabus copy in, putting in some type of schedule, adding some readings or other passively received content. Instructors who approach the same work with a design thinking mentality are going to begin by asking themselves questions in order to determine key elements of the student experience.

QUESTIONS FOR USER-CENTRIC DESIGN SCAFFOLDING

(also see Table 5.1 to clarify user-centric design as compared to "content dump" setups)

1. What are the naming conventions for my course?
   a. What do I define as a quiz, test, exam, assignment, homework, journal, project, et cetera? How will I communicate my expectations around this to my students?
   b. What should my file names look like in order to be comprehensible and align with the same word choices I use in lectures or other parts of the course delivery (e.g., "syll_engcomp-spring2019-FINAL.doc" should probably be "English Composition 1110 Syllabus – 2019.doc" if students are expected to use it)?
2. If the full semester is a forest of content, activities, and examinations, what does my students' path through that forest look like? In other words, how do they navigate my course? (Also see Table 5.2 for suggestions of how to mindfully add course content)
   a. Do I expect students to look through a "Files" or "Documents" section? If so, is the content in there well organized with standardized naming conventions and extraneous content removed?

TABLE 5.1

USER-CENTRIC ONLINE LEARNING ENVIRONMENT DESIGN	"CONTENT DUMP" COURSE SETUP
a. Offers students a clear path through the course via simplified navigation. b. Organizes all content around the path, e.g., via chronological modules or folders labeled "Week 1: Subtopic" with all relevant materials, activities, and content housed within. c. Identifies a space in the course for help and support resources, linking or providing information for accessing these; points students back to that space as needed throughout the term. d. Uses color and imagery to enable wayfinding in the course. e. Communicates each expectation, including any required student work, clearly and in a consistent manner. f. Minimizes how many clicks important information is away from initial entry into the environment.	a. Assumes that it's the students' job to find content and assignments, wherever it may be in the course. b. Organizes content in "Files" or "Documents," or organizes content by file type (e.g., a folder for PDFs, a folder for quizzes, a folder for images). c. Drops help and support resources throughout the course sporadically as the need arises. d. Chooses color or images quickly for emphasis, or avoids using them altogether. e. Communicates only "the big" expectations, like exams and major deadlines, and suggests students view the syllabus for other details. f. Takes no measure of how students click through the environment.

TABLE 5.2

FILE TYPE (ENDING OF FILE NAME, LIKE EXAMPLEFILE.DOC)	WHAT'S IMPORTANT TO KNOW
HTML, CSS, other codes	These are web-based files that operate within browsers, like Safari, Chrome, and Firefox. HTML can also be copy/pasted into editable content fields within some LMSs. For the most part, faculty don't use these as frequently as other file types.
PNG, JPG, JPEG, HEIC	These are image file types, with PNG most notably being the only image file that can have a transparent background. This means if you want to add a circular image, you'll need it to be a PNG, because all other file types would include a white or grey rectangle as the background.
MP4, MOV	These are the most common video file types, including videos you record on your smartphone. When using a video creation software for the first time, people are often concerned about their ability to export the final product and where they can put it. You will have many export options, but either of these will display across most platforms and devices.
PDF, DOC, DOCX, TXT	These document files vary in accessibility and size, and whether they require specific software or technology to open. In general, PDFs are often favored because they are not editable. However, PDFs are less accessible than information displayed in HTML and less readable on small screens like smartphones. The others are editable, with TXT being universal and requiring no software specifically; however, TXT also doesn't allow formatting, so text is plain.
URL	In short, a website or link; the unique URL is what you paste into a browser bar or hyperlink from text to ensure that students view a specific website or video. Anything online, even a specific image file, has a URL.

b. Do I want students to work through the course chronologically, meaning we are all moving from week 1's content and assignments to week 2's content and assignments, not hopping around? If so, is my content organized accordingly?
   c. Do I have distracting elements in the course, such as links to things students don't need?
   d. Do I have redundant elements in the course, such as a syllabus link in eight different locations?
   e. How can I simplify the students' navigation experience in the course?
3. What resource expectations do I hold for students, and where am I communicating these?
   a. Do I expect them all to have laptops?
   b. Do I require them to access certain technologies?
   c. Are there specific web browsers they should use or avoid for an optimal experience?
   d. Are there mobile apps I will suggest? Do I have alternatives for students without smartphones?
   e. What assumptions about internet accessibility and speed do I make for students in an online course, and how do I communicate this?
4. What skill expectations do I hold for my students, and where am I communicating these?
   a. Is there a minimum level of software skills I expect?
   b. What about math, language, or other applied skills?
   c. How do I measure the baseline skill level students will need to succeed in this course so they can be aware up front?
   d. What resources can I share with students needing to develop their skills in order to complete this course?
5. Does my course display the same across devices and software?
   a. How does it appear differently on different browsers?
   b. How does it appear differently in the LMS app for mobile experience (if available)?
   c. How does it work on an iPad?
6. Is the homepage or landing page of the course used effectively?
   a. Is the information on the homepage important and functional to all students and something they will consult throughout the term?
   b. How do I capitalize on the most visible real estate within the learning environment? What student needs could be satisfied here?
7. What key information requires more than two clicks, and how can I fix that?
   a. What do my students repeatedly do through the term (e.g., check due dates or grades, check calendars), and how many clicks does it take to reach that?
   b. What information is buried that could be more surface available?
   c. What expectations do I hold that are not represented anywhere in the course? (For example, academic integrity practices, ability to use the library systems, or knowledge of certain campus resources.)

Mindfully Adding Course Content

Before examining how to add content and why, it's helpful to establish basic literacy in what types of files and content you might bring into a course (see table 5.2).

The Case Against Documents

It is always a hard battle to suggest that folks retire long-held conventions, especially if they perceive the transition as one that may require additional work or time. With that in mind, an alternative would be to view change as inevitable—especially with technology, where progress means improved user experience and more effective learning.

Twenty years ago, it was the standard to put formal information into a static document, and this normalized the creation of Word documents and PDFs for student assignment prompts. These were perfect file types for print—a mode of information dissemination restricted by standard 8.5″ × 11″ commercial paper. We needed printable documents, so we made them in abundance, and we carried them in folders to class where we handed them out—which many instructors may still do. However, the printable document has no benefits on the digital screen. Today, paper copies of information are most likely to be lost by students, while digital copies will be revisited multiple times.

Let's consider the rectangular display of such a document and what happens when you open it on a smartphone: it remains a rectangle, just smaller. Now consider what happens when you visit a news article on a browser on your laptop, then view the same news article on your phone. The text, which is stacked from top to bottom, shifts to accommodate the screen it is being displayed on as well as any settings (like contrast, font size) that have been adjusted by the user for best readability. That ability for text to adjust for optimal display is interchangeably called "responsive" or "dynamic," meaning that it does not retain one static format but recognizes the parameters of the screen when loading and adjusts accordingly. If the information is at all important, students need to be able to view it in a responsive format, and students can export it for printable formats as needed.

Your school's LMS has some type of text-box fields in which you can type text, add images, and build content directly into the system itself. These too often go ignored and unused, and yet they will transform your content into dynamic, responsive content that is web based and displays to each device and user's needs (see Table 5.3 for clarification on static documents and those in the

TABLE 5.3

	WHAT HAPPENS IF THE PROMPT IS IN A STATIC DOCUMENT:	**WHAT HAPPENS IF THE PROMPT IS IN THE SYSTEM'S CONTENT EDITOR:**
Instructor completes it and shares it with the class	The document will be uploaded into the LMS as a PDF, DOC, or DOCX attachment. Students may be notified that it is ready and where to find it.	The text, hyperlinks, and any included content will be drafted in the system or pasted from an external program, then display as part of the web-based system.
Students receive it and open it	Students will log into the LMS, download the file, then open the file in a third-party viewer. Some systems may allow a preview of the document. The document will remain the 3–4 ratio, displaying in rectangular format.	Students will log into the LMS and click on the appropriate link or tab. The prompt will adjust to display on whatever device or software the students are each using; students can increase and decrease font sizes easily.
Instructor is notified of a mistake that requires revising the prompt	Instructor must return to a device that has the original authoring software (Microsoft Word, commonly), open the editable file, edit the file, log into the LMS, delete the old file, upload the new version with corrected information, then notify students that the information has been updated. Some students will still have old copies downloaded.	Instructor can log into the LMS from whatever device is nearest, correct the erroneous information, and save. Now the information is updated immediately on the display that all students have.

system's content editor). To explain further, let's take a typical practice and look at how it impacts instructors and students to deliver it in different formats:

Course: a third-year history general education course

Assignment: a 10-page essay over a specific unit subtopic

Document: an essay prompt that specifies all requirements and details of the assignment

Chapter Summary

Crafting the online learning environment is a matter of intentional design of the student experience and attention to accessibility, in all the ways we understand creating equal access in learning technologies. The instructor's primary task is to prioritize the students' experience over their own workflow while making decisions within the LMS to craft the most effective learning environment that facilitates ease and universality of use. It is worth nothing that the first semester of a major course redesign will have the most up-front investment of time for the instructor, with subsequent terms requiring significantly less. Good course design allows the learner to engage with the content directly and actively, and the system and tools through which they do so become almost invisible. When well employed, the LMS assists in conveying instructional information, facilitating communication among participants, and updating students about changes, and presents the instructor as an invested human presence.

Online Resources

37 Great Resources on Instructional Design

A site containing links to academic resources, multimedia resources, and blogs about instructional design: http://www.studentguide.org/37-great-resources-on-instructional-design/

ADDIE Model

For an overview of the ADDIE model and its iterative instructional design process, check out the information at this link: https://www.lib.purdue.edu/sites/default/files/directory/butler38/ADDIE.pdf

All About Learning Objectives for E-learning

This site provides guidance on how to write learning objectives for e-learning: https://community.articulate.com/articles/how-to-write-good-e-learning-objectives-for-your-online-course

Family Education Right and Privacy Act (FERPA)

This U.S. Department of Education site provides an overview of FERPA: https://www2.ed.gov/policy/gen/guid/fpco/ferpa/index.html

In Search of the Secret Handshakes of ID

This essay by Ellen Wagner grapples with the complexities of defining instructional design as a process, discipline, and science: https://docs.wixstatic.com/ugd/c9b0ce_4c5d961291de41e58e08576d3c9ee868.pdf

Timeline of Computer History

This site provides an overview of the history of computers: https://www.computerhistory.org/timeline/computers/

References

Davis, B., Carmean, C., & Wagner, E. (2009, October 15). *The evolution of the LMS: From management to learning; Deep analysis of trends shaping the future of e-learning.* The Learning Guild. https://www.learningguild.com/insights/137/the-evolution-of-the-lms-from-management-to-learning/

De Salvo, A. (2002). *The Rise and fall of the university correspondence college: Pioneer of distance learning.* National Extension College.

Nonyongo, E. P. (2002). Changing entrenched learner support systems. In A. Tait and R. Mills (Eds.), *Rethinking learner support in distance education: Change and continuity in an international context.* Routledge.

Peterson, C. (2003). Bringing ADDIE to life: Instructional design at its best. *Journal of Educational Media and Hypermedia, 12*(3), 227–241.

Threstha, G. (1997). *Distance education in developing countries: Definition.* United Nations Development Programme.

CHAPTER SIX

Accessibility in the Online Classroom for Student Success

Megan Fogel, MLT

Part of our mission as educators is to "level the playing field" and ensure equitable access to learning opportunities for all our students. We already do this in small ways, so frequently that we may not think twice. We provide study guides, presentation slides, guided notes, and practice quizzes. We give our students opportunities to learn in different ways, ways that may better match their learning styles, habits, or accommodate their unique challenges. These accommodations are so commonplace that they feel like a natural part of teaching. With practice, digital accessibility accommodations can feel the same.

Accessibility accommodations are already all around us, such as in sidewalk curb cuts, automatic doors, crosswalks with visual and audio signals, and widened doorways for wheelchairs, to name a few. These examples are all accommodations that affect the physical world, making it easier to navigate for those with disabilities impacting mobility, vision, or hearing. As educators, we can appreciate these considerations made to the design of our classrooms, buildings, campuses, and communities. But when teaching online, how do we ensure the same careful consideration is made to digital spaces and materials? How do we ensure that those with vision, hearing, mobility, and cognitive differences can equally and efficiently access our online classrooms and content?

Digital accessibility work begins with identifying the unique challenges of those with disabilities and the barriers that can exist when interacting with digital materials. For example, those with hearing differences will need to rely on captions and transcripts to access video and audio material. A lack of captioning on a video would be considered an **access barrier** and would require the student to do more work than others to gain equal access to the learning materials. The most common and easiest to spot access barriers are ones that impact students with vision or hearing differences. This chapter will equip you with the skills to not only identify and remediate those most common barriers, but also to identify less obvious accessibility issues in online courses.

Unique Challenges

To understand the unique challenges of students with disabilities, it helps to learn how they might interact with their physical and digital environment. Starting to see these barriers in your everyday life can be empowering in your journey toward more accessible teaching and learning. The lists below outline just a few of the challenges faced by those with vision, hearing, mobility, and cognitive differences.

Vision Differences

- Graphics can pose a challenge no matter the severity of vision loss. Students must rely then on alternate text for images that provide a text description of what the graphic is and how it relates to the content.
- Sometimes color is used to convey meaning without a text explanation, which is meaning lost on those with color blindness.
- Some websites and web-based technologies contain links without descriptions and that display as long messy URLs to a **screen reader**, which many visually impaired students rely on (Taylor, 2009).
- Some videos rely heavily on graphics and visuals without audio narrative to explain what's happening. Without proper narration, the student misses out on whatever valuable information is being shared.
- Assignments that require visual presentations can be an unfair challenge to those with vision differences and are therefore not a great assessment of their learning.
- Some PDF content is simply a scanned image of text that is not readable to those who rely on a screen reader to read the content back to them.

Hearing Differences

- Extra sounds, background noise, or lack of clear audio can ruin the listening experience for those anywhere on the range of hearing differences, even with hearing aids or cochlear implants.
- Videos that do not include captions require students to gather meaning from visuals alone, meaning that most points are missed without the additional audio.
- Anytime audio is central to gathering meaning or giving a message, the message is not conveyed unless there is also a visual element or text version.

Mobility Differences

- Websites built without accessibility in mind can be difficult to navigate for those relying on a keyboard, directive speech, or other assistive technology to navigate instead of a mouse. Websites may not allow for tabbing from link to link or may include drag-and-drop features that are difficult or impossible without a mouse.
- Websites and programs that do allow for keyboard or directive speech commands may not prompt a user with a warning before taking an action. This means that accidental keystrokes or voice commands can have unintended consequences and add delays to the user experience.

Cognitive Differences

- When there are few to no graphics that support the written word, those with cognitive differences may miss out on any helpful visual cues related to comprehending the content.
- Content that contains sarcasm, satire, parody, and metaphor it is particularly challenging to comprehend.
- If an author implies meaning indirectly without stating it explicitly in the writing, the message may be lost.

Other Differences

Accessibility challenges are not always related to a disability and, often, accommodating one access barrier can benefit many students regardless of ability. For example, communication differences and language barriers are by no means a disability but can have a profound impact on the user's ease of accessing materials. Communication differences are especially challenging in an online forum and may include the following:

- Videos that contain new terminology that is harder to learn without text support via captions.
- The speed of some videos can be too fast for those learning a language or struggling to process the instructor's accent.
- Course content that contains lengthy paragraphs without headings for meaning or organization can be difficult to process.
- Metaphors, sarcasm, and references to aspects of American culture without providing additional context or explanation can be frustrating.
- Courses that require tons of public speaking can be an unnecessary challenge.

Proactive Approach

Reading through the unique challenges above can help us to anticipate the access barriers that our students may face in our online learning spaces. This enables us to take a **proactive approach to digital accessibility** as opposed to a reactive approach. For example, a proactive approach is captioning videos you create for your class, whereas a reactive approach is waiting for a student to ask for a captioned video. A proactive approach is important because it helps us to meet the diverse needs of our students even when they may not disclose a disability. We can minimize the need for retroactive, rushed fixes (Scott et al., 2003). While both approaches are valid and necessary, in this chapter you'll be given tips for practicing the proactive approach. But because we cannot anticipate everything, it is important to know your responsibility and the resources available to you, should you need to solve a problem reactively.

Higher Ed Context

At most higher education institutions, you will find two big players in digital accessibility. First, a **disability services center**, operating under federal funding to provide accommodations to students with a disability on file. These centers can usually only provide accommodations and remediation of course materials if a student submits a formal request. They serve a vital role, and often provide proctoring services for students who need extra time on exams, provide in-class American Sign Language, or ASL, interpreters, and match students to appropriate **assistive technologies**. Because some of their functions are focused on in-person contexts, and because they can only intervene at the request of a student, they are usually not a proactive resource for online instructors looking to make their courses more accessible.

Second, you will find a digital accessibility policy outlining the responsibilities of the university to comply with the **Americans with Disabilities Act (ADA) guidelines** (U.S. Department of Justice, n. d.). The ADA was enacted in 1990 to act as an equal opportunity law for Americans with disabilities. These ADA compliance policies vary widely from campus to campus, as does their implementation and support resources. Most institutions have some form of digital accessibility resources for faculty, whether maintained by their ADA compliance office, IT department, teaching and learning center, or elsewhere. Reach out to your institution to get clarity on the accessibility expectations for your role, even while you practice the proactive approaches outlined here.

K–12 Context

Usually alike in many ways, the K–12 context differs greatly from higher ed when it comes to digital accessibility. By no fault of its own, mainstream K–12 education has not spent much time diving into online teaching and learning. Therefore, some of the supports that are in place in higher ed for digital accessibility are much rarer in K–12. It should be noted that fully online K–12 experiences exist and have adapted with the needs of their learners but are typically separated from the traditional K–12 conversations. Elementary, middle, and high schools do, however, have a secret advantage in digital accessibility.

Individualized Education Plans (IEPs) are widely supported and encouraged for many students, giving them extra support and creative strategies to succeed in school. The Individuals with Disability Education Act (U.S. Department of Education, 2001) passed in 1997 requires the consideration of assistive technologies and accessibility accommodations for each student with an IEP. Some of these plans lead to special education classes for the student, while others involve the existing teacher in conversations about accommodating the student's needs. Special education teachers are typically very familiar with the various assistive technologies (wheelchairs, hearing aids, etc.) used by their students but are historically focused on how those help the student navigate the physical world. Online courses require different mobilization of IEP meetings, assistive technology conversations, and IT support than does traditional face-to-face education. Teachers should communicate early and often with administrators and tech support personnel to proactively accommodate students in online courses.

Accessibility and Universal Design for Learning

Accessibility refers to the ability of a device, product, service, or environment to be usable by as many people as possible. This is an important aspect of **universal design for learning** (UDL) and they often go hand in hand. UDL, in the context we use, refers to the process of making learning effective and usable for all and can extend beyond accessibility to addressing learner preferences, styles, and methods of instruction that meet students' needs. Often, accessibility is considered when integrating technology into the learning environment. Universal design involves the usability of that technology and extends to how the technology is integrated into the learning plan, along with the other elements of the course.

Universal design for learning is a proactive process of designing learning experiences in order to achieve the highest level of functionality and positive user experience for the widest audience possible (Burgstahler, 2013). For UDL to be effective, it requires purposeful consideration and strategy in all areas of course planning and design. The result will be online learning that allows students to access, interact, and learn in a variety of ways, addressing the learning styles and learning needs of a wide variety of students. UDL is an approach that takes practice and frequent evaluation of the learning objectives and teaching strategies being employed in your online course. The value added to a course can be impressive, and UDL often reinforces the best teaching habits you may already be practicing. The following principles of UDL are outlined by Burgstahler (2013, para. 7):

- Equitable use: Design is appealing and usable for all.
- Flexibility in use: Choice in methods of use and consideration of preferences is part of the design.
- Simple and intuitive use: Consistency and ease of use are considered in design.
- Perceptible information: Information is presented in several ways to accommodate various learner needs. Information is clear and well organized.
- Tolerance for error: Guidelines and instructions help to steer the learner away from errors or hazards.

- Low physical effort: Navigation is clear and requires no unnecessary redundancies.
- Size and space approach and use: Appropriate space to accommodate various learner needs is made available.

These principles help guide more than just the design of assessments and activities but also the navigation of the online course space. The following pillars of UDL (CAST, n.d.) were outlined to help put these principles into action in the design of assessments and activities. In order to think critically and creatively about applying UDL, we must provide for multiple means of representation, expression, and engagement.

Multiple Means of Representation

Part of the complexity in how people learn involves how information is perceived and comprehended. Additionally, the rate at which information is grasped may occur quickly in one individual but require more time in another. Both will likely end up achieving the same learning goals but at different points in time or in a different sequence. Certain learning styles and preferences also come to play as the learner processes information. Some learners may grasp information best when it is presented visually while others may require both auditory and visual cues. Students with disabilities will certainly be more inclined toward certain means of accessing and ingesting information.

Present information in multiple ways and provide options for learners. Here are some examples:

- Provide captions for all videos and transcripts for all audio recordings or podcasts.
- Make key information stand out by highlighting big ideas and by indicating relationships between concepts.
- Provide background information and context through a story or an example.
- Offer alternatives for visual and auditory information.
- Explain an image or graph that illuminates a concept in the caption or in corresponding text.

Multiple Means of Expression

Just as learners differ in how they process new information, they also differ in how they can best demonstrate learning. Some students struggle with writing skills while others excel. Some students can describe their learning verbally quite well while others do not. By limiting the means by which a student can demonstrate their learning, we may not get a true indication of what the student has learned because it is hidden by areas of weakness. Furthermore, some means of expression may translate better to the job world or to a particular field. For instance, someone whose work will involve giving presentations to large groups of people may benefit from a presentation approach in the classroom instead of a written assignment.

Provide a variety of opportunities and methods for students to demonstrate their learning. Here are some examples:

- Instead of just a written assignment, provide other options for presentation like PowerPoint, screencast, video, or audio recording.
- Research ways to make assignment options professionally relevant.
- Provide multiple types of materials to support completion of assignments (video, audio, written instruction).
- Embed opportunities for students to "stop and think" about strategies and concepts they've learned before applying them in assessments.

Multiple Means of Engagement

The factors that impact how a student engages with content are numerous and may include race, gender, socioeconomic standing, sexual orientation, mental health, and many more. These factors can influence whether learners prefer to work alone or in groups and what aspects of the content will draw the most interest. If learners are not deeply engaged with the content, they are less likely to transfer knowledge and skills in a meaningful way.

Provide multiple ways for students to connect and interact with the content. Here are some examples:

- Give learners choice and autonomy in such things as tools used, methods of reflection and self-assessment, types of rewards and recognition, level of challenge.
- Provide opportunities for both group work and independent work and create a community of thinkers.
- Allow learners to set meaningful personal goals related to the impact of the content to their lives and professions.
- Provide opportunities for instructor-student and student-student support and coaching.

Applying these principles and pillars is not a one-time fix. It takes reflection and feedback from students to best understand if they are being given the best chance to learn. This work hinges on understanding and addressing your students' possible access barriers, providing multiple means of representation, expression and engagement in course work, and being open to constant improvement. In theory, many of the changes you make following UDL principles will benefit all students. Similarly, any accessibility accommodations you make often end up being beneficial to all students regardless of ability.

When thinking about the UDL approach to course design and online teaching, consider the following design strategies at a course level:

- Plan for differences: familiarize yourself with the unique challenges of those with disabilities and identify possible access barriers in your course.
- Give options and variety for assessment: leave as much flexibility in assignment instructions as your learning objectives allow; write instructions and rubrics that allow for multiple formats.
- Present information in multiple ways: provide video, audio, and text for as many resources as possible, making sure they are all accessible.
- Make key points stand out: organize your course, course pages, and materials in ways that are easy to process; provide to-do lists and clear instructions; use templates for consistent formatting.
- Give options and variety for interactions: mix up the amount of individual and group work opportunities in the course; allow for student choice and ownership of their learning.

Assistive Technology

Digital accessibility work and UDL work hinges on understanding how your students interact with their devices long before they even interact with your course. Assistive technologies in this context are what enable students with specific disabilities to interact with devices such as smartphones, tablets, and computers. As you might expect, the landscape of the assistive technology industry has changed drastically alongside the advances in computing devices. More than just providing braille keyboards, schools and universities are now well versed in the technologies available and can help to match students to the appropriate solutions. Special education teachers in K–12 are often very familiar with things like specialized wheelchairs, voice synthesizers, and hearing aids that make in-person learning more equitable for their students. But in the online context, there are a few key players in assistive technology that enable equitable interaction with an online course:

- **Screen readers** are types of software that operate on a student's device in order to read aloud the information on the screen as the user navigates. Screen readers provide text-to-speech experiences that make digital content immediately accessible to users with vision differences. There are many screen readers on the market that are more and less compatible with different combinations of operating system, software, and web browser.
- **Optical character recognition** (OCR) is a technology designed to scan images of text and convert to digital text that is then ready to be read aloud by a screen reader or used in other digital spaces. OCR is most often performed on a PDF document to make it more accessible. The same technology behind OCR is available in optical character readers that vary from large office scanners to handheld devices used to scan print text and convert to digital text or auditory speech.
- A standard keyboard is often an assistive technology used for navigation when a mouse cannot be used. A user with mobility or vision differences would use their tab key and certain other keys to navigate their computer, software systems and the internet. Specialized keyboards also exist in compact sizes or with larger keys or high-contrast keys depending on the needs of the user.
- **Speech-to-text** functions are crucial to allow users with mobility and vision differences to dictate text. This may be used in word processing systems, course Learning Management Systems (LMS), or even on a phone to dictate a text message.
- **Voice command** functions use the same underlying technology as speech-to-text functions to allow users with mobility and vision differences to control their device using their voice.

Two important takeaways emerge from learning about assistive technologies relevant to online courses. First, many of these technologies, and even more that aren't listed, were developed initially to assist those with disabilities but have since become mainstream features. Without voice command technologies, we would not have digital assistants like Amazon Alexa or Google Assistant. Second, each of these technologies requires a certain level of accessibility to be built into the operating systems, software, web browsers, websites, and even online courses in order to function properly. Individual instructors must rely on an accessible LMS but must also follow accessibility best practices within their course and within their materials, and look for accessible external websites and tools if they choose to use them.

Accessibility Best Practices

The good news is that most LMSs are already fairly accessible, that is to say they are already compatible with most assistive technologies a student might be using. Creators of popular platforms like Blackboard, Canvas, or Moodle have needed to constantly incorporate accessibility into the design of new features. The educator's responsibility is to be aware of the accessibility best practices that are within their control. The following best practices (U.S. General Services Administration, n. d.) are a starting point that will lead to a more accessible online course if combined with a UDL approach to course design. These common issues and solutions are not an exhaustive list, but rather some of the easiest changes you can make to improve the accessibility of your online course. The following categories are described quickly and then explored in more detail:

- Course pages—while your LMS is accessible, individual pages and course navigation need to be designed with key accessibility considerations.
- Documents—documents that are uploaded to your course come in various formats, whether they are slide decks, readings, data sheets or otherwise and must be authored accessibly.

- Websites—websites that you link to from your online course may be for readings, researching, or participating in an activity and must be chosen carefully based on their accessibility.
- Hyperlinks—links that are accessed from your course via highlighted text like "click here" need to be reworded for a more accessible student experience.
- Alt text—images included in your course are often decorative, but sometimes convey a lot of meaning and need to have appropriate alt text added to give a user context.
- Captions—videos and audio materials require closed captions or transcripts in order to be accessible.

Course Pages

Course pages can be utilized heavily to communicate expectations with students, provide instructions and resources, and set up the context of the course. In more robust uses, course pages become like a mini textbook, providing readings, images, and videos all in one webpage with the course LMS. Regardless of how packed your pages, they still need to be built with accessibility in mind. Most LMSs will provide a content editor that allows you to set heading styles alongside your font settings. Marking certain text as headings can help screen reader users better navigate the course and help sighted students better process the information. It is important to organize your pages themselves but also to organize the navigation of your course. Make sure that students can easily find what they need. Do files have consistent naming conventions? Are assignments always found in the same place? Does each week or unit provide a list of to-do items for your students to work through? Students have too much learning to do to spend time being frustrated about navigation and organization. Removing these barriers can help all your students succeed.

Documents

Documents of various formats are the meat of your course and are typically uploaded with careful thought to the quality of the resource but very little thought about the accessibility of the document. Whether you are the author of the content or are just choosing the resource to share with your students, there are accessibility factors to consider. The possible access barriers in this category are endless, but there are a few key things to keep in mind for each format. Each of these tasks can be completed quickly and easily in most software you may be using. Conduct a quick internet search to find accurate step-by-step instructions for each tip.

PDFS

- Run OCR to convert images of text to selectable text so that it is readable by screen readers.
- Start with an accessible document in an authoring tool (Word, PowerPoint, InDesign, etc.) and then export as an accessible PDF.
- Add tags to indicate heading structure to help users navigate long and complex documents.
- Set or correct reading order to prevent the user from jumping all over the page when using a screen reader.
- Add alt text to images within the PDF to give context to screen reader users.
- Set the language of the document and a title for the document to help screen readers get started.
- Run an automated accessibility checker built into software like Adobe Acrobat Pro.

DOCUMENTS, PRESENTATIONS, AND SPREADSHEETS

- Use document templates that may be provided by your school to ensure a cohesive look and a more accessible setup.
- Set heading styles to indicate titles, subtitles, and headings to provide visual organization as well as easier navigation for screen reader users.
- Add alt text to images within the document to give context to screen reader users.
- Provide a file name and title that will help screen reader users to better identify the document.
- Write in a way that is appropriate for your audience and is organized for easy reading.
- Avoid using only color to convey meaning so that users with vision differences (e.g., color blindness) can still understand. Use a combination of color and text or symbols, which can be interpreted by a screen reader while color cannot.
- Write descriptive hyperlinks when linking to other files and webpages within the document.
- Provide a title for each slide in a slide deck so that screen reader users can more easily navigate between slides without getting lost.
- Set header rows and columns in tables to provide visual organization and easier navigation for screen readers.
- Run an automated accessibility checker built into software like Microsoft Word, Microsoft PowerPoint or Microsoft Excel.

Websites

While most instructors don't need to know the details of accessible web design and development, it is important for them to understand how to evaluate websites for accessibility. Just as you would evaluate a possible student resource based on its timeliness, bias, accuracy, and credibility, accessibility is an important factor. There are a multitude of automated web accessibility checkers available that provide varying levels of detail. A good starting point is the web accessibility evaluation tool WAVE, developed by WebAIM at Utah State University. Most instructors just need an accessibility checker, like WAVE, that indicates when indicators of accessibility concerns (missing alt text, poor navigation, inaccessible form fields, etc.) are present. Educators should keep looking to find the most accessible resource that meets their needs. If for some reason an accessible version does not exist, consider saving webpage content as a Word document, which you can more easily control, while properly citing the source. This could be available to all your students or available by request if a student has an issue with the less-than-perfect site.

    Some websites to which you send students are intended for use in an activity or collaborative experience. For example, you may send students to a site where they can record a quick video, interact with their peers, and curate resources. This sounds like an amazing addition to your course but could create a massive access barrier for some students. It is crucial in these instances—when participation and grades are on the line—to choose sites that are designed with accessibility in mind. Some of these learning technologies may be harder to evaluate than others, depending on their complexity. A good practice is to do a bit of research on the tool's accessibility, reading through the vendor's information as well as any reviews or commentary from other educators. Have others found this tool to be inaccessible? Does the vendor seem to prioritize accessibility?

    Most learning technologies that educators use in a class setting will be free and will not require students to create a login or download software. However, when this is not the case, be sure to contact an IT professional from your school to help investigate accessibility and security concerns. Most schools will encourage you to stay within the general bounds of the school's supported technologies (the ones that have been vetted and for which IT provides tech support). If you simply must use an external tool, it is important to think ahead about how you would accommodate a student if they weren't able to use that tool. Would they be missing a major chunk of learning, big participation points, or peer interaction? Is there another format that you can design that would give them an equivalent experience and opportunity to demonstrate their knowledge? Having a course designed based on learning objectives and not based on the use of a specific tool will allow you to pivot much easier when trying to accommodate a student who runs into an issue with an inaccessible tool.

Hyperlinks

Hyperlinks are ubiquitous in our daily lives; we may not think twice about how descriptive they are. For example, "read the article about digital accessibility" is much more descriptive than "click here." Unfortunately, short descriptors like "click here" and "read more" are a bad habit all over the internet and create an annoying and inaccessible experience for screen reader users. When a screen reader user is navigating a webpage or document, they are often using their keyboard to jump between heading levels, between images, and between links on a page to get a better sense of what the page is all about. As they jump around, they may come across a hyperlink that reads out like "external link … click here," giving them no context about where the link might take them. They're very unlikely to proceed to that link and may need to start at the top of the page, listening to every line in order to get context to know where the link goes.

Instead, writing descriptive hyperlinks using the page title or a quick description of the link will speed up the experience. Now a screen reader user may stumble upon "external link … read the article about digital accessibility" and be able to make a more informed decision about whether to visit the link. To edit hyperlink text, simply grab the relevant link URL, write your more descriptive text in your sentence, highlight the new text, and insert the hyperlink using what is typically a chain link icon in your toolbar. Look for step-by-step instructions on inserting hyperlinks based on the software or site you are using.

Alt Text

Alt text is one of the most common access barriers all over the internet. Just like screen reader users jump from link to link on a page, they may jump from image to image on a page to better understand the layout and information. However, a student with vision differences may not be able to physically see the image to glean its meaning or context, or even understand why it was included.

Alt text is a short description of an image that gets included in the metadata of the photo and does not appear as a visual text caption. Instead, it is read out by a screen reader when the user lands on the image in their navigation. The default alt text in some platforms is the file name or is left blank—both of which provide very little explanation to the user. Some images are decorative and can be marked as such in certain software. Images that add meaning to the resource or page should be given a short two-to-three sentence description giving the student an equivalent understanding as if they had seen the image visually. Some images like infographics and charts are more complex than others and may require a longer description. Alt text should still be included, but a longer caption beneath the image can also be added. This may benefit all your students and aid with their understanding of the image. Some instructors go even further to provide an audio description of the image directly below. This can be especially useful when describing an equation or complex problem that is better read aloud. If you include an audio description, be sure to also include a transcript so that you do not exclude any students with hearing differences. To add alt text to your materials, search for a step-by-step tutorial on adding alt text in whatever software you are using.

When an activity relies heavily on the student's ability to visually identify or objects or characteristics, such as anatomy or biology activities, you may need to get creative in accommodating your students with vision differences. Can they work with a partner to "use their eyes" but still actively contribute to the nonvisual components of the activity? Can the activity be adapted from the learning objectives to focus more on nonvisual skills?

Captions

Video and audio resources are impactful and valuable in your online course. Whether they take the form of a video lecture, a podcast, or a virtual field trip, they give your students a new perspective and spark interest. But these resources are better for everyone when they include captions or transcripts. Not only do captions support those with hearing differences, they also support those with communication and cognitive differences. Captions are so prevalent in our modern media environment that they are considered a convenience for any user. But adding captions to video and developing transcripts for audio can be daunting if you don't know where to begin.

There are two main sources of captions: paid captioning services and DIY options.

The vendors available for paid services are numerous but are usually only cost effective after negotiating a contract on a larger scale for an entire school or department. These vendors typically have their services integrated with YouTube or other media management systems like Mediasite or Kaltura to more quickly receive and return captioning jobs. From these vendors you can also receive text files of the captions for use as transcripts, and certain caption file types that may be compatible with other hosting platforms if you'd like to relocate your videos. For example, an instructor may want to download a captioning file from the vendor to attach to the same video hosted in Mediasite because they prefer the security or features of that platform.

DIY captioning options exist on a spectrum of difficulty. On the more difficult and time-consuming end, you can manually type out transcripts for a video that can then be adapted into captions in YouTube. Some instructors are able to incorporate this into their workflow by working from an online script or even creating a script. On the easier end of the spectrum, we can rely on the technology to do the work. With a free YouTube account (all Google accounts have a YouTube account), a video can be uploaded and captioned in a few steps. These videos can be set to any privacy level you prefer. As an owner of this video, you can go into the editing platform and choose automatic captions, selecting the appropriate language. These captions can take anywhere from a few minutes to a few hours to appear on the video when the CC button is enabled. The accuracy is much better than it used to be and the captions can be easily edited to correct spelling mistakes.

It is important to note that this option relies on artificial intelligence and the accuracy can decrease with accents or complex terminology. From YouTube you can download the same captioning files to attach to your video in whatever platform you prefer. Search for step-by-step tutorials on creating and editing captions in YouTube as well as for getting those captions into another platform if you so choose.

Recap

The following quick questions should be in your mind when evaluating and creating resources for use in online courses:

- Do documents have a structure that is easy to navigate?
- Do websites have a structure that is easy to navigate?

- Do hyperlinks have descriptive text?
- Do images have alternate text?
- Do videos have closed captions?

Even if you are not the creator of the content, it is important to select accessible materials for your students.

Getting Started

You may notice that many of these tips, apart from captions, focus on the needs of screen reader users. Students with vision differences are not necessarily more prevalent nor more important, but there are certainly more access barriers that arise for them in online courses. Many of the UDL ideas and strategies more directly support students with mobility, cognitive, and communication differences. It is important to understand that accessibility best practices in your online course are necessary for legal and ethical reasons but also create a better online experience for all your students. Combining these tips with thoughtfully designed activities and assessments will leave your students feeling more supported, more aware of course expectations, and more able to demonstrate what they've learned.

Start from where you are. Do not try to overhaul your course in one night, but instead slowly adopt more accessible content creation and curation habits. Lean on peers to brainstorm the UDL ideas that can fundamentally change your course. Start with just one assignment at a time to try out new approaches. Ask for feedback from your students. In all that you add and evaluate, ask these questions:

- What is useful about this content or activity?
- What do students need to do with it to show that they've learned?
- What might be a barrier to their success?

Chapter Summary

Digital accessibility is an important and often neglected aspect of online teaching. Accessibility issues directly impact students with disabilities in both online and face-to-face contexts. Educators must do the creative work of anticipating access barriers, finding solutions, and accommodating their students. All of this begins with awareness and practice in their own course materials and teaching practices. Accessibility and UDL work are an iterative process that requires practice and the ability to keep up with the changes in technology that online courses are sure to experience. Access barriers can be subtle or very tangible and impact our learners in different ways. Diving into applying accessibility best practices will make an immediate difference in an online course and help to bridge the gap between teachers and learners, making learners feel more supported. Investing time proactively and paying attention to the need of students, instructors strive to provide an even playing field upon which all students may gain education, skills, and insights equally.

Online Resources

Acrobat PDF Accessibility

The link below provides access to information about pdf accessibility: https://webaim.org/techniques/acrobat/

CAST.org Website

This link provides access to information about the CAST organization, which is credited with creating the UDL framework and guidelines: http://www.cast.org/

Web Accessibility Initiative

The link below provides access to information about making presentations accessible for all and provides some suggestions for professional presentations and conferences: https://www.w3.org/WAI/teach-advocate/accessible-presentations/#slides

WebAIM

This website provides resources for individuals and organization to create accessible online content: https://webaim.org/

Web Content Accessibility Guidelines

The link below provides access to recommendations for making web content accessible: https://www.w3.org/TR/WCAG20/

WAVE Web Accessibility Tool

The link below provides access to the WAVE web accessibility tool and serves as a resource to determine the accessibility of web pages: https://wave.webaim.org/about

References

Burgstahler, S. (2013). Preface. In S. Burgstahler (Ed.). *Universal design in higher education: Promising practices*. DO-IT, University of Washington. https://www.washington.edu/doit/sites/default/files/atoms/files/Universal%20Design%20in%20Higher%20Education_Promising%20Practices_0.pdf

CAST (n. d.). *About universal design for learning*. http://www.cast.org/impact/universal-design-for-learning-udl

Scott, S. S., Mcguire, J. M., & Shaw, S. F. (2003). Universal design for instruction. *Remedial and Special Education, 24*(6), 369–379. https://doi.org/10.1177%2F07419325030240060801

Taylor, M. A. (2016). Improving accessibility for students with visual disabilities in the technology-rich classroom. *Political Science and Politics, 49*(1), 122–127. https://doi.org/10.1017/S1049096515001134

U.S. Department of Education. (2001, October). *Individuals with Disabilities Education Act (IDEA) 1997/Services to parentally placed private school students with disabilities*. https://www2.ed.gov/about/offices/list/oii/nonpublic/idea1.html

U.S. Department of Justice. (n.d.). *Information and technical assistance on the Americans with Disabilities Act*. https://www.ada.gov/ada_intro.htm

U. S. General Service Administration. (n. d.). *Government-wide IT accessibility program: Create accessible digital products*. https://www.section508.gov/create

CHAPTER SEVEN

Developing an Online Syllabus

Tricia M. Mikolon, PhD, CRC, LPC, BC-TMH
Brooke Murphy, MS, LPC, NCC, CCTP

Caughlin (2014) describes a course syllabus as a contract between the instructor and the student, existing as an opportunity for the instructor to offer the student all the requirements necessary to succeed in the course. The syllabus is a distinct communication tool that allows the instructor to provide their best intentions for the course (Stanny et al., 2015), while empowering the student with clear and predictable expectations. Therefore, a syllabus holds a unique importance to both the student and the instructor. This communication includes both an understandable explanation of the content by the instructor and an accurate comprehension of the content by the student, an exchange which may occur in a different manner in a distance learning class than in an in-person class. For example, in an in-person course, a student may be familiar with and expect the instructor to pass out paper copies of the syllabus to review in class (Caughlin, 2014), yet this familiar process would not be conducted in an online class. In this case, a syllabus can serve as a solution to this problem by clearly providing the instructor's contact information and unique ways to access the instructor from a distance. A distance-learning instructor should consider any barriers to successful communication, such as unfamiliarity of the process, with online students. As a result, syllabi developed for distance learning courses should include distinct considerations to ensure successful communication of course expectations and intentions.

Student academic success has been found to be positively correlated with the amount of information provided by instructors regarding the course expectations of student responsibilities and assessment of student learning in a course (Grunert O'Brien et al., 2009). This information is disseminated via the **syllabus**, which sets the tone for a course by outlining the goals of the course, the structure in which the course will take place, and the expectations to which the students will be held both behaviorally and academically (Ko & Rosen, 2001; Smith 2005). The syllabus provides students with an overview of the course and its schedule, the **method of instruction**, and the course objectives and required texts (Palloff & Pratt, 2001; Smith, 2005). Communication between the instructor and students is an important aspect of the course to outline in the syllabus, along with the importance of confidentiality for both the students in the course and any clients which may be discussed (Ko & Rosen, 2001; Smith 2005). A detailed explanation of the course requirements governing attendance and participation, the expectation of professionalism, and the writing, submission, and assessment of assignments is important to set the standards for the course from the start (Ko & Rosen, 2001; Palloff & Pratt, 2001; Smith, 2005). For online courses, a review of the platform used, internet and software requirements, and specifications regarding video conferencing are important to allow students preparation time prior to the first class with technology (Palloff & Pratt, 2001; Smith, 2005). An overview of the school and departmental policies and procedures, as well as accommodations available for students in need, rounds out the student's introduction to the course and provides a valuable reference resource throughout the semester.

Overview of Syllabi Use and Importance

Distance learning, or **distance education**, is designated as such when the instructor and the student are not physically together (Kentnor, 2015). While distance learning may utilize different methodologies, such as mail, radio, and television (Kentnor, 2015), to connect the instructor to the student, current distance learning is mostly conducted via online education where the internet is the utilized delivery system (Kentnor, 2015). Distance learning requires a different teaching approach than face-to-face teaching, and Roberts (2019) explains the importance of adapting learning resources to accommodate for separation of the instructor and the student, one such resource being the syllabus. An important duty posed to distance learning instructors is the creation of an equal learning outcome for students enrolled in online courses as opposed to in-person courses (Trammell et al., 2018). Trammell et al. (2018) states that equal outcomes for online and in-person students are possible, but the process will be different for each experience. In examination of the online syllabus, Roberts (2019) discusses that online courses involve transactional distance, in which there is a not only a physical gap between the instructor and the student but the potential for communication gaps as well, increasing the possibility for miscommunication and confusion. However, a successful syllabus could be the solution to this problem by providing thorough information for the student to reference throughout the course.

Importance to Instructor

The syllabus content, while partially dictated by the academic institution, provides an opportunity for the instructor to express the personality of the instructor and the tone of the course (Stanny et al., 2015). The syllabus can be valuable to the instructor by offering an opportunity to express their teaching philosophy (Caughlin, 2014). In an online setting, the syllabus may be a supplemental way for the instructor to emphasize important tenets of their teaching philosophy in text format to compensate for any communication that an in-person environment would allow.

Distance learning is often characterized by the presence of independent learning for the students (Roberts, 2019) and freedom for the instructors to post learning materials from virtually anywhere the internet is present (Goralski & Falk, 2017). This is a learning exchange where instructional procedures and academic learning are separated by distance and even time (Roberts, 2019). For this reason, an online syllabus gains additional importance to the instructor as a means to connect communication between instructor and student. For example, Stanny (2015) reports that many student grade appeals are granted when the syllabus is unclear. In a distance learning situation, a well-structured syllabus can serve as evidence of clear communication from instructor to student, therefore having great importance to an instructor in such cases as grade appeals and student disputes.

Importance to Student

It is important to keep in mind that the primary intention of any course is to ultimately result in student learning. The syllabus provides an opportunity for the student's educational success when it offers clearly written, relevant, and well-organized information. The syllabus can outline the unique ways the course will utilize distance learning methods to offer the student quality learning opportunities. Caughlin (2014) suggests a well-written syllabus will favor too much information over too little, while avoiding being too laborious, to empower the student with knowledge and predictable expectations. Also, from the viewpoint of the student, the presentation of the syllabus during the first class session invites the student to engage in making an informed choice about agreeing to the course expectations (Caughlin, 2014). Part of the informed decision to participate in an online learning experience is defined by the acceptance of responsibility for learning on the part of the student (Roberts, 2019). Goralski and Falk (2017) explain that modern industry and business are favoring critical thinking, a trait bolstered in students by online learning modalities. Since online classes create the unique occasion for independent, self-directed learning (Roberts, 2019), a well-constructed syllabus may be an additional learning tool for motivated students to access to encourage responsibility for learning outcomes.

Fundamental Components of the Syllabus

Information included in the syllabus provides students with a guide for content of the course, the expectations of their responsibilities and behaviors, and a reference for the procedures of the course (Parkes & Harris, 2010). The content of a syllabus needs to be tailored to each course topic and instructional design. The foundational components of a syllabus are outlined here to provide instructors with a well-informed structure upon which to build their course syllabus.

MISSION STATEMENT

The **mission statement** of both the institution and the specific department are important to include in the syllabus, as they provide a summary of the goals of the department. The mission statement connects the instructor and learner through a shared mission in learning, skill development, and ethical practice in their field of study. This motivational statement also provides insight into the purpose of the content of the rest of the syllabus.

COURSE DESCRIPTION

The **course description** would be provided from the institutional course catalog. This provides the students with a focused summary of the course allowing for a cursory overview of topics discussed. This preview of the course allows students to prepare themselves for topics that will come up throughout the course, consider their own reactions to each, and formulate a plan on how to share their views with their instructor and peers.

REQUIRED TEXTS

Required textbooks and other academic sources, such as articles or video pertinent to class, would be listed here. Necessary information includes the authors names, book title, edition if applicable, and publisher. Providing the **International Standard Book Number** (**ISBN**) allows the students to locate the correct source quickly and reduces misunderstanding of editions or versions of materials.

While institutional bookstores provide the first point of access to students in purchasing course-required materials, providing this information allows the consumer the ability to choose where they purchase the required materials for each course and could reduce student cost.

METHOD OF INSTRUCTION

This section of the syllabus provides students with an introduction to the delivery of the course. The instructor will want to provide insight into how, when, and where the course will be provided, perhaps by stating "Students are expected to read their assigned reading prior to class and be prepared to discuss the assigned topics. Assignments will be submitted via the assignments link." Clarification of the time zone is important as not all students in an online class will be in the same region as the instructor.

Outlining the various modes of instruction throughout the semester will assist the student in fully understanding the requirements of the course but also in appreciating the number of hours outside of class necessary to be successful in the course. Instructors may outline that readings of the textbook and assigned literature will be expected along with attending synchronous lectures at the scheduled class meeting time. Asynchronous classes would need to address expected due dates for reviewing prerecorded lectures. A brief statement regarding the expectation of assignments being completed on time with attention to the assignment focus (skills development, case conceptualization, and the like), as well as how students will be assessed for learning—for example, "Class presentations and completed assignments will evaluate the student's incorporation of the material into their skill set."—should also be included.

NATURE OF AN ONLINE COURSE

Increased flexibility and adaptability are characteristic of online education (Bailey et al., 2014; Bates, 2005; Brown, 1997; Johnson, 2015; Roddy et al., 2017); however, these exist within different parameters for different courses. **Synchronous classes** occur with the instructor and students meeting together on an online platform at the same time, sharing information and discussion in live time (Cleveland-Innes & Ally, 2004; Skylar, 2009). **Asynchronous classes** occur over a set period of time during which students may log into class when it is convenient for them to view prerecorded lectures by the instructor; however, an asynchronous class lacks live interaction with instructors and peers (Cleveland-Innes & Ally, 2004; Skylar, 2009). Clarification of the type of course and the degree of flexibility and adaptability regarding expectations for attendance and due dates are important to include in the syllabus (Palloff & Pratt, 2001, Smith, 2005).

Another consideration is the **course length**. Some institutions provide standard 16-week **semester** while others use the 8-week **biterm**. If using the shorter biterm, it may be beneficial to provide a statement clarifying the expected workload and amount of time required to successfully complete required readings, assignments, and projects. This may be presented as "Eight week courses address the same materials as longer courses, just in a shorter time with assignments due closer together. The same expectations for student work are maintained."

Trimesters, or breaking the academic calendar down into fall, spring, and summer sections, may also occur. Postsecondary education conceptualizes these as semesters, with some institutions using the trimester, while others maintain the traditional fall and spring semesters with only minimal classes and students enrolled for summer courses.

CONTACT INFORMATION FOR INSTRUCTOR

Clarification on how to contact the instructor as well as when the student can expect a response from their instructor is important to include in the syllabus. If your institution has a policy on only responding to students via their institutional emails, clarification is necessary. Perhaps a statement such as "Students are expected to use only their institutional email when contacting the instructor, other emails may be missed." A simple statement such as this added to the syllabus serves as a reminder to students and may reduce frustration from unanswered emails.

Providing specification for emails also assists in facilitating effective communication between the instructor and students. A reminder statement such as "Students are expected to check their emails daily throughout the semester, as this is the primary means of communication between you and your instructor." Clarification of adding either the course number and name of student to the subject line or the student's first and last names in the signature outlines expectations for students and sets the standard of clear and effective communication for the course.

Best times and methods for contacting the instructor are important additions to any syllabus. Providing students with the instructor's email address, the expected time frame of a response, and the means by which to schedule a meeting time, if necessary, facilitates open communication. Office hours, if applicable, can be provided here as well. If, as an instructor, you are more flexible with availability and do not provide structured office hours, a statement clarifying this can help students understand that you are available, and a lack of structured office hours is not an issue. This can be accomplished by a statement identifying your willingness to meet with them at a mutually agreed upon time scheduled via email. Instructors may want to include their contact number if they accept phone calls or texts, a link to their virtual office if they engage in video conferencing, or an email address. It is also valuable to indicate the preferred or primary source of communication to facilitate efficient communication response times. Some instructors may wish to email their phone number or virtual office link on an as-needed basis rather than initially providing this information in the syllabus for all students to be able to reference.

COURSE OBJECTIVES

Course objectives summarize what the student will learn by completing the course work guided by national and state credentialing requirements. Some national accrediting bodies include the Association of Advanced Rabbinical and Talmudic Schools, the Accreditation Commission Council on Occupational Education (COE), the Accrediting Commission of Career Schools and Colleges (ACCSC), the Accrediting Council for Continuing Education and Training (ACCET), the Accrediting Council for Independent Colleges and Schools (ACICS), and the Distance Education Accrediting Commission (DEAC). Credentialing requirements vary by state and program. Many programs have specific credentialing bodies for their specific field of study, including the American Psychological Association (APA) for psychology, the Counsel for the Accreditation of Education Preparation (CAEP) for education, the Council for Accreditation of Counseling and Related Educational Programs (CACREP) for counseling, the International Accreditation Counsel for Business Education (IACBE) for business, and the Occupational Safety and Health Association (OSHA) for various careers, to name a few. Reinforcement of the need for privacy and confidentiality regarding clients past or present in any assignments, class discussions, or other course-related activities is important as it sets the stage for both ethical compliance and professionalism in the course.

CONFIDENTIALITY FOR CLIENTS

Some fields of study, including human services, counseling, social work, psychology, and nursing, and professional preparation programs such as counseling, psychology, nursing, and medicine, require case discussion of work with clients or patients. In any academic setting wherein protected health information (PHI) might be discussed, outlining the ethical need for **confidentiality of clients** is important. Citing the applicable code of ethics serves as a reminder to students that confidential information remains as such in the learning environment (Palloff & Pratt, 2003; Smith, 2005). For those courses in the human services, additionally citing the requirements of Health Insurance Portability and Accountability Act (HIPAA) would be beneficial.

CONFIDENTIALITY FOR STUDENTS IN CLASS

Privacy and confidentiality also extend to the students in the classroom, as they may choose to share personal information during discussions. Instructors need to set a standard for this by highlighting its importance in the syllabus and reiterating it regularly in class. This can be accomplished by a statement such as "Students are expected to be in a quiet and professional setting with good internet access, a working camera and microphone and to check these elements prior to each class." This important aspect of professionalism is often overlooked in course syllabi, but is important, especially in the online learning classroom environment (Ko & Rosen, 2001; Smith, 2005).

Course Requirements: In developing the **course requirements**, consider it as a recipe for success provided to students. This section of the syllabus needs to outline, in detail, the expectations and responsibilities of the students to succeed in the course. Providing students with clear parameters and expectations allows them to make informed decisions regarding various aspects of their participation, such as attendance, professionalism, writing, and technology requirements, and to prepare prior to the first class meeting.

For synchronous classes, clarification of being on time for the start of the live class, being on camera, and staying in class and on camera the entire time is important to state (Palloff & Pratt, 2001; Smith, 2005). Clarification on the use of chat features in class, if applicable, is necessary so students are aware of expected communication methods. The more detailed explanation of expectations the better, so consider outlining what constitutes active and appropriate participation in class. Asynchronous classes may need to include expectations for discussion boards or mandatory logins that constitutes participation for the course.

Attendance and participation: When outlining course expectations for **attendance and participation,** the more specific the instructor is in the syllabus, the better set the student's expectations are (Palloff & Pratt, 2001; Smith, 2005). Providing a clear expectation depends on the type of class. Being detailed in the syllabus provides the students with an introduction to and a reference for these expectations as well as a firm foundation for grading on these variables for the instructor. Attaching a rubric for attendance and participation is an effective way to assist students in clarifying what is expected and what constitutes points in a class for these areas (Palloff & Pratt, 2001; Smith, 2005).

Professionalism: **Professionalism** is defined differently in various fields of study, but the foundational aspects of it are consistent across the board. If the class is experiential, interpersonal, and/or intrapersonal in nature, professionalism is critical within class discussions. Students will need to use the ability to display appropriate behavior, accept constructive feedback, and get along with their peers to promote a meaningful learning experience (Grunert O'Brien et al., 2009).

Appropriate language for professional students is expected regardless of topic or course focus, so avoiding vulgarity is necessary. Encouraging students to attempt to improve their professional vocabulary and verbal communication skills throughout the course assists in meeting this goal as well as increasing their effective communication in the field. Clarification of professionalism expectations, be it in class, emails, discussion boards, or assignments, is imperative. Lack of professionalism may result in loss of points from both the assignment and attendance and participation grade if it is incorporated into the specific syllabus. Attaching a rubric for attendance and participation is an effective way to assist students clarify what is expected and what constitutes points in a class for professionalism.

The advent of online learning brings a need for appreciation of **netiquette, or internet etiquette**. Addressing netiquette in the syllabus helps to guide students, who may feel less restricted by social norms in online classes, to consider appropriate interactions with their peers and instructors (Mintu-Wimsatt et al., 2009). Considerations of professional background choices, whether in your actual workspace or virtual, is necessary for video conferences. Other important considerations include sharing screen time, time management during discussions, maintaining professional vocabulary, and facial expressions and behaviors. Instructors may choose to address these topics, as they complement professionalism expectations previously set forth in the online syllabus.

Writing: Each field of study brings with it a specific **writing style**. APA is the preferred writing style of the education, psychology and counseling, and science fields while MLA is preferred for the study of the humanities. Business, history, and finance use the Chicago/Turabian style of writing. Each writing style brings its own expectations regarding formatting, citations, and references. Providing the students with the required writing format and including the manual as a required textbook clarifies expectations and assists understanding of the importance of the chosen writing style as an effective communication skill in their field. Including the writing expectations in each assignment explanation and associated rubric provides a reminder to students of its importance as well as simplifies grading for the instructor.

Copyright statements: Consideration of **copyright** is important in academic and professional writing and presentations. This statement provides a summary of the expectations of students regarding their use of images and materials written by another, be it an artist, musician, or institute of higher education. A reminder of the importance of copyright reminds students to keep this in their forethoughts when developing projects or presentations.

Submission of assignments: Most assignments for online courses will be completed by students through **assignment links** tethered to the course platform and attached to the grade book. Explanation of the location of these links assists students in submitting their assignments on time. Some links are associated with plagiarism programs such as SafeAssign or Grammarly. Clarifying this requirement, as it applies to students, allows for transparency between instructor and students. Such a program, if used, may allow students to view their scores after submission, depending on instructor preference. Allowing students this option assists them in learning more about plagiarism and the professional manner for avoiding it in their writing.

Other forms of submission include the use of group access files such as Box, Dropbox, Google Drive, or Microsoft OneDrive. Regardless of chosen platform, it is beneficial for instructors to introduce students to the expected means of assignment submission in the syllabus and explore this further in their class time together to ensure proficient use. Specifications of the platform needs, such as certain types or sizes of documents, needs to be outlined to avoid problems closer to due dates.

Policies and Procedures: Carefully follow course **policies and procedures** regarding writing, academic honesty, submission of assignments, formatting, and other matters to assist in student success. Since following directions is a crucial skill for higher-learning graduates and the smooth operation of a course depends on meeting expectations, adherence to policies can positively or adversely affect a student's grade. Students' expectations regarding writing and other course-specific requirements are reiterated here, allowing for a reminder reinforcing the necessary components for success in the course.

Academic honesty and ethical considerations: Institutions of higher education pride themselves on committing to academic integrity and ethical decision-making practices. Outlining the ethical guidelines students are expected to adhere to strengthens their understanding and appreciation of the role those play in their academic and future professional careers. Providing a hyperlink in the syllabus to the applicable **professional code of ethics**—for example, the American Counseling Association (ACA), the National Society for Professional Engineers (NSPE), or the Association for Computing Machinery (ACM)—streamlines access for students. Providing a link to the college or university's academic catalog will also support the student's learning and appreciation of ethical expectations governing their behavior. The impact of unethical behaviors needs to be outlined with the logical consequences, such as a discussion with departmental faculty. Formal probation and remediation needs to be outlined, as well as the impact of a second offense, or for both single and multiple offenses, such as failure of the course or dismissal from the program, depending upon the severity of the offense(s). Remaining transparent with students from the start via the syllabus dismisses any confusion and places responsibility for behaviors firmly on the student from the start.

Accommodations statement and procedures: Inclusion in academics is paramount, affording all students the equal opportunity for success. Students may need to request reasonable accommodations for disabilities by contacting the designated staff member at the institution (Grunert O'Brien et al., 2009). Some schools place this responsibility on the **student services office or student success office**. Procedures differ by institution, but, fundamentally, for accommodations to be awarded, a student must complete an application and provide documentation of the disability to the assigned department or office. Any accommodations for disabilities often must be recertified each semester by that same office before course adjustments are made by individual instructors. Providing a link for students to the correct office or department, as well as the student handbook, provides support and information on the process in a more detailed form.

Platform used: Colleges and universities chose various **platforms** for the administration of online courses. Some of the most popular include Blackboard, alentLMS, Canvas, Schoology, Brightspace, Google Classroom, SAP Litmos, and Cornerstone Learning, to name a few. Regardless of the chosen platform, they all exist to provide the following fundamental purposes: for students to receive information from the instructor through assignments or grades, for interactions to occur between the student and the instructor, and for students to complete forms of academic evaluation—for example, quizzes and examinations (Ko & Rosen, 2001; Palloff & Pratt; 2001, Smith, 2005). These formats also provide a location for students to submit assignments, gain access to additional information provided by the instructor, and even meet in a virtual classroom. Administrators often determine what aspects of the platform are used or not, but the syllabus provides a resource for the instructor to share this information with students as well as guide them in the location of content within the system. Should an instructor be using a system off the chosen platform for classes, such as choosing Zoom over the Collaborate feature in Blackboard, clarification of this needs to be provided to students as well as a link to the alterative platform if registration is required.

Internet and software requirements: **Internet and software requirements** need to be explained in the syllabus to provide students with a clear expectation and time to prepare their technology to meet expected standards. Specifications are determined by administration or instructors but need to be clearly communicated to students with regards to working and dependable internet, and reliable email software with attachments receiving/sending enabled, as well as specific software such as Microsoft Word, Open Office Writer, PowerPoint, Prezi, or Google Slides.

Institutional IT departments often offer free downloads of specific programs to students for their academic use. Check with the institution to be sure that those options include those required for the course. Being very specific in a statement such as "Student assignments are expected to be completed in (chosen program, IE: Microsoft word or Google docs). Failure to do so may result in a failing grade. Please see the IT Department link for details on program downloads," clarifies expectations, and adding a link to the school's IT department, where the downloads are available, reduces confusion.

Course Schedule: The **course schedule** needs to be included in the syllabus but also provided within the platform for easy reference by both students and the instructor. Placing it under the content or information tabs may be useful, and referencing its placement in the syllabus connects the two locations for student accessibility. Key components of the course schedule include the week of the semester with the specific date and the topics of discussion for that week, as well as any assigned readings and assignments due during that period (Smith, 2005). Please see the example syllabus provided in this chapter for a suggested layout.

***Assignments and Rubrics:* Assignments and rubrics** work in collaboration to provide assessment for courses. The syllabus provides the instructor with the modality to outline assignment expectations as well as the grading procedure via the associated rubric. Assignment descriptions need to be thorough, outlining the various aspects of the assignment with an explanation of expectations. See the example assignment and corresponding rubric for a model of this.

Grading procedures: The rubrics that correspond to each assignment provide a clear explanation of the **grading procedure** for each assignment. The rubrics provide the students a clear guide to the evaluation process and provide the instructor an objective means by which to grade students (Palloff & Pratt, 2001; Smith, 2005). The consistently applied grading procedures place all students on the same playing field, reducing concerns of inequitable assessment for each assignment. An explanation of how quickly grades will be returned and if feedback will be provided needs to be explained to provide structure to the assessment process (Merisotis & Phipps, 1999; Smith, 2005). Inclusion of detailed feedback, with the expectation of its inclusion in future assignments, increases student learning. This expectation, if included in the course, should be explicitly stated (Pepicello & Rice, 2000, Smith 2005).

Disclaimer statement: The syllabus is noted not to be a legal contract (Rumore, 2016) but an agreement between instructors and students serving as a pathway to success. A disclaimer statement allows the instructor to notify students that certain aspects, such as the course schedule or deadlines for assignments, may change during the semester. This is done to allow for the course to evolve during the biterm or semester as needed due to "extraordinary events or circumstances" (Rumore, 2016, p. 4). Changes made should benefit both the instructor and student, such as extending assignment deadlines or reducing work assigned. A disclaimer statement may be as simple as "This syllabus is subject to change."

Multicultural/Ethical and Social Justice Considerations Regarding Syllabi

Multicultural and **social justice** considerations are two different dimensions to consider in developing a syllabus. **Multiculturalism** is often considered "a wide range of multiple groups without grading, comparing, or ranking them as better or worse than one another and without denying the very distinct and complementary or even contradictory perspectives that each group brings with it" (Pedersen, 1991, p. 4), while a working definition of social justice may be "the scholarship and professional action designed to change societal values, structures, policies, and practices, such that disadvantaged or marginalized groups gain increased access to these tools of self-determination" (Goodman et al., 2004, p. 795). Whenever applicable to a course topic, instructors need to attempt to include both multicultural and social justice considerations into the development of their course and presentation of the course material (Pieterse, 2009). Instructors may accomplish this by seizing opportunities to use content and illustrations from various cultures as well as incorporating various approaches to teaching to consider individual differences "in developmental status, learning styles, and varying frames of reference for interpretation and application of concepts and skills being learned" (Ramsey et al., 2003, p. 153). Consideration of inclusion of these topics that are in compliance with accreditation requirements is also recommended. These topics are explored at length in Chapter 3.

Example of Rubrics

ATTENDANCE/PARTICIPATION RUBRIC Students are expected to attend each class and actively participate. Lack of professionalism, attendance or participation will result in loss of points as noted below.

Note: There is a range of points for items, these are dependent upon the extent of the behavior exhibited.

WEEK	10 POINTS	9-5 POINTS	4-1 POINT	0 POINTS
1	Attends class on time, stays for whole class, on camera entire while, contributes to class discussion in professional manner.	Attends entire class and is always on camera, participates in chat only, not involved in verbal discussions.	Attends class but does not participate fully or is unprofessional. May not always be on camera, distracted by things off camera at times.	Fails to attend class and/or fails to add anything to the learning process
2	Attends class on time, stays for whole class, on camera entire while, contributes to class discussion in professional manner.	Attends entire class and is always on camera, participates in chat only, not involved in verbal discussions.	Attends class but does not participate fully or is unprofessional. May not always be on camera, distracted by things off camera at times.	Fails to attend class and/or fails to add anything to the learning process
3	Attends class on time, stays for whole class, on camera entire while, contributes to class discussion in professional manner.	Attends entire class and is always on camera, participates in chat only, not involved in verbal discussions.	Attends class but does not participate fully or is unprofessional. May not always be on camera, distracted by things off camera at times.	Fails to attend class and/or fails to add anything to the learning process
4	Attends class on time, stays for whole class, on camera entire while, contributes to class discussion in professional manner.	Attends entire class and is always on camera, participates in chat only, not involved in verbal discussions.	Attends class but does not participate fully or is unprofessional. May not always be on camera, distracted by things off camera at times.	Fails to attend class and/or fails to add anything to the learning process
5	Attends class on time, stays for whole class, on camera entire while, contributes to class discussion in professional manner.	Attends entire class and is always on camera, participates in chat only, not involved in verbal discussions.	Attends class but does not participate fully or is unprofessional. May not always be on camera, distracted by things off camera at times.	Fails to attend class and/or fails to add anything to the learning process
6	Attends class on time, stays for whole class, on camera entire while, contributes to class discussion in professional manner.	Attends entire class and is always on camera, participates in chat only, not involved in verbal discussions.	Attends class but does not participate fully or is unprofessional. May not always be on camera, distracted by things off camera at times.	Fails to attend class and/or fails to add anything to the learning process
7	Attends class on time, stays for whole class, on camera entire while, contributes to class discussion in professional manner.	Attends entire class and is always on camera, participates in chat only, not involved in verbal discussions.	Attends class but does not participate fully or is unprofessional. May not always be on camera, distracted by things off camera at times.	Fails to attend class and/or fails to add anything to the learning process
8	Attends class on time, stays for whole class, on camera entire while, contributes to class discussion in professional manner.	Attends entire class and is always on camera, participates in chat only, not involved in verbal discussions.	Attends class but does not participate fully or is unprofessional. May not always be on camera, distracted by things off camera at times.	Fails to attend class and/or fails to add anything to the learning process

(continued)

CHAPTER SEVEN Developing an Online Syllabus

WEEK	10 POINTS	9-5 POINTS	4-1 POINT	0 POINTS
9	Attends class on time, stays for whole class, on camera entire while, contributes to class discussion in professional manner.	Attends entire class and is always on camera, participates in chat only, not involved in verbal discussions.	Attends class but does not participate fully or is unprofessional. May not always be on camera, distracted by things off camera at times.	Fails to attend class and/or fails to add anything to the learning process
10	Attends class on time, stays for whole class, on camera entire while, contributes to class discussion in professional manner.	Attends entire class and is always on camera, participates in chat only, not involved in verbal discussions.	Attends class but does not participate fully or is unprofessional. May not always be on camera, distracted by things off camera at times.	Fails to attend class and/or fails to add anything to the learning process
11	Attends class on time, stays for whole class, on camera entire while, contributes to class discussion in professional manner.	Attends entire class and is always on camera, participates in chat only, not involved in verbal discussions.	Attends class but does not participate fully or is unprofessional. May not always be on camera, distracted by things off camera at times.	Fails to attend class and/or fails to add anything to the learning process
12	Attends class on time, stays for whole class, on camera entire while, contributes to class discussion in professional manner.	Attends entire class and is always on camera, participates in chat only, not involved in verbal discussions.	Attends class but does not participate fully or is unprofessional. May not always be on camera, distracted by things off camera at times.	Fails to attend class and/or fails to add anything to the learning process
13	Attends class on time, stays for whole class, on camera entire while, contributes to class discussion in professional manner.	Attends entire class and is always on camera, participates in chat only, not involved in verbal discussions.	Attends class but does not participate fully or is unprofessional. May not always be on camera, distracted by things off camera at times.	Fails to attend class and/or fails to add anything to the learning process
14	Attends class on time, stays for whole class, on camera entire while, contributes to class discussion in professional manner.	Attends entire class and is always on camera, participates in chat only, not involved in verbal discussions.	Attends class but does not participate fully or is unprofessional. May not always be on camera, distracted by things off camera at times.	Fails to attend class and/or fails to add anything to the learning process
15	Attends class on time, stays for whole class, on camera entire while, contributes to class discussion in professional manner.	Attends entire class and is always on camera, participates in chat only, not involved in verbal discussions.	Attends class but does not participate fully or is unprofessional. May not always be on camera, distracted by things off camera at times.	Fails to attend class and/or fails to add anything to the learning process
16	Attends class on time, stays for whole class, on camera entire while, contributes to class discussion in professional manner.	Attends entire class and is always on camera, participates in chat only, not involved in verbal discussions.	Attends class but does not participate fully or is unprofessional. May not always be on camera, distracted by things off camera at times.	Fails to attend class and/or fails to add anything to the learning process
Total Points Earned:				

Instructor feedback:

Points Summary:
- 10 points: Attends class on time, stays for whole class, on camera entire time, contributes to class discussion in professional manner
- 9-5 points: Attends session, participates in chat only
- 4-1 point: Attends, participation is not voluntary, or lacks professionalism
- 0 points: Fails to attend or participate, fails to act as a collaborate agent in the learning process

Points will be deducted for late arrivals:
- Late < 5 minutes -1
- Late > 5 minutes but <10 minutes -3
- Late <10 minutes -5

Failure to attend two or the equivalent of two classes will result in a failing grade for this course. Example of instructor feedback for Attendance/Participation rubric:

When providing feedback to students regarding attendance, participation, or professionalism the more specific information you can provide to students the better to provide clarification on what is needed to improve but also to highlight what they are doing well on.

Examples for consideration include:

Great participation in class in weeks 1, 2, and 3, however you were 4 minutes late to class, so you lost one point per the rubric. Please make every attempt to be on time for class.

I appreciate your sharing in class tonight and you maintained a great level of professionalism when receiving your feedback from your peers. Nice work!

This week you attended class on time, but you weren't on camera the entire time. Please be sure to review the attendance policy and trouble shoot your camera prior to the start of class. I hate to see you lose points due to technology. IT may be able to assist you, you can reach them at ITDepartment@levaiuniversity

I've notice you were late for the last two weeks to class. Let's schedule a time to meet at your convience so we can discuss your attendance and brainstorm any possible solutions. Email me at tricia.mikolon@levaiuniversity and we will schedule time to meet.

DOCTORAL STUDENT GROUP PROJECT Doctoral students will work in assigned group to develop an online teaching module and demonstration.

This project will include:

1. a paper identifying the evidence-based modification necessary to teach the topic online
2. A recorded presentation provided to the professor on the finding of the necessary modification related to the chosen topic and a demonstration of the modifications completed in a classroom setting.

Student groups will pick one topic in which they plan to teach (i.e.: science, math, etc.) and complete a paper summarizing the skills necessary to teach this course in person, the necessary modification to instruct this course online, and the evidence -based practices to support this.

This paper will contain at least 20 professional references within the last 7 years to support the presented information.

Students will then complete a presentation, along with a PowerPoint to summarize their paper findings as well as a 30-minute demonstration of how these skills would be enacted in the classroom. Total presentation time is 60–70 minutes.

Doctoral Group Project Paper Rubric

CRITERIA	40 POINTS	30 POINTS	15 POINTS	0 POINTS
Necessary skills to teach topic online	Fully addresses the necessary skills to teach the topic online	Mostly addresses the necessary skills to teach the topic online	Minimally addresses the necessary skills to teach the topic online	Fails to address the necessary skills to teach the topic online
Modifications are appropriate and evidence based	Fully addresses the modifications and each is appropriate, and evidence based	Mostly addresses the modifications and each is appropriate, and evidence based	Minimally addresses the modifications and not all are appropriate, and evidence based	Fails adequately address the modifications or provides a majority which are not appropriate, or evidence based
Discussion connects purpose of skills and modification to student success	Fully addresses how the discussion connects the purpose and skills to the modification and student success	Mostly addresses how the discussion connects the purpose and skills to the modification and student success	Minimally addresses how the discussion connects the purpose and skills to the modification and student success	Fails to fully address how the discussion connects the purpose and skills to the modification and student success
At least 20 references, all of which are recent	20 references, all are current and no more than 7 years old	15–19 references and/or no more than 8 years old	10–14 references, majority no more than 8 years old	Less than 10 references and majority are more than 8 years old
APA formatting and references	APA is error free, contains 30 or more references	APA has minor errors and/or contains 25–29 references	APA as significant errors and/or contains 15–24 references	Lacks APA formatting and/or contains less than 15 references
Total 200 points				

Professor Comments:

COMPLETED EXAMPLE RUBRIC FOR CONSIDERATION

Doctoral Student Group Project

Doctoral students will work in assigned group to develop an online teaching module and demonstration.

This project will include:

1. a paper identifying the evidence-based modification necessary to teach the topic online
2. A recorded presentation provided to the professor on the finding of the necessary modification related to the chosen topic and a demonstration of the modifications completed in a classroom setting.

Student groups will pick one topic in which they plan to teach (i.e.: science, math, etc.) and complete a paper summarizing the skills necessary to teach this course in person, the necessary modification to instruct this course online, and the evidence-based practices to support this.

This paper will contain at least 20 professional references within the last 7 years to support the presented information.

Students will then complete a presentation, along with a PowerPoint to summarize their paper findings as well as a 30-minute demonstration of how these skills would be enacted in the classroom. Total presentation time is 60–70 minutes.

Doctoral Group Project Paper Rubric

CRITERIA	40 POINTS	30 POINTS	15 POINTS	0 POINTS
Necessary skills to teach topic online	Fully addresses the necessary skills to teach the topic online	Mostly addresses the necessary skills to teach the topic online	Minimally addresses the necessary skills to teach the topic online	Fails to address the necessary skills to teach the topic online
Modifications are appropriate and evidence based	Fully addresses the modifications and each is appropriate, and evidence based	Mostly addresses the modifications and each is appropriate, and evidence based	Minimally addresses the modifications and not all are appropriate, and evidence based	Fails adequately address the modifications or provides a majority which are not appropriate, or evidence based
Discussion connects purpose of skills and modification to student success	Fully addresses how the discussion connects the purpose and skills to the modification and student success	Mostly addresses how the discussion connects the purpose and skills to the modification and student success	Minimally addresses how the discussion connects the purpose and skills to the modification and student success	Fails to fully address how the discussion connects the purpose and skills to the modification and student success
At least 20 references, all of which are recent	20 references, all are current and no more than 7 years old	15–19 references and/or no more than 8 years old	10–14 references, majority no more than 8 years old	Less than 10 references and majority are more than 8 years old
APA formatting and references	APA is error free, contains 30 or more references	APA has minor errors and/or contains 25–29 references	APA as significant errors and/or contains 15–24 references	Lacks APA formatting and/or contains less than 15 references
Total 200 points				

Professor Comments:

You earned 190 points out of 200.

Great work on this. You clearly provided information on the skills and modifications needed for the topic.

I would have liked to have seen you add more about how these relate to student success. This is an important aspect of all teaching, so consider this in the future when choosing interventions or teaching skills.

Your APA was error free, well done!

You also provided great references, you did your research and it shows.

Syllabus Outline

Institutional logo

COURSE Number _____
Course Title _____
Institution Program _____
Course Syllabus _____
Semester/term _____
Day/time of course (clarify time zone) _____

Instructor: Instructor name and credentials
Telephone: Number
Office Hours: Days/times
Email: Instructor email address
Mission Statement

Course Description

Required Text(s)

Method of Instruction

Email

Best times and methods to contact instructor:

Prerequisites

Course Objectives

ACCREDITATION STANDARDS	ASSIGNMENTS	PRACTICAL APPLICATIONS

Client and student confidentiality (as applicable to course)

GENERAL COURSE REQUIREMENTS

Understanding the following will assist you in completing all assignments thoroughly and doing well in this course.

1. Attendance and Participation:
   Institutional Attendance and Participation Policy
   Professionalism:

2. Assignments:
   Writing
   Grading/Professional Development

3. Policies and Procedures:
   Platform Specifics (e.g., Blackboard or Google classroom)
   Submission of Assignments
   Internet and Software:
   Institutional Policies
   Academic Honesty and Ethics Statement

Copyright Statement:
Students Seeking Accommodation:

Schedule and Evaluation

Method of Evaluation

Method of Evaluating Student Performance (All assignments are to be fully described below)

Course Schedule

Tentative Course Schedule

NOTE: Due dates and meeting times are posted in Eastern Standard Time.

WEEK	TOPIC/ASSIGNMENTS	READINGS OR ASSIGNMENTS FOR THIS WEEK'S CLASS
Week 1 Date		

Example Syllabus

EDU 822

EDUCATING STUDENTS IN THE ONLINE PLATFORM

LEVAI UNIVERSITY
School of Education
Autumn 2022 Semester Course Syllabus
Mondays 8:30–10:00 p.m. EST

Primary Instructor: Tricia M. Mikolon, PhD, CRC, LPC, BC-TBH
Phone: 914.111.5822
Office Hours: By appointment
Email: tricia.mikolon@levaiuniversity

Mission Statement
Levai University strives to educate students to become professionals in their field. Levai students excel in their chosen careers and view others as their equals, encouraging the best from those around them.

Course Description
This course will train educators to understand the nuances of teaching in the online environment. It is designed to assist students in understanding the needs of students from primary school through secondary school and beyond into college and graduate programs. Students will learn to appreciate the unique needs of online students, adjust their teaching skills to enhance student success and increase their own skills in communicating course expectations to students.

Required Texts
Mikolon, T. M., & Hatfield, T. (Eds). (2022). *Foundations, principles, & techniques of online teaching.* (12th ed.). Cognella.

Suggested/supplemental texts
Talipski, A. M., & Mikolon, E. J. (2054). *Online Platforms and Education.* (88th ed.) Cognella.

American Psychological Association. (2020). *Publication manual of the American Psychological Association* (7th ed.).

Some outside readings and/or videos will also be required.

These will be provided by your instructor in the course shell.

Method of Instruction
Students will attend weekly classes via the Levai online platform. Course materials are provided through the class shell in Blackboard. Students are expected to attend each class on time, actively always participate and be on camera.

Students are expected to read their assigned reading prior to class and be prepared to discuss the assigned topics. Assignments will be submitted via the assignments link. Class presentations and completed assignments will evaluate the student's incorporation of the material into their teaching.

Email
Students are expected to use only their Levai University email when contacting the instructor, other emails may be missed. Please check your emails daily throughout the semester, as this is the primary means of communication between you and your instructor. Course announcements will be posted in Blackboard but will also be directed to your email for review.

For quicker responses, please include your course number and section in your emails. This will expediate responses from your professor.

Best Times and Methods for Contacting the Professor
Email is the most efficient way to reach your professor. Please use the email tricia.mikolon@levaiuniversity. Responses will occur within a few hours based on class schedules.

If you would like to discuss a topic or concern in more depth, you may request a video conference or phone call, as not all communication needs to be written. If this option fits your needs, please email me to schedule a time and clarify the means of communication, as well as a few dates/times that may work for you. I'm confident we can schedule an appointment in a short time to meet your needs.

Prerequisites
Students need to have obtained a passing grade in the following courses prior to being enrolled in this course. Failure to verify successful completion of both courses will result in the removal from this course until the prerequisites are completed.

Please check with your academic advisor and the registrar to ensure fulfillment of the following courses:

EDU 2015

EDU 0724

COURSE OBJECTIVES

ONLINE PLATFORM TEACHING AND EDUCATION STANDARDS	ASSIGNMENTS	PRACTICAL APPLICATION
1-A-11 Instructors will understand educational needs and how to facilitate learning for their students	Discussion boards Exams Papers	Class discussions Class presentations
1-B-11-c Instructors will understand the foundations of the chosen online platform and modify teaching skills to enhance both student understanding and success	Discussion boards Exams Papers	Class discussions Class presentations
3-x-265-q Instructors appreciate the unique world view of their students as well as their needs, and increase accessibility in classes to ensure student success	Discussion boards Exams Papers	Class discussions Class presentations
4-ab-A-n Instructors personalize their pedagogy to match the students who comprise their classes, basing their teaching on fundamental principles but matching student needs and background	Discussion boards Exams Papers	Class discussions Class presentations
4-abc-A-nb Instructors encourage communication between students, their families and themselves. Understanding is the primary goal.	Discussion boards Exams Papers	Class discussions Class presentations
7-7-14-tmm Instructors modify their teaching skills to match their student needs according to grade and ability levels	Discussion boards Exams Papers	Class discussions Class presentations
8-we-d-22 Instructors create a welcoming and professional online classroom environment to benefit themselves as well as their students	Discussion boards Exams Papers	Class discussions Class presentations
9-14-tmml Instructors understand and appreciate the multicultural history of their students and strive to enhance incorporation of different views in their classroom	Discussion boards Exams Papers	Class discussions Class presentations
9-ej-29-Oo Instructors understand and appreciate both social justice and ethical applications of skills in the classroom and work hard to ensure their daily use	Discussion boards Exams Papers	Class discussions Class presentations
11-15-fal Instructors understand the importance of collaboration with peers and the role of administration in guiding education	Discussion boards Exams Papers	Class discussions Class presentations

CLIENT AND STUDENT CONFIDENTIALITY

Application of the Online Platform Teaching and Education standards specify that educators will strive to provide students with quality education free from judgement and supporting and encouraging their unique skills and viewpoints. For this reason, instructors and students will maintain confidentiality of shared information by students during class or in their presentations or other assignments.

GENERAL COURSE REQUIREMENTS

Students are expected to review the following in student guidebook. A thorough explanation of each of the following is provided there.

Attendance and Participation: Students are expected to attend each class and actively participate in all discussions and complete all assignments by their due date. The attendance policy is available in the student guidebook and students are expected to be aware of its content. Professionalism is expected and assessed, see appendix A for details.

Professionalism: Students are expected to be in a quiet and professional setting with good internet access, a working camera and microphone and to check these elements prior to each class. Professionalism will be displayed in setting, actions, and language. Be sure to be visible with in the screen always and mute your microphone when not sharing. Lack of professionalism will result in points being deducted from your class participation grade.

Student Course Expectations:
These are provided to students in detail in their course shell under the content tab for review. Students are expected to have read them completely prior to the first class meeting.

Students are expected to ask for clarification or assistance as needed.

Failure to attend full classes will result in loss of points (see appendix A for details).

Students are not permitted to miss more than 2 classes per semester.

Technology is the responsibility of the student. Please check your camera, microphone and access to the online platform prior to the start time of each class.

Levai University Attendance, Participation and Professionalism Policy
Regular class attendance and active participation enhance student learning at Levai University. Your attendance will be noted, and late arrivals or early departures will result in loss of points.
Students are expected to:
  Prepare for each class by completing reading and assignments
  Check their emails and course announcements to stay up to date with the course
  Review the course schedule regularly to ensure timely submission of assignments
  Attend class on time, cameras on and contact their instructor should they feel the need for additional clarification or assistance about course materials or expectations.

Assignments: Be sure to check the course schedule, emails, and announcements so you don't miss any aspect of the class or due dates. Pay close attention to due dates and note that all assignments are due in Eastern Standard Time regardless of your location. Late assignments will lose points as noted on the rubric.

Writing: APA will be the writing style of this course. Please refer to the APA 7th edition manual. We will use the professional paper outline, as you will only be a student for a short time but a professional for the rest of your career.

Be sure to keep in mind the professional paper requires a cover page with a header, an abstract, citations and references. We will use these in all our assignments as practice as practice makes perfect.

Be sure to incorporate your instructors' feedback, as failure to incorporate it will result in points lost.

Grading and Professional Development: If you are struggling at any point during the semester, your instructor will ask to meet with you to develop a plan of improvement. This is not a punitive meeting, but instead an opportunity for you to gain insight into problem areas and share these with your instructor while brainstorming ways to improve. These meeting will be scheduled at a convenient time for you and your instructor.

Policies and Procedures: Be sure to review the policies and procedures of both Levai University and your particular course. Questions allow us to gain clarity and learn, so bring them to your instructor so your education will blossom.

Blackboard: For this course, Blackboard will be used for discussion board as well as a central place for all course information. For discussion board, which are meant to mimic conversations with your peers like in a brick and mortar classroom before or after class, the initial post is due by 11:59 p.m. EST on Monday, and the two responses to your peers' initial post are due by 11:59 pm EST on Wednesday.

Discussion boards will strive to be through yet concise, so strive to maintain a word limit of between 240–300 words. Points will not be deducted for those slightly above or below but will be if they exceed the limits by more than 25 words. Questions will be posted in Blackboard under the discussion tab.

Discussion board format: Students will answer the prompt provided by the instructor for their initial post and support their assertions with appropriate citations from current peer reviewed literature (peer reviewed journals are available through the Levai University library) and must be within the last 4–7 years to allow the discussion to be based in current trends and issues. Initial posts require at least 3 references.

Students will also respond to at least 3 peers initial post by Wednesday of the discussion board week. The same format will prevail, but this time only 2 references are required to support your statements. Be sure to keep your responses substantial, containing at least 5–6 sentences and reflecting you have read the post and are continuing the conversation points raised by your peer.

Submission of Assignments

All assignments must be completed thoroughly and will be submitted via the assignment link in Blackboard. Be sure to use the correct assignment link that matches the title of the assignment on the rubric to avoid loss of points and confusion in grading.

Assignments must contain the APA elements discussed under the writing expectations for this course, and must used the appropriate software, which is available through the University's IT department for students to use.

Internet and Software: You must have continuous access to a working and dependable internet provider as well as reliable email software that can send and receive attachments. You must also have access to Microsoft Word 2022 or later or PowerPoint 2021 or later for writing assignments.

Levai University Online Platform:

Students are required to activate their Levai University Online Platform to be able to access their course shells in Blackboard and attend classes. This may be downloaded at LevaiUniversityOnlinePlatform/download/student-access

Levai University Policies
Academic honesty and ethical teaching Statement

Levai University strives to provide students with an understanding and appreciation of academic honesty and ethical teaching. Students are expected to read the Levai University Academic Honesty and Ethical handbook and abide by the guidelines set forth. You can access this at LevaiuniversityAHandES.pdf

Any unethical behavior such as cheating, plagiarism or disregard for peers/student confidentiality may result in various outcomes including remediation with faculty to academic probation or failure of the course, depending upon the individual offense or pattern thereof.

Copyright Statement

Awareness of copywrite rules and regulations are expected by both faculty and students. Levai University expects all students to behave in a lawful and ethical manner to protect the rights of others.

Students Seeking Accommodation

Accommodations to assist students in succeeding are provided by contacting Mrs. Sherri Howe, Coordinator of Supporting Students through Accommodations office. An application must be completed and reviewed by Mrs. Howe. Any granted accommodations need to be re-evaluated each semester as requirements for classes vary and to ensure the appropriate accommodations are provided.

Instructors must be contacted by Mrs. Howe for the accommodations to go into play. The student guidebook contains additional information on this matter, or you may contact Mrs. Howe at mshowe@levaiuniversity.

SCHEDULE AND EVALUATION
COURSE SCHEDULE

Be sure check the course schedule regularly so you don't miss due dates. Late assignments lost points according to the associated rubric.

Notes:
- Online classes scheduled below will be on Monday from 8:00–1030 p.m. Eastern Standard Time.
- Individual meetings with the instructor may be scheduled by emailing the instructor your name, course number, a brief summary of the topic of discussion and at least two days and times that are convenient for you to meet. Please include your local time zone for reference and preference to discuss your questions/concerns in a phone call or video conference.
- Due dates and meeting times are posted in Eastern Standard Time.
- All assignments will be submitted via the assignment's links in blackboard
- Any changes to the course schedule will be posted in course announcements
- Failure to utilize the email address provided on this syllabus or from your Levai University student email account may result in emails being missed; please utilize tricia.mikolon@levaiuniversity for all course communications.

METHOD OF EVALUATION

Assignments will be graded and provided back to students within 7–10 days (depending on the assignment length). Feedback will be provided and is expected to be incorporated in future assignments.

Meeting with your instructor for clarification are always available by appointment.

COURSE REQUIREMENTS

ASSIGNMENT	DESCRIPTION

Attendance/ Participation, and Professionalism
 	
See Appendix A for grading rubric.
 	
10 points/class for a total of 160 points
	Students are expected to attend each class and actively participate in all discussion and complete all assignments.
	
	The attendance policy is available in the student guidebook and students are expected to be aware of its content.
	
	Professionalism is expected and assessed, see appendix A for details.
	
	Students are expected to be in a quiet and professional setting with good internet access, a working camera and microphone and to check these elements prior to each class.
	
	Professionalism will be displayed in setting, actions, and language. Be sure to be visible with in the screen at all times and mute your microphone when not sharing.
	
	Lack of professionalism will result in points being deducted from your class participation grade.
	
	Students are expected to ask for clarification or assistance as needed.
	
	Failure to attend full classes will result in loss of points (see appendix A for details).
	
	Students are not permitted to miss more than 2 classes per semester.
	
	Regular class attendance and active participation enhance student learning at Levai University.
	
	Your attendance will be noted, and late arrivals or early departures will result in loss of points.
	
	Students are expected to:
	    Prepare for each class by completing reading and assignments
	    Check their emails and course announcements to stay up to date with the course
	Attend class on time with cameras on
	    Contact their instructor should they feel the need for additional clarification or assistance about course materials or expectations.

(continued)

ASSIGNMENT	DESCRIPTION
Class Discussion and Discussion Boards See Appendix B for grading rubric. **Discussion boards are 100 points each.** **There are six for a total of 600 points.**	Students will attend weekly classes via the Levai online platform. Course materials are provided through the class shell in Blackboard. Students are expected to attend each class on time, actively participate and be on camera at all times. Students are expected to read their assigned reading prior to class and be prepared to discuss the assigned topics. Assignments will be submitted via the assignments link. Class presentations and completed assignments will evaluate the student's incorporation of the material into their teaching. For this course, Blackboard will be used for discussion board as well as a central place for all course information. For discussion board, which are meant to mimic conversations with your peers like in a brick and mortar classroom before or after class. The initial post is due by 11:59 p.m. EST on Monday, and the two responses to your peers' initial post are due by 11:59 pm EST on Wednesday. **Discussion boards** will strive to be through yet concise, so strive to maintain a word limit of between 240–300 words. Points will not be deducted for those slightly above or below but will be if they exceed the limits by more than 25 words. Questions will be posted in Blackboard under the discussion tab. **Discussion board format:** Students will answer the prompt provided by the instructor for their initial post and support their assertions with appropriate citations from current peer reviewed literature (peer reviewed journals are available through the Levai University library) and must be within the last 4–7 years to allow the discussion to be based in current trends and issues. Initial posts require at least 3 references. Students will also respond to at least 3 peers initial post by Wednesday of the discussion board week. The same format will prevail, but this time only 2 references are required to support your statements. Be sure to keep your responses substantial, containing at least 5–6 sentences and reflecting you have read the post and are continuing the conversation points raised by your peer. APA will be the writing style of this course. Please refer to the APA 7th edition manual. We will use the professional paper outline, as you will only be a student for a short time but a professional for the rest of your career. Be sure to keep in mind the professional paper requires a cover page, abstract, citations and references. We will use these in all our assignments as practice as practice makes perfect. Be sure to incorporate your instructors' feedback, as failure to incorporate it will result in points lost.

(continued)

ASSIGNMENT	DESCRIPTION
Online Teaching Project Outline See Appendix C 200 points	Students will develop an outline (lesson plan/course schedule) for 1 week of classes in primary or secondary school OR 5 weeks of classes for a college or graduate course Students will provide all the following elements: Learning modalities Assigned reading <ul><li>from a real textbook the student has researched Assigned supplemental reading</li><li>from real articles with APA references provided for each Discussion/lecture topics</li></ul>At least 1 of each of the following assignments:<ul><li>introduction discussion board</li><li>summary paper of a related topic</li></ul>
Integrating Teaching Skills to the Online Platform See Appendix D 200 points	Students will complete a summary checklist of necessary teaching skills and modifications to the online platform Students will develop the checklist of all necessary teaching skills for teaching a class of the topic of their choice Each adaption will be supported by evidence-based research from peer reviewed journals Journals will be from the last 4–7 years A total of 7 teaching skills with at least 2 modifications each will be provided Each modification will contain at least 1 peer reviewed reference to support it
Sample Syllabus Assignment See Appendix E 200 points	Students will develop a sample syllabus for the college or graduate course of their chose. Students will include all necessary information for the course including but not limited to: Course title Class meeting times Instructor's name and email Telephone: Number Office Hours: Days/times Mission Statement Course Description Required Text(s) Method of Instruction Email Best times and methods to contact instructor: Prerequisites Course Objectives <ul><li>citing related standards to the topics</li></ul>Client and student confidentiality (as applicable to course) GENERAL COURSE REQUIREMENTS 1. Attendance and Participation: Institutional Attendance and Participation Policy Professionalism:

(continued)

ASSIGNMENT	DESCRIPTION
	2. Assignments: Writing Grading/Professional Development 3. Policies and Procedures: Platform Specifics (e.g., Blackboard or Google classroom) Submission of Assignments Internet and Software: Institutional Policies Academic Honesty and Ethics Statement Copyright Statement: Students Seeking Accommodation: Schedule and Evaluation Method of Evaluation Method of Evaluating Student Performance (All assignments are fully described below.) Course Schedule
Accessibility and the Online Platform Presentation and Paper See Appendix F 200 points	Students will complete a 5–7-page paper discussing possible accessibility issues which may arise in their online classroom and how they plan to address each to enhance student learning and student success Students will include references to support their accessibility interventions 3–5 interventions will be explored minimally
Midterm Examination See Appendix G for grading rubric 100 points	Midterm examination will occur in week 9 It will cover all information from weeks 1–8 It will contain multiple choice, true and false and short fill ins to test student understanding of course materials. The textbook, PowerPoints and notes are permitted during the examination, but this is an individual not group project.
Final Examination See Appendix H for grading rubric. 100 points	Final examination will occur in week 16 It will cover all information from weeks 9–15 It will contain multiple choice, true and false and short fill ins to test student understanding of course materials. The textbook, PowerPoints and notes are permitted during the examination, but this is an individual not group project.
Total points: 1860	

Keep in mind that if you have handed in assignments previously related to our topics, be sure to paraphrase your information, not just copy and paste it. Self-plagiarism is handing in prior published words for new credit. For our class, we are going to practice avoiding this by always using new references or paraphrasing those we have previously used.

Practice will assist you in teaching this same skill to your students in the future.

GRADING SCALE	LETTER GRADE
95–100	A
89–94	A-
82–88	B+
77–81	B
70–76	B-
65–69	C
<64	F

DOCTORAL PROJECTS

Doctoral Students Taking this course will complete an additional project to enhance their learning beyond that of the master's students.

These students will complete either an individual OR group project, depending upon the number of doctoral students in the course.

The instructor will determine which project will be completed and will notify students in the first class.

Either project will result in an additional 500 points for the doctoral student's total possible points to equal **2360 points**.

Doctoral Group Project	Group Project:	Doctoral students will work in assigned group to develop an online teaching module and demonstration.
As noted above doctoral students will complete **ONE** *of these assignments as directed by the instructor*	Online teaching module and demonstration See Appendix I for details and rubrics	This project will include: 1. A paper identifying the evidence-based modification necessary to teach the topic online 2. A recorded presentation provided to the professor on the finding of the necessary modification related to the chosen topic and a demonstration of the modifications completed in a classroom setting.
		Student groups will pick one topic in which they plan to teach (i.e.: science, math, etc.) and complete a paper summarizing the skills necessary to teach this course in person, the necessary modification to instruct this course online, and the evidence-based practices to support this.
		This paper will contain at least 20 professional references within the last 7 years to support the presented information.
		Students will then complete a presentation, along with a PowerPoint to summarize their paper findings as well as a 30-minute demonstration of how these skills would be enacted in the classroom.
		Total presentation time is 60–70 minutes.
	Individual Project: Teaching philosophy presentation See appendix J for details and rubrics	Individual doctoral students will complete a paper on their teaching philosophy, addressing all of the following areas: Pedagogy Classroom management Supporting student success Student assessment Accessibility Multicultural classroom considerations Ethical classroom considerations Social Justice classroom considerations Remediation Professional Growth This paper will contain a minimum of 30 references Students will be assigned a week during the semester to their teaching philosophy to the class during class time and lead a discussion on the importance of each element explored.
Additional Points: 500		

Changes in the syllabus prior to the first day of class will be communicated through course announcements. Please check these and your email regularly.

SCHEDULE AND EVALUATION

COURSE SCHEDULE:
Please refer to the course schedule regularly so that you will be up to date on expectations, assigned reading and assignments.

TENTATIVE COURSE SCHEDULE

Class time and due dates are in Eastern Central Time, regardless of your local time zone.

WEEK	TOPICS	READINGS OR ASSIGNMENTS FOR THIS WEEK'S CLASS
Week 1	Introduction to class Review of the syllabus and course expectations Review of assignments and rubrics	Introduction **Completion of Discussion Board 1: class introductions** No references necessary for this discussion board.
Week 2	Preparing teach online Why teach online? Pros/cons Considerations Home office and technology needs	Chapter 1
Week 3	Pedagogy and its history Traditional pedagogy Heutagogy E-pedagogy Inclusive frameworks Trauma informed pedagogy	Chapter 2
Week 4	Online pedagogy Effective teaching strategies Building community and co-creating knowledge	Chapter 2 continued **Discussion Board 2 due**
Week 5	Diversity and inclusion in the online classroom Multicultural issues/factors Critical cross-education Intersectionality	Chapter 3
Week 6	Fostering student success online Classroom management Supporting student success Communication Building a sense of community and connectedness Assessment and Remediation	Chapter 4
Week 7	Online course design Online learning environments vs. storage closets	Chapter 5 **Discussion Board 3 due**

(continued)

WEEK	TOPICS	READINGS OR ASSIGNMENTS FOR THIS WEEK'S CLASS
Week 8	Accessibility in the online classroom for student success Unique challenges and proactive approaches	Chapter 6 **Accessibility assignment due**
Week 9	**Midterm Examination** link available under the assignments link	**Midterm Examination due by Tuesday at 1159 pm EST.**
Week 10	Developing the online syllabus Necessary elements and considerations	Chapter 7 **Syllabus assignment due**
Week 11	Online teaching and learning in primary education Student engagement Communication Assessment Remediation	Chapter 8 **Discussion board 4 due**
Week 12	Online teaching and learning in secondary education Student engagement Communication Assessment Remediation	Chapter 9 **Discussion board 5 due**
Week 13	Online teaching and learning in post-secondary education Student engagement Communication Assessment Remediation	Chapter 10 **Online teaching outline assignment due**
Week 14	Legal and ethical issues in online teaching Principles of ethics Moral distress Ethical decision making Gatekeeping	Chapter 11 **Discussion board 6 due**
Week 15	Administration of online teaching Leadership Building a team Student engagement and support services Legal and ethical considerations for administrators	Chapter 12 **Integrative teaching assignment due** **Doctoral group or individual project due if applicable**
Week 16	**Final Examination**	**Final Examination due by Tuesday at 1159 pm EST.**

Appendix A

Attendance and Participation

Weekly attendance will be required. Absences must be excused prior to class and make-up assignments may be required to receive partial credit for a missed class.

Note: There is a range of points for items, these are dependent upon the extent of the behavior exhibited.

Week	10 points	9-5 points	4-1 point	0 points
1	Attends class on time, stays for whole class, on camera entire while, contributes to class discussion in professional manner.	Attends entire class and is always on camera, participates in chat only, not involved in verbal discussions.	Attends class but does not participate fully or is unprofessional. May not always be on camera, distracted by things off camera at times.	Fails to attend class and/or fails to add anything to the learning process
2	Attends class on time, stays for whole class, on camera entire while, contributes to class discussion in professional manner.	Attends entire class and is always on camera, participates in chat only, not involved in verbal discussions.	Attends class but does not participate fully or is unprofessional. May not always be on camera, distracted by things off camera at times.	Fails to attend class and/or fails to add anything to the learning process
3	Attends class on time, stays for whole class, on camera entire while, contributes to class discussion in professional manner.	Attends entire class and is always on camera, participates in chat only, not involved in verbal discussions.	Attends class but does not participate fully or is unprofessional. May not always be on camera, distracted by things off camera at times.	Fails to attend class and/or fails to add anything to the learning process
4	Attends class on time, stays for whole class, on camera entire while, contributes to class discussion in professional manner.	Attends entire class and is always on camera, participates in chat only, not involved in verbal discussions.	Attends class but does not participate fully or is unprofessional. May not always be on camera, distracted by things off camera at times.	Fails to attend class and/or fails to add anything to the learning process
5	Attends class on time, stays for whole class, on camera entire while, contributes to class discussion in professional manner.	Attends entire class and is always on camera, participates in chat only, not involved in verbal discussions.	Attends class but does not participate fully or is unprofessional. May not always be on camera, distracted by things off camera at times.	Fails to attend class and/or fails to add anything to the learning process
6	Attends class on time, stays for whole class, on camera entire while, contributes to class discussion in professional manner.	Attends entire class and is always on camera, participates in chat only, not involved in verbal discussions.	Attends class but does not participate fully or is unprofessional. May not always be on camera, distracted by things off camera at times.	Fails to attend class and/or fails to add anything to the learning process
7	Attends class on time, stays for whole class, on camera entire while, contributes to class discussion in professional manner.	Attends entire class and is always on camera, participates in chat only, not involved in verbal discussions.	Attends class but does not participate fully or is unprofessional. May not always be on camera, distracted by things off camera at times.	Fails to attend class and/or fails to add anything to the learning process
8	Attends class on time, stays for whole class, on camera entire while, contributes to class discussion in professional manner.	Attends entire class and is always on camera, participates in chat only, not involved in verbal discussions.	Attends class but does not participate fully or is unprofessional. May not always be on camera, distracted by things off camera at times.	Fails to attend class and/or fails to add anything to the learning process

(continued)

Week	10 points	9-5 points	4-1 point	0 points
9	Attends class on time, stays for whole class, on camera entire while, contributes to class discussion in professional manner.	Attends entire class and is always on camera, participates in chat only, not involved in verbal discussions.	Attends class but does not participate fully or is unprofessional. May not always be on camera, distracted by things off camera at times.	Fails to attend class and/or fails to add anything to the learning process
10	Attends class on time, stays for whole class, on camera entire while, contributes to class discussion in professional manner.	Attends entire class and is always on camera, participates in chat only, not involved in verbal discussions.	Attends class but does not participate fully or is unprofessional. May not always be on camera, distracted by things off camera at times.	Fails to attend class and/or fails to add anything to the learning process
11	Attends class on time, stays for whole class, on camera entire while, contributes to class discussion in professional manner.	Attends entire class and is always on camera, participates in chat only, not involved in verbal discussions.	Attends class but does not participate fully or is unprofessional. May not always be on camera, distracted by things off camera at times.	Fails to attend class and/or fails to add anything to the learning process
12	Attends class on time, stays for whole class, on camera entire while, contributes to class discussion in professional manner.	Attends entire class and is always on camera, participates in chat only, not involved in verbal discussions.	Attends class but does not participate fully or is unprofessional. May not always be on camera, distracted by things off camera at times.	Fails to attend class and/or fails to add anything to the learning process
13	Attends class on time, stays for whole class, on camera entire while, contributes to class discussion in professional manner.	Attends entire class and is always on camera, participates in chat only, not involved in verbal discussions.	Attends class but does not participate fully or is unprofessional. May not always be on camera, distracted by things off camera at times.	Fails to attend class and/or fails to add anything to the learning process
14	Attends class on time, stays for whole class, on camera entire while, contributes to class discussion in professional manner.	Attends entire class and is always on camera, participates in chat only, not involved in verbal discussions.	Attends class but does not participate fully or is unprofessional. May not always be on camera, distracted by things off camera at times.	Fails to attend class and/or fails to add anything to the learning process
15	Attends class on time, stays for whole class, on camera entire while, contributes to class discussion in professional manner.	Attends entire class and is always on camera, participates in chat only, not involved in verbal discussions.	Attends class but does not participate fully or is unprofessional. May not always be on camera, distracted by things off camera at times.	Fails to attend class and/or fails to add anything to the learning process
16	Attends class on time, stays for whole class, on camera entire while, contributes to class discussion in professional manner.	Attends entire class and is always on camera, participates in chat only, not involved in verbal discussions.	Attends class but does not participate fully or is unprofessional. May not always be on camera, distracted by things off camera at times.	Fails to attend class and/or fails to add anything to the learning process
Total Points Earned:				

Instructor comments:

Points Summary:
   10 points: Attends class on time, stays for whole class, on camera entire while, contributes to class discussion in professional manner.
   9-5 points: Attends session, participates in chat only
   4-1 point: Attends, participation is not voluntary, lacks professionalism
   0 points: Fails to attend or participate, fails to add to discussions

Points will be deducted for late arrivals:
   Late < 5 minutes -1
   Late > 5 minutes but <10 minutes -3
   Late <10 minutes -5

Failure to attend two or the equivalent of two classes will result in a failing grade for this course.

Appendix B

Discussion Board Grading Rubric
Please read and respond to the prompt under the discussion tab in blackboard

CRITERION	15	10	7	4	0
Initial post	Initial post is completed on time, formatted according to APA directions, addresses the prompt completely and contains the full number of references. Citations are appropriate to the topic and from appropriate sources.	Initial post is completed on time but lacks some APA formatting, or addresses most of the prompt, or contains total number of necessary references with appropriate citations, but sources are not all peer reviewed or too old.	Initial post is 1 day late and lacks one of the following: Appropriate number of references, References from appropriate sources, or Contains significant APA errors	Initial post is 2 days late and lacks two of the following: Appropriate number of references, References from appropriate sources, or Contains significant APA errors	Initial post is 3 or more days late and lacks all of the following: Appropriate number of references, References from appropriate sources, or Contains significant APA errors

CRITERION	17	10	6	4	0
Responses to peers' initial posts	Completed on time	Completed with 2 hours of deadline	Completed within 12 hours of deadline	Completed within 1 day of deadline	Not completed or completed over a day late
Citations and responses are related to topic.	Citations and responses are related to topics	Citations and responses are mostly related to topics	Citations and responses are somewhat related to topics	Citations and responses are minimally related to topics	Citations and responses are not related to topics
Response is related to peers' initial post and adds to the conversation	Responses to post add significantly to the conversation	Responses to post add mostly to the conversation	Responses to post add somewhat to the conversation	Responses to post add little to the conversation	Responses to post do not add to the conversation

(continued)

Additive and substantial responses	Response is additive and substantial. Contains at least 2 paragraphs of 3 sentences each.	Response is mostly additive and responsive	Response is somewhat additive and responsive	Response is minimally additive and responsive	Response is not additive or responsive.
APA	APA is error free	Contains minimal APA errors	Contains some APA errors	Contains significant APA errors	Lacks APA formatting
Total: 100					

Professor Comments:

Appendix C

Online Teaching Project Outline

Students will develop an outline (lesson plan/course schedule) for 1 week of classes in primary or secondary school OR 5 weeks of classes for a college or graduate course

Students will provide all the following elements:

Learning modalities
Assigned reading

- from a real textbook the student has researched

Assigned supplemental reading

- from real articles with APA references provided for each

Discussion/lecture topics
At least 1 of each of the following assignments:

- introduction discussion board
- summary paper of a related topic

ONLINE TEACHING PROJECT OUTLINE RUBRIC

CRITERIA	40 POINTS	30 POINTS	15 POINTS	0 POINTS
Learning modalities	Learning modalities are clearly outlined with pedagogy explained and contain at least three of the following: • lecture with handouts/PowerPoint, • classroom discussions with or without break out rooms • reflective assignments/journal • in class activities	Learning modalities are clearly outlined with pedagogy explained and contain at least two of the following: • lecture with handouts/PowerPoint, • classroom discussions with or without break out rooms • reflective assignments/journal • in class activities	Learning modalities are somewhat outlined with pedagogy explained minimally and contain at least one of the following: • lecture with handouts/PowerPoint, • classroom discussions with or without break out rooms • reflective assignments/journal • in class activities	Learning modalities are not outlined and/or pedagogy is not explained and/or failed to include means of sharing or processing information with students

(continued)

CRITERIA	40 POINTS	30 POINTS	15 POINTS	0 POINTS
Assigned readings and supplemental readings	Assigned readings and supplemental readings are actual sources verified and provided with APA formatted references	Assigned readings and supplemental readings are actual sources verified but not provided with APA formatted references	Assigned readings and supplemental readings are not all actual sources (over 50% are) verified and some may not be provided with APA formatted references	Assigned readings and supplemental readings are not actual sources verified and failed to provided with APA formatted references
Discussion/lecture topics	Discussion/lecture topics are clearly outlined and appropriate to the topics	Discussion/lecture topics are somewhat clearly outlined and appropriate to the topics	Discussion/lecture topics are minimally outlined and appropriate to the topics	Discussion/lecture topics are not clearly outlined and/or not appropriate to the topics
Introduction discussion board prompt	Introduction discussion board prompt is clear and concise	Introduction discussion board prompt is somewhat clear and concise	Introduction discussion board prompt is minimally clear and concise; may cause some confusion in interpretation or is too wordy	Introduction discussion board prompt is neither clear nor concise
Outline of summary paper on related topic	Outline of summary paper on related topic is clear and complete	Outline of summary paper on related topic is somewhat clear and complete	Outline of summary paper on related topic is minimally clear and complete; may cause some confusion or contains incomplete thoughts	Outline of summary paper on related topic is unclear and/or incomplete
Total points: 200				

Appendix D

Integration of Teaching Skills to Online Platform

Students will complete a summary checklist of necessary teaching skills and modifications to the online platform

Students will develop the checklist of all necessary teaching skills for teaching a class of the topic of their choice

Each adaption will be supported by evidence-based research from peer reviewed journals

Journals will be from the last 4–7 years

A total of 7 teaching skills with at least 2 modifications each will be provided

Each modification will contain at least 1 peer reviewed reference to support it

Integration of Teaching Skills to Online Platform

CRITERIA	40 POINTS	30 POINTS	15 POINTS	0 POINTS
Class topic	Clearly identified class topic	Class topic identified but is somewhat unclear	Class topic is unclear or too complicated	Class topic is not stated
Modifications	Modifications are appropriate to the online platform	Modifications are somewhat appropriate to the online platform	Modifications are minimally appropriate to the online platform	Modifications are not appropriate to the online platform
Evidence-based support for modifications	Each modification is supported clearly by evidence-based literature	Each modification is supported to some degree by evidence-based literature	Each modification is supported minimally by evidence-based literature	Each modification is not supported clearly by evidence-based literature
7 teaching skills with 2 modifications each	7 teaching skills with 2 modifications each are provided	6 teaching skills with 2 modifications each are provided	5 teaching skills with 2 modifications each	4 teaching skills with less than 2 modifications provided for each
Journals are 4–7 years old	Journals are current with 7 years oldest	Journals are current with 8–9 years oldest	Journals are current with 10 years oldest	Journals are either not provided or are older than 10 years
Total points: 200				

Appendix E

Sample Syllabus

Students will develop a sample syllabus for the college or graduate course of their chose.

Students will include all necessary information for the course including but not limited to:

Course title

Class meeting times

Instructor's name and email

Telephone: Number

Office Hours: Days/times

Mission Statement

Course Description

Required Text(s)

Method of Instruction

Email

Best times and methods to contact instructor:

Prerequisites

Course Objectives

- citing related standards to the topics

Client and student confidentiality (as applicable to course)

GENERAL COURSE REQUIREMENTS

1. Attendance and Participation
   Institutional Attendance and Participation Policy
   Professionalism

2. Assignments
   Writing
   Grading/Professional Development

3. Policies and Procedures
   Platform Specifics (e.g., Blackboard or Google classroom)
   Submission of Assignments
   Internet and Software
   Institutional Policies
   Academic Honesty and Ethics Statement
   Copyright Statement

   Students Seeking Accommodation
   Schedule and Evaluation
   Method of Evaluation
   Method of Evaluating Student Performance (All assignments are fully described.)
   Course Schedule

(continued)

Sample Syllabus Rubric

CRITERIA	20 POINTS	10 POINTS	5 POINTS	0 POINTS
Class meeting times Instructor's name and email Telephone: Number Office Hours: Days/times	Fully addresses each of the prompts noted in the criteria	Mostly addresses each of the prompts in the criteria	Fails to fully address each prompt in the criteria or fails to address 1 or more prompts	Fails to address prompts
Mission Statement Course Description Required Text(s) Method of Instruction	Fully addresses each of the prompts noted in the criteria	Mostly addresses each of the prompts in the criteria	Fails to fully address each prompt in the criteria or fails to address 1 or more prompts	Fails to address prompts
Email Best times and methods to contact instructor: Prerequisites Course Objectives	Fully addresses each of the prompts noted in the criteria	Mostly addresses each of the prompts in the criteria	Fails to fully address each prompt in the criteria or fails to address 1 or more prompts	Fails to address prompts
Attendance and Participation: Institutional Attendance and Participation Policy Professionalism:	Fully addresses each of the prompts noted in the criteria	Mostly addresses each of the prompts in the criteria	Fails to fully address each prompt in the criteria or fails to address 1 or more prompts	Fails to address prompts
Assignments: Writing Grading/Professional Development	Fully addresses each of the prompts noted in the criteria	Mostly addresses each of the prompts in the criteria	Fails to fully address each prompt in the criteria or fails to address 1 or more prompts	Fails to address prompts
Policies and Procedures: Platform Specifics (e.g., Blackboard or Google classroom) Submission of Assignments Internet and Software Institutional Policies Academic Honesty and Ethics Statement Copyright Statement	Fully addresses each of the prompts noted in the criteria	Mostly addresses each of the prompts in the criteria	Fails to fully address each prompt in the criteria or fails to address 1 or more prompts	Fails to address prompts
Students Seeking Accommodation	Fully addresses each of the prompts noted in the criteria	Mostly addresses each of the prompts in the criteria	Fails to fully address each prompt in the criteria or fails to address 1 or more prompts	Fails to address prompts
Schedule and Evaluation Method of Evaluation	Fully addresses each of the prompts noted in the criteria	Mostly addresses each of the prompts in the criteria	Fails to fully address each prompt in the criteria or fails to address 1 or more prompts	Fails to address prompts
Method of Evaluating Student Performance	Fully addresses each of the prompts noted in the criteria	Mostly addresses each of the prompts in the criteria	Fails to fully address each prompt in the criteria or fails to address 1 or more prompts	Fails to address prompts

(continued)

CRITERIA	20 POINTS	10 POINTS	5 POINTS	0 POINTS
Course Schedule	Fully addresses the topic and provides detailed examples addressing each important element	Mostly addresses the topic and provides detailed examples addressing each important element	Minimally addresses the topic and provides detailed examples addressing each important element	Fails to address prompts
Total points: 200				

Appendix F

Accessibility and the Online Platform

Students will complete a 5–7-page paper discussing possible accessibility issues which may arise in their online classroom and how they plan to address each to enhance student learning and student success

Students will include references to support their accessibility interventions

3–5 interventions will be explored minimally

Accessibility and the Online Platform Paper Rubric

CRITERIA	40 POINTS	30 POINTS	15 POINTS	0 POINTS
Accessibility issues are identified	Accessibility issues are identified fully	Accessibility issues are identified somewhat	Accessibility issues are identified minimally	Accessibility issues are not identified
Interventions are provided to enhance student learning and student success	Interventions to enhance student learning and success are provided and explained fully	Interventions to enhance student learning and success are somewhat provided and explained	Interventions to enhance student learning and success are minimally provided and explained	Interventions to enhance student learning and success are not provided and nor explained fully
Intervention are supported by evidence-based references	Interventions are fully supported by evidence-based references.	Interventions are mostly supported by evidence-based references.	Interventions are somewhat supported by evidence-based references.	Interventions are not supported by evidence-based references.
3–5 interventions are explored minimally	4–5 interventions are explored	3 interventions are explored	2 intervention is explored	Less than 2 intervention are explored
APA formatting	APA is error free	APA has minor errors	APA as significant errors	Lacks APA formatting
Total 200 points				

Appendix G

Midterm Examination
The midterm examination is worth 100 points.

Midterm examination will occur in week 9

It will cover all information from weeks 1–8

It will contain multiple choice, true and false and short fill ins to test student understanding of course materials.

The textbook, PowerPoints and notes are permitted during the examination, but this is an individual not group project.

Appendix H

Final Examination
The final examination is worth 100 points.

Final examination will occur in week 16

It will cover all information from weeks 9–15

It will contain multiple choice, true and false and short fill ins to test student understanding of course materials.

The textbook, PowerPoints and notes are permitted during the examination, but this is an individual not group project.

Appendix I

Doctoral Student Group Project
Doctoral students will work in assigned group to develop an online teaching module and demonstration.
This project will include:

1. a paper identifying the evidence-based modification necessary to teach the topic online
2. A recorded presentation provided to the professor on the finding of the necessary modification related to the chosen topic and a demonstration of the modifications completed in a classroom setting.

Student groups will pick one topic in which they plan to teach (i.e.: science, math, etc.) and complete a paper summarizing the skills necessary to teach this course in person, the necessary modification to instruct this course online, and the evidence-based practices to support this.

This paper will contain at least 20 professional references within the last 7 years to support the presented information.

Students will then complete a presentation, along with a PowerPoint to summarize their paper findings as well as a 30-minute demonstration of how these skills would be enacted in the classroom. Total presentation time is 60–70 minutes.

Doctoral Group Project Paper Rubric

CRITERIA	40 POINTS	30 POINTS	15 POINTS	0 POINTS
Necessary skills to teach topic online	Fully addresses the necessary skills to teach the topic online	Mostly addresses the necessary skills to teach the topic online	Minimally addresses the necessary skills to teach the topic online	Fails to address the necessary skills to teach the topic online
Modifications are appropriate and evidence based	Fully addresses the modifications and each is appropriate, and evidence based	Mostly addresses the modifications and each is appropriate, and evidence based	Minimally addresses the modifications and not all are appropriate, and evidence based	Fails adequately address the modifications or provides a majority which are not appropriate, or evidence based
Discussion connects purpose of skills and modification to student success	Fully addresses how the discussion connects the purpose and skills to the modification and student success	Mostly addresses how the discussion connects the purpose and skills to the modification and student success	Minimally addresses how the discussion connects the purpose and skills to the modification and student success	Fails to fully address how the discussion connects the purpose and skills to the modification and student success
At least 20 references, all of which are recent	20 references, all are current and no more than 7 years old	15–19 references and/or no more than 8 years old	10–14 references, majority no more than 8 years old	Less than 10 references and majority are more than 8 years old

(continued)

CRITERIA	40 POINTS	30 POINTS	15 POINTS	0 POINTS
APA formatting and references	APA is error free, contains 30 or more references	APA has minor errors and/or contains 25–29 references	APA as significant errors and/or contains 15–24 references	Lacks APA formatting and/or contains less than 15 references
Total 200 points				

Doctoral Group Presentation Rubric

CRITERIA	50 POINTS	40 POINTS	30 POINTS	0 POINTS
Presentation is well prepared and within time limits	Presentation is well prepared and within time limits	Presentation is somewhat prepared and within time limits within 2 minutes	Presentation is minimally prepared and within time limits within 3–4 minutes	Presentation is not well prepared and is not within time limits by more than 5 minutes
Presentation provides a summary of necessary modifications to modification related to the chosen topic	Presentation provides a thorough summary of necessary modifications to modification related to the chosen topic	Presentation provides a mostly complete summary of necessary modifications to modification related to the chosen topic	Presentation provides a minimally complete summary of necessary modifications to modification related to the chosen topic	Presentation does not provides a summary of necessary modifications to modification related to the chosen topic
Presentation contains a demonstration of the modifications completed in a classroom setting.	Presentation contains a complete and appropriate demonstration of the modifications completed in a classroom setting	Presentation contains a mostly complete and appropriate demonstration of the modifications completed in a classroom setting	Presentation contains a minimally complete and appropriate demonstration of the modifications completed in a classroom setting	Presentation does not contain a complete and appropriate demonstration of the modifications completed in a classroom setting
Presentation is engaging for the viewer	Presentation is engaging for the viewer	Presentation is mostly engaging for the viewer	Presentation is minimally engaging for the viewer	Presentation is not engaging for the viewer
Presenters are professional and well prepared	Presenters are professional and well prepared	Presenters are mostly professional and/or well prepared	Presenters are minimally professional and/or well prepared	Presenters are either not professional and/or not well prepared
Presenters maintain audience attention and engagement	Presenters maintain significant audience attention and engagement	Presenters maintain good audience attention and engagement	Presenters maintain minimal audience attention and engagement	Presenters fails to maintain audience attention and/or engagement
Total 300 points				

Appendix J

Doctoral Student Individual Project

Individual doctoral students will complete a paper on their teaching philosophy, addressing all the following areas:

Pedagogy

Classroom management
Supporting student success
Student assessment

Accessibility

Multicultural classroom considerations
Ethical classroom considerations
Social Justice classroom considerations

Remediation

Professional Growth

This paper will contain a minimum of 30 references

Students will be assigned a week during the semester to their teaching philosophy to the class during class time and lead a discussion on the importance of each element explored.

Doctoral Student Individual Project Paper Rubric

CRITERIA	40 POINTS	30 POINTS	15 POINTS	0 POINTS
Pedagogy	Fully addresses pedagogy and explains personal choices and applications	Mostly addresses pedagogy and explains personal choices and applications	Minimally addresses pedagogy and explains personal choices and applications	Fails to address pedagogy and explains personal choices and applications
Classroom management Supporting student success Student assessment	Fully addresses each of the prompts in the criteria	Mostly addresses each of the prompts in the criteria	Fails to fully address each prompt in the criteria or fails to address 1 or more prompts does not fully expand on the presented ideas	Fails to address prompts
Accessibility Multicultural classroom considerations Ethical classroom considerations Social Justice classroom considerations	Fully addresses each of the prompts noted in the criteria	Mostly addresses each of the prompts in the criteria	Fails to fully address each prompt in the criteria or fails to address 1 or more prompts or does not fully expand on the presented ideas	Fails to address prompts
Remediation Professional Growth	Fully addresses each of the prompts noted in the criteria	Mostly addresses each of the prompts in the criteria	Fails to fully address each prompt in the criteria or fails to address 1 or more prompts or does not fully expand on the presented ideas	Fails to address prompts

(continued)

CRITERIA	40 POINTS	30 POINTS	15 POINTS	0 POINTS
APA formatting and references	APA is error free, contains 30 or more references	APA has minor errors and/or contains 25–29 references	APA as significant errors and/or contains 15–24 references	Lacks APA formatting and/or contains less than 15 references
Total 200 points				

Presentation Rubric

CRITERIA	50 POINTS	40 POINTS	30 POINTS	0 POINTS
Classroom presentation addressed pedagogy and its importance related to the topic	Classroom presentation thoroughly addressed pedagogy and its importance related to the topic	Classroom presentation significantly addressed pedagogy and its importance related to the topic	Classroom presentation mostly addressed pedagogy and its importance related to the topic	Classroom presentation failed to address pedagogy and its importance related to the topic
Classroom presentation addressed classroom management, supporting student success and student assessment	Classroom presentation thoroughly addressed classroom management, supporting student success and student assessment	Classroom presentation significantly addressed classroom management, supporting student success and student assessment	Classroom presentation mostly addressed classroom management, supporting student success and student assessment	Classroom presentation failed to address classroom management, supporting student success and student assessment
Classroom presentation addressed accessibility in the classroom	Classroom presentation thoroughly addressed accessibility in the classroom	Classroom presentation significantly addressed accessibility in the classroom	Classroom presentation mostly addressed accessibility in the classroom	Classroom presentation failed to address accessibility in the classroom
Classroom presentation addressed multicultural, social justice, and ethical considerations related to the topic	Classroom presentation thoroughly addressed multicultural, social justice, and ethical considerations related to the topic	Classroom presentation significantly addressed multicultural, social justice, and ethical considerations related to the topic	Classroom presentation mostly addressed multicultural, social justice, and ethical considerations related to the topic	Classroom presentation failed to address multicultural, social justice, and ethical considerations related to the topic
Classroom presentation addressed remediation and professional growth	Classroom presentation thoroughly addressed remediation and professional growth	Classroom presentation significantly addressed remediation and professional growth	Classroom presentation mostly addressed remediation and professional growth	Classroom presentation failed to address remediation and professional growth
Classroom presentation addressed all student questions in a thorough and professional manner, good classroom and time management was evident	Classroom presentation addressed all student questions in a thorough and professional manner, good classroom and time management was evident	Classroom presentation addressed all student questions in a mostly thorough and professional manner, and/or mostly good classroom and time management was evident	Classroom presentation addressed all student questions in a somewhat thorough and professional manner, and/or somewhat good classroom and time management was evident	Classroom presentation failed to address all student questions in a thorough and professional manner, or good classroom and time management was not evident
Total 300 points				

Chapter Summary

The course syllabus provides both structure for the course and an effective means of communication between the instructor and students during the course. Providing the syllabus prior to the first class meeting allows students to review course requirements and to prepare their schedules to incorporate time for classes and assignments. Additionally, the syllabus serves as an outline of course expectations, thus allowing each student to make an informed decision regarding their responsibilities necessary to succeed in the course. The more detailed the information provided, the firmer foundation upon which the course is built. Reviewing the syllabus with students in the first meeting allows for clarification, as necessary, and solidifies expectations for both instructors and students. A well-written syllabus serves as a fundamental course guide throughout the course and as a reference for course schedules, assignments, and expectations, and provides a safeguard for course communication.

Online Resources

Useful resources for consideration in the development of an online syllabus are provided below:

Accreditation Commission Council on Occupational Education

Various program accreditations: https://council.org/manuals/

Accrediting Commission of Career Schools and Colleges (ACCSC)

Standards of Accreditation, Section IX- Distance Education, Standards C and D: http://www.accsc.org/UploadedDocuments/1954/ACCSC-Standards-of-Accreditation-and-Bylaws-070120.pdf

Accrediting Council for Continuing Education and Training (ACCET)

Standard V- Curricula, Standard V- Instructional Delivery: http://docs.accet.org/downloads/docs/doc2.pdf

Accrediting Council for Independent Colleges and Schools (ACICS)

Title 3 Evaluation Standards, Chapters 2–6: https://static1.squarespace.com/static/5ce58a38738b880001909396/t/5e305b667204aa2d261bc883/1580227431231/January+2020+ACICS+Accreditation+Criteria.pdf

American Psychological Association (APA)

For psychology; Accreditation for Programs in Health Service Psychology, Section II. Aims, Competencies, Curriculum, and Outcomes, Standards B, C, and D1: https://www.apa.org/ed/accreditation/about/policies/standards-of-accreditation.pdf

Association of Advanced Rabbinical and Talmudic Schools (AARTS)

https://www.chea.org/association-advanced-rabbinical-and-talmudic-schools-accreditation-commission

Council for Accreditation of Counseling and Related Educational Programs (CACREP)

For counseling; Section 2: Professional Counseling Identity, Counseling Curriculum, Standards D, E, F1–8: https://www.cacrep.org/section-2-professional-counseling-identity/

Council for the Accreditation of Education Preparation (CAEP)

For education; Standard 1. Content and Pedagogical Knowledge, 1.1–1.5: http://caepnet.org/~/media/Files/caep/standards/caep-standards-one-pager-0219.pdf?la=en

Council for Higher Education Accreditation (CHEA)

Clearing house for information regarding accreditation on various programs: https://www.chea.org/about-accreditation

Distance Education Accrediting Commission (DEAC)

Accreditation Handbook, Section 3: Accreditation Standards, Standard III: Program Outcomes, Curricula, and Materials, Core Components A-J: https://www.deac.org/UploadedDocuments/Handbook/Accreditation-Handbook-Part-Three.pdf

International Accreditation Counsel for Business Education (IACBE)

For business; Section 3: New Program Accreditation Principles, Principle 2: Curriculum, sections 2.1-2.1: https://iacbe.org/wp-content/uploads/2017/08/new-program-accreditation-manual.pdf

Simple Syllabus

Policy and content guide: https://simplesyllabus.com/what-policies-should-i-include-in-my-syllabus/

References

Bailey, M., Ifenthaler, D., Gosper, M., & Kretzschmar, M. (2014). Factors influencing tertiary students' choice of study mode. In B. Hegarty, J. McDonald, & S.-K. Loke (Eds.), *Rhetoric and reality: Critical perspectives on educational technology* (pp. 251–261). ASCILITE.

Bates, A. W. (2005). *Technology, e-learning and distance education*. Routledge.

Brown, A. (1997). Designing for learning: What are the essential features of an effective online course? *Australian Journal of Educational Technology, 13*(2), 115-126. https://doi.org/10.14742/ajet.1926

Caughlin, D. E. (2014). Enhancing your teaching experience: Developing your teaching philosophy, course syllabus, and teaching portfolio. *TIP: The Industrial-Organizational Psychologist, 52*(2), 94–99.

Cleveland-Innes, M., & Ally, M. (2009). Affective learning outcomes in workplace training: A test of synchronous vs. asynchronous learning environments. *Canadian Journal of University Continuing Education, 30*(1), 15-35. https://doi.org/10.21225/D5259V

Johnson, G. M. (2015). On-campus and fully-online university students: Comparing demographics, digital technology use and learning characteristics. *Journal of University Teaching and Learning Practice, 12*(1), 11–51.

Goodman, L. A., Liang, B., Helms, J. E., Latta, R. E., Sparks, E., & Weintraub, S. R. (2004). Training counseling psychologists as social justice agents: Feminist and multicultural principles in action. *Counseling Psychologist, 32*(6), 793–837. https://doi.org/10.1177%2F0011000004268802

Goralski, M. A., & Falk, L. K. (2017). Online vs. brick and mortar learning: Competition or complementary. *Competition Forum, 15*(2), 271–277.

Grunert O'Brien, J., Millis, B. J., & Cohen, M. W. (2009). *The course syllabus: A learning-centered approach* (2nd ed.). Wiley.

Kentnor, H. E. (2015). Distance education and the evolution of online learning in the United States. *Curriculum and Teaching Dialogue, 17*(1–2), 21–34.

Ko, S., & Rosen, S. (2001). *Teaching online: A practical guide*. Houghton Mifflin.

Merisotis, J. P., & Phipps, R. A. (1999). What's the difference? *Change, 31*(3), 12–17.

Mintu-Wimsatt, A., Kernek, C., & Lozada, H. R. (2010). Netiquette: Make it part of your syllabus. *MERLOT Journal of Online Learning and Teaching, 6*(1), 264-267.

Palloff, R. M., & Pratt, K. (2001). *Lessons from the cyberspace classroom: The realities of online teaching*. Jossey-Bass.

Parkes, J., & Harris, M. B. (2010) The purposes of syllabus. *College Teaching, 50*(2), 55–61. https://doi.org/10.1080/87567550209595875Pedersen, P. B. (1991). Multiculturalism as a fourth force in counseling. *Journal of Counseling and Development, 70*(1), 6–12. https://doi.org/10.1002/j.1556-6676.1991.tb01555.x

Pepicello, B., & Rice, E. (2000). Reshaping teaching and learning: The role of liberal arts in online education. In K. W. White & B. H. Weight (Eds.), *The online teaching guide: A handbook of attitudes, strategies, and techniques for the virtual classroom* (pp. 45–56). Allyn and Bacon.

Pieterse, A. L., Evans, S. A., Risner-Butner, A., Collins, N. M., & Mason, L. B. (2008). Multicultural competence and social justice training in counseling psychology and counselor education: A review and analysis of a sample of multicultural course syllabi. *Counseling Psychologist, 37*(1), 93–115.

Ramsey, P. G., Williams, L. R., & Vold, E. B. (2003). *Multicultural education: A source book* (2nd ed.). Routledge.

Roberts, J. J. (2019). Online learning as a form of distance education: Linking formation learning in theology to the theories of distance education. *HTS Teologiese Studies/Theological Studies, 75*(1), e1–e9.

Roddy, C., Amiet, D. L., Chung, J., Holt, C., Shaw, L., McKenzie, S., Garivaldis, F., Lodge, J. M., & Mundy, M. E. (2017). Applying best practice online learning, teaching, and support to intensive online environments: An integrative review. *Frontiers in Education.* https://doi.org/10.3389/feduc.2017.00059

Rumore, M. M. (2014). The course syllabus: Legal contract or operator's manual? *American Journal of Pharmaceutical Education, 80*(10), 1–7. https://doi.org/10.5688/ajpe8010177

Skylar, A. A. (2009). A comparison of asynchronous online text-based lectures and synchronous interactive web conferencing lectures. *Issues in Teacher Education, 18*(2), 69–84. ERIC. https://files.eric.ed.gov/fulltext/EJ858506.pdf

Smith, T. C. (2005). Fifty-one competencies for online instruction. *Journal of Educators Online, 2*(2), 1–18. https://doi.org/10.9743/JEO.2005.2.2

Stanny, C., Gonzalez, M., & McGowan, B. (2015). Assessing the culture of teaching and learning through a syllabus review. *Assessment and Evaluation in Higher Education, 40*(7), 898–913. https://doi.org/10.1080/02602938.2014.956684

Trammell, B. A., Morgan, R. K., Davies, W., Petrunich-Rutherford, M. L., & Herold, D. S. (2018). Creating an online course shell: Strategies to mitigate frustration and increase student success across multiple campuses. *Scholarship of Teaching and Learning in Psychology, 4*(3), 164–180. https://doi.org/10.1037/stl0000109

Credits

Img. 7.2: Copyright © 2016 Depositphotos/brainbistro.

PART III

Online Teaching from Primary to Post-Secondary

CHAPTER EIGHT

Online Teaching and Learning in Primary Education

Jason Creekmore, EdD

Students in today's primary classrooms are experiencing an educational model that is highly dependent on the use of technology. While it is relatively easy to see how older students utilize various types of technological resources for learning, primary students, too, engage in routine use of technology, despite their young age and level of skill development. One obvious fact that must be acknowledged is that more and more students are introduced to technology at an earlier age, therefore giving them the opportunity to practice with the manipulation of basic devices. From viewing pictures on an iPhone to playing games and making videos, even toddlers are developing a rudimentary understanding of how certain types of technology can be used.

A recent study showed that 52% of 3- and 4-year-olds spend an average of 9 hours online each week (Ofcom, 2018). Survey results indicated that some children in this age range not only have their own cell phone but also have a social media profile (Ofcom, 2018). This early introduction to technology at home is resulting in primary students entering schools with a higher level of technological skill at an unprecedented rate. Consequently, it is the responsibility of teachers to leverage their students' use of technology skills to make learning fun and improve overall academic performance.

In the last decade, P–12 school administrators and teachers have changed their view on electronic devices. For instance, when cell phones became the norm for middle and high school students, most schools implemented polices that prohibited cell phones and other electronic devices at schools, as these devices were thought of as a distraction. However, it did not take long before school leaders reconsidered their stance. In fact, shortly after schools created polices to prohibit personal technological devices, they saw the need to leverage these free resources as more and more students brought them to school. Ironically, this led to the development of the **Bring Your Own Device**, or BYOD, policy, which is commonplace in schools today.

Currently, teacher and student use of technology is increasing and considered the norm, but this was not always the case. Like with any fundamental change, online teaching and learning went through a developmental process. Today, most schools have many technological devices and resources at their disposable, but there was a time when one basic computer lab was the only technology schools had to offer. Consequently, it is important to review the history of online teaching and learning and how it developed over the decades.

History of Online Learning in Primary Education

The implementation of online learning grew naturally, as did the growth of technology within society. By the mid- to late-1980s, technology within schools began to see an uptick. Schools began to utilize basic computers to support their students' learning, although there was not a true online component during this time. While there were educational games loaded onto computers, these games could not tailor instruction so that students could receive an individualized experienced based on their academic skill level. Frankly, these early educational games where nothing more than worksheets on a monitor. However, this quickly changed with the inception of the internet. The World Wide Web opened to the public in 1991 and proved to be a game changer. By 1996, email had surpassed the postal service in the number of documents sent and received, per Jeremy Norman's History of Information (https://www.historyofinformation.com). In 1998, Google debuted and helped to bridge the gap from the technology age to the information age. Suddenly, students could do meaningful and effective research on virtually any topic online. With the increase in information availability, and the decrease in the price of computers, students found themselves on computers more and more during school hours. This led educators and computer software programmers to consider how students' learning experiences could be improved. The concept of individualized instruction via technology began to emerge to support both teachers' instruction and, more importantly, the students' learning. In the following years, a multitude of online learning programs emerged to support primary-level students. Some of the more widely used programs include Lexia Core5 Reading, ABC Mouse, Moby Max, iReady, Study Island, Edmentum, and Khan Academy. These online programs are enticing to younger students as they feature colorful images, sounds, and cartoon characters during the learning experience.

In response to the ever-increasing use of online programs, the technology industry soon created smaller computer devices now known as tablets. Apple's iPad was introduced in 2010, and Amazon's Kindle Fire the following year. These tablets and others like them have become common in primary schools across the nation. The availability of tablets was vital in the development of online learning as no longer did students have to be walked down the hall to a computer lab; rather, the computers came to them and students could utilize them from their seat in any classroom. Around this same time period, Chromebooks also became widely available in schools and were seen as a perfect marriage between the price and convenience of a tablet with the functionality of a laptop.

Online learning among primary students continues to rise. In fact, a recent study indicates that 42% of students 5 to 7 years old have their own tablet at home (Ofcom, 2018). Moreover, 67% of this same age group reported they are online at least 9 hours each week. These data steadily increase for older students. Of primary students ages 8 to 11, 47% report they have their own tablet and 93% report they spend at least 9 hours per week online (Ofcom, 2018).

While virtually every study suggests that primary students are using online instruction at an ever-increasing rate (Chauhan, 2017; Fernandez, 2020), most schools were not prepared for the sudden shift to almost total reliance on technology that occurred in the spring of 2020 due to COVID-19. The pandemic affected most aspects of people's lives, and education was certainly one of those. For decades, online learning was viewed as a supplement to the educational process but never as the primary method of learning. However, that suddenly changed as schools across the nation closed their doors and were forced to rely on virtual means to educate students.

The following months proved to be difficult, or at least different, as students used online learning to a degree that was unusual even to them. Schools soon realized the importance of organizing instruction, providing clear directions, and communicating with students in a virtual world. Perhaps the most important lesson learned from this time period was the value that should be placed on assisting students as they navigate the online world of learning.

Assisting Students with Technology

Teachers must first understand that online learning is different than traditional, in-seat learning. Small corrections in page numbers and other minor clarifications can easily be made in a matter of seconds in the actual classroom, but this is not necessarily the case for online learning. There are also organizational tasks within online learning that students must master such as where to submit an assignment or what file folder to review a PDF document in. In the traditional classroom these tasks are much easier to complete because students simply "hand in" their assignments. These are only some of the issues that primary students must master if they are to be successful at online learning. The following are suggestions for how to aid primary students who are in an online learning experience.

Clear Learning Targets

Just like in the traditional classroom, communicating clear learning targets in the online classroom is also critical to the success of students. Primary students must understand exactly what they are supposed to be learning. While there are several ways to organize a virtual classroom (synchronous, asynchronous, or hybrid), learning targets should be clearly listed and referred to frequently from the first lesson to the summative assessment. Many teachers use some type of bullseye clipart with the learning targets to help their students make the connection to the term and concept of *target*. Learning targets simply provide meaning to the lesson and help the teacher and the students focus on what is important (Moss & Brookhart, 2019). Additionally, it is important that learning targets are aligned to specific academic standards. Teachers can replace difficult academic language with more student-friendly terms, especially for primary students, but the content and skill level should remain the same.

Tutorials and Instructional Videos

The importance of communicating clear and precise directions regarding an assignment are a given. To some degree, online teaching and learning hinges on the teacher's ability to articulate and communicate clear and correct directions. The online environment provides little opportunity to quickly correct an oversight such as a page number or the name of a document, for example. As a result, the directions that are provided to primary students must be essentially perfect.

Additionally, it is recommended to provide directions using multiple methods, as oftentimes primary students have difficulty in reading and comprehension, particularly at the early grades. Directions should be available in writing but also via video recording. This can be done either in a live class (synchronously) or as a recording (asynchronously). Either way, primary students, more than older students, want to see and hear their teacher as much as possible. An audio/video file of the directions is always recommended.

Likewise, written directions and video recordings are needed to assist primary students to navigate the online setting. Instructional tools such as Google Classroom and Zoom can be of enormous benefit, but students will not automatically know how to navigate within these platforms. As a result, written directions and recorded video tutorials are needed to help promote confidence in primary students.

Managing Time

Managing one's time is certainly a skill that applies to all ages, but as students progress through their school career, this skill grows in importance. Younger primary students may have not developed an understating of time and how that time must be properly allocated to complete tasks. This is a skill that students become more accustomed to as they get older, but the earlier grade teachers can also make them aware of its importance. In fact, Dr. Lynn Meltzer perhaps said it best: "When we teach children strategies for time management from an early age, they internalize them, which sets them up for lifelong success" (Estroff, 2020, para. 1).

Teachers can do several things to assist students with their overall time management. For starters, they can indicate an approximate time it will take to complete assignments. This could be something as simple as including a suggested time as part of the directions on an assignment. Secondly, they can encourage students use, or provide them with, a timer. Many learning platforms will have some type of timer that can be utilized if desired. These simple techniques can help primary students balance their learning time so that all of their required assignments can be completed in a timely manner.

Managing Materials

The success of online instruction and learning depends heavily on the degree to which students are able to manage their class materials. Fortunately, there are platforms such as Google Drive and Dropbox that can assist students in saving and retrieving documents. Just as primary students can sometimes have difficulty placing important papers in the correct folder and ultimately into their backpack, students can oftentimes struggle to manage and organize their materials in an online class setting. The aforementioned platforms can be of great benefit to students, but as previously discussed, these tools are sometimes not intuitive. Therefore, a tutorial video provided by the teacher would go a long way in helping students utilize these managerial tools efficiently.

The Virtual Classroom Environment

Regarding the virtual classroom environment, there are two separate but equally important issues to consider. As the teacher, you will need to communicate these issues to the student and the parent, as the parent must assist in this area. First, the student should have a designated workspace to participate in online learning. This space should be separate from where students watch television and play games. Students should be able to differentiate between when it is time to play, as opposed to when it is time to work. Providing a workspace will help students make this transition to work time. Secondly, the virtual classroom should be organized and neat. Too much stimuli and too many opened windows can confuse and frustrate students. Students should monitor the number of windows, or tabs, they have open at any given time. Also, students are encouraged to work on one assignment at a time, as opposed to working on multiple assignments without completing any single one. Students will gain confidence with every assignment they complete, which is why they need to maintain focus on a single assignment until completion.

Student Engagement

There is perhaps nothing more important in the learning process than student engagement. Students can have a wealth of resources and a teacher with tremendous content knowledge, but unless students are truly engaged in their work, they will never achieve at the highest possible level. Student engagement increases student satisfaction and motivation and assures them that they are part of the class (Martin & Bollinger, 2018). Even in a virtual environment, there are several strategies teachers can use which will improve the overall performance of primary students.

Creating a Virtual Classroom

Just like adults, primary students form opinions based largely on first impressions. With this thought in mind, it becomes paramount for teachers to create a visually appealing classroom for their young students. One tool that works well in this department is the **Bitmoji classroom**. Teachers can use this feature to, in a sense, make a replica of the actual classroom. The Bitmoji classroom can feature a caricature of the teacher, the teacher's desk, bookshelves, a whiteboard, and much more. The teacher can implement links within the Bitmoji classroom where students can navigate to different resources by simply clicking a word or image. Creating an environment that is inviting and similar to the actual classroom gives students a sense of connection.

Scavenger Hunts

A virtual scavenger hunt is an excellent way to engage primary students in the learning process. This instructional game plays on young students' natural curiosity to find answers, as well as compete against others. This activity requires a fair amount of preparation time as the teacher must visit multiple websites and create questions from the content on those specific sites. Ultimately, students are given a document with multiple websites to visit in order to answer questions. This activity gives students clear direction and allows them to "move outside" the classroom in order to investigate different reading materials. Furthermore, based on the rigor of the questions asked, students can also engage with higher-order thinking skills.

Learning Stations via Breakout Rooms

Many learning platforms, such as Blackboard Collaborate, have a breakout room feature that allows an entire class of students to break into smaller groups with different instructional activities. The teacher begins the lesson by having all students log in to the virtual main room. During this time, the teacher will discuss overall learning targets and give directions on what the students are to do. After this initial meeting, students then move to their breakout rooms and began their rotation so that they experience each breakout room. For example, Breakout Room #1 may be a video students watch regarding the executive branch of the government. After students watch this video and take notes, they then would move to Breakout Room #2, which features a graphic organizer of the responsibilities of the judicial branch. There could be multiple breakout rooms, but the lesson ends with everyone returning to the main room for one final assignment that would typically be assigned as homework. Breakout rooms are also an excellent way to give students the opportunity to meet and discuss their project and to take advantage of peer tutoring in a safe environment.

Guided Notes

Summarizing and notetaking are skills with which primary students have little experience. While it is easy for teachers to assume that students should be able to identify the most important details from a lesson, this assumption would be wrong. Many primary students have difficulty organizing their thoughts and are unable to recognize verbal cues that teachers provide regarding what is important in a particular lesson. *Should I write this down? Was the last thing the teacher said the most important, or was it the first thing the she said?* These are the types of questions that go through the mind of primary students. According to Marzano et al. (2008), the skills of summarizing and notetaking are collectively the second most effective strategy to raising student achievement. With such a significant pay off in student achievement, teachers need to ensure that students have the resources to take notes effectively.

One method often used in online instruction is guided notes. **Guided notes** are prepared by the teacher and contain some of the key information from a lecture or audiovisual presentation, while intentionally omitting some of the other information. The notes are often in an outline format to assist students as they listen to a lesson. Students review the guided notes prior to the lesson so they can better follow the lecture as they anticipate the missing essential information to be introduced by the teacher. Guided notes give primary students structure and encourage overall engagement as they follow along with the lesson with an actual person. Guided notes are particularly effective for online learning where students are more likely to be unengaged in a virtual environment. However, if implemented properly, guided notes can be a great match for the online learning as they pair perfectly with PowerPoint or Prezi presentations.

Communication

In any endeavor that requires people working together to accomplish a goal, effective communication is essential. Teaching primary students is certainly no different. There are several common practices that can help teachers improve the quantity and quality of communication, as well as increase the accessibility of information for students.

Make Videos Personable

Whether teachers livestream lessons and/or utilize prerecordings, they should always make it a point to show their face in the videos. Primary students want to actually see their teachers, as this makes the online experience more real to them, as well as more meaningful. Studies have shown that face-to-face communication results in an increase in neural synchronization between people involved in the communication, which leads to better comprehension and a better overall understanding of the discussion (Jiang et al., 2012).

Create Recordings

Most online instructional platforms have the option to record class sessions. By recording class sessions, teachers give students the ability to replay important lectures and listen to directions multiple times, which is very important for primary students. The recordings remove the excuse of "I can't remember what the teacher said" that sometimes arises in traditional classrooms. By recording their lessons, teachers simply give their students more support.

Limit the Length of Recordings

While recordings are recommended, it also recommend that the recordings are limited in time. Most studies show that primary students' attention span is typically 10–15 minutes. This is important to keep in mind when planning recordings for students to access. It is recommended to plan recordings to last approximately 10 minutes, and if need be, use multiple recordings as a way to break up the content and allow students to departmentalize in their minds. This strategy not only addresses what the research says about attention spans but will also aid in the organization and comprehension of the content.

Assessment

Assessment is one of the foundational pillars of education. After all, how do teachers know what their students have learned, and their overall depth of knowledge unless they utilize quality assessments? Whether the educational setting is in the traditional classroom or in a virtual classroom, the same theoretical underpinnings of assessment practices are in play. Teachers still must prepare both formative and summative assessments. Additionally, assessments must be clearly aligned to academic standards. One of the more recognized methodologies regarding assessment practices is referred to as the Five Keys to High-Quality Classroom Assessment. These keys, according to Chappuis et al. (2012) include the following:

- Clear Purpose
- Clear Targets
- Sound Design
- Effective Communication
- Student Involvement

If further research on this topic is conducted, one will find there are guided questions to help teachers create quality assessments. The Five Keys to High-Quality Classroom Assessments addresses both formative and summative assessment, as well as standard alignment (Chappuis et al., 2012).

Once teachers have thought through the assessment development process, the next step is to put their assessment plans in action. Fortunately, the online learning environment is conducive to student assessment. The following are assessment strategies that can be used in the online classroom. These assessment strategies are simple, but effective. Moreover, primary students can receive immediate feedback, which is both needed and, honestly, expected in today's society.

Quizzes

Quizzes are a time-honored assessment practice, and just because the term has been in the educational lexicon for decades does not mean that it is not effective. Quizzes are an excellent method of formative assessment, especially if the quizzes are created in a such a way that students receive immediate feedback, just as the teacher does. It is recommended to keep quizzes short, comprising 5–10 questions, and utilized often if they are being used as ongoing formative assessment. There are several programs that are great for quiz development. Some of these include Quizlet, Google Forms, and Kahoot. Additionally, instructional programs such as Edmentum also have quiz applications.

Essays and Open-Ended Responses

While quizzes are easily graded and quick to setup, essays and open-ended responses require more time, especially to grade. Even though students do not get the immediate feedback as they do with quizzes that feature multiple choice questions, essay-type questions can provide meaningful insight on the depth of knowledge students have on a particular topic. In order to make essays powerful, the teacher must provide specific feedback and be as encouraging as possible—especially to primary students. Oftentimes, primary students struggle with the organization and overall quality of writing in regard to the basic writing conventions. While writing is important, the level of content knowledge primary students portray is more important. Essays are an effective measure of content knowledge and can be easily implemented in online learning.

Drag and Drop

Another form of assessment that primary students enjoy is the concept known as **drag and drop**. As the name suggests, this activity asks students to literally drag vocabulary or comments into one of several boxes which have a heading or matching description. Basically, this activity requires students to categorize by determining how a comment or vocabulary word is different from the others. Drag and drop is quick, effective, and somewhat more interactive, as students are required to manipulate text boxes on the screen. From a theoretical perspective, the act of identifying similarities and differences is the single most effective teaching strategy, according to Marzano's high yield strategies (Marzano et al., 2008).

Polling

Polling is another quick but effective method for teachers to formatively assess students. Polling works just as well in the online learning arena, and perhaps even better, as primary students can sometimes be embarrassed to admit they don't understand something in person as the rest of the class raises their hands signifying they do understand. Primary students love to share their opinions on virtually anything, and this gives them the opportunity to do so in an emotionally safe environment. As with quizzes, teachers receive instant feedback from their students, which helps them quickly make adjustments to their instruction during online class time. Furthermore, polling can be done in a variety of ways, including on a personal level, where the teacher can see the specific responses from specific students, or anonymously, which promotes the most honest answers. Most online instructional platforms have a polling feature; however, polleverywhere.com is an alternative method to implementing polling in the virtual classroom.

Remediation

Remediation, also known as reteaching, is a very common practice in education. Some students will always need further support if they do not master the content. This will obviously be true in the online classroom as well. Since so many educational concepts rely on scaffolded learning, it is important that students meet their educational goals in the early years so they can be successful later in their career. There are several strategies that teachers can use in the online classroom to assist with remediation of skills.

Direct Instruction

While direct instruction is the foundation for the traditional classroom, this is not necessarily true for the online classroom. Nevertheless, it is a vital aspect of education and, as such, must be accounted for in virtual learning. **Direct instruction** is one of the most effective remediation teaching strategies and can be implemented in the online environment. For example, after reviewing formative assessment data, teachers may find that a few students have not mastered one or more key concepts and are in need of remediation. Direct instruction can be used to address the students' needs by combining it with another feature of online learning, such as breakout rooms. The teacher could schedule a time and breakout room just for the few students who are struggling and provide further explanation and more modeling at a pace that is more suitable for the students.

Chunking Work

Another great strategy to use for remediation is simply chunking the work. Some students get overwhelmed when numerous activities are presented to them for completion. Anxiety takes over, attention spans decrease, while frustration levels increase, which results in poor academic performance. To help alleviate this difficult situation, teachers, when possible, should divide the amount of work into smaller chunks, and rather than presenting everything that must be done by the end of the week, just present what has to be completed over a 2-day period, perhaps. Chunking the work will encourage students and give them motivation to carry on.

Learning Styles

Educators can all agree that students are unique. Every child is special in each and every way, including the way in which they learn. Theories regarding learning styles have been around for quite some time, but they are as relevant today as they have ever been. One of the most recognized theories is Howard Gardner's multiple intelligences. Gardner maintains that learners simply learn best when the content is presented in a way in which they learn the easiest—that is, the way in which they are most intelligent (Gardner, 2006). According to Gardner, these intelligence areas include visual-spatial, bodily-kinesthetic, musical, interpersonal, intrapersonal, linguistic, and logical-mathematical. Needless to say, volumes and volumes have been written on this subject, but just a cursory review of this information can help teachers construct lessons with learning styles in mind.

In the online classroom, teachers could create folders for some or all of the aforementioned types of intelligences with the same content within the folder, just presented in a way that aligns with a specific learning style. While there will not always be a perfect match for all intelligent styles, teachers can address more of the styles than probably first perceived. Most online formats have many tools that can be used to better align to students' individual learning styles. An intentional focus on student learning styles to address remediation needs is an effective and practical method.

Self-Assessment

Another excellent form of remediation that can easily be implemented in the online learning environment is self-assessment. Primary students are generally very concerned about their performance and want to be "in the know" about their grades. Self-assessment leverages this innate desire primary students exhibit to become aware of their performance and, as a result, is also an excellent tool to promote remediation. If students are aware of their performance level and, more importantly, are able to articulate why they are at the level, they will be more receptive to remediation. In fact, self-assessment itself is a form of remediation if done properly. Online classrooms are suited nicely to facilitate student self-assessment in a variety of ways.

One effective self-assessment method is the reflection log. Reflection logs give students the ability to reflect on what they have learned and, just as importantly, give them a chance to articulate what they have learned. Reflection logs can also be easily combined with discussion boards, which allow for other students' feedback. Discussion boards are common among online learning platforms.

Another self-assessment strategy is an emoji worksheet. Emoji worksheets utilize happy faces, intuitive faces, and sad faces from which students can choose as a visual representation of their confidence level or comprehension level of an academic skill. This allows students to truly consider how they are feeling, as well as gives the teacher formative feedback so that necessary adjustments can be made based on student responses.

Lastly, students can utilize a self-evaluation of their time management, use of study strategies, and other related issues in regard to the learning process. A simple Google Form can be used for this strategy. Sample questions on a self-evaluation include: *Did I allocate sufficient time for this assignment? Did I follow all the directions? Did I use all the available resources when completing this assignment?* These types of questions help students reflect on their own preparation for learning—that is, they begin to truly own their work and accept responsibility for their performance.

Chapter Summary

Essentially, online teaching and learning are no different than traditional in-seat teaching and learning. Primary students have to be given assistance on an on-going basis, but especially upfront. While this is true in all learning environments, it is especially true in online learning. Assisting students with technology is vital if students are to achieve at high levels. Issues with which students typically need assistance include establishing clear learning targets, managing time and materials, and navigating the virtual classroom.

Student engagement is also crucial for online learning. There are several issues for teachers to keep in mind including the presentation and appearance of the overall virtual classroom. Also, there are tools to promote student engagement such as scavenger hunts, learning stations via the use of breakout rooms, and the use of guided notes. All of the tools help engage leaners and will help students stay focused on the task at hand.

As discussed earlier in the chapter, communication is extremely important for online learning to occur. One common approach many teachers use to communicate virtually is to record videos. Students, especially primary students, really want to actually see their teacher. If students can see their teacher, the online classroom becomes more real. Teachers need to be aware of the length of the recordings and keep the recording brief and on point.

Assessment is one of the fundamental aspects of teaching and learning. Just like in the traditional classroom, online assessments should be of high quality and aligned to identified academic standards. Teachers can use basic quizzes and essays to assess students, but they can also use the popular online drag and drop feature as a quick method to assess student learning.

Finally, remediation is also required in an online learning environment. There will always be students who are in need of further instruction and support in order to improve their skill level. Online teachers have several strategies, including direct instruction (even in the online setting), chunking work, emphasizing learning styles, and utilizing self-assessments. These remedial strategies are effective in supporting students who need additional assistance in reaching academic success. Online teaching and learning is not easy, but it is very rewarding. While every classroom is different and students will have different needs for a variety of reasons, the aforementioned topics are universally recognized as fundamental in planning for a successful online teaching and learning experience.

Online Resources

9 Articles to Help Primary Teachers Engage Learners Online

From Pearson English, links to nine different articles to assist in various aspects of teaching online for primary school-level students: https://www.english.com/blog/9-articles-to-help-primary-teachers-engage-learners-online/

Common Sense Education: 10 Great Free Websites for Elementary School

Provides various links for educational sites for students K–12: https://www.commonsense.org/education/top-picks/10-great-free-websites-for-elementary-school

Future Learn: COVID-19: The Best Resources for Online Teaching During Coronavirus

Provides resources with for online teaching anytime: https://www.futurelearn.com/info/blog/resources-for-online-teaching-during-coronavirus

Supporting Every Teacher: How to Teach Primary-Level Learners Online

From Cambridge University Press, useful tips for teachers to help primary school students learn online: https://www.cambridge.org/elt/blog/2020/04/08/supporting-every-teacher-how-teach-primary-level-learners-online/

Teacher Toolkit: 47 Ideas: How to Teach Online

Includes links to videos and resources for both students and teachers: https://www.teachertoolkit.co.uk/2020/03/15/how-to-teach-online/

U.S. Department of Education: Use of Technology in Teaching and Learning

A review of resources and schools and how they use technology in education: https://www.ed.gov/oii-news/use-technology-teaching-and-learning

References

Chappuis, J., Stiggins, R., Chappuis, S., & Arter, J. (2012). *Classroom assessment for student learning: Doing it right—using it well*. Allyn and Bacon.

Chauhan, S. (2017). A meta-analysis of the impact of technology on learning effectiveness of elementary students. *Computers and Education, 105*, 14–30. https://doi.org/10.1016/j.compedu.2016.11.005

Estroff, S. (2020). *The age-by-age guide to teaching kids time management*. Scholastic. https://www.scholastic.com/parents/family-life/parent-child/teach-kids-to-manage-time.html

Fernandez, N. (2020). *Primary education and the use of technology* (Publication No. 744) [Capstone project, California State University, Monterey Bay]. Capstone Projects and Master's Theses. https://digitalcommons.csumb.edu/caps_thes_all/744

Gardner, H. (2006). *Multiple intelligences: New horizons in theory in practice*. Basic Books.

Jiang, J., Dai, B., Peng, D., Zhu, C., Lu, L., & Lu, C. (2012). Neural synchronization during face-to-face communication. *Journal of Neuroscience, 32*(45), 16064–16069. https://doi.org/10.1523/jneurosci.2926-12.2012

Martin, F., & Bolliger, D. U. (2018). Engagement matters: Student perceptions on the importance of engagement strategies in the online learning environment. *Online Learning, 22*(1), 205–222. https://doi.org/10.24059/olj.v22i1.1092

Marzano, R. J., Pickering, D. J., & Pollock, J. E. (2008). *Classroom instruction that works: Research-based strategies for increasing student achievement*. Association for Supervision and Curriculum Development.

Moss, C. M., & Brookhart, S. M. (2019). *Advancing formative assessment in every classroom: A guide for instructional leaders*. Association for Supervision and Curriculum Development.

OFCOM. (2018). *Children and parents: Media use and attitudes report, 2018*. https://www.ofcom.org.uk/__data/assets/pdf_file/0024/134907/children-and-parents-media-use-and-attitudes-2018.pdf

CHAPTER NINE

Online Teaching and Learning in Secondary Education

Shannon Deaton, EdD

Students in today's secondary classrooms are digital natives. From the moment they become aware of the world around them, they begin swiping devices, flipping switches, and staring into the myriad screens that compose our digital world. These are students who understand technology in the same way that they understand the function of a pencil and paper. To these students who stand on the forefront of history, technology is no longer something that integrates into society; rather, technology has become society itself. In the age of online learning, educators must adapt to the changing landscape around them and embrace learning in all its modes and formats.

Context of Technology and Online Learning

Consider modern smartphones. In 2015, 82% of high school students consistently used smartphones (Pearson, 2015), a number that has increased over the last 5 years as access to mobile technology and the internet has expanded. Students are using smartphones to communicate with friends and family across the world, research answers to homework, play massive multiplayer online games, and even create and share their own content on platforms such as YouTube, Facebook, Instagram, and TikTok. Access to the world's entire body of knowledge is accessible from a device that students already have in their pockets and already know intrinsically how to use.

But how have these devices been leveraged in the classroom? Historically, possession of electronic devices has been at odds with administrative policies in P–12 schools. In some instances, smartphones and tablet devices are banned outright, or their uses are limited to recreational rewards that do not overlap with instructional outcomes. Administrators and teachers have sometimes labeled electronic devices as instructional distractions that have no place or function in the secondary classroom. While these results are disheartening to those who understand the value of leveraging educational technology, the future is not hopeless.

As the use of electronic devices by both students and teachers becomes more ubiquitous in daily life, restrictions on such devices for educational use have started to recede. The National Center for Education Statistics (2019) found that the percentage of public schools banning cell phones dropped from 91% in 2010 to 66% in 2016, and restrictions have continued to loosen. This transition signals a change in the mindset of educators and policymakers, indicating that the value of learning can be complemented when students use electronic tools toward enhancing classroom learning. But have educators changed their minds and policies quickly enough to adapt to the urgent need for educational technology in our present landscape?

In the spring of 2020, schools across the nation began closing their doors amid fears of the COVID-19 pandemic, thrusting thousands of teachers and students into digital learning environments in which they were unprepared to thrive. Over the course of a few weeks, students closed the door on the only school structure they had ever known and opened their laptops, powered-up their smartphones, and for some, connected to their first virtual learning experience in a P–12 setting. Teachers struggled to bring their students together inside learning management systems like Google Classroom and Blackboard. Smartphones and tablets, once ostracized from schools and relegated to lockers and backpacks, were now the lifeblood of the educational system, allowing students and teachers to connect and facilitate the learning experience.

Although students are more equipped for the challenges of online education than they have ever been, there is still a great divide between current implementation of online learning and how the system must evolve to ensure success for all. As teachers scramble to develop new skills needed to overcome the digital wilderness, their struggles are not without precedent. The following sections provide guidance on how best to implement teaching and learning strategies for secondary students in an online environment.

Assisting Students with Technology

One of the first obstacles that teachers will encounter when transitioning to online instruction is issues with student access to and use of technology. To connect to the online learning environment, students will need one or more electronic devices, and they will also need to be proficient with those devices. Unfortunately, the reality is that many students, especially those from low socioeconomic backgrounds, do not have access to technology needed to engage with and sustain online learning. From an educator's perspective, this poses a significant hindrance to the educational process.

Identification

To begin solving this first dilemma, educators must take an individualized approach toward understanding the students they serve. For most, this will mean identifying the technology that students have available to them through personal, community, and school-based means. At the onset of learning, it will be necessary to provide a survey to students, requesting information about the types of technology that can be accessed from home, how often the technology can be used, and whether the student has expertise in operating the technology.

This process of **identifying student needs** will lead to a broader understanding of the educational landscape and will provide educators with information needed to begin moving all students toward the online platform. If the survey identifies that students are lacking access to internet-ready devices at home, community-based options should be explored. For example, many local libraries offer internet access to local students, and if parents/guardians are made aware of the need for educational technology, they can assist in getting students online. Additionally, school buildings often house computer labs and other resources that are available to students before and after school hours. Students who have limited access to internet-ready technology at home can arrange to work at a school location before or after hours, often under the supervision of dedicated education faculty.

Training

For students who already have access to technology, it will be necessary to gauge their level of proficiency with the technology. For example, if a student has access to a tablet device at home but has never used the device, it might be necessary to provide a demonstration or to send instructional literature home. Creating a module within the school's learning management system (LMS) that provides instructions for common internet-ready devices (iPads, Chromebooks, personal computers, laptops, etc.) will provide students and parents/guardians with support needed to ensure all students are able to engage in online learning.

In addition to providing a module with instructions for utilizing common technology, video demonstrations can also be provided, or the educator can provide weblinks to relevant technology resources. When considering which online video platforms should be used, be sure to consider the accessibility of each platform. Instructional videos should only be used when they are linked from free public websites such as YouTube, Vimeo, Dailymotion, ReadWriteThink, et cetera. This will ensure that parents/guardians and students are able to access relevant instructional videos without the need to pay for website registration.

Student Engagement

In a traditional classroom setting, there are many tools available to the classroom teacher to ensure students remain engaged. For example, common pedagogical practices involve breaking students into groups to complete assignments, allowing students to read and present information in a diversity of formats (PowerPoint, Excel, Word), and, among many other strategies, allowing students to engage in scholarly debate. When an educator considers online teaching, it is a natural tendency to believe these student engagement strategies will not translate to online learning. However, online learning tools have made significant strides in the last decade, and as a result, both synchronous and asynchronous online classrooms can be just as engaging as traditional classroom settings. The following sections outline specific student engagement strategies that are pedagogically sound and can be translated easily into the online teaching classroom.

Energy Shifts

One primary goal of student engagement is to ensure that students are paying attention, that they are interested in the material being presented, and ultimately that they retain information relevant to content mastery. This fundamental aspect of learning relies on ensuring that students maintain focus on a given task for a sustained amount of time. The key to maintaining this focus is through the concept of **energy shifts**, which employ a strategic redirection of the classroom flow at defined intervals. Energy shifts contribute to student engagement by encouraging an **autonomous-supportive teaching style** (Inayat & Ali, 2020).

For example, in a synchronous online class meeting, the lesson may begin with a "bell ringer" assignment wherein students independently answer two to three multiple-choice questions associated with learning objectives from a previous class session. Once students have been given 3–5 minutes to respond to each multiple-choice question, the teacher performs an energy shift, whereby students are then asked to partner with another student in the class to discuss their answers. After 3–5 additional minutes have passed, the teacher performs another energy shift, asking students to share some of the items they discussed with their partner. This process of allowing students 3–5 minutes (and up to 20 minutes) to work on a focused activity before redirecting attention to another activity increases student engagement.

Students naturally desire to accomplish a task, move to a new next task, accomplish the new task, and continue moving forward. This creates learning momentum, which enables students to capitalize on the success of previous achievements and compound their momentum to accomplish increasingly more difficult tasks. As another example, consider that an educator may want students in the online classroom to begin creating an organized outline for a short story. The students have never worked on a short story before, so they have little experience with the task. However, through the process of strategic energy shifts, the online instructor can gradually build student understanding of the overall process, which culminates in the creation of a short story outline.

AN ENERGY SHIFT EXAMPLE

In this example, the instructor begins the 60-minute class session with a short essay question, asking students to each write one paragraph, explaining something they find mysterious about the world. The paragraph can be written in a Word document, and the instructor will use a short, 5-minute timer to track the activity. Once time is up, the instructor will use an energy shift and ask students to use the chat functionality within the virtual classroom to distill their thoughts into one sentence. The instructor will then set a 10-minute timer and facilitate a discussion among the students (using the sentences entered into the chat window), prompting students to explain why their entry is mysterious.

The instructor will then divide the students into response groups (which is discussed in the following section), and another energy shift is employed for 15 minutes, wherein students are asked to work within response groups to discuss a series of questions related to their individual topics. At the end of the 15 minutes, another energy shift is used, and students return to a whole group setting to share responses for 10 minutes. At the end of the class, the instructor has 5 minutes remaining to provide directions to students on how they can synthesize their original answer from the Word document with class discussions to begin constructing an outline for the short story activity. By refocusing student attention at strategic intervals, student engagement is encouraged and learning momentum is established.

Student Response Groups

In a traditional classroom setting, collaborative learning is a regular occurrence, as learning is often enhanced through multiple perspectives and social interaction. In the traditional setting, it is easy to maneuver students in and out of collaborative groupings since the space of the classroom can be physically manipulated. Students can rearrange their chairs and desks to fit many group configurations, and when the collaborative activity is completed, students can simply move back to their original locations. With online learning, the same strategies can be implemented, but the process of designing, initiating, and returning from collaborative groupings is different.

When designing **student response groups**, the online instructor should first consider the number of students in the classroom and how many divisions of students are necessary. For example, if a virtual classroom has 30 students, the instructor, depending on the activity, could divide the students into three groups of ten, six groups of five, or a variety of other combinations. In general, response groups should be as small as the assigned group activity will allow. Students should always feel that they are a contributing member of the group and that their perspective is important. This positive feeling associated with one's personal contribution to a group is best accomplished in smaller group configurations.

Once the group design has been determined, the instructor will then determine how the response group will be initiated (i.e., how students will "move" into the assigned groups). As when collaborative grouping is implemented in the traditional classroom, instructions for students should be explicit before students move into groups and begin interacting with one another. In the least, the instructor should provide the following instructions before response groups are initiated:

1. When students move into groups, who will speak first, and how will the next speaker be determined?
2. What task must be accomplished in order for students to know that they are "finished" with the assigned group activity?
3. When students are finished with the assigned group activity, what should they do with their remaining time?

WHO WILL SPEAK FIRST?

It may seem straightforward, but secondary education students often find it difficult to "get started" when working in groups. This stems from social development stages associated with the secondary age group, but the issue can also arise when clear directions are not provided by the instructor. Best practice is to let students know that the person whose name appears first (alphabetically) in the response group's list of participants should begin the group conversation. This might involve the first student reading a question, answering a question, or sharing a response that they constructed for a previous prompt. In this arrangement, the student whose name appears second (alphabetically) in the response group's list of participants will speak next, and the process will continue until everyone has completed the activity.

WHEN ARE STUDENTS "FINISHED"?

Students should be given clear direction on how they will know when the response group activity is "finished." These directions will be dependent on the given activity, but in general, the response group activity will finish when all students have had a chance to complete their portion of the activity. This might mean that every student has an opportunity to answer a question, share a response, and/or read a passage, depending on the nature of the assignment. Additionally, the instructor should provide a definitive time limit for the activity, and if possible, within the virtual classroom, the timer should be visible to students while they work in the response groups.

WHAT SHOULD STUDENTS DO WHEN "FINISHED"?

In any educational setting, traditional or online, there will be times when students finish their assignments ahead of schedule. This could mean that 10 minutes was given for an activity and the students finished the activity in 5 minutes. In this scenario, students must be clear on how they should use their remaining time to continue productivity and not break learning momentum. When possible, the instructor can account for students who finish early by providing extension activities. These extension activities should be a natural progression of the activity that was already completed (i.e., add an additional, more complex question to a set of questions the students were answering). This strategy ensures that students work at a moderate pace rather than rush through the assigned task, and it also ensures that students who finish early are given an opportunity to extend their learning.

Random Selection

Randomly selecting students to answer questions, respond to prompts, or engage in classroom discussion is a staple in all educational settings. Although there are some challenges to consider with random selection, which will be discussed later in this chapter, this method increases student engagement and can ensure that everyone in the class is actively participating. This is especially important in the online classroom, as students are not physically present, and therefore the usual markers of student alertness are not present either. For example, some virtual classroom configurations do not utilize cameras, which means that the teacher will not be able to see students in the classroom. In this configuration, engagement can only be determined when students actively respond to questions and engage in classroom activities.

PROCESS FOR RANDOM SELECTION

There are several methods for randomly selecting students in an online classroom, which might include arbitrarily calling a student's name, using software that randomly generates names, and/or using **Nth name selection** in which every Nth name is chosen from a list. The most effective **random selection method** will ensure that all students in the class have an opportunity for being selected. Although this may not occur in every class meeting, all students should be selected equally within the duration of the course.

Arbitrary Selection: With this method, the instructor glances at the class roster and chooses a student to call upon, usually based upon intuition, at first. This method can be viable for random selection if the instructor keeps a list of students in the class, marks the students who have been selected, and makes an effort to select each student in equal frequency.

Random Name Generator: With this method, student names are entered into a software program, and students are randomly selected by the program. Depending on the software used, student names can be removed as candidates for random selection after an initial selection. A random list generator that can be employed for randomly selecting student names can be accessed at https://www.random.org/lists/. To protect student confidentiality, it is recommended that a number be assigned to students in the random list generator rather than entering student names explicitly.

Nth Name Selection: With this method, the instructor arbitrarily chooses a number between 1 and 10 and counts from the first student on the class roster to the student whose position on the roster is equal to the selected number. That student is selected, and future selections are determined by using the same number, starting from the previously selected student and repeating the process. For example, if the number "3" is arbitrarily selected, the instructor will select the third student on the class roster. When it is time to select another student, the instructor will count three positions down from the previously selected student. If the end of the list is reached, the instructor will begin at the top of the list again, and the instructor will also skip names of previously selected students.

CHALLENGES WITH RANDOM SELECTION

There are a few challenges with random selection that must be considered. Random selection creates tension within students, as they never know when their name will be randomly selected for a response. This positively affects student engagement because students are more likely to pay attention and focus on content if they know that they may be asked to respond to questioning related to the content. However, for some students, especially those who struggle with anxiety issues, the tension created by random selection can have negative effects. When an instructor becomes aware of students who experience negative feelings associated with random selection, accommodations can be made. For example, the instructor can omit the student from the random selection process but require that the student volunteer to participate regularly in class discussions.

Another challenge of random selection is that students may become disengaged after their name has been randomly selected and the instructor has moved on. Students will assume that the instructor will not randomly select them again, so the tension associated with random selection will ease, thus leading to lower engagement. This issue can be overcome by ensuring that the course uses a variety of student engagement strategies and does not depend on random selection exclusively. As an extension of this idea, the instructor should employ strategic energy shifts and allow students other opportunities to actively participate in class discussions, such as in the context of a student response group.

2-Minute Response

In the online classroom, time constraints are often an issue. In traditional class settings, students may have more time in-seat than they do in online settings, which means that online instructors must use class time wisely. Everything that must be accomplished in the online classroom, including formative assessments, must be accomplished according to a strict timeline with strategic intent. Given the limited timeline associated with synchronous class meetings, a **2-minute response** strategy might be appropriate.

In the 2-minute response, students are given a prompt with one or two content-related questions. The instructor reads the question aloud to the students and then explains that students should type their answers to the question into the chat window. The following instructions should also be provided to students before they respond:

- Students should type their answers into the chat window, but they should not "send" the response until the instructor notifies the class that 2 minutes have elapsed.
- Students should use the entire 2 minutes to construct their response, and if they finish early, they should review their response for grammatical mistakes and consider other ways to improve their response.

By allowing students to work on their responses for 2 minutes without actually sending the responses to the class, the instructor accomplishes adequate **wait time** and decreases **answer bias**. When students are asked to use the chat functionality in an online classroom, they are often tempted to do so with the same brevity in which they would send a text message. However, meaningful answers to complex questions can seldom be answered without appropriate "wait time" and reflection. Giving students an expectation for the amount of time that should be given to a particular response creates a buffer between the student's gratification in sending a response in the chat window and the cognitive processes that need to take place for the student to adequately reflect. Additionally, when the student is unable to see the responses of their peers, the student is more likely to provide a genuine response that may draw different conclusions than others in the class.

THINK, PAIR, SHARE

The 2-minute response strategy discussed in the previous section can also be combined with response groups. Students may be asked to complete a **think, pair, share** activity that will allow for collaborative learning while still providing the benefits mentioned previously (Prahl, 2017).

Think: To begin this modification of the 2-minute response strategy, the instructor shows the students a question, sets a timer for 1 minute, and asks the students to spend the time "thinking" about the answer to the question.

Pair: When the time has elapsed, the instructor pairs each student with another student and asks the students to each take 30 seconds to share their thoughts with their partner. In total, this should take one additional minute.

Share: When the time has elapsed, the instructor brings the students back into the whole-group setting, and responses are shared from two to three groups before moving onto the next section of the lesson.

Flipped Classroom

The benefit of online instruction when compared to traditional instruction is that the online format provides opportunities to invert (or flip) the traditional lecture and homework model (Zheng et al., 2020). In a traditional classroom setting, especially in a secondary education classroom, the instructor often allots time to lecturing each day. Following the lecture, the instructor may provide individualized or group activities for students to complete, and any remaining assignments are assigned as homework. When completing homework, students may have limited access to content assistance in their homes because the instructor is not present, and parents/guardians may not be able to provide needed support. Lack of support with homework can lead to student frustration, which can lead to not completing homework—or worse, spending hours repeating mistakes on homework that would not have occurred if a parent or instructor was available to assist.

In the **flipped classroom** model, the lecture and homework paradigm are inverted. The instructor records the lecture and provides students with a link so that they can access the recording at home. Students watch the lecture before attending class, and the actual class session is focused on the students engaging in various activities related to the content of the lecture. The benefit of this model is that the instructor, as the content expert, is available to assist students with what would ordinarily be the homework portion of the course. Students also have fewer tasks to complete at home because they will primarily just be watching the video lecture.

BENEFITS OF THE FLIPPED CLASSROOM MODEL

Students who have engaged in the flipped classroom model often express higher levels of satisfaction in their courses (Strelan et al., 2020). They cite being able to relax at home while watching video content that would ordinarily be delivered in a rigid classroom setting. This enables students to learn at their own pace, rewind video content, and/or fast-forward through sections they have already mastered. Additionally, since some students do not have parents/guardians who are available to assist with homework (for work-related or other reasons), the flipped classroom model eliminates the worry some students feel in having to complete challenging homework items in isolation (and often with limited mastery). Also, time can be more effectively used in online class sessions since the instructor will not need to allot time for lecturing.

CHALLENGES OF THE FLIPPED CLASSROOM MODEL

The flipped classroom model has several benefits, but there are some challenges associated as well. For example, the premise of the model is that students will watch recorded video lectures at home so that they can more actively engage with content (with instructor assistance) while in the live class session. However, if students fail to watch the video lecture, they will have difficulty engaging with class activities because they will not be familiar with the expected content. To remedy this issue, instructors should set high expectations for students watching the recorded lectures, and parental support should be solicited when possible. Parents/guardians should be aware that students will be expected to watch video lectures at home, and resources should be provided for parents/guardians to assist students in viewing the video lectures.

Communication

Communication is a key component of online learning, especially when working with P–12 students and their families. Since traditional means of communication are not always available in an online setting, it is necessary that educators familiarize themselves with the tools available to ensure success for all students. The following sections outline communication strategies that have proven successful in online learning environments.

Visuals

Visualization is important when communicating with students and parents/guardians. In traditional classroom settings, this facet of student learning is often addressed through classroom decorations, **manipulatives**, and PowerPoint presentations. In the online classroom, visuals can be incorporated in similar ways, but they must be adapted for the virtual context. Foremost, synchronous class sessions should always include a PowerPoint presentation and/or the sharing of relevant electronic files associated with the course content (PDFs, Word documents, images, etc.). PowerPoint presentations should use no more than three colors for representing text (one color for normal text, one color for emphasized text, and one color for headings). Images should be strategically placed, and in general, no more than one or two images should appear on a given slide.

Learner Feedback

To ensure students are making acceptable strides in their learning, it is necessary that the instructor creates a feedback loop. In this feedback loop, the instructor should provide specific instructions for communication during class (if the class occurs in a synchronous setting) and throughout the instructional week. Strategies for ensuring learner feedback are provided in the following sections.

LEARNING SIGNALS

Each learning management system (LMS) has a different method for allowing students to respond in a live class session. In some LMS systems, the student can click a "Thumbs Up" button to indicate agreement with the instructor or peers, or the student can click a "Thumbs Down" button to indicate disagreement. This functionality may alternatively be represented as a checkmark, green/red light, or some other variation that indicates a positive response or a negative response. The instructor can use these incorporated learning signals within a live class session to formatively assess students, to quickly request student opinions on a given topic, or to simply check whether the technology is working correctly at the beginning of class.

ELECTRONIC MESSAGING

There are a variety of methods that students can use to contact the instructor through electronic means. The most readily available tool for online communication is email. For best practice, instructors should respond to all email messages from students within 24 hours. If the instructor requires more time to evaluate a student's question or needs to seek additional information before providing a response, the instructor should send the student a message, indicating that they are seeking additional information and will respond as soon as possible.

Most LMS systems also include a means for communicating with students through discussion boards or internal messaging systems. If these modes for communication will be utilized in the course, the instructor should provide students with instructions on how to use them. These instructions can be provided in a live class session, in a prerecorded orientation video, or via email. As with email, the instructor should communicate an average response time to students regarding internal modes of communication, and the response time to student inquiries should not exceed 24 hours.

Screensharing Best Practices

Whether the instructor is recording a video for students to view or conducting a live class session, it will often be necessary to utilize **screensharing**. Screensharing is the process of using a communication management system (Zoom, Skype, Microsoft Teams, etc.) to share a document or an entire view of one's desktop with an external audience. In the educational context, the instructor might be sharing a document related to course content, or they may be sharing a view of their desktop to demonstrate a process associated with the course (e.g., accessing assignment submission folders or using the discussion board).

When screensharing is used, there are best practices that should be considered to ensure confidentiality, a meeting of instructional objectives, and effective time management. First, instructors should only share as much information as is necessary to accomplish a goal. For example, if the instructor only needs to share a single PDF page with students, they should share the single document via screensharing rather than share an entire view of the desktop in order to display the PDF. The desktop can sometimes include confidential information (such as filenames that include sensitive information or other open documents on the computer that are outside the scope of the lesson). For this reason, the instructor should exercise caution when sharing the entire desktop.

If the goal of the screenshare necessitates that the instructor shares their entire desktop, such as might be the case if the instructor is demonstrating a process rather than sharing a single file, the instructor should take care to close sensitive information before sharing the screen. Sensitive information might include the instructor's email, personal webpages that are open, search history that might prepopulate when the instructor clicks in a search box, spreadsheets that might display identifiable student information, et cetera. If screensharing will be utilized in a lesson, time should be taken to plan ahead and prepare the desktop and open files on the computer beforehand.

Assessment

In online education, as in all forms of education, assessment practices are needed to ensure learning outcomes are being met. Thankfully, there are a variety of tools available that simplify the process of data monitoring, collection, and analysis within the online environment. Some of these tools are embedded within common LMSs, and others are available externally (usually for free). The following sections discuss best practices for assessment in online secondary education, and tools are provided to facilitate the assessment process.

Polling

One of the most common assessment strategies in traditional education is **polling**. In a traditional setting, an instructor will ask a question and then ask students to raise their hand or give a "Thumbs Up" or "Thumbs Down" to indicate agreement or disagreement. In more advanced traditional settings, the instructor might employ a virtual polling system in the classroom or use a technology like Plickers. In the online instructional setting, the concept of polling can be adapted to fit the needs of the virtual classroom. Two of the most common polling systems used in online instruction are Survey Monkey (used in asynchronous instruction) and Poll Everywhere (used in synchronous instruction).

SURVEY MONKEY

Survey Monkey is a website polling system that can be used in asynchronous instruction to create surveys, quizzes, and polls. Much of the functionality of the tool is available by creating a free account on the Survey Monkey website (https://www.surveymonkey.com). The tool allows the poll designer to create a survey of one or more questions and provide a list of answers to the user for each question. Answers can be framed as multiple choice, true/false, yes/no, or any other selected response type. Visuals can also be added to polling questions and/or answers to supplement the content of the poll. Once the poll has been created, it can be distributed to students via web link, email, social media, website embedding, and a variety of other platforms. Survey Monkey also provides analytical tools, which include question summaries, insights and data trends, and individual responses. Instructors can use these analytical data for formative or summative instructional purposes.

POLL EVERYWHERE

Poll Everywhere is a website polling system that can be used during synchronous instruction to capture feedback instantly and to provide real-time analytics to the instructor and students. The software can be accessed by creating a free account on the Poll Everywhere website (https://www.polleverywhere.com). The polling question must be designed prior to the lesson and include relevant answers in a multiple-choice, true/false, or yes/no format. Students are then able to use their phones or web browsers to access the poll via a unique link provided by the instructor. As students record their responses to the question, poll results populate on a visual bar graph that the instructor can use for formative assessment purposes and for general class discussion.

Differentiation and Extension

All students learn differently and have unique characteristics and abilities that must be accounted for during instructional design. In an online class setting, there are several strategies that can be employed to ensure success for students of all mastery levels. These strategies can be described as **differentiation** and **extension** strategies because they involve differentiating instruction to meet specific student needs as well as providing more rigorous extension content for students who have already demonstrated mastery. The following sections highlight the most common strategies for promoting student success through differentiation and extension.

HIGHER-ORDER THINKING QUESTIONS

Higher-order thinking is a teaching approach based on Bloom's taxonomy that involves establishing a baseline for student understanding with the intent of pushing students to higher levels of thinking. The process begins by asking questions related to remembering information (Level 1) and understanding information (Level 2). These questions help students recall factual information and explain information in a manner that is relevant to the concepts being studied. Level 1 questions might include creating a list, matching terms with definitions, or identifying a concept from memory. Level 2 questions might include asking students to differentiate between concepts, explain the main idea of a reading passage, or create a summary.

Once these basic levels of thinking are accomplished, instructors can then push students to consider concepts at higher levels of thinking, such as through application (Level 3), analysis (Level 4), evaluation (Level 5), and creation (Level 6). Figure 9.1 illustrates the hierarchical structure associated with higher-order thinking.

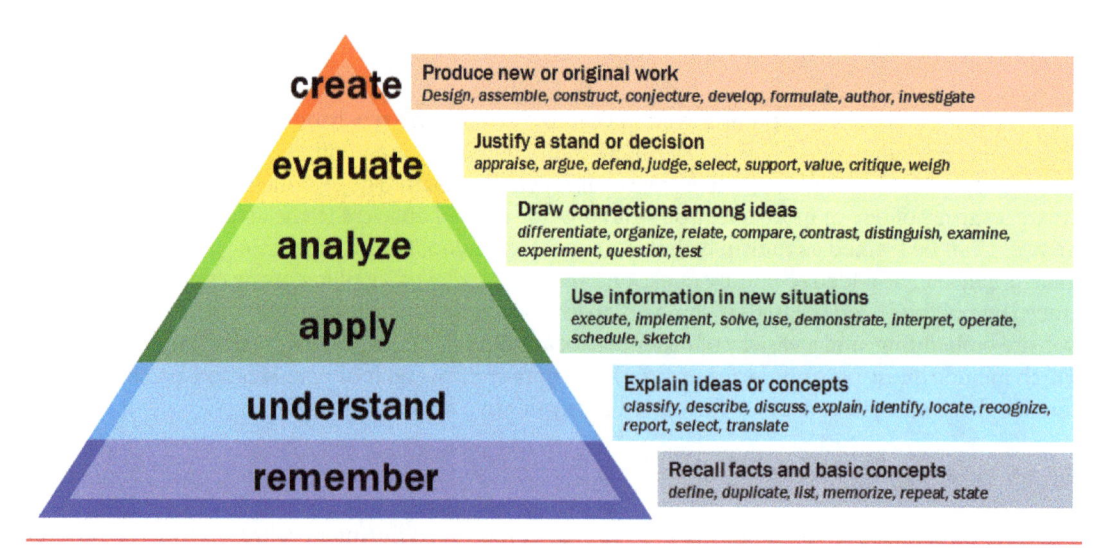

create — Produce new or original work
Design, assemble, construct, conjecture, develop, formulate, author, investigate

evaluate — Justify a stand or decision
appraise, argue, defend, judge, select, support, value, critique, weigh

analyze — Draw connections among ideas
differentiate, organize, relate, compare, contrast, distinguish, examine, experiment, question, test

apply — Use information in new situations
execute, implement, solve, use, demonstrate, interpret, operate, schedule, sketch

understand — Explain ideas or concepts
classify, describe, discuss, explain, identify, locate, recognize, report, select, translate

remember — Recall facts and basic concepts
define, duplicate, list, memorize, repeat, state

FIGURE 9.1 Bloom's Taxonomy

In an online setting, questioning techniques can be adapted into various energy shifts by using student response groups, Survey Monkey, and Poll Everywhere. Understanding a student's mastery of a topic in relation to the Bloom's taxonomy model for higher-order thinking enables online instructors to differentiate instruction in a manner that is relevant for all learners. For example, consider three students who each have different levels of mastery on the topic of poetry. By understanding higher-order questioning techniques, the instructor can design questions at different levels to meet students at their unique mastery level.

For the first student, whose mastery level of poetry is poor, the instructor could design questions that involve defining poetic terms (Level 1) or describing poetry using relevant vocabulary (Level 2). For the second student, whose mastery level of poetry is meeting the grade-level target, the instructor could design questions that involve interpreting poetry (Level 3) or comparing two poetic works (Level 4). For the third student, whose mastery is above grade level, the instructor could design questions that involve defending the merits of a poetic work (Level 5) or constructing a poetic work based on a set of guiding philosophies and concepts (Level 6). As student mastery increases, the online instructor can differentiate questions to ensure that students are being pushed to perform at higher levels relative to current mastery.

ONLINE VIDEOS FOR REMEDIATION AND EXTENSION

In the online classroom, instructors have leeway to provide students with many options for engaging with technology to enhance instruction. One of the most fundamentals methods for engaging students in the use of technology is through online videos. These videos can be created by the instructor, based on content relevant to the classroom, or the videos can be procured from various websites that contain educational content. Whatever the means for selecting and providing online videos, the goal of the video should be to meet students at their current mastery level and to push them to the next level of understanding.

There are several websites that can be used for procuring videos, and some of the websites provide grade-level-specific designations that are searchable by content area. These grade-level designations should be used by the instructor to locate content that meets the individual needs of each student. Examples of websites that allow for grade-level designation when searching include ReadWriteThink (http://www.readwritethink.org/), Khan Academy (https://www.khanacademy.org/), and Edutube (https://www.edutube.org/). Instructors can use formative assessment data to determine the mastery level of each student in the online classroom. Then, students can be categorized according to the following mastery levels: (1) Below Grade Level, (2) At Grade Level, and (3) Above Grade Level. Email distribution lists can be created for each mastery level, and students can be sent assignments that include differentiated videos to supplement understanding.

QR CODES

Another method for distributing resources to students is through the use of **quick response (QR) codes**. QR codes are machine-readable barcodes that can be scanned by modern smart devices (usually phones or tablets) to produce a website link. These codes can be created via specialized QR code-generating websites such as QR Code Generator (https://www.qr-code-generator.com/) or QR Code Monkey (https://www.qrcode-monkey.com/).

Instructors can use these codes to share videos, informational websites, Survey Monkey links, and any media that is accessible via a dedicated hyperlink. QR codes are especially useful for providing links to supplemental homework resources (especially for parents/guardians of students). Once generated, the code can be uploaded to a LMS such as Google Classroom, displayed at the top of an electronic assignment file (such as a Word document containing homework problems), or sent to students and parents/guardians via electronic communication. Varied assignments and resources can also be provided to students through QR codes based on whether the assignment is designed for remediation or extension (depending on student mastery).

Chapter Summary

Through a variety of online instructional strategies, educators can adapt instruction to the virtual landscape. The first step is to identify the technology available to students and parents/guardians and provide adequate training on technology needed to access coursework. Once all students have access to relevant technologies, student engagement strategies should be implemented to ensure focused attention and effort that leads to achievement. The results of achievement, as well as resources needed for online learning in the secondary classroom, can be shared electronically and should be visually appealing to students and parents/guardians. Additionally, student achievement can be monitored and analyzed through online assessments, which can include polling software such as Survey Monkey and Poll Everywhere. When implementing assessment, it is important to provide differentiation and extension activities when appropriate to ensure the needs of all learners are met.

Online Resources

Edutube

A source for educational videos: https://www.edutube.org

Khan Academy

https://www.khanacademy.org

Poll Everywhere

Take real time polls to assess student attitudes and thoughts: https://www.polleverywhere.com

QR Code Generator

https://www.qr-code-generator.com

QR Code Monkey

https://www.qrcode-monkey.com

Random.org

A list randomizer: https://www.random.org/lists/

ReadWriteThink

Examples of websites that allow for grade-level designation when searching: http://www.readwritethink.org

Survey Monkey

Assists in completing surveys of students: https://www.surveymonkey.com

References

Inayat, A., & Ali, A. Z. (2020). Influence of teaching style on students' engagement, curiosity and exploration in the classroom. *Journal of Education and Educational Development, 7*(1), 87–102.

National Center for Education Statistics. (2019). *Percentage of public schools with various safety and security measures: Selected years, 1999–2000 through 2017–18.* https://nces.ed.gov/programs/digest/d19/tables/dt19_233.50.asp

Pearson. (2015). *Pearson mobile device survey 2015.* https://www.pearsoned.com/wp-content/uploads/2015-Pearson-Student-Mobile-Device-Survey-Grades-4-12.pdf

Prahl, K. (2017). Best practices for the think-pair-share active-learning technique. *American Biology Teacher, 79*(1), 3–8. https://doi.org/10.1525/abt.2017.79.1.3

Strelan, P., Osborn, A., & Palmer, E. (2020). Student satisfaction with courses and instructors in a flipped classroom: A meta-analysis. *Journal of Computer Assisted Learning, 36*(3), 295–314.

Zheng, L., Bhagat, K., Zhen, Y., & Zhang, X. (2020). The effectiveness of the flipped classroom on students' learning achievement and learning motivation: A meta-analysis. *Journal of Educational Technology and Society, 23*(1), 1–15.

Credits

Fig. 9.1: Copyright © by Vanderbilt University Center for Teaching (cc by 2.0) at https://cft.vanderbilt.edu/guides-sub-pages/blooms-taxonomy/.

CHAPTER TEN

Online Teaching and Learning in Post-Secondary Education

Adrienne Sarise Baggs, PhD
Laura N. Moore, MEd, NBCC, LPC

According to the National Center for Education Statistics in 2018, over 19.6 million students were enrolled in college and graduate educational programs, referred to as postsecondary education, with nearly 7 million students taking some or all distance education courses (National Center for Education Statistics, 2020, n.d.). With the onset of COVID-19 in 2020, nearly all U. S. higher education institutions shifted abruptly to online education for some period of time as a requirement to protect public health. Although the long-term implications of this global pandemic as it relates to **online learning** is unknown, it can be argued that online learning is here to stay and likely to grow in coming years. Because of the relatively young nature of online education, it is likely that many online educators completed their education in traditional, brick-and-mortar classrooms and are being challenged to teach in an environment in which they did not learn. Creating a rich, dynamic learning environment is not necessarily intuitive, and developing systems, resources, and tools for students and education is a skill and an intentional process. The purpose of this chapter is to equip postsecondary educators with some pedagogical inspiration, practical tools, and current resources to successfully facilitate an online course. This chapter begins with a brief history of the evolution of online learning. Then, definitions of various types of online learning are presented, followed by relationship, connection, and communication strategies for developing an **online learning** community. Next, a conceptual framework for teaching online in postsecondary education is discussed, followed by concrete steps in creating an online classroom and technology resources.

Evolution of Distance Education and Online Learning

Distance education has historically been referred to as "independent study, correspondence education, home study, educational study, teaching at a distance, off campus study, open learning, outreach education, and many others" (Schulte, 2011, p. 35). Distance education is defined as a method of teaching and learning where the instructor and learner are separated by a geographical distance, and teaching and learning are facilitated through technology (American Association of University Professors, 1999; Escotet, 1980; Keegan, 1986; Moore 1973, 1977;

Moore & Thompson, 1997; Phipps et al., 1998; Roffe, 2004; Wedemeyer, 1973). **Virtual learning** alongside the emergence and availability of new technologies led to the transformation of traditional teaching methods, demanding adaptation of pedagogical methods for the virtual classroom. There are three phases of evolution in distance education:

1. correspondence learning utilizing the postal service,
2. audio and visual media learning utilizing the radio and television, and
3. online learning through use of the internet. (Kentnor, 2015; Schulte, 2011)

Correspondence Learning Utilizing the Postal Service

Although some argue that evidence of distance learning occurred in 1728, when Caleb Phillips placed an advertisement in the *Boston Gazette* for the opportunity to learn shorthand through the postal service, most agree that distance learning began over 150 years ago, 1840 to be exact, with Sir Isaac Pitman who offered shorthand courses through the postal service in England. Evidence exists that Pitman mailed assignments to individuals and requested they be returned to him for evaluation. This type of distance education is referred to as correspondence education (Kentnor, 2015; Schulte, 2011).

Audio and Visual Media Learning Utilizing the Radio and Television

The advent of the radio paved the way for the next era of development in distance learning. The University of Wisconsin–Extension became the first "distance teaching unit" in 1906. Throughout the next decade, 176 higher learning institutions obtained broadcasting licenses to offer educational content, as well as programs dedicated to the performing arts and competitive sport activities via radio broadcasts. In the United States, several regulations were passed to ensure that educational institutions were able to secure a broadcasting frequency. The Radio Act of 1912 required all equipment owners to obtain a broadcasting license; however, an amendment was needed due to the limited number of frequencies available to utilize the radio to disseminate information. Thus, the Radio Act of 1927 created the Federal Radio Commission to oversee the broadcasting agency. Around 1930, the National Committee on Education by Radio sought to coordinate educational efforts in radio broadcasting (Kentnor, 2015).

The use of visual media for educational purposes predates the actual implementation of visual technologies in higher education. Frederick Smith (1913) cited Thomas Edison as anticipating the use of visual media in public education, possibly leading to the obsolescence of books. Visual technologies were incorporated in higher education at the University of Iowa (Koenig & Hill, 1967) and in military education between 1932 and 1937. Although educational television in institutions of higher education continued to expand, the Federal Communications Commission could not meet the demand for licenses due the rapid growth for educational television, similar to the growing pains of radio broadcasting. In 1952, the Sixth Report and Order (Federal Communications Commission, 1952) reserved channels specifically for local educational systems, higher education institutions, and community organizations (Koenig & Hill, 1967). The Corporation for Public Broadcasting, charged with the expansion of public radio and television broadcasting, was established by the Public Broadcasting Act (1967). Despite the growth of these technologies in education as a supplement to traditional instruction in classrooms, as well as in family gatherings around the television for educational purposes, educational television did not achieve the same success in distance education. However, with assistance in curricula development from the British

Broadcasting Company and the incorporation of computers to deliver educational content, the possibilities for distance learning broadened. Unfortunately, educators were not convinced of the ability of computers and television to promote or enhance the quality of learning experiences (Kentnor, 2011).

As the availability of computers exploded in the 1980s, the business world quickly embraced the use of computer programs to train employees. The University of Phoenix, a for-profit educational institution, utilized CompuServe to offer online educational courses in 1989 (Hanford, n.d.; Kentnor, 2015). The year 1991 marked the premiere of the World Wide Web, with the University of Phoenix leading the way in online education programs through the internet. Other institutions developed asynchronous learning networks to provide an option to learners who faced barriers to traditional learning. Online education is interpreted as "a form of distance education that uses computers and the internet as a delivery mechanism, with at least 80% of the course content delivered online" (Kentnor, 2015, p. 28).

Online Learning Through Use of the Internet

By the mid to late 1990s, institutions of higher learning developed online education courses. In 2008, an estimated 4.8 million students were enrolled in online higher education programs at the University of Phoenix (Allen & Seaman, 2008). It is important to note that many brick-and-mortar institutions initiated online programs but many failed. Contributing factors to the failed sustainability of these online programs suggest an insufficient engagement of faculty by leadership, deficient understanding of online pedagogy and learning styles, and skepticism regarding the efficacy and quality of online instruction (Bernard et al., 2004; Carlson & Carnevale, 2001; Marcus, 2004; Shelton & Saltsman, 2005). Literature including that of Dykman and Davis (2008), Gaytan and McEwen (2007), and Palmer and Holt (2008) supports that a key factor in successful online learning relies on instructor facilitation of purposeful engagement with the students (Kentnor, 2015). Chatterjee and Correia (2020) highlight studies including those by Baker and Moyer (2019), Blanchard (2007), and Dawson (2006), concluding that students who expressed a sense of community, communicate more frequently, and rated higher in the traits conscientiousness and inherent motivation to succeed rated satisfaction with online courses more favorably. A study conducted by Chatterjee and Correia (2020) concluded that a positive correlation exists between students with positive attitudes toward collaborative learning and a sense of community, more so with graduate students than undergraduate students.

Staying the Course: Online Education in the United States (Allen & Seaman, 2008) is the sixth annual report in a series compiled to describe the evolution of online learning. In the fall semester of 2007, 3.9 million students were enrolled in at least one online course, equaling 20% of the U.S. higher education student population. This represents a 12.9% growth rate for online enrollments in higher education. In *Digital Learning Compass: Distance Education Enrollment Report*, Allen and Seaman (2017) state that the number of students in higher education taking at least one online course rose to 29.7%, and of those, 14.3% percent were enrolled in distance learning programs offering an exclusive online curriculum. Allen and Seaman (2017) cited the downward trend of enrollment in traditional learning at higher education institutions with an increase in online learning. The total number of students studying on campus, defined as those not taking any distance course or taking a combination of distance and nondistance courses, dropped by almost one million (931,317) between 2012 and 2015. The largest declines were at for-profit institutions, which saw a 31.4% drop, followed by 2-year public institutions, which saw a 10.4% decrease. Seaman et al. (2018) cited a continuing downward trend in traditional learning enrollment, with those studying in **traditional courses** or hybrid courses on campus decreasing by over one million (1,173,805, or 6.4%) between 2012 and 2016.

Legon et al. (2019) gathered statistics regarding distance education, eliciting responses from 280 chief online officers from a variety of higher education institutions. The authors note the ambiguity in defining traditional, online, hybrid, and MOOC learning courses, highlighting that the institutions define the terms individually, some based on number of on-campus meetings and some according to the number of hours of instruction time. The same authors also found that **asynchronous learning** proves to be the dominant methodology of online teaching at most institutions, with the use of student materials being the main form of instruction. Legon et al. (2019) state that "cutting-edge techniques such as simulations and games remain exceptional" (p. 21). The authors also highlight that **synchronous learning** that includes "peer learning, mentoring, or role-play" is correlated with increased quality in online courses (p. 21).

Definitions

Boettcher and Conrad (2016) define four types of courses in higher education: traditional; **lightly blended or hybrid**, also referred to as a **flipped course**; **blended or hybrid course**; and online course, also referred to as a **massive open online course** (**MOOC**).

TRADITIONAL COURSES

Boettcher and Conrad (2016) argue that very few courses are taught without the use of technology. The authors report that up to 14% of content may be delivered online through the use of course management systems or other technologies, especially in emergent situations. However, most traditional face-to-face courses include synchronous meetings on a consistent day and time throughout the course of a semester where the majority of the curriculum is taught orally, with the instructor and learners in the same space in real time.

LIGHTLY BLENDED, LIGHTLY HYBRID, OR FLIPPED COURSES

Fifteen to thirty-nine percent of course content is online through the use of course management systems for the dissemination of course materials, submission of student assignments, and grading. Asynchronous assignments, such as readings and viewing lectures, are available to the learner, with regular **face-to-face meetings** utilized for discussion.

Blended or hybrid courses are described by Boettcher and Conrad (2016) to include 40% to 70% of the content to be online through the use of course management systems for mostly synchronous learning sessions but continue to include face-to-face learning sessions periodically throughout a semester.

ONLINE COURSES

Eighty percent or more of the content is delivered online through the use of course management systems and includes both asynchronous and synchronous learning opportunities. Online courses typically include face-to-face **meetings** in a virtual space throughout the semester (Boettcher & Conrad, 2016).

Allen and Seaman (2016) agree that massive open online courses (**MOOC**) share commonalities with online courses, yet they assert a differentiation exists due to the following reasons:

- Those participating are not registered students at the school.
- The courses are designed for unlimited participation and open access via the web—no tuition is charged.
- There is typically no credit given for completion of the MOOC. (p. 8)

Glance et al. (2013) conclude that MOOCs are web-based platforms that offer online courses free of charge, often from universities and higher education institutions. MOOCs are based on pedagogical principles using quizzes, videos, peer and self-assessment, and online forum discussions to facilitate learning. Glance et al. (2013) suggest that MOOCs are just as effective as online courses in achieving learning objectives. Examples of MOOC providers include Coursera, edX, Khan Academy, and Udacity (Berg & Simonson, n.d.).

For the purposes of this chapter, writers will be referring to online learning environments as defined by Boettcher and Conrad (2016), where 80% or more of the course content is delivered online through the use of course management systems and includes asynchronous learning and regular synchronous online meetings throughout the semester.

Relationship, Connection, and Communication in Online Learning

Relationship and Connection

Depending on the course and educational content, there is variability in how important the relationships between faculty and students and among students will be to the learning process. For example, in graduate courses in the helping professions, such as counseling and education, one would expect a great detail of discussion and relational engagement as a part of the learning process. However, an undergraduate course in biology, for example, might require less relational engagement and more of a need to have students demonstrate mastery of rote concepts. This chapter is written with the underlying assumption that no matter the content, the relationship between faculty and students and among students will enhance and facilitate the learning process.

Schwartz (2020) references hooks (1994) and Noddings (2003) in her statement about the content and processes of teaching:

> We are always teaching on at least two levels. Clearly, we teach the essence of our disciplines, and at the same time, by virtue of our presence and approach, we model ways of being in the world. In this time of uncertainty, anxiety, and fear, we have the potential to model acceptance of imperfection in ourselves and our students and teaching as an act of care. (para. 2)

This statement illustrates how educators and students are engaged in education in the context of their lives outside of the learning environment. It is powerful to imagine a mother reading journal articles while nursing a baby; a father writing out a discussion post in the early morning hours before the family wakes up; a rural student driving half an hour into town to get reliable internet connection before logging into live class; a student in potential crisis, watching the progress of an encroaching wildfire while writing a list of items to pack and finishing up a paper.

Schwartz (2020) encourages educators to consider providing steady presence in the midst of dynamic, potentially chaotic life circumstances and to remain authentic in our own realities that we too, as educators, face challenging life circumstances at times. Schwartz states,

> As we engage with students remotely, we construct learning spaces (synchronous and asynchronous), and then through each interaction, we create small moments of big possibility. Every communication has the potential to say: "I see you," "I care," and "you matter." And we are connected, even from afar. (para. 9)

Communication in Online Learning

A traditional classroom environment is typically characterized by in-person interactions of students and educators. Nonverbals are present, and informal relational experiences happen naturally such as sharing books, chatting at the coffee station, or meeting up after class. However, in online learning environments where written discussions often dominate the ways in which conversations are held, communication is impacted by other factors, such as students' writing skills and time, and the frequency and timing of when a student logs into the class shell. Whether students are logging into a synchronous video classroom or are engaging in asynchronous written discussions, the learning environment can be used to facilitate the acquisition and application of knowledge and explore practical applications of content that integrates students' experiences, identities, and backgrounds. As it relates to creating this kind of learning space, the term **safe space** has been used as a way to communicate that students are ensured a comfortable learning environment.

In *Teaching to Transgress*, hooks (1994) challenged our notion of "safe" classrooms, which likely entail a quiet, small group of students being called upon after raising their hands. She discusses that educators have long feared conflict, as it may contribute to "uncontrollable" classrooms and that "emotions and passions will not be contained" (p. 39). She challenges educators to reconsider this notion that learning environments should be free from conflict and maintains that educators who include awareness of diverse identities including race and ethnicity, sexual orientation, gender, and the like can create a sense of community where students share a desire to learn and each individual voice is recognized and heard. hooks writes:

> Rather than focusing on issues of safety, I think a feeling of community creates a sense that there is shared commitment and common goods that binds us. What we all ideally share is the desire to learn—to receive actively knowledge that enhances our intellectual development and our capacity to live more fully in the world. It has been my experience that one way to build community in the classroom is to recognize the value of each individual voice. In my classes, students keep journals and often write paragraphs during class which they read to one another. This happens at least once irrespective of class size. Most of the classes I teach are not small. They range anywhere from thirty to sixty students, and at times I have taught more than one hundred. To hear each other (the sound of different voices), to listen to one another, is an exercise in recognition. It also ensures that no student remains invisible in the classroom. (p. 40)

Ali (2017) addresses the problematic nature of encouraging safe spaces (p. 3) in the classroom and recommends the following in order to create brave spaces (p. 3) instead. Brave spaces have five main elements:

"Controversy with civility," where varying opinions are accepted

"Owning intentions and impacts," in which students acknowledge and discuss instances where a dialogue has affected the emotional well-being of another person

"Challenge by choice," where students have an option to step in and out of challenging conversations

"Respect," where students show respect for one another's basic personhood

"No attacks," where students agree not to intentionally inflict harm on one another. (pp. 3–4)

In addition, Boettcher and Conrad (2016) present ten best practices for teaching online. In the second practice, the authors present the importance of creating a supportive online course community and encouraging learner-to-learner dialogue with some specific strategies that include some of the following recommendations: launching the class with introductions among students that include some personal interests to facilitate connection; setting up peer-to-peer open forums for learners to engage with one another, brainstorm, and support each other; and dividing the class into smaller study groups where students can create supportive networking (Boettcher & Conrad, 2016). Some additional ideas include eliciting intentional discussion in synchronous classes where authenticity is encouraged and identities are validated and acknowledged as a valuable part of the learning process and directly applied to the content in relevant ways; creating chat rooms that serve as student learning hubs where students can collaborate, as well as support and challenge each other in constructive ways relevant to the course content and/or learning process; and offering standing days/times for educator office hours where the educator is on a video call ready for students to hop on and available to answer questions and support students. Educators can also elicit recommendations from students in the class about ways to create brave learning spaces in which students can engage in learning that allows them to engage in honest discussion, practically apply course content to their life contexts, and challenge content and each other in ways that cultivate transformational learning experiences.

Online Engagement Framework

When preparing to deliver an online course in postsecondary education, it may be helpful to conceptualize the various types of engagement for students and how this might apply in concrete ways in the online learning environment. Based on these findings, the online engagement framework (Figure 10.1) was developed to assist academics and researchers as it relates to online engagement. This framework supports the idea that viewing and engaging with students holistically can promote learning in authentic and transformational ways. Five major elements emerged from the data: social engagement, cognitive engagement, behavioral engagement, collaborative engagement, and emotional engagement. Each element is briefly summarized below as presented by Redmond et al. (2018) and associated concrete strategies are provided by the authors of this chapter.

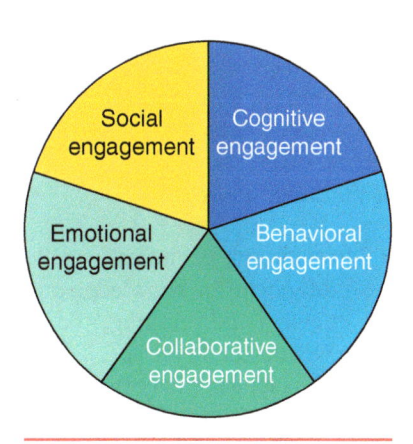

FIGURE 10.1

SOCIAL ENGAGEMENT

In traditional, **in-person learning** environments, social engagement happens naturally. Students and faculty chat before and after class, and students may develop study groups, grab coffee after class, or plan a dinner after a big test to decompress and process their experiences. These opportunities to connect outside of the formal learning environment can facilitate learning by meeting needs for emotional support, collaborative learning experiences, and meaningful connection. Redmond et al. (2018) found that social engagement included five major indicators: building community, creating a sense of belonging, developing relationships and establishing trust. In online learning environments, however, informal connection and building supportive communities must be an intentional effort. Some ideas on how to cultivate these connections are presented below:

- Develop intentional discussion in live, synchronous classes where authenticity is encouraged. When students can engage authentically with one another, they are likely to discover like-minded students to whom they can reach out and develop their own supportive learning networks in ways that accommodate their contact preferences and availability.

- Consider enabling the chat feature available in many video platforms. In this chat function, students contribute to the discussion in text or private message each other to comment on the discussion and/or course content in nonverbal ways or make plans to connect outside of class. Depending on the size of the class, a running chat thread can be distracting to students and/or the instructor, who may feel the need to facilitate the verbal discussion as well as the chat thread. Set parameters that allow students to connect via chat in ways that do not distract from the central conversation (e.g., only attending to the chat when certain content has been presented, at a specific time in the course).
- Create chat rooms or separate discussion threads that serve as student learning hubs where students can collaborate, support each other, and double-check logistical elements of the course. Some learning platforms allow for areas, such as discussion threads, to remain open and active throughout the duration of the course.
- Encourage students to create profiles, with photos, that may include elements of their identity that may be meaningful to share.
- Learn students' names and use them, in all aspects of the course, including, for example, qualitative grading feedback, live video classes, online discussion forums.

COGNITIVE ENGAGEMENT

Cognitive engagement includes the mental elements to the acquisition of knowledge, and researchers found six indicators for cognitive engagement: thinking critically, activating metacognition, integrating ideas, justifying decisions, developing deep discipline understandings, and distributing expertise (Redmond et al., 2018). Some strategies that might facilitate cognitive engagement include the following:

- Provide opportunities for reflection in class and/or built into assignments where students can integrate prior knowledge and new knowledge gained from the course, challenge old ways of knowing and thinking, and process how the course content and process will apply to future education and practice.
- Offer supplemental content and reading that supports the contextual and holistic understanding of content. For example, instead of only including the text chapters, perhaps there is an interesting biography, memoir, or video that illuminates the learning objectives in a human story, or an organizational success case study.
- Provide a culminating capstone assignment or experience where students can reflect on the course content and learning process.
- Offer one or more assignments where an alternative assignment is presented. For example, if a portfolio is required for course completion, perhaps students can choose to submit either a recorded video presentation or a written portfolio. Promoting autonomy in learning can help students self-select assignments that will serve them well.

BEHAVIORAL ENGAGEMENT

Behavioral engagement is characterized by "students who develop academic skills, identify opportunities and challenges, develop multidisciplinary skills, develop agency, uphold online learning norms and support and encourage peers" (Redmond et al., 2018, p. 190). Strategies that might facilitate behavioral engagement may include the following:

- Assignments and discussions that recommend students collaborate to process the content and learn diverse perspectives on the same content.

- Provide course content that integrates other disciplines and challenges students to apply and demonstrate the skills they have learned in practical ways.
- Create timelines and scaffolding of large assignments, so students can work through big projects in a developmentally supported way, noting challenges and successes along the way.

COLLABORATIVE ENGAGEMENT

Collaborative engagement includes "learning with peers, relating to faculty members, connecting to institutional opportunities, developing professional networks" (Redmond et al., 2018, p. 190).

- Create assignments that help students beyond the classroom, such as integrating assignments that contribute to the field—for example, working toward conference submissions, article submissions, community projects, et cetera.
- Provide regular days/times of the week where there are standing faculty office hours. Similar to a student walking by an open door with a faculty member ready to support students and answer questions, you can sit in a video platform working on various tasks but be available for students to pop by.
- Distribute a list of institutional resources that include not only support related to writing, library, tutoring, and the like but also ones that support students holistically, such as counseling and cultural communities within the institution and community wide.

EMOTIONAL ENGAGEMENT

Emotional engagement includes "managing expectations, articulating assumptions, recognizing motivations, and committing to learning" (Redmond et al., 2018, p. 190).

- Attend to the emotional experiences of individual learners and trends among classes. Manage expectations by speaking to the emotional elements of the learning experiences and activities (e.g., anxiety provoking, enjoyable), normalizing the reactions and offering support when needed.
- Anchor learning experiences and activities to practical, real-world value. Address how each assignment is connected to something important the student may use in their future job, relationships, progress in academics, et cetera.
- Attune to students' potential experiences outside of the classroom. Depending on the span of where your students reside, students may be facing any number of natural disasters, political unrest, access to resources in rural areas, et cetera. Post announcements and reach out to students individually, if possible, to extend your support and offer awareness and empathy of these unique situations.

Creating the Online Classroom

Imagine an elementary school classroom, equipped with various learning areas, each designed with a specific purpose. The entry way might include a cubby with the students' name and picture, a hook to hang her coat, and drawer for her lunch. To the left of the classroom entryway is an area with desks and chairs to facilitate formal tasks with structured instruction, and equipped with various writing utensils, art supplies, science tools, et cetera. Then, to the right of the entryway, there might be some beanbags, blankets, and bookshelves to encourage students to informally connect, relax, and read. On the chalkboard is the agenda for the day, broken down by time and task. Elementary school teachers may have mastered the elements of online course design without even realizing it.

These teachers create classrooms, each area with a specific purpose, attention to students' unique identity, and a clear, focused agenda for the learning to take place.

For instructors new to teaching online, setting up the online classroom is likely an unfamiliar concept, and without adequate time and training to prepare and create an online learning environment, course learning shells can be fragmented, empty, and unorganized. Copying course shells from previous semesters, neglecting to take the time to engage in introductions and build relationships, and being unprepared due to other academic roles and responsibilities can lead to a rough start to an online course. Online faculty and educators have a responsibility to begin a course that will be conducive to a clear and effective learning environment. Alward and Phelps (2019) conducted a qualitative phenomenological inquiry on successful leadership traits of academic leaders leading virtual teams. Many themes emerged from the research, such as training and development, trust, emotional intelligence, communication and team building, technology, employee recognition and motivation, leadership styles, and virtual leadership competencies unique to higher education, but overall, researchers state "organizational success partially hinges on comprehensive training for virtual leaders, the significance of trust, emotional intelligence, and effective, respectful communication" (p. 72).

Although this study was directly applied to academic leaders of virtual teams and not online postsecondary education, the important elements identified may be relevant to educators leading a classroom: the need for training, trust, emotional intelligence and respectful communication. Online educators are challenged to consider how to create a classroom environment that allows for the holistic student identity to emerge and the learning environment to flourish. The following areas are recommended to include in your online classroom to encourage organization, communication, and connection: course policies and procedures (as explained in detail in Chapter 7), weekly announcement hubs, weekly module folders, informal chatrooms, and university/college resources.

Course Policies and Procedures

In the course policies and procedures section, you will want to ensure you have listed all the course policies and procedures related to the course. Depending on the institution, this may include solely a comprehensive syllabus that addresses critical elements to include the following: attendance and participation policies; nature of the course (synchronous or asynchronous); days, times, and location of the in-person sessions; student and faculty responsibilities and expectations; technology requirements and prerequisite skill requirements, and the like. Examples of these are explored in Chapter 7.

Weekly Announcement Hub

Depending how much material is provided in the course shell, accessing it all at once can be overwhelming for students. Therefore, including weekly announcements that point to the important module-specific requirements and supplemental resources is helpful in allowing students to access important information in a manageable way. Weekly announcements can also be a way for instructors to connect with students, providing support in various stages of the course and approaching assignments that may be particularly high-stakes and/or anxiety provoking for students.

Weekly Module Folders

Weekly module folders include all resources for each module. Each week, students can access the required supplemental course content, including reading assignments, videos, PowerPoints, et cetera in a progressive way. This provides student access to materials in an asynchronous format, exposing students to content outside of class allowing time for reflection, then reexposure in synchronous class in which they can question and facilitate discussion on content.

Informal Chatroom

This is an area in the course shell where students can come to ask questions about the course content, process any learning experiences, and/or offer support to one another. The room can be accessed anytime and is loosely monitored by the instructor, meaning that several times a week the instructor might log in to answer questions or offer support, but the room is more of a student-led, student-focused environment. This provides an opportunity to empower students to take responsibility for their learning, creating a brave space allowing for peer-to-peer interactions (Ali, 2017).

University/College Resources

Recognizing students are at various developmental levels and have different needs, connecting students to university/college resources can promote their success. Although potentially included in the syllabus, it is helpful for students to have a central point to learn of and access contact information for various resources, including writing centers, instructional technology, disability resource centers, plagiarism resources (e.g., Turnitin), and tutorials specific to the classroom management platform. In addition to the various elements of your course construction, we have included a beginning-of-course checklist for faculty.

- Consider creating a welcome video that allows students to see and hear you. Included in this video may be elements such as your teaching philosophy, your relationship to the course topic, what has led you to teaching this course, what meaning you derive from teaching, and how this course content will serve the students outside of the learning environment. Inform students about your standing office hours and the best way to reach you if they have questions or need support. Include your profile picture, bio, contact information, and office hours.
- Most colleges and universities have specific institution-wide policies and procedures. Your syllabus will need to align with those, but you also need to distinguish between university-wide policies and classroom policies of which you want students to be aware. Make sure to include a list of support resources for students, such as technology support, disability services, and writing support services. This is discussed in detail in Chapter 7.
- Include a clear, week-by-week course schedule in your syllabus, or perhaps offer it as a separate document. A course schedule may include any number of the following: assigned required and optional readings, assignments due, live classes scheduled and their video platform location, and additional recorded video content. An example of this is available in Chapter 7.
- Post a welcome announcement. Include a message to orient students to you, the process of the course, and the location of important items such as the syllabus and areas of the course shell including discussion board, weekly announcement hub, university/college resources, and the like.
- Develop systems that flag students who may be struggling and develop a reach-out and retention plan to support their progress in your class. Many classroom management programs have ways to monitor the progress of students, so instructors can review a data report or graph and identify students who are excelling or struggling to keep up in time-efficient ways.
- Identify students using disability accommodations and document how those accommodations will apply to your specific course assignments.

Mastering Technology in Online Learning in Higher Education

John Sener (2014) coined the term *cybersymbiosis* referring to "education's and society's irretrievable dependence on online and digital technologies" (p. 92). The origin of distance education is rooted in a mission to expand opportunities to learners lacking access and resources to traditional educational resources. In 2020, a global pandemic unveiled an opportunity to improve the quality of distance education, not only through improvements in the infrastructure of the internet and increased access to technological devices to rural and impoverished communities, but also to motivate educators to revolutionize teaching and learning through innovative, creative online pedagogical methodologies in the virtual classroom. Table 10.1 presents some technology tools to assist with the facilitation of the online course, for the educator as well as the students.

TABLE 10.1

PRESENTATION TOOLS (OTHER THAN POWERPOINT)	Sutori (https://sutori.com)—an online instructional tool where students and faculty can create creative, timeline-structured presentations that allow users to integrate features such as videos, quizzes, and comments from the audience.
	Prezi (https://prezi.com)—an online presentation tool highlighting creative spatial design and ability to see a video of the presenter alongside the presentation.
	Google Slides (https://google.com/slides/about/)—a free, cloud-friendly way to create and collaborate on slide presentations.
VIDEOCONFERENCING SOFTWARE	Zoom (https://zoom.us)—a free, entry-level video platform that provides capabilities in meetings and chats, video webinars, and conference rooms.
	Cisco Webex (https://cisco.com)—an online platform for content sharing and audio and video meeting capabilities.
	Microsoft Teams (https://www.microsoft.com/en-us/microsoft-teams/group-chat-software)—for users of Microsoft Office 365, this business platform allows for video meetings, chat-based communication, and file sharing.
CONTENT SHARING	Dropmark (https://dropmark.com)—a visual and remote content sharing platform that allows teams to collaborate to save various forms of content, including videos, images, and documents, and comment or annotate on the work.
	Dropbox (https://dropbox.com)—a file sharing and organization platform with cloud capabilities.
	Google Docs (https://docs.google.com)—a free, user-friendly way to share and edit files in real time.

Chapter Summary

This chapter has outlined various elements to assist educators in postsecondary education with ways to facilitate an authentic, organized, and holistic learning experience for students. Although organization, structure, and intentional content are critical to an effective online learning environment, learning can be maximized when students feel connected to fellow students and the educator. As online pedagogy and resources continue to evolve, these elements will certainly evolve as well. With the rapid pace of technology development, perhaps online educators' willingness to adapt and openness to change are the most important characteristics of a successful online educator in higher education.

Online Resources

Online Learning Resources

National Communication Association; downloadable online learning resources for educators: https://www.natcom.org/academic-professional-resources/teaching-and-learning/classroom/online-learning-resources

Resources and Tools for Teaching Students

Affordable College Online; resource links for instructors: https://www.affordablecollegesonline.org/degrees/education-and-teaching-programs/resources/

Resources for Instructors

Online Learning Insights; online faculty resources: https://onlinelearninginsights.wordpress.com/resources-2/

The Top 10 Online Teaching Resources

Top Hat; lecture and digital tools for instructors: https://tophat.com/blog/the-top-10-online-teaching-resources/

The Ultimate Guide to Online Resources for Educators

The Faculty; 20 free apps for online teaching: https://medium.com/the-faculty/free-online-tools-for-remote-teaching-ba6aa4447c24

Websites for Educators

Harvard Graduate School of Education; websites and resources for educators separated by topic/course of study: https://www.gse.harvard.edu/library/educator-resources

References

Ali, D. (2017, October). *Safe spaces and brave spaces: Historical Context and Recommendations for Student Affairs Professionals.* NASPA Research and Policy Institute. https://www.naspa.org/report/safe-spaces-and-brave-spaces-historical-context-and-recommendations-for-student-affairs-professionals

Allen, I. E., & Seaman, J. (2008). *Staying the course: Online education in the United States, 2008.* Sloan Consortium. ERIC. https://files.eric.ed.gov/fulltext/ED529698.pdf

Allen, I. E., & Seaman, J. (2016). *Online report card: Tracking online education in the United States.* Sloan Consortium. https://onlinelearningsurvey.com/reports/onlinereportcard.pdf

Allen, I. E., & Seaman, J. (2017). *Digital learning compass: Distance education enrollment report, 2017.* Sloan Consortium. ERIC. https://files.eric.ed.gov/fulltext/ED580868.pdf

Alward, E., & Phelps, Y. (2019). Impactful leadership traits of virtual leaders in higher education. *Online Learning, 23*(3), 72–93.

American Association of University Professors. (1999). *Reports and publications: Statement on online and distance education.* https://www.aaup.org/report/statement-online-and-distance-education

Andresen, M. A. (2009). Asynchronous discussion forums: Success factors, outcomes, assessments, and limitations. *Journal of Educational Technology and Society, 12*(1), 249–257.

Baker, K. Q., & Moyer, D. M. (2019). The relationship between students' characteristics and their impressions of online courses. *American Journal of Distance Education, 33*(1), 16–28.

Berg, G. A., & Simonson, M. (n.d.). *Distance learning.* Britannica. Retrieved October, 10, 2020, from http://www.britannica.com/topic/distance-learning

Bernard, R. M., Abrami, P. C., Lou, Y., Borokhovski, E., Wade, A., Wozney, L., Wallet, P. A., Fiset, M., & Huang, B. (2004). How does distance education compare with classroom instruction? A meta-analysis of the empirical literature. *Review of Educational Research, 74*(3), 379–439.

Blanchard, A. L. (2007). Developing a sense of virtual community measure. *Cyber Psychology and Behavior, 10*(6), 827–830. https://doi.org/10.1089/cpb.2007.9946

Boettcher, J. V., & Conrad, R. M. (2016). *The online teaching survival guide: Simple and practical pedagogical tips.* Wiley.

Carlson, S., & Carnevale, D. (2001). Debating the demise of NYUonline. *Chronicle of Higher Education, 48*(16).

Chatterjee, R., & Correia, A. P. (2020). Online students' attitudes toward collaborative learning and sense of community. *American Journal of Distance Education, 34*(1), 53–68. https://doi.org/10.1080/08923647.2020.1703479

Dawson, S. (2006). A study of the relationship between student communication interaction and sense of community. *The Internet and Higher Education, 9*(3), 153–162. https://doi.org/10.1016/j.iheduc.2006.06.007

Dykman, C. A., & Davis, C. K. (2008). Online education forum—part three: A quality online educational experience. *Journal of Information Systems Education, 19*(3), 281–289.

Escotet, M. A. (1980). Adverse factors in the development of an open university in Latin America. *Programmed Learning and Educational Technology, 17*(4), 262–270. https://doi.org/10.1080/0033039800170410

Federal Communications Commission. (1952, April 14). *Sixth report and order, Part II.* Broadcasting Telecasting. https://worldradiohistory.com/Archive-BC/BC-1952/BC-1952-04-14-Pt-II-TV-Freeze-Lift.pdf

Gaytan, J., & McEwen, B. C. (2007). Effective online instructional and assessment strategies. *American Journal of Distance Education, (21)*3, 117–132. https://doi.org/10.1080/08923640701341653

Glance, D. G., Forsey, M., & Riley, M. (2013). The pedagogical foundations of massive open online courses. *First Monday, 18*(5). https://doi.org/10.5210/fm.v18i5.4350

Hanford, E. (n.d.) *The story of the University of Phoenix.* American Public Media. http://americanradioworks.publicradio.org/features/tomorrows-college/phoenix/story-of-university-of-phoenix.html

hooks, b. (1994). *Teaching to transgress.* Routledge.

Keegan, D. (1986). *The foundations of distance education.* Croom Helm.

Kentnor, H. E. (2015). Distance education and the evolution of online learning in the United States. *Curriculum and Teaching Dialogue, 17*(1), 21–34.

Koenig, A. E., & Hill, R. B. (1967). *The farther vision: Educational television today.* University of Wisconsin Press.

Legon, R., Garrett, R., & Fredericksen, E. E. (2019). *CHLOE 3: Behind the numbers: The changing landscape of online and education.* Quality Matters. https://www.qualitymatters.org/sites/default/files/research-docs-pdfs/CHLOE-3-Report-2019-Behind-the-Numbers.pdf

Marcus, S. (2004). Leadership in distance education: Is it a unique type of leadership—A literature review. *Online Journal of Distance Learning Administration, 7*(1). Advance online publication. https://www.westga.edu/~distance/ojdla/spring71/marcus71.html

Moore, M. G. (1973). Toward a theory of independent learning and teaching. *Journal of Higher Education, 44*(9), 661–679. https://doi.org/10.1080/00221546.1973.11776906

Moore, M. G. (1977). *On a theory of independent study.* Fernuniversitat DIFF. https://ub-deposit.fernuni-hagen.de/servlets/MCRFileNodeServlet/mir_derivate_00000218/ZIFF_16_Moore_Theory_of_Independet_Study_1977.pdf

Moore, M. G., & Thompson, M. M. (1997). The effects of distance learning (Rev. ed.) [Research monograph No. 2]. *American Journal of Distance Education.* Pennsylvania State University. ERIC. https://files.eric.ed.gov/fulltext/ED330321.pdf

National Center for Educational Statistics [NCES]. (2020, April). *Characteristics of Postsecondary Students.* https://nces.ed.gov/programs/coe/indicator_csb.asp

National Center for Educational Statistics [NCES]. (n.d.) *Fast facts: Distance learning.* https://nces.ed.gov/fastfacts/display.asp?id=80

Noddings, N. (2003). *Caring: A feminine approach to ethics and moral education* (2nd ed.). University of California Press.

Palmer, S. R., & Holt, D. M. (2009). Examining student satisfaction with wholly online learning. *Journal of Computer Assisted Learning, (25)*2, 101–113.

Philipps, C. (1728, March 25-April 1). Caleb Philipps teacher of the new method of short hand. *The Boston Gazette, 436*(2).

Phipps, R. A., Wellman, J. V., & Merisotis, J. P. (1998). *Assuring quality in distance learning: A preliminary review.* Council for Higher Education Accreditation. http://www.ihep.com/sites/default/files/uploads/docs/pubs/assuringqualitydistancelearning.pdf

Public Broadcasting Act, 47 U.S.C. § 396 (1967).

Redmond, P., Abawi, L. A., Brown, A., Henderson, R., & Heffernan, A. (2018). An online engagement framework for higher education. *Online Learning, 22*(1), 183–204.

Roffe, I. (2004). *Innovation and e-learning: E-business for an educational enterprise.* University of Wales Press.

Schulte, M. (2011). The foundations of technology distance education: A review of the literature to 2001. *Journal of Continuing Higher Education, 59*(1), 34–44.

Schwartz, H. (2020, September 17). *Authentic teaching and connected learning in the age of COVID-19*. The Scholarly Teacher. https://www.scholarlyteacher.com/post/authentic-teaching-and-connected-learning-in-the-age-of-covid-19

Seaman, J. E., Allen, I. E., & Seaman, J. (2018). *Grade increase: Tracking distance education in the United States*. Babson Survey Research Group. http://onlinelearningsurvey.com/reports/gradeincrease.pdf

Sener, J. (2014). Using the Seven Futures framework for improving educational quality. *e-mentor, 53*(1), 92–97.

Shelton, K., & Saltsman, G. (2005). *An administrator's guide to online education*. Information Age Publishing.

Shelton, K., & Saltsman, G. (Eds.). (2005). *An administrator's guide to online education*. Information Age Publishing.

Smith, F. J. (1913, July 9). The evolution of the motion picture: VI—Looking into the future with Thomas A. Edison; An exclusive interview with the master inventor. *The New York Dramatic Mirror*, 24. http://www.laviemoderne.net/images/forum_pics/2017/20171116%20New%20York%20NY%20Dramatic%20Mirror%201913%20Mar-Apr%201914%20Grayscale%20-%200690.pdf

Wedemeyer, C. (1973). The use of correspondence education for post-secondary education. In A. Kabwasa & M. Kaunda (Eds.), *Correspondence education in Africa* (pp. 72–79). Routledge and Kegan Paul.

Credits

Fig. 10.1: Copyright © by Petrea Redmond, Amanda Heffernan, Lindy Abawi, Alice Brown, and Robyn Henderson (CC by 4.0) at https://olj.onlinelearningconsortium.org/index.php/olj/article/view/1175.

PART IV

Legal, Ethical, and Other Administrative Considerations

CHAPTER ELEVEN

Legal and Ethical Issues in Online Education

Gary L. Patton, PhD

A brief overview of online education might not include ethical issues as an area of either relevance or concern. Yet, in a closer examination, several topics of ethical interest would surface. This chapter addresses that closer examination and provides introductory material for online educators to be aware of. While the practice of online education could seem relatively sterile and benign related to interpersonal encounters, the engagement of educators with students presents similar circumstances and concerns as that of professional counseling. As noted by Wheeler and Bertram, "counselor educators and clinical supervisors of counselors are exposed to an array of legal and ethical challenges" (2012, p. 259). A similar observation could be made about educators overall. The focus of this chapter is how ethical issues can arise in online education formats.

Portions of this chapter address the format of online counselor education. Included in this chapter are also ethical issues that pertain to any educational setting. In both areas, the approach is not on how to teach ethics. As important as courses in ethics are in the counseling curriculum, it is equally important to have online educators to be prepared to recognize and respond to ethical issues that may, and likely will, present in teaching online classes of pertaining to many topics. Ethics is a matter of importance in online education.

In education, there is disproportionate power. Students are vulnerable to the degree that they are dependent on others for training and instruction. Educators have power by virtue of their credentials, status, and experience. In any setting where levels of power are not equal, someone in the encounter is more vulnerable. As students have paid for the opportunity to learn, it is incumbent on the educators to be competent and provide the best instruction possible, in both content and design. Issues of how students are treated as individuals, how grades are assigned, and how appeals of grievances are managed are important areas for sound ethical decisions and conduct.

In any endeavor with human beings, whether it be health care, research, financial guidance, mental health counseling, or education, a foundational consideration is to not injure or adversely impact anyone. The equation of risk versus benefit is a core concept for helping professionals to fully understand. Included in this would be educators. The goal of working with others is to practice with zero risk and high benefit. Since that is the ideal and yet sometimes unfortunate things happen, professionals often must settle for practicing with minimal risk and the intent of greater benefit. Ethical considerations often involve those delicate matters in which the attempt is to achieve some benefit, yet a level of risk is apparent or evident. A process of ethical reasoning must be followed to reach a decision that maximizes benefit and minimizes risk.

Principles of Ethics

There are numerous approaches and theories of ethical reasoning. In this chapter, attention will be given to the work of Kitchener in the realm of principled ethics. A way of thinking about this model is that there is a certain aspirational quality about abiding by principles to make ethical decisions. The assumption is that while people may not demonstrate these consistently, there is a value in striving to exemplify these principles. Also, the notion is proposed that these are good ways to treat people. Kitchener (1984) identified principles related to ethics that have wide application for any helping profession. Adherence to these principles, while not exclusive or legislated for online education, can improve the learning environment for students and ensure that they are being considered and treated in the most ethical manner possible.

Autonomy

According to this principle, people are entitled to have some degree of independence and control over their lives and decisions. While everyone has to yield to higher authorities, and at times to the will of the majority, there is still a value in allowing people to have as much self-direction as is feasible and permissible.

Beneficence

This principle conveys the idea of providing good to others. Essentially, if we are going to serve others, then some good should be the outcome.

Nonmaleficence

According to this principle, people should not be harmed. If harm is the likely result of an action, then that action should not be done.

Justice

This principle assures everyone of equal access. The main point is not the everyone is treated the same. While that may sound like a violation in itself, not being treated like everyone else, the real issue is that everyone does not need or even want the same thing(s). Yet, based on what a person does need or seek, everyone is given access to an equal degree.

Fidelity

This principle holds that those who are in a position of service to others follow a practice of truthfulness and honesty with others. The reasoning behind this principle is that even withholding truth or practicing deception for what might be considered good reasons is detrimental to others and to the relationship with them.

Moral Distress

Moral distress is becoming a topic of research interest in some professions. Sometimes a professional is faced with situations that do not have a single morally defensible solution. The conflict contained in this encounter is what becomes distressing to the professional. In essence, whether one does nothing or takes action, there remains some part of the problem that is not satisfactorily resolved. The work of Holland and Kilpatrick (1991) indicated that professionals can experience a profound awareness of loneliness in regard to addressing ethical and moral issues. It is reasonable to conclude that educators in an online setting may encounter a similar sense of isolation and loneliness as ethical issues emerge in education.

When a difficult decision must be made that involves the future of a person or persons, the weight of having to make that decision can seem overwhelming. Thus, there is a practice in the field of health care that is applicable to education as well. That practice is to seek consultation. The practice of consulting with other professionals can be beneficial by assisting with different perspectives on a problem, encouraging an educator to act in a courageous and responsible manner, and providing incentive to implement an ethical choice (Kempworth, 2005). While considering a course of action with issues that pose a moral dilemma, "consultation may also reduce distress as well as the moral and emotional isolation that clinicians feel" (Welfel, 2016, p. 50). Educators in online settings will find benefit of insight and reassurance in discussing issues of concern with colleagues to see what others think and explore their suggestions.

Ethical Decision-Making Model

Addressing an ethical dilemma can be very time consuming. There are also times, when due to the urgency of a situation, decisions must be made expeditiously. Some ethical issues are easy to make rather quickly and do not require extensive analysis. It is also important to be aware of some type of decision-making model for certain situations. The use of decision-making models is especially important when situations have long-term ramifications, numerous parties are involved, conflicting values are operative, or the risks are high of serious consequences if a thorough process is not followed. It is important to note that there is not a right or wrong model. Personal preference or compatibility with organizational policy can guide the selection of a model. Some authors who have developed decision-making models are Corey et al. (2015) and Remley and Herlihy (2010). A model that is often used is the format developed by Kitchener and Anderson (2011). This is a 10-step model based on a critical evaluative approach. A general listing of some of these models would include the collaborative model, the Kenyon model, and the ethical principles screen.

Professionals should also be aware of what constitutes an appeal. While decisions can always be revisited or reviewed, a formal appeal process is typically based on one of three situations: (a) new evidence has emerged, (b) there was flaw in the process, or (c) a sanction does not fit the offense. This approach moves away from the common practice of seeking an appeal based on someone not agreeing with a decision that has been made. As mentioned above, having used a decision-making model can be useful in establishing how the original decision was made and can be explained and even defended accordingly.

Another important dimension of decision-making models is culture. Sue and Sue (2012) identified three competencies for professionals to demonstrate the ability and awareness to work with multicultural awareness and sensitivity. These are (a) self-awareness, (b) understanding without negativity and judgment, and (c) skills in responding appropriately to diversity. These skills are relevant to decision-making models, especially to increase the assurance of treating all people with justice and integrity.

Federal Regulations

It is beyond the scope of this overview of ethics in online education to provide an exhaustive explanation of federal regulations. It is important to identify and remind educators of the existence of such laws so that they can be both aware of and informed of their pertinence. This matters in times of accreditation visits, when challenges to administrative or classroom decisions are raised, and most of all to manage the educational process in a manner that is right and ethically sound. Welfel (2016) suggests that the primary regulations to be informed of and to have general working knowledge of are FERPA, HIPAA, HITECH, and the Clery Act. The following is a brief explanation on each of these as they apply to education.

Family Educational Rights and Privacy Act (FERPA)

All educators must be knowledgeable about the federal statute known as Family Educational Rights and Privacy Act of 1974, or FERPA. This law is also known as the Buckley Amendment. While most educators are likely aware of FERPA, many are quickly puzzled by probing questions about what the law does and does not require. In general, this law protects the privacy of students and their parents. It also guarantees that students can access their educational records and even challenge content in their records. While FERPA allows for directory information to be shared and provided to others, sharing any information that discloses a student's personal information is prohibited. The concept of "legitimate educational interest" is a guideline for what can be shared with others about a student. Educators in any venue need to be on guard that a person believing that they have a legitimate educational interest and meeting the law's definition of legitimate need to know do not always align.

All educational institutions should hold a mandatory training each year on the basic points of FERPA. The reason for such a strict directive would be that there are new educators coming in each year who may or may not have an adequate mastery of the concepts of FERPA. Furthermore, the complexity of this federal law is such that it is likely that some points will be easily remembered from year to year while other critical elements of the law may not be recalled as readily. If there are lapses in the compliance with FERPA requirements, it will be in the best interest of educators, administration, and the board of the organization to be able to show that ongoing training is required and that any such lapse can be explained as human error rather than simply not even trying to uphold FERPA statutes.

Health Care Portability and Accountability Act (HIPAA)

Most people are aware of the federal law known as HIPAA. This legislation applies to business practices of health care organizations and how health care information is managed and protected by health care professionals and organizations, such as hospitals and clinics. What many people are not aware of is that there are several provisions in HIPAA that are known as exceptions to confidentiality. Links are included in this chapter that educators can access for more information on HIPAA.

While online education is not a primary focus of HIPAA legislation, it is important for educators and administrators to know that in FERPA, records or even in communication with students, matters such as "I'd like an extension on that assignment ... I'm going through chemotherapy" or

"My child has been diagnosed with … and I may have to withdraw from this class" also belong to protected health information. It is important to be familiar with HIPAA requirements that might interface with educational records and communications with students.

Health Information Technology for Economic and Clinical Health Act (HITECH)

This federal legislation of 2009 continues the regulations from HIPAA in order to address the conduct and business practices of hired entities and business associates related to confidentiality, breaches of privacy, and how protected health information is managed. While the online educator may not have direct need to know about this legislation and what it requires, recognition of the name and purpose of the act is useful and important for all professionals in education. This is especially the case since HITECH relates to electronic health records that an educator could have access to. Organizations that are found to be in violation of HIPAA and HITECH requirements may be faced with fines that total millions of dollars. Persons who are found responsible for breaches of privacy in records also face loss of employment and financial penalties.

Clery Act

This federal law is mentioned here mainly for educators to recognize the name and basic purpose of the law. The Clery Act relates to student safety, which, of course, is not a prime focus of online education in terms of danger on campus. However, educators may hear the term and be in conversations where a general awareness of the law could be helpful. Two main points of the Clery Act are

- warning systems on campus to notify people of imminent danger of violence, storms, et cetera; and
- the requirement of postsecondary educational institutions to publish reports about on-campus violence.

Title IX

Educators in all schools that receive federal funding need to be familiar with the Title IX Act. This law protects everyone from any type of gender or sexual discrimination or harassment. Since this law is very complex and critical for educators to be aware of, a link is provided for more information. The link provided at the end of the chapter under Online Resources will take the reader to a fact sheet on this important legislation. There are numerous ethical considerations in Title IX. Even a casual reading of the law and its stipulations will reveal that compliance with this law is the good and right thing to do. Additionally, to add stringency to the ethical issues contained in Title IX, any school that is not compliance with this law can lose federal funding. Schools must have training for faculty and staff and develop policies to show that Title IX is being adhered to. All of this clearly applies to online education as well as traditional classrooms.

Privileged Communication

Privileged communication is a legal and ethical term to convey that certain information is to remain private. There are conditions that must exist in order for a claim of "privilege" to be established.

Confidentiality is the practice by a professional of honoring that privileged communication. It is important for any professional who served others to know that privileged communication belongs to the client, patient, or in the case of education, the student.

Frequently, professionals in human service fields such as teachers, counselors, social workers, psychologists, physicians, and nurses, are called upon to appear in court for testimony in matters of parenting, well-being of students or patients, competency of a client or patient, and other concerns. It is also a common occurrence for records created by these professionals to be subpoenaed for release. Welfel (2016) provides a very clear overview of what a professional could receive from a court. This includes professionals in education. First, a subpoena is a requirement to appear in court to provide a testimony. A specific type of subpoena is a subpoena duces tecum. This is not only a requirement to appear in court but also to produce designated records.

Finally, distinct from a subpoena is a court order. This is issued by a judge. Laws vary from state to state as to how subpoenas must be responded to. Even in a state where privileged communication is recognized and upheld, professionals need the assistance of an attorney in responding to these mandates from the court. The existence of privileged communication does not mean that a subpoena can be ignored. While professionals have time to respond to directives from the court, it is important to understand that requirements of the court to appear for testimony or to release records cannot be ignored.

One legal precept that every professional need to have awareness of is the **Wigmore test**. The basic point of the Wigmore test is that the court is asked—usually by a person who is being required to provide records of a student, client, or patient—to balance the benefit that may be obtained from the records against the harm that could be done to a person's reputation, status, family ties, et cetera. The four criteria of Wigmore according to Sheppard (n. d.) are as follows:

1. "The communications must originate in a confidence that they will not be disclosed.
2. This element of confidentiality must be essential to the full and satisfactory maintenance of the relation between the parties.
3. The relationship must be one that, in the opinion of the community, ought to be sedulously fostered.
4. The injury to the relationship that disclosure of the communications would cause must." (p. 2)

There have been times when a judge has ruled in favor of the request and has only required a testimony or summary letter of the documents instead of calling for the full record to be released. This has resulted in private matters or details of person's life remaining confidential while the court was able to secure only the information needed for the question(s) most pertinent to the case.

Mandated Reporting/Duty to Warn

All educators need to be informed of the laws in their state about mandatory reporting. This concept refers to the duty of professionals to report the risk of harm of others to law enforcement and protective agencies. In general, these statutes apply to any population that is not able to defend or protect themselves from harm. Specifically, children, elderly, individuals with physical or mental challenges, and pregnant women are the focus of such laws. As specifics of the laws vary from state to state, the ethical issue is that all people deserve a safe environment, and if threats to physical and emotional safety are determined, then health care professionals, educators, and others who have knowledge of such threats need to intervene by reporting. A general concept is that a reasonable suspicion that is reported in good faith is what is expected. Suspicion of abuse is enough to base a report on; we do not need evidence to make such a report.

Educators have a duty to act in response to indicators of self-harm for students. The case of *Eisel v. Board of Education of Montgomery County* (1991) was a confounding and yet insightful process that dealt with educators notifying parents if there is a safety risk for students. The issues of foreseeability and the need for educators to act in the absence of parents while a student is under their care were critical elements in the Maryland Court of Appeals overturning a ruling of the circuit court that had ruled in favor of the school system. Subsequently, the case was remanded back to the original court and again the school system was found to have no liability for the death of the student. One issue that continues to remain a troubling matter for educators was not the question of responsibility for Ms. Eisel's death. The case revolved around the point that the school system did not communicate with the student's parents about the information they had related to Ms. Eisel's comments of self-harm.

Educators and educational systems still must be knowledgeable of and follow institutional policy about how to manage and communicate information about self-harm pertaining to students. It is likely that more cases like this will surface. Training in ethics about student safety, mandated reporting, and organizational policy will be important in protecting students in need. Also, if a complaint does arise from an unreported event of self-harm, defense of the school system will be built on whether state laws about reporting and organizational policy were followed. The personal impact on the professional of not addressing self-harm behaviors in a client weigh heavy for the professional and their peers. For these reasons, it is always to better to err on the side of caution than to avoid addressing self-harm behaviors with a student.

Closely related to the mandated reporting is the concept of **duty to warn**. While this may sound similar to mandated reporting, the distinction is that a person could be in danger without being identified as in a vulnerable population. Such is the case, if an educator or health care professional has information regarding a threat to a person's safety. A review of what is commonly referred to as the Tarasoff case (*Tarasoff v. Regents of the University of California*, 1976) would be helpful to get a broad understanding of what the duty to warn laws are about. In the case of Tatiana Tarasoff, the University of California was found liable for her death due the counseling center having heard threats against her life by Potter. While attempts to notify Ms. Tarasoff were initiated, contact with her was never actually made. Potter did end Ms. Tarasoff's life. The enduring message of this unfortunate case as cited is that "the privilege ends where the public peril begins" (*Tarasoff v. Regents of the University of California*, 1976, p. 347). As already mentioned, these issues could seem to be very removed from the online education format. However, an educator who gains knowledge about a student's risk or about a threat against a student through an email, a text, or in an online class setting could still be one who needs to assist in securing safety for a student.

Preventing Violations of HIPAA/HITECH

Both HIPPA and HITECH have sections that pertain to business partners. Of particular interest and to show the impact of one regulation on another, Doll (2011) explained the details of how two federal laws relate in education and summarized that "HIPAA regulations do not apply if an individual's records are subject to FERPA" (pp. 259–263). Additionally, Pauldi (2008) has provided extensive review of the cases and issues related to matters such as disability claims by students who have been dismissed from educational programs. Claims that come under accommodations of the Americans with Disability Act need attention at the juncture of both students' needs for accommodations and ethical reasoning in policy formation.

While every educator in the health care professions has some general knowledge about HIPAA, it may be that the term HITECH is not easily recognized by many educators. The Health Information Technology for Economic and Clinical Health Act (HITECH Act) accompanies HIPAA in that it requires that health care organizations and professionals carefully monitor and remain vigilant in their business partnerships. This is especially relevant to any business that is involved in the technology of a counseling practice, university, or health care agency. Essentially, in cases of breach of personal information about clients, students, customers, or patients, an organization can no longer assume that this is a problem for companies they hired for encryption or technology management. Investigations related to privacy breaches now address the contractual agreements between health care agencies and their business partners, as well as the due diligence of the hiring organization as to the practices of the partners they contract with. This material is pertinent for online educators to both protect the privacy of students as well as to be informed and vigilant about the privacy practices of any business partner that they associate with in the course of their educational processes. For counseling, psychology, or social work programs, this would include activities such as online meetings, interviews, and recordings for training purposes, as well as student records.

HITECH requires the application of HIPAA security and privacy provisions and penalties directly to business associates of covered entities. Before HITECH, the security and privacy requirements were imposed on business associates through contractual provisions with covered entities. HITECH requires business associates to restrict the use and disclosure of protected health information and subjects business associates directly to civil and criminal penalties for violating HIPAA requirements in the same manner as covered entities. Another key requirement imposed by HITECH is for covered entities and business associates to notify individuals and the U.S. Department of Health and Human Services if an individual's unsecured or unencrypted protected health information "has been, or is reasonably believed ... to have been, accessed, acquired, or disclosed as a result of such breach" (HIPPA Survival Guide, n. d., Sec. 13402(b)).

While these laws relate to health care information, it is prudent to address them in this material as educators—and certainly including online educators—engage with students on various issues. Included in these would be students dealing with illnesses, and students' family and personal problems and excuses for missing class. How many educators have heard instances of students who cannot attend class due to side effects of chemotherapy or surgery and hospital admissions? Even the death of student in an online program can create far reaching implications. Questions of what happened and when it happened, and general concern for a fellow student can border on violating privacy for a family.

Gatekeeping

"While the requirement for counselor educators to fulfill the gatekeeping function is clear, discharging that responsibility can be fraught with complexities and legal risks" (Wheeler & Bertram, 2012, p. 262). Every educator knows that hard decisions on ability have to be made in teaching. When students have difficulty, it is often good teaching that helps them to remediate and recall lessons. However, when there is ongoing difficulty that can even resemble learning problems, an educator often must consider if it is right or fair to accept tuition from a student who has repeated difficulties that prompt remediation. Occasionally, teachers even question a student's ability to succeed in a profession. Every educational institution has been faced with this dilemma and struggled to find acceptable answers. Each organization and each instructor will probably continue to struggle with this practical and ethical question. In the spirit of genuine ethical reasoning, this struggle probably should not be solved in a "one-answer-fits-all model." Facing the uncertainties and puzzle in a straightforward way with honest inquiry and wrestling with the magnitude of the problem will result in better outcomes and fairness for each student involved. Nonetheless, some guidelines, interventions, policies, and even dismissal processes will be useful to address and formulate.

An example to consider comes from the counseling field. While it may be easy to ignore or even fail to notice professional, personal, or placement problems that students present, the American Counseling Association *Code of Ethics* (2014) addresses in strict language that "counselor educators may require students to address any personal concerns that have the potential to affect professional competency" (F.8.d., p. 14). According to F.5.b, both supervisors and students are under ethical requirements to monitor and address any indicators of impairment "when such impairment is likely to harm a client or others" (American Counseling Association, p. 13). This ethical duty stipulates that not only should supervisors and students seek assistance for any impairment that affect their professional functioning, but they should also "limit, suspend, or terminate their professional responsibilities until it is determined they may safely resume their work" (F.5.b, p. 13).

Some additional sections of the ACA *Code of Ethics* that address how counselor educators are instructed to ethically respond to students' difficulties moving through the curriculum are provided here. Counselor educators provide students with ongoing feedback regarding their performance throughout the training program. This section identifies that levels of competence, timing of evaluations, and appraisal processes for progress will be followed (F.9.a, p. 15). Counseling supervisors are directed to recommend dismissal from programs for those students who cannot give evidence of providing competent services to clients (F.6.b, p. 13). Closely aligned with this is section F.9.b, which states through the evaluative process, educators are aware of and address "the inability of some students to achieve counseling competencies" (p. 15). Educators are encouraged to assist their students in understanding and applying their field of study's governing code of ethics.

Decision-Making Capacity

An area that is closely related to health care, which would include mental health counseling services, is decision-making capacity. There are ramifications of this concept that could apply to educators as well. The concept of being able to make decisions in health care relates to the larger concept of informed consent. In essence, health care professionals cannot rely on the agreement of a patient for services if that patient lacks the capacity to make decisions concerning their care. Here is an overview of the criteria for determining decision-making capacity.

A client who has decision-making capacity, in a health care sense, will be able to demonstrate the following:

- Comprehension, or what is often referred to as ability to appreciate, of the situation or need that they are in.
- Comprehension, or appreciation, of the treatment and/or intervention options that are available and viable for them.
- Comprehension, or appreciation, of what will likely occur if no treatment and/or intervention is done.
- A process of deliberation.
- Ability to communicate their decision in an unambiguous manner.

A client who cannot give evidence of each of these steps is determined to lack decision-making capacity. In such instances, a surrogate needs to assist in the process of deciding health care decisions. Obviously, online education is several steps removed from the environment of health care. However, this concept and the steps used to determine a person's capacity is relevant in the practice of online education in several of points.

First, for informed consent to be provided for health care to take place, there has to be some credible method of determining that the client has the ability to provide that consent. In other words, does the client have the decision-making capacity to provide the informed consent that is required for services to be provided? Educators may be asking students for information that is highly sensitive or personal. If through their interactions with students, educators have reason to question a student's ability to provide this information in a reliable and appropriate manner, assistance may be indicated. That assistance could be a more in-depth conversation with the student. It could be a referral to counseling services provided by the institution. In extreme situations it could be a contact with law enforcement to provide what is known as a wellness check for the student.

Second, assessing for the ability to make health care decisions is somewhat nebulous in an in-person setting. The variables and nuances for determining decision-making capacity are only complicated further when the client and counselor are not in each other's presence. That is not to suggest that the assessment of decision-making cannot be done in distance counseling, but only that careful attention to details and creative approaches to arriving at that conclusion will be extremely important to follow and adhere to.

Third, health care providers must be aware that the process of determining decision-making capacity is not the same as a mental status exam. Furthermore, a history of substance abuse or mental health diagnosis does not in itself prove that a person lacks decision-making capacity. Capacity is also distinct from the legal concept of competency. Competency is determined in a legal process and assesses whether a person has the ability to manage business and financial matters and to function in their own best interest. It is possible that an individual could have the competency to live alone and manage their daily affairs but not demonstrate the capacity to make good decisions for their best interest. From one perspective it could be argued that this happens every day, as people make poor decisions. According to the virtue of autonomy, it could be further argued that persons even have the right to make poor decisions. However, from an ethical perspective and in striving for the highest level of professional conduct, it could also be held that if educators notice trends and examples that students are not making decisions that are conducive to successful outcomes for their advancement in learning and careers, some intervention is warranted.

A lack of decision-making capacity could be temporary, and this suggests even more that if educators notice a change in a student's demeanor and behavior as an outcome of their decision-making, at least some further inquiry is warranted regarding the necessity of referral for assistance. The focus on capacity is not only to assess whether a person has the ability to make decisions that are deemed "good," which is vague, circumstantial, and even a matter of judgment. It is also critical to assess that a person has the ability to make decisions that foster their best interest and professional functioning. Lest this sound like a remote and infrequent concern, consider the actual experience of a graduate intern who was dismissed by three agencies for problems ranging from lack of skill, to awkward personal engagements, to client complaints, and occasional eccentric behavior. This was a graduate student who had succeeded in all of the course work. When faculty addressed these terminations with the intern and asked what the intern thought this meant, the response was "I think another site will be better for me." Clearly, the intern lacked insight and awareness. Furthermore, it could be noted that borrowing from the health care concept of decision-making capacity, this intern lacked the capacity by several of those precepts.

This experience required not only administrative guidance about the determinations for the career of this person so near to graduation, but also ethical guidance on the issues of justice, nonmaleficence, fidelity, and beneficence. This situation can and should be reviewed to see if there were indicators of problems with this student earlier in the program of study that needed to be addressed. At the same time, with passing grades and without the spotlight of regular evaluation of clinical skills, it also demonstrates that some students can move through a curriculum under the radar, so to speak, until the situation reaches a very unfortunate point. Does this reveal something about entrance criteria into graduate educational programs? Does this identify that earlier and more practical assessments be done to gauge a student's likelihood of success in the chosen profession? Does this call into question how interventions are being done and should be done with students who on margin of developing or managing problems? If the answer is yes to any of these questions, then accordingly there are ethical issues to also be reviewed and policy revisions that need to be constructed with ethical awareness and interventions. Again, if these points are pertinent to residential programs, how much more critical are these points for online educational programs?

The issue of decision-making capacity relates to another ethical issue known as informed consent. Informed consent requires that a person be told about what will happen to them, in a medical treatment for example, and they have an opportunity to ask questions. Consent has to be voluntary, and special attention to make sure that a person is willingly participating is provided to any person who is considered to be in a vulnerable population. Students with special needs or who require accommodations could be considered to be in a vulnerable population. If a person is determined to lack the capacity to make decisions, then special arrangements have to be made to make certain that a person's wishes are followed or that the person understands what is happening in their life.

Some examples of informed consent in education include the following. Does the person grasp that education, especially in a field of mental health or health care, can be an experience and environment that will likely activate challenging and even traumatic memories from one's past? Does the person understand that enrollment in a counselor education curriculum, or any health care field, does not guarantee successful completion and placement in that profession? Does the person understand that legal and ethical difficulties in one's history could impact whether a state will even grant a license to practice if one graduates from a counseling program?

Educators who are training students in health professions, including mental health professions, hold the ethical duty to provide informed consent to students and to assess the capacity of the student to comprehend the informed consent as it applies to them. Nearing the end of completing their program of study is not a time to hear a student say, "Nobody told me that" or "I didn't understand that." Communication is important in education to assist both educators and students to be successful. Chapter 4 in this textbook discusses this topic in more detail.

Syllabus

As all educators know, a syllabus for a course is essentially a contract. What many educators may not have considered that a syllabus is in many respects a document of ethical direction and behavior for both the student and the educator. In online education, this agreement is critical to avoid misunderstandings, complaints, and even lawsuits. If such unfortunate situations do arise, the syllabus will be one of the main documents to be reviewed and explored that impact the outcome of the complaint or litigation.

In situations of grievances, complaints, appeals, or litigation, a syllabus will be one of the first discoverable documents to referenced. The material in the syllabus—or, unfortunately, material not addressed in the syllabus—may decide the outcome of a disagreement on expectations or grades in a course. In online programs, face-to-face discussions and impromptu meetings in a hallway to clarify misunderstandings are not possible. Obviously, the avoidance of such conflicts or disagreements would be advisable. The detailed elements of the syllabus are explored in Chapter 7.

Vicarious Liability

In the practice of online education, including online supervision, the issue of vicarious liability must be thought through carefully and managed well. The legal term for being responsible for a subordinate's actions is *respondeat superior*. "Supervisors may be named as defendants in malpractice suits on the basis that the supervisor is 'vicariously' liable for the acts of the supervisee" (Wheeler & Bertram, 2012, p. 266). Clearly, documentation on every supervisory session is critical, including what was addressed in the session and the direction that was given for cases where an intern or student is in obvious need of direction. Additionally, policies on how urgent situations are to be managed, what constitutes an emergency, and immediate steps for an intern or student to follow are important ethical elements for good practice as well as protection for learner and educator. Most educators will be knowledgeable about the seriousness of liability in teaching students. The point for consideration in online education is that this issue only magnifies and enlarges when the teaching and supervision occurs when the supervisor is not in physical proximity to the place where care is provided.

Boundaries in Online Education

All educational programs fall under their respective code of ethics, and each focus on healthy boundaries between educators and students, and as applicable, practitioners and clients. For example, personal and professional boundaries is a topic of intense focus in the ACA *Code of Ethics* (2014). Material in this section relates to counselor education and supervision. The material, however, can be a template for other educators to consider in their decisions and relationships with students. Given the dynamics of online education being done at a distance with typically no personal proximity, it could be questioned why and how the term *boundaries* would apply. Basically, if two people are not in physical contact, how does a need for a boundary exist? Through the various mechanisms of the virtual world, people can essentially be close without being close in person.

The ACA *Code of the Ethics* provides guidance to counselors and counselor educators that demonstrates how boundary violations are to be avoided and thereby addresses how violations can occur if these guidelines are not followed. While these points apply to the profession of mental health counseling, the points can be applicable to any educational setting and by any educator. Section F of the ACA *Code of Ethics* addresses the topics of supervision, training, and teaching. All educators should carefully read and know the implications of this section, or the respective ethics of their profession. Rather than recite this entire section, relevant material for online counseling and student-instructor relationships will be reviewed. Section F.8 of the ACA *Code of Ethics* is dedicated to the topic of student welfare.

The entire F.10 section of the ACA *Code of Ethics* addresses roles and relationships between counselors, educators, and students (2014). In this section, sexual and romantic relationships are prohibited "with students currently enrolled and over whom they have power and authority" by a definitive statement that "this applies to both in-person and electronic interactions or relationships" (F.10.a; p. 15). Regarding former students, the *Code of Ethics* directs that faculty members discuss with former students potential risks when they consider engaging in social, sexual, or other intimate relationships (F.10.c). Associated with this, sexual harassment is prohibited by the ACA code (F.10.b).

The counseling profession addresses issue of boundaries with the terms *boundary crossings*, *boundary extensions*, and *boundary violations* (Gutheil & Gabbard, 1993). As has been addressed, boundaries are often considered in terms of physical closeness and proximity. However, relationships that cross boundaries that can often result in boundary violations can begin in written communication. Online educators need to be cognizant of boundary issues and how to act in ethical ways to stay within professional boundaries.

The following are some discussion questions and topics for faculty meetings of online educators:

> How do colleagues respond to awkward or inappropriate messages from students?
>
> What is the best way of responding to requests from students that are questionable in terms of professional boundaries?
>
> How can attention seeking by dependent students be balanced with diplomacy, discretion, caution, and firmness as needed?

It is an obvious and yet important reminder to mention that ethical problems are not usually the result of a sudden or impromptu decision to do something wrong or questionable. While impulsivity and poor judgement can result in very problematic circumstances, it is often the case that those problematic circumstances have a trail of lesser and simultaneously mounting events behind them.

One ill-advised comment leads to another and then another. Ultimately, judgement is clouded, and people say and do things in this escalated environment with emotions that are skewed. Reason becomes tainted and people find themselves in predicaments that they never consciously intended to be in. Or even if they did have some vague intent to press the limits, they now realize that this has moved beyond what was initially intended.

An interesting way to think about why and how people are attracted to risky behavior is by considering Morin's erotic formula (Morin, 1995). Jack Morin constructed an equation that stated that attraction + obstacles = excitement. This equation is not only pertinent for sexual matters. A review of human nature according to the author reveals that, in general, people chose to entertain a certain level of risk in their lives. This could be driving over a speed limit, pushing financial matters too far, or not following policies or regulations. This could even include being capricious with a professional code of ethics. Essentially, Morin's work teaches that when an attraction encounters an obstacle, something of a challenge rises in a person's mind. Closely associated with this challenge are the emotions of risk and the rush of adrenaline that is associated with trying something new, demanding, or even dangerous. Even with this brief introduction, the concerns of ethical behavior or violations thereof become visible and apparent.

Educators, and especially online educators, may be confronted with questionable behavior. This is because people often express themselves differently through the use of technology and the sense of anonymity that this conveys. Without being suspicious of every student's actions or intentions, it is prudent for online educators to have an awareness of the reality that social media can be a means for inappropriate behavior to surface.

The aerial model in Figure 11.1 presents a way to visualize steps educators can take in responding to students who appear to pose boundary extensions or violations.

This brief incremental outline conveys a generic way that anyone can use to respond to questionable comments or initiatives by others. **Discretion** basically means that others' behavior can be ignored, time can be allowed to see if a behavior or comment happens again, or the behavior can be gently questioned in an open-ended way to try to assess what was intended. **Diplomacy** means that in dealing with others we can make requests for certain behaviors to cease, name other behaviors that are expected to start, and state personal limits and preferences. **Caution** would involve avoiding individuals who could pose a threat or cause one to feel uncomfortable. This could also involve having a witness present if encounters must be maintained. Also, keeping documentation of what has occurred would be a way to use caution in case behaviors continue to be uncomfortable and threatening. Finally, if one has advanced through these steps or if an encounter is clearly provocative, confronting a person's comments or behavior directly may be the best option. While the model is obviously basic and is not intended to be detailed, the simplicity of it also allows for a quick recall and easy formulation as to what may seem to be the most effective response at the time.

If an educator uses a personal example of how they managed a challenging experience in life, it may be a meaningful learning opportunity. However, such disclosures may be misquoted, misunderstood, or maligned by others. Educators would be wise to consider that any use of situations

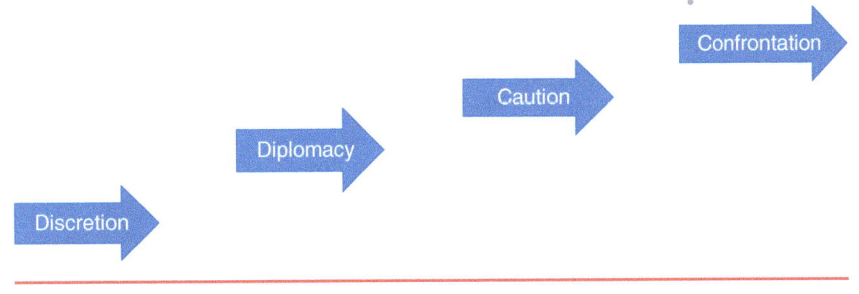

FIGURE 11.1

from their own life should be shared only with the full recognition that there are risks of disclosure beyond the setting of the classroom. The best decision process for such disclosures would be to first consider whether there could be any adverse consequences realized by the educator or their institution if this example is shared publicly.

Social Media

The environment of social media, including both the means and the type of messaging that can be shared, is changing daily. New technology and devices constantly alter the types of messages and details of messages that can shared. How many times have professionals in any vocation been cautioned about the need for discretion and careful thought before posting pictures and messages only to disregard that advice and act impulsively? Careers have been ruined through posting messages that was insensitive, pictures that were indecent, and personal information that was inappropriate. Rosen (2010) explained the decision by a university to deny a degree to an education major for posting pictures of themselves online depicting a drunken condition. The student sued the university under the clause of freedom of speech. The university maintained that this was not behavior becoming to a professional and could even promote drinking behavior to an underaged audience, such as students. A federal court upheld the denial of the degree.

The preceding suggestions may not appear to be directly associated with ethical behavior. Closer analysis would suggest something different. As the principles of ethical reasoning were discussed in this chapter, it is a smooth transition to consider that questionable actions on social media can result in harm to careers, relationships, innocent persons, and the educational institutions a person represents. An online classroom is an environment through which people can be bullied, disrespected, and even threatened. Educators acting with an awareness of ethics will be vigilant to monitor for such events. Furthermore, ethical behavior would dictate that educators themselves set an example of appropriate conduct and decision making in their online behavior also. Experience has shown far too many times that what was thought to not do any harm in the world of social media has in fact caused harm to oneself or to others. Even something that begins in an innocuous way, can often escalate or be construed as much more virulent, offensive, or hostile manner.

National Council for State Authorization Reciprocity Agreements (NC-SARA)

The State Authorization Reciprocity Agreements, commonly known as SARA, provides a voluntary, regional approach to state oversight of postsecondary distance education.

Postsecondary schools that participate in NC-SARA provide information to students about requirements that they will have to comply with after graduation in order to qualify for a license or certification. The ethical aspect of this relates to making sure that a person knows those requirements before paying tuition and meeting the rigors of a curriculum. One component of the ethics of this is people will also know what could disqualify them from obtaining their desired credentials. For example, some professions will not credential a person who has certain types of legal convictions. Therefore, before a person pays tuition and earns a degree, they will know if they will or will not qualify in certain professions. Ideally, according to the *SARA Policy Manual* (National Council for State Authorization Reciprocity Agreements, 2020) guidelines, a school would post the requirements for each state for every license or certification that can be obtained by earning a degree in a major from their school. Students and prospective students can then search this site for specific credentials they will be seeking in states of interest to them.

Chapter Summary

In this chapter, ethical concepts have been introduced that may be unfamiliar for educators. Other points may have been more familiar, and this chapter has provided a review of that material. While part of the focus has been related to counselor education, the concepts have application to a wide variety of educational settings. Of particular interest in this chapter is for online educators to gain a working knowledge of this material so that their work can be done in compliance with sound ethical practice and adherence to policies and laws that will protect and serve students, families, and educational institutions, as well as the educators.

Online Resources

Family Educational Rights and Privacy Act (FERPA)

This website provided by the U.S. Department of Education provides readers with information on FERPA; they can locate guidelines for FERPA as well as connection to how it applies to topics such as laws, student loans and grants: https://www2.ed.gov/policy/gen/guid/fpco/ferpa/index.html

National Council for State Authorization Reciprocity Agreements (NC-SARA)

This website provides information on NC-SARA and links to resources including the NC-SARA Manual 20.2, the NC-SARA Applications for States and Institutions, the 2020 Data Reporting Handbook, and the NC-SARA 2019 Data Report: Enrollment & Out-of-State Learning Placements: http://nc-sara.org/content/faqs

Online Training Modules

This U.S. Department of Education website provides online training modules for educators and students on how to protect student privacy: https://studentprivacy.ed.gov/content/online-training-modules

Protecting Student Privacy

This U.S. Department of Education website provides resources useful to educators for protecting student privacy: https://studentprivacy.ed.gov/resources

TITLE IX

The Myra Sadker Foundation website provides information on Title IX as it applies to education: https://www.sadker.org/TitleIX.html

U.S. Department of Health and Human Services

These websites provide information on HIPPA for professionals, including information on the security and privacy rules: https://www.hhs.gov/hipaa/index.html

https://www.hhs.gov/hipaa/for-professionals/index.html

https://www.hhs.gov/hipaa/for-professionals/security/laws-regulations/index.html

https://www.hhs.gov/hipaa/for-professionals/privacy/laws-regulations/index.html

References

American Counseling Association. (2014). *2014 ACA code of ethics*. http://www.counseling.org/resources/aca-code-of-ethics.pdf

Corey, G., Corey, M. S., Corey, C., & Callahan, P. (2015). *Issues and ethics in the helping professions* (9th ed.). Brooks/Cole.

Doll, B. (2011). Youth privacy, school records, and the ethical practice of psychology in schools. *Professional Psychology: Research and Practice, 42*, 259–263.

Eisel v. Board of Education, 324 Md. 376, 597 A.2d 447 (1991). https://casetext.com/case/eisel-v-board-of-education

Gutheil, T. G., & Gabbard, G. O. (1993). The concept of boundaries in clinical practice. *American Journal of Psychiatry, 150,* 188–196.

HIPPA Survival Guide. (n. d.). *HITECH breach notifications: Sec. 13402(b).* http://www.hipaasurvivalguide.com/hitech-act-13402.php

Holland, T. P., & Kilpatrick, A. C. (1991). Ethical issues in social work: Toward a grounded theory of professional ethics. *Social Work, 36,* 138–144.

Kempworth, T. J. (2005). *Collaborative consultation in the schools* (3rd ed.). Pearson.

Kitchener, K. S. (1984). Intuition, critical evaluation and ethical principles: The foundation for ethical decisions in counseling psychology. *Counseling Psychologist, 12,* 43–45.

Kitchener, K. S., & Anderson, S. K. (2011). *Foundations of ethical practice, research and teaching in psychology* (2nd ed.). Lawrence Erlbaum.

Morin, J. (1995). *The erotic mind: Unlocking the inner sources of passion and fulfillment.* Harper Collins.

National Council for State Authorization Reciprocity Agreements. (2020). *SARA Policy Manual.* https://nc-sara.org/resources/nc-sara-manual-202

Paludi, M. A. (2008). *Understanding and preventing campus violence.* Praeger.

Remley, T. P., & Herlihy, B. (2010). *Ethical, legal, and professional issues in counseling* (3rd ed.). Pearson-Merrill.

Rosen, J. (2010, July 25). The web means the end of forgetting. *The New York Times Magazine.* http://www.nytimes.com/2010/07/25/magazine/25privacy-t2.html?pagewanted=all&_r=0

Sheppard, G. (n.d.). *Notebook on ethics, standards, and legal issues for counselors and psychotherapists: Confidentiality and the Wigmore criteria.* Canadian Counselling and Psychotherapy Association. https://www.ccpa-accp.ca/wp-content/uploads/2016/05/NOE.Confidentiality-and-the-Wigmore-Criteria.pdf

Sue, D. W., & Sue, D. (2012). *Counseling the culturally diverse: Theory and practice* (6th ed.). Wiley.

Tarasoff v. Regents of the University of California, 17 Cal. 3d 425, 131 Cal. Rptr. 14, 551 P.2d 334 (1976). https://www.lexis-nexis.com/community/casebrief/p/casebrief-tarasoff-v-regents-of-univ-of-cal

Welfel, E., (2016). *Ethics in counseling and psychotherapy: Standards, research, and emerging issues.* Cengage.

Wheeler, A., & Bertram, B. (2012). *The counselor and the law: A guide to legal and ethical practice* (7th ed.). American Counseling Association.

CHAPTER TWELVE

Administration of Online Teaching

Matthew Lyons, PhD
Marina Bunch, MA, LMHC

This chapter is written against the backdrop of the Covid-19 global pandemic. The effects of the pandemic are well known, still active, and certainly will punctuate the pages of history for generations to come. The pandemic impact is multifaceted and far reaching for individuals and organizations worldwide. However, educational institutions have uniquely felt the impact. In fact, at the time of writing these words, the United States and numerous other countries around the world are facing a second wave of the pandemic in which education institutions nationwide are considering alternatives to in-person classes and events for the second time in a year. According to a UNESCO report, approximately 1.2 billion students around the world have experienced disruptions to their education as a result of the pandemic (Giannini, 2020).

One strategy for coping with the pandemic has been to turn traditional education into online education. K–12 institutions and institutions of higher education alike pivoted to variations of online and hybrid delivery formats. In fact, the United States Census Bureau, in a report titled *Schooling During the COVID-19 Pandemic*, suggests that approximately 93% of families with school-aged children reported using online delivery modalities (Mcelrath, 2020). The speed of the pivot cannot be understated, as it has implications for our discussion later in the chapter. Only a few months ago the topic of administration of online programs would have been applicable to those who were either already running online programs or were considering the development of online programs.

Given the current cultural milieu, the following pages have application to nearly every education administrator. It is a unique time in which we can arguably say that most administrators around the world have now wrestled with the realities of online education either by choice or by consequence of the Covid-19 pandemic. Accordingly, the pandemic response has affirmed the legitimacy of programs already online. It has forced many who were resistant to online models to embrace the virtual delivery formats. This forced response has opened the door to more serious inquiry and provided the opportunity to look at the phenomenon from every angle. Online education is now, more than ever, a permanent reality in the landscape of education at every level.

It would be insufficient to proceed without acknowledging the impact of our nearly universal rapid shift online. However, this chapter is not on the response to the pandemic. Online academic programs were prolific long before the pandemic. They have proliferated over several decades. The Integrated Postsecondary Education Data System (IPEDS), established as the primary higher education data collection program of the U.S. Department of Education, is charged with responsibility for data, research, and evaluation (Institute of Education Sciences, n.d.). IPEDS started tracking online enrollment in 2011, and by 2018 found 35.3% of students in degree-granting institutions who participate in Title IV had at least one distance education course (National Center for Education Statistics, n.d.).

Online programs frequently operate with decentralized organizational structures (Lundberg & Sheridan, 2015), which means that frequently an individual's only contact with faculty, staff, and certainly students may be in virtual spaces. The shift signifies the terrain for relationships, accountability, and handling ethical considerations must be navigated differently. The pace of change seems to be faster and the demand on response times shorter. The ever-present need to understand new technology and thus provide support for those learning technologies for the first time occurs more frequently. Finally, the lack of parity in access to technological resources continues to be a challenge for online learners.

Many programs and administrations have gone to the online platform by choice; others have done so by influence of forces outside their control. Regardless, the discourse related to online education is more accessible and more relevant. Certainly, the conversation is more welcomed than ever. Therefore, administrators rather new to online delivery, or those to which this is familiar terrain, have a unique opportunity to explore and further develop online offerings.

The administration of online programs is a robust topic deserving a full textbook of its own. This chapter explores the major considerations for the administration of online programs across K–12 and higher education, which is such a vast range; that alone is a challenge given the limitations of a book chapter. However, what follows is, in the authors' view, the primary considerations for administrators who lead or aspire to lead online programs.

Leadership Matters

Leadership is a vast topic and the literature is replete with attempts to define it effectively. In fact, it can be argued that there are as many definitions of leadership as there are leaders (Lyons, 2012). However, understanding the applicable literature and having a clear theoretical approach to leadership is important for any administrative leader. It is especially important for those of online programs given the decentralized leadership structure that typifies online learning.

A plethora of scholars have endeavored to explain leadership over the years. There are robust musings about leadership lining the shelves of our bookstores and libraries. Much of that literature is based on anecdotal accounts and personal experience. Everyone from military officers, business CEOs, politicians, and the like have offered their perspectives. However, the most helpful writing about the topic comes from the academic literature, where you find two primary lines of inquiry. Those lines are related to **leader traits** and **leader behaviors** and their relative effectiveness in leadership (DeRue et al., 2011). In fact, the academic inquiry begs an answer to the question of which is more important -what a leader does or who a leader is?

DeRue et al. (2011) developed an integrative framework to explore the interaction of leader traits and behaviors through a large-scale meta-analysis. The authors found that within the trait paradigm, **conscientiousness** proved most important. Conscientiousness refers to the "extent to which a person is dependable, dutiful, and achievement oriented, and is often associated with deliberate planning and structure" (DeRue et al., 2011, p. 14). However, the results suggest that despite the trait of conscientiousness, overall, leader behaviors are more important than leader traits. According to the same authors, "overall, we found that leader behaviors had a greater impact on leadership effectiveness than did leader traits" (2011, p. 37). The results are encouraging because we know that behaviors can be learned; however, it leaves us with the question of which behaviors are most important. The same study points to the effectiveness of behaviors rooted in transformational leadership theory.

Transformational Leadership

Transformational leadership has four key concepts that guide the leader: individualized consideration, idealized influence, inspirational motivation, and intellectual stimulation (Bass, 1999; Northouse, 2010). A brief summary is appropriate, yet the reader is encouraged to pursue the literature on this theory further and to consider the implications for education administration. **Individualized consideration** refers to how a leader tends to follower needs. Through this lens, faculty and staff are seen as contributors and their wellness is a key consideration on the mind of the leader (Kouzes & Posner, 2006, 2010).

The concept of **idealized influence** takes into consideration how a leader compels the best from the faculty and staff (de Vries & Engellau, 2010; Herzog & Zimmerman 2009). Third, **inspirational motivation** reflects the energy invested in setting and pursuing a vision. Finally, the fourth tenet, **intellectual stimulation**, suggests the leader is key in stimulating innovation, creating an environment that fosters critical questions, and fostering creativity in solutions (Lyons, 2012). In total, transformational leadership theory might be best summed up in a quote from Kouzes and Posner when they state that "the most significant contributions leaders make are not to today's bottom line but to the long-term development of individuals and intuitions that adapt, prosper, and grow" (2006, p. 18).

Authentic Leadership

The principles of transformational leadership are not the only model worth study. The concepts of transformational leadership arguably paved the way for authentic leadership theory to emerge. Accordingly, authentic leaders are effective because their approach creates work environments that empower others to be their best. As such, authentic leaders are generally balanced, have high levels of self-awareness, extend empathy, and act with transparency (Lyons, 2012). Authentic leaders, because they act out of the best of their true selves, are able to cultivate the best in others (George, 2007; Northouse, 2010).

Bill George (2007) developed an integrated **authentic leadership** model that includes the interaction of values and principles, motivations, support team, integrated life, and self-awareness. Well-developed interaction between these domains points to what he calls one's "true north." Ultimately, your "true north" is your purpose for leadership. However, it cannot be understated, George places high importance on self-awareness and personal transformation as essential to the development of an authentic leadership style.

Self-awareness is especially key to effectively leading online programs. The traditional face-to-face conversations, full of verbal and nonverbal cues, are often replaced with an email, instant message, or online meetings where cameras may or may not be activated. Therefore, input from colleagues, students, and even supervisors can be harder to read, synthesize, and understand accurately.

Online programs frequently operate with decentralized structures, which means a shift in how we relate to others, the pace at which we interact and respond, and the need to both understand and use technology effectively while assisting others to do the same. For these reasons and others, it is imperative that online leaders have a clear sense of self and a well-developed set of guiding principles for their approach to leadership. This chapter provides a preliminary review of the topic of leadership, and, suffice it to say, administrative leaders of online programs should consider investing the time in studying the forementioned leadership models. It is further advised that such leaders consider personal counseling or professional coaching, or minimally seek mentors that can help facilitate the necessary growth and resulting self-awareness.

Building the Team—Faculty and Staff

Following the importance of a well-developed leader with an integrated sense of self and intentional leadership strategy comes the importance of developing a high-caliber faculty and staff team. It is possible to build an online team with great faculty and staff who have experience only in traditional programs and delivery modalities. Certainly, training and professional development can bridge any existing gaps; however, online education has been well established and there are faculty and staff at all levels who have significant experience teaching in online environments. It is particularly important to build a team with experts in online learning and to welcome their experience and insights to help fulfill the overall vision.

Portugal (2015) notes the importance of having a faculty who both affirm the value of online education and can be successful in the online environment in order to meet the growing demand for online education. As such, the administrative leader need have intentional and focused recruiting strategies, faculty teambuilding and development, and a clear evaluation and accountability processes. This comprehensive approach is essential to supporting online education programs.

Recruiting and Retention

Recruiting practices designed with online success in mind are essential (Parsons & Shelton, 2019). The research is clear that there are particular skills and characteristics necessary for success in the online environment. Portugal (2015) suggests that online instructors have the following: "(a) good organizational skills (b) effective time management, (c) positive work attitude and behavior (e.g., patience, diligence), (d) ability to be comfortable in an online learning environment, (e) technological competence, and (f) flexibility in dealing with student needs" (p. 37). The traditional interview process may not accurately assess for these skills.

It serves administrators well to examine their own practices and make sure the hiring processes accurately reflects the proposed work environment. It is important that prospective faculty demonstrate the ability to establish meaningful connections and work effectively in the virtual space. Portugal (2015) offers some helpful suggestions for making the process more accurate for staffing online programs. Notably, the authors suggest online teaching demonstrations, handling first assignment submission, and even walking through the online faculty review process as part of the interview.

The primary author's institution, when hiring online faculty, conducts the full interview process online. In fact, there are no on-campus requirements prior to hiring if the teaching assignment is 100% online. The interview process continues to evolve but is designed very much to demonstrate potential faculty members' ability to successfully engage in online education. It is a real misconception that the traditional interview process can accurately vet high caliber online faculty.

In addition to quality faculty and support staff, administrators need to focus resources on hiring experts in instructional design and online program management. As educators learn to teach online, they likely will not have the instructional design skills to present courses in the learning management system (LMS) that are appealing, professional, and effective. Or if they do, the time spent is prohibitive given the expectations of the role. Effective instructional designers can roll out systems that will support all educators within an organization, while also providing individual collaborative faculty support (Parsons & Shelton 2019).

Also, hiring a director for online education, or similar roles, serves as a clear indicator of the serious intent to deliver quality online education. Because of the various technological platforms used in online programs and the decentralized structure of faculty and staff, oversight and use of data becomes of paramount importance. Online program directors or managers can facilitate the dissemination of the unique expertise and resources required in online education and help administrators monitor assessment data and promote student success.

Faculty and Staff Training and Engagement

The decentralized nature of online program administration makes faculty training and engagement important. The criteria listed above have been found to be important skills for online faculty. The list is in no way exhaustive. In fact, the research is meager in the area of specialized skills needed for online educators and much work is yet to be done to further explore the area, although there are some basic criteria as offered in the literature. Many online administrators are growing programs, have the support to hire, and have developed hiring strategies for bringing on dedicated expertise and experience. Others are more likely to work with an existing faculty who have varied experience with online education and must continue to integrate the necessary skills as they transition from traditional classrooms. In either case, leading a group of faculty and staff to teach students online requires active and ongoing attention to training and faculty engagement.

TRAINING

Professional development of faculty through ongoing training and access to resources is an important part of the academic administrator's role. In fact, Fredericksen (2018) found it ranked with the top three concerns for administrators, followed closely by student support and strategic planning. It is especially important for administrators of online programs to recognize the different needs of online educators. Additionally, it is necessary to ensure that professional development and training offer both faculty and staff every opportunity for the ongoing development of required expertise and skills to be successful in online education (Hammond et al., 2018).

In fact, it is increasingly likely to see the requirement for ongoing training featured in faculty job recruitment materials and position announcements (Bates & LaBrecque, 2019). This is consistent with Roache et al. (2020) who suggest that training be formally integrated as a matter of policy. The recommendation allows for training to move from being a recommendation that is dependent upon the individual motivation of the faculty and staff, to building a culture of professional development that standardizes both the expectation and the experience across faculty and staff group to ensure movement toward best practices.

Johnson et al. (2020) offer a glimpse at the type of training online faculty desire. Their research suggests faculty requested resources for supporting remote students, access to dedicated online educational materials, training related to best practices for working online, and, of course, technology. However, this is in no way an exhaustive list.

Having surveyed our large online faculty group regarding training needs, the requests have been diverse and include curriculum-specific requests such as best practices for grading discussion boards, discerning plagiarism in online education, and supporting struggling or unengaged students. However, their requests also include more personal topics such as faculty wellness and remaining connected in the virtual workplace. It is important to offer training on the specific technological platforms being used by the program.

Whether a matter of policy or not, it is clear that a robust and consistent approach to professional development is essential. The administrator might start by surveying their faculty and staff to inquire about the areas in which they would like to see additional training. However, it is the responsibility of the administrator to work with institutional resources and decide how best to incentivize and ensure ongoing improvement through consistent training.

Faculty and Staff Connection

Due to the decentralized nature of working online, the traditional points of professional connection are less possible, or certainly less frequent. Hammond et al. (2018) state, "the geographic separation from campus may prevent online faculty from the benefits of daily interaction, community, and opportunities for collaboration that are inherent in campus-based teaching position" (p. 4). Yet, such restricted opportunities can impact faculty wellness and effectiveness. In fact, research suggests that connection with colleagues is an important factor in faculty satisfaction (Hammond et al., 2018).

It is important that faculty and staff feel connected to the institution, the vision and mission of the programs, to students, and to one another. The online venue forces us to think about connecting differently. The truth of the matter is connection in the online environment must be scheduled. It is incumbent upon the administrator to set the expectation for meetings and faculty and staff participation in said meeting structure.

Evidence suggests that faculty desire to connect (Hammond et al., 2018). How faculty and staff achieve a feeling of connectedness varies significantly. Strategies for connection must connect back to one's understanding of leadership and thus be informed by it. One approach to developing faculty and staff connectedness is to have meetings that are high in frequency but low intensity. As such, connecting frequently is important but heavy agendas are not required all the time. For example, weekly staff meetings and bi-weekly or monthly faculty meetings may be helpful. It is important to be in regular contact but said meetings can become dreaded if they are heavy with content and expectation. On the other hand, faculty and staff may resent the time spent if it does not prove valuable. The leader's goal is then to strike a balance between the importance of relationship and productivity.

It can be helpful to include team-building moments as part of a meeting agenda. This can be achieved by regularly using breakout rooms to offer opportunities to connect in small groups. For example, small group discussion centered around the question, "If you could return to yourself in your first year of teaching and give yourself some advice, what would it be?" This type of discussion allows for variously experienced faculty and staff to share with one another their learning experiences and form deeper connection. Furthermore, individual faculty and staff can be encouraged to start various types of meetings or support groups that increase opportunities for faculty to find connection and mutual support.

Vulnerability is a key tenet in authentic leadership (George, 2007). Honoring vulnerability goes a long way to fostering meaningful connections in professional environments. As leaders, we add value to our teams when we ensure that we tend to the basic needs of those with whom we work. Handwritten notes, emails just expressing thanks, brief text messages, and personal phone calls are an important part of the way we conceptualize and foster faculty connection, engagement, and wellness. Especially when we know of faculty and staff facing challenges, picking up the phone and calling them is still a profound way to communicate care and concern and encourage authentic connection.

Evaluation

Evaluation of faculty and staff is a primary function for administrators. The expectations for online faculty and staff differ than those of traditional faculty and staff; however, there is certainly overlap that occurs depending significantly on institutional expectations. That said, it is imperative that administrators ensure that the evaluation is consistent with the expectations of working online (Thomas et al., 2018). Faculty and staff may experience an exercise in frustration when their work is not accurately reflected in the evaluation criteria.

The upside of evaluation in online education is the ready access to data. Generally, the administrator has easy access to recorded class lectures and engagement data through the LMS, along with student course evaluations. The faculty and staff evaluation processes are best when aligned with the stated job descriptions of the positions.

Understanding the difference in job responsibilities and having these reflected in evaluations is particularly important for more traditional organizations and institutions who transition to online education. It takes purposeful and intentional effort to transition the evaluation measures. Not only do annual performance evaluations need to be revisited but so do all promotion, tenure, and ranking systems. The criteria for these processes and the means of evaluation that were typically based on traditional understandings of education now need to reflect the online working environment, expectations, and responsibilities. It is important to work with relevant organizational/institutional entities, including human resources and legal departments, to revise and make equitable processes consistent with the reality of online education.

Student Engagement and Support Services

Ultimately, all education programs are evaluated in terms of student success. This focus does not change for online versus traditional programs; therefore, online programs must consider the wholistic development of student support services that parallel their traditional counterparts. Online programs today must consider employing online advisors, tutors, tech support staff, and more (Parsons & Shelton, 2019). The services may be similar in nature but will call for different delivery, as strategies for student success and engagement will vary across K–12, four-year colleges, and graduate programs.

That said, there are two key components of student success to consider: engagement and support services. Wide-ranging opinions exist on how to define student engagement, as it is the precursor to student success—and ultimately, retaining students and fostering their success is the common goal guiding all of education. A consensus does not exist when it comes to defining student engagement (Blakely & Major, 2019). However, Blakely and Major offer a general way of conceptualizing the concept stating that "engagement is students' willingness and desire to contribute and be successful in a learning process that leads them to higher-level thinking and long-term understanding" (2019, p. 3). Student engagement is both a process and a goal. The strength of online education is in accessibility and flexibility, although both are also part of the challenge when it comes to student engagement.

Synchronous and asynchronous programs have necessary benchmarks for student engagement and ways to support such. There are models such as that offered by Salmon (2016) that help conceptualize engagement, while Mason's (2011) research offers specific recommendations of tasks that will foster engagement in online education. Both the forementioned are geared toward the asynchronous learning environment. For those synchronous or hybrid designs, the criteria for engagement are different.

In fact, for synchronous modalities, engagement may look more like traditional in-person delivery. It can be argued that attendance in online meetings is an essential part of engagement. Administrators must wrestle with policy regarding attendance and more importantly presence or deciding what it means to be present for a live class meeting held online. It is a common occurrence to find students attending while driving in their vehicles, lying in bed, or sitting in the bleachers at a baseball game actively cheering for child's success. It is also common to find students with their cameras off with no clear sense of if they are engaged. Student success and engagement are further explored in Chapter 4.

Administrators must carefully consider what it means to be engaged, how policy will impact engagement and how attendance needs to be defined and evaluated. Given the potential for variation in student engagement and ways they may or may not participate, it is recommended that there be clear policies that remove the burden from faculty while allowing them to communicate what the program or organization has decided. Policies should be clearly explained as early as orientation and repeated frequently, perhaps at the start of each semester in each class. Chapter 7 contains some examples of how to disseminate these expectations to students though use of the syllabus.

Support Services

Parsons and Shelton (2019) point out the need for a robust support structure for online students. Support services are those resources that are available to students such as advising, library and tutoring, mental health services, and much more (Budash & Shaw, 2017; Roache et al., 2020). Traditional programs have a full spectrum of offerings that ensure student needs are met; online programs must think through all the same considerations.

An early alert system and associated remediation policies and procedures are very important. The literature reveals that online students may struggle, making retention a challenge (Rose & Moore, 2019). Faculty and staff may have less interaction in order to understand the students' struggles. Therefore, it is advisable to have a clearly defined early alert system and associated support mechanism formalized through program policy and procedures. This way a student who is struggling can be identified very early, and when identified, there is a clearly defined set of actions that take place to support the student.

Mental health services can be a particularly challenging service to provide for online learners. We know that college and the associated stress can increase mental health concerns (Liu et al., 2019). However, issues of licensed providers working across state lines can make it very difficult for campus-based counseling centers to serve students who are dispersed. Therefore, administrators will benefit from adding expertise to their counseling centers related to telemental health and online counseling services. There are numerous solutions to the challenges, but they are best pursued by hiring the expertise or requiring existing providers to pursue the requisite professional development.

Legal and Ethical Considerations

This chapter would not be complete without a dedicated exploration of the legal and ethical concerns that should be on the forefront of the mind of any administrator of online education programs. As discussed previously, while there are similarities with traditional in-person delivery, administrators must think about online education as a completely different phenomenon. Therefore, while many of our structures, systems, policies, and procedures might be applicable, they likely will not be applicable in the same way. This is especially true in the areas of information security and student safety.

Information Security

Anyone reading this chapter is likely conversant with the requirements of the Federal Educational Rights and Privacy Act (FERPA) and likely the Health Insurance Portability and Accountability ACT (HIPPA). They offer protection for information related to student academic and health records respectively. Each institution and organization will have varied needs related to HIPPA but certainly will be accountable to FERPA laws.

As such, online programs must increase the expertise in the area of data protection and digital security. Online programs use numerous technological platforms from learning management systems, video conferencing platforms, cloud storage, application and academic record management tools, and much more. Early conversations, before any implementation, should explore data protection capabilities in order to ensure FERPA compliance. Part of faculty development is well spent orienting faculty and staff on data protection requirements and how to use built-in features in the various platforms to ensure privacy.

While it may seem like a given that faculty and staff will use resources provided by the institution or organization, it is not uncommon to find remote faculty opting to use their own computers, Zoom accounts, or cloud storage. Again, as a matter of policy, it must be stated that only those systems, accounts, and resources provided by the organization meet the required standards and that the use of outside resources is strictly prohibited.

Student Safety and Crisis Management

As noted previously, college student experience stress that can increase mental health needs (Liu et al., 2019). Faculty and staff generally have well-developed acumen for handling student safety crisis on a campus. Elementary school teachers through college professors are well trained on the potential concerns that might come up and how they should respond. Generally, geographic proximity allows for some immediacy of response and the support of well-established policies and procedures.

Working in online education, the phenomenon is quite different. Students are generally not in front of us, and if they are, it is by video where they are only a mouse click away from being out of touch. The phenomenon of concern is vastly different across grade levels and yet, similarly to the refrain heard throughout this chapter, policies and procedures upon which faculty and staff can rely must be clearly delineated. It is advisable that online education programs have a crisis management team and a well-developed crisis management plan specific to the population of online students. The crisis management plan should address data needed for students in case of an emergency and delineate clear and specific actions a faculty and staff should take, the required levels of communication, and any follow-up requirements following the report. Administrators must work closely with their related legal counsel and law enforcement to assist with the develop and approval of said plans. Chapter 11 provides a more in-depth discussion of legal and ethical considerations of online education.

Special Consideration for Clinical Programs

There are programs that have special considerations related to placement of students in community organizations and agencies for the purposes of gaining clinical experience. This is especially true in the social and medical sciences. Medicine, nursing, counseling, social work, and many others require that students accrue hours in the field. Traditionally, these placements are generally located in the same community of or at least near the educational institution or through partnerships with the institution. However, with online education, programs might be endorsing clinical placements around the country or even around the world and at a magnitude where developing existing partnerships is prohibitive.

Programs with such considerations must invest time into planning and creating systems, policies, and procedures to facilitate placement at a distance. At the most basic level is the responsibility to verify placement, proper educational experience, and onsite supervision. This is often straightforward but becomes complicated in the cases of states or countries that have very different professional standards in the related field.

Supervision is a significant part of student clinical experiences and typically requires viewing students work, case presentations, and more. As such, these programs must navigate HIPPA compliance in addition to FERPA. While some platforms are adequate for FERPA compliance, they may not suffice for HIPPA compliance. Internet technology security specialists need to be involved from the beginning to ensure adequacy of systems and compliance.

Due to the myriad special consideration in clinical programs, it is best to have a dedicated clinical or field placement director if possible. The director should have experience in the relevant field and have a highly refined capacity for ethical decision-making. The scenarios that emerge in the clinical space continue to be the most varied and require the most time and consideration at the administrative level.

Chapter Summary

Online education is a growing phenomenon. Not only is the number students engaging in online education and programs offering online opportunities growing, but the robust resources for online learning, and research related to best practices, continues to grow as well. Certainly, the growth has been propelled recently in part due to the COVID-19 global pandemic. As Plato said, "Our need will be the real creator." Our need has exacerbated the phenomenon of online education. However, the phenomenon is here to stay and holds much promise for the future. That is true across all levels, from K–12 through graduate school.

It is easy to conceptualize online education through the lens of traditional in-person education delivery. While there are some parallels, the whole online education enterprise must be thought about differently and approached with the intention of developing policies, procedures, and expert teams that are specifically tailored to online education. That is not to say that as an administrator must have said expertise. However, administrators of online programs will be judged by their ability to bring the expertise to build adequate systems and their ability to discern the ongoing need for professional development to support ongoing student success.

There are many incentives for pursuing online education for students, faculty and staff, and institutions. It remains the most accessible, flexible, and in many cases affordable option. For those reasons, the trend to turn to online education does not have an expiration date. From all accounts, it appears to be a phenomenon that will continue to grow. It is deeply rewarding to build and implement systems that do remove traditional barriers to educational opportunities. As stated from the outset, online education is a permanent reality in the landscape of education in the United States and around the world. It is more than ever worth exploring, further developing, and investigating through rigorous research.

Online Resources

Boxlight: Top 25 Resources for School Administrators

Resources with links for school administrators: https://blog.mimio.com/top-25-resources-for-school-administrators

Capterra: 27 Best School Administration Resources

Helpful links to blogs, publications, apps, and events for school administrators: https://blog.capterra.com/top-27-school-administration-resources/

EdIncites: Top 5 Resources for Principals and School Administrators

Resources for primary and secondary principles and school administrators: https://educationincites.com/top-5-resources-for-principals-and-school-administrators/

Edutopia: School Leadership: Resource Roundup

Videos, blogs, and articles on effective leadership: https://www.edutopia.org/school-leadership-principals-teachers-resources

The Edvocate: 10 Ed-Teach Resources for School Administrators

Suggestions and helpful links for school administrators: https://www.theedadvocate.org/10-ed-tech-resources-school-administrators/

Wabisabi Learning: 10 Free (and Awesome) Online School Administrator Resources

Online resources and advise for online school administrators: https://wabisabilearning.com/blogs/professional-development/10-free-online-school-administrator-resources

References

Bates, R. & LaBrecque, B. (2019). Full-time from afar. *Online Journal of Distance Learning*, 22(2).

Bass, B. M. (1999). Two decades of research and development in transformational leadership. *European Journal of Work and Organizational Psychology*, 8(1), 9–32.

Blakely, C. H., & Major, C. H. (2019). Student perceptions of engagement in online courses: An exploratory study. *Online Journal of Distance Learning Administration*, 22(4).

Budash, D., & Shaw, M. (2017). Persistence in an online master's degree program: Perceptions of students and faculty. *Online Journal of Distance Learning Administration*, 20(3).

DeRue, D. S., Nahrgang, J. D., Wellman, N., & Humphrey, S. E. (2011). Trait and behavioral theories of leadership: An integration and meta-analytic test of their relative validity. *Personnel Psychology*, 64(1), 7–52. https://doi.org/10.1111/j.1744-6570.2010.01201.x

de Vries, M. K., & Engellau, E. (2010). A clinical approach to the dynamics of leadership and executive transformation. In N. Nohria & R. Khurana (Eds.), *Handbook of leadership theory and practice* (pp. 183–222). Harvard Business Press.

Fredericksen, E. E. (2018). A national study of online learning leaders in U.S. community colleges. *Online Learning*, 22(4), 383–405. https://doi.org/10.24059/olj.v22i4.1458

George, B. (2007). *True north: Discover your authentic leadership*. Jossey-Bass.

Giannini, S. (2020). *COVID-19: Education is the bedrock of a just society in the post-COVID world*. UNESCO. https://en.unesco.org/news/covid-19-education-bedrock-just-society-post-covid-world

Hammond, H. G., Coplan, M. J., & Mandernach, B. J. (2018). Administrative considerations impacting the quality of online teaching. *Online Journal of Distance Learning*, 21(4).

Herzog, V. W., & Zimmerman, E. P. (2009). Transformational leadership and building relationships with clinical instructors. *Human Kinetics*, 143(3), 39–41.

Institute of Education Sciences. (n.d.). https://ies.ed.gov/aboutus/

Johnson, N., Veletsianos, G., & Seaman, J. (2020). U.S. faculty and administrators experiences and approaches in the early weeks of the COVID-19 pandemic. *Online Learning*, 24(2), 6–21. https://doi.org/10.24059/olj.v24i2.2285

Kouzes, J. M., & Posner, B. Z. (2006). *A leader's legacy*. Jossey-Bass.

Kouzes, J. M., & Posner, B. Z. (2010). *The truth about leadership: The no-fads, heart-of-the-matter facts you need to know*. Jossey-Bass.

Liu, C. H., Stevens, C., Wong, S. H. M., & Yasui, M. (2018). The prevalence and predictors of mental health diagnoses and suicide among U.S. college students: implication for addressing disparities in service use. *Depression and Anxiety*, 36, 8–17. https://doi.org/10.1002/da.22830

Lyons, M. L. (2012). *Leadership in the counseling profession: A qualitative study of CACREP counselor education programs* [Doctoral dissertation, Ohio University]. Electronic Theses and Dissertations Center. https://etd.ohiolink.edu

Lundberg, C. A., & Sheridan, D. (2015). Benefits of engagement with peers, faculty, and diversity for online learners. *College Teaching*, 63(1) 8–15. https://doi.org/10.1080/87567555.2014.972317

Mason, R. (2011). Student engagement with, and participation in, an e-forum. *Educational Technology and Society*, 14(2), 258–268.

Mcelrath, K. (2020, August 26). *Schooling during the COVID-19 pandemic*. U.S. Census Bureau. https://www.census.gov/library/stories/2020/08/schooling-during-the-covid-19-pandemic.html

National Center for Education Statistics. (n.d.). *Digest of education statistics 2019*. U.S. Department of Education. https://nces.ed.gov/fastfacts/display.asp?id=80

Northouse, P. G. (2010). *Leadership: Theory and practice* (5th ed.). Sage.

Portugal, L. M. (2015). Findings identifying how administrative leaders might recruit, select, train, motivate, and support online faculty. *International Journal of Online Pedagogy and Course Design*, 5(4), 27–46.

Parsons, P., & Shelton, K. (2019). Organizational sustainability in online higher education: Reframing through the viable systems model. *Online Journal of Distance Learning*, 22(3).

Roache, D., Rowe-Holder, D., & Muschette, R. (2020). Transitioning to online distance learning in the COVID-19 era: A call for skilled leadership in higher education institutions (HEIs). *International Studies in Educational Administration*, 48(1), 103-110. https://www.researchgate.net/publication/347495846_Transitioning_to_Online_Distance_Learning_in_the_COVID-19_Era_A_Call_for_Skilled_Leadership_in_Higher_Education_Institutions_HEIs#fullTextFileContent

Rose, M., & Moore, A. (2019). Student retention in online courses: University role. *Online Journal of Distance Learning Administration*, 22(3).

Salmon, G. (2016). *The five stage model*. http://www.gillysalmon.com/five-stage-model.html

Thomas, J. E., Graham, C. R., & Pina, A. A. (2018). Current practices of online instructor evaluation in higher education. *Online Journal of Distance Learning Administration*, 21(2).

GLOSSARY

2-minute response strategy: Strategy where the instructor asks a question and provides students with two minutes to "think" about the question, draft a response, and then send the response electronically (usually into a chat window) for further class discussion. (Ch. 9)

academic honesty and ethical considerations: Outlining the policies and procedures for academic honesty/plagiarism and ethical considerations as they apply to the course for students. (Ch. 7)

access barrier: Such as lack of captioning on a video and would require the student to do more work than others to gain equal access to the learning materials. (Ch. 6)

accessibility accommodations: Accommodations that affect the physical world making it easier to navigate for those with disabilities impacting mobility, vision, or hearing. (Ch. 6)

accommodations statement and procedures: Inclusion of students who may need to request reasonable accommodations for disabilities by contacting the designated staff member at the institution. (Ch. 7)

ADDIE model: Analyze, Design, Development, Implement, Evaluate, with this being a circular repeating process not a philosophy of teaching but a structure through which one can develop your online course building practices; creating an online course hinges on the instructor's intent to experiment with methods and continually revise approaches in order to discover what is most effective (Peterson, 2003). (Ch. 5)

Americans with Disabilities Act (ADA) guidelines: The ADA was enacted in 1990 to act as an equal opportunity law for Americans with disabilities; these ADA compliance policies vary widely from campus to campus, as does their implementation and support resources. (Ch. 6)

andragogy: The practice of teaching adult learners. (Ch. 2)

androcentric: Centered on or dominated by men. (Ch. 2)

answer bias: The influencing of someone's opinion prior to that person answering a question. (Ch. 9)

anti-Black racism: Deeply imbedded prejudice against people of African descent. (Ch. 2)

assignments and rubrics: Work in collaboration to provide assessment for courses by providing an outline of assignment expectations, including various aspects of each with an explanation of expectations, and the grading procedure via the associated **rubric**. (Ch. 7)

assignments links: Where assignments for online courses completed by students are submitted; often tethered to the course platform and attached to the grade book. (Ch. 7)

assistive technologies: Assistive, rehabilitative, or adaptive technology used to assist students in gaining equal access for success by assisting with completion of tasks that their disability may limit their performance in. (Ch. 6)

asynchronous classes: Occur over a set period, but students may log into class when it is convenient for them to view prerecorded lectures by the instructor and lack the live interaction with their instructors and peers. (Ch. 7)

asynchronous learning: A form of learning where the instructor and students access the online classroom, materials, assignments, and discussions at their own convenience. One example of asynchronous learning would be prerecorded lectures that are viewed by students at any time. (Ch. 1); Learning that occurs independently, indicating that the student and the teacher are not in the same geographical location or present in the same space at the same time. (Ch. 10)

attendance and participation: For synchronous classes, clarification of being on time for the start of the live class, being on camera and staying in class and on camera the entire time, clarification on the use of chat features. For asynchronous classes this includes expectations for discussion boards or mandatory logins that constitutes participation for the course. (Ch. 7)

authentic leadership: Includes the interaction of values and principles, motivations, support team, integrated life, and self-awareness. (Ch. 12)

autonomous-supportive teaching style: Teaching style whereby students are given a choice in classroom tasks, which can stem from a variety of instructional strategies being offered in each class session (see "energy shifts"). (Ch. 9)

autonomy: People are entitled to have some degree of independence and control over their lives and decisions. (Ch. 11)

backwards design: A method of designing course curriculum by first determining key objectives for learners to reach in the course, then choosing instructional methods and forms of assessment. (Ch. 5)

beneficence: The idea of providing good to others. (Ch. 11)

biterm: The academic schedule comprised of 8-week condensed courses. The work of a traditional 16-week semester course is condensed into 8 weeks, allowing for students to take fewer classes in each biterm but still complete a full course load in the 16-week overall session. (Ch. 7)

Bitmoji classroom: The Bitmoji classroom is an interactive virtual representation of a classroom, complete with bookshelves, a dry erase board, teacher desk, and customizable teacher avatars. This resource is available through the Bitmoji app. (Ch. 8)

blended learning environment: A form of learning that incorporates both synchronous and asynchronous instruction. One example of hybrid learning would be live video lectures combined with other prerecorded lessons. (Ch. 1)

blended or hybrid courses: 40% to 79% of course content is presented through a synchronous or asynchronous online format but continue to include **face-to-face** or **in-person** learning sessions periodically throughout a semester. (Ch. 10)

brave space: A term defined by Arao & Clemens (2013) that describes the process of creating a space that allows for dialogue about emotionally laden and sensitive topics with the goal of fostering the development of critical consciousness. (Ch. 2); A virtual or **in-person** space, facilitated and governed by the instructor, where participants function as community members, adhering to established ground rules, and engage in sharing personal reflections and experiences, allowing for vulnerabilities to further learning objectives. (Ch. 10)

bring your own device (BYOD): BYOD is a philosophy that has been adopted by many districts which allows students to bring their own computer devices (cell phones, tablets, laptops, etc.) into the classroom to be used as an educational resource. This philosophy is regulated by school and/or school district policy. (Ch. 8)

caution: A sense of thoughtfulness and consideration about one's actions and comments in a situation that could be demanding, difficult, or dangerous. (Ch. 11)

classroom management: "The act of supervising relationships, behaviors, and instructional settings and lessons for communities of learners" (Iverson, 2003, p. 4). (Ch. 4)

code-switching: A process during which speakers of more than one language or dialect move back and forth between those languages or dialects. (Ch. 2)

colonialism: A complex power structure that shifts power, possession, and resources from indigenous people to those who are invading and conquering. (Ch. 2)

colonization: An event with a start and end date, during which one group of people traveled to another geographical area, conquered and dominated another group of people and then instituted colonialism. (Ch. 2)

community: Having a sense of belonging in a group; collaboration with others. (Ch. 4)

confidentiality of clients: Application of the code of ethics mandating confidential information regarding clients remains as such in the learning environment. (Ch. 7)

confidentiality of students in the classroom: The extension of confidentiality and privacy to what students choose to share in class. (Ch. 7)

connectedness: Feeling of being close or connected to others; having shared goals and expectations. (Ch. 4)

conscientiousness: The leadership trait referred to as the "extent to which a person is dependable, dutiful, and achievement oriented, and is often associated with deliberate planning and structure" according to DeRue et al. (2011, p. 14). (Ch. 12)

constructivist remediation: "Compensatory education, direct instruction, corrective teaching, adaptive instruction, diagnostic-prescriptive teaching, and individualized instruction" (Johnson, 2004, p. 76). (Ch. 4)

copyright statements: A statement provides a summary of the expectations of students regarding their use of images and materials copywritten by another, be it an artist, musician, or institute of higher education. (Ch. 7)

correspondence school model: A form of distance education in which the materials are mailed between the student and educator. (Ch. 1)

course description: A focused summary of the course allowing for a cursory overview of topics discussed. (Ch. 7)

course length: Amount of time required to successfully complete required readings, assignments, and projects; may be the standard 16-week semester or the condensed 8-week biterm. (Ch. 7)

course objectives: What the student will learn by completing the course work guided by national and state credentialing requirements. (Ch. 7)

course requirements: The recipe for success provided to students outlining in detail the expectations and responsibilities of the students to succeed in the course. (Ch. 7)

course schedule: Includes the week of the semester with the specific date and the topics of discussion for that week, as well as any assigned readings and assignments due during that period. (Ch. 7)

critical consciousness: An awareness of social inequalities and one's position within systems of oppression and marginalization, and the ability to critically reflect on the sociopolitical environment that results in taking action to promote equity and social justice. (Ch. 2)

critical pedagogy: A teaching approach based on critical thinking that seeks to question and challenge the oppressive aspects of education, and has an aim to promote critical consciousness development among students and thereby promote social justice action. (Ch. 2)

cultural assumptions: Biases or assumptions based on one's culture. (Ch. 4)

culturally responsive classroom management: Teaching with cultural sensitivity and awareness. (Ch. 4)

culturally responsive pedagogy: An educational philosophy that recognizes the influence of culture and adapts teaching to integrate student culture and social location. (Ch. 2)

custom resources: Each school's unique instance of the LMS they use, and therefore whatever resources are available should be sought out. These may include workshops, tutorials, templates, or guides and documentation. (Ch. 5)

decoloniality: "A method and paradigm of restoration and reparation that aspires to restore, elevate, renew, rediscover, and acknowledge and validate the lives, live-experiences, cultural and knowledge of indigenous people, People of Color, and colonized people as well as decenter hetero/cis normativity, gender hierarchies and racial privilege" (William & Mary, n.d., para.2). (Ch. 2)

decolonization: The process of dismantling power hierarchies and oppressive educational practices, promoting inclusive practices and policies, and valuing diverse ways of knowing, being, and doing (in this chapter, decolonization and decolonialization are used interchangeably). (Ch. 2)

deficit approach to pedagogy: Emerged in the 1960s and is based on the belief that the languages and cultural practices of BIPOC students are deficient and inferior; therefore, the role of education is to teach superior models based on Eurocentric cultural and educational approaches. (Ch. 2)

difference pedagogies: Emerged in the 1970s and 1980s and recognized that the cultural languages and beliefs systems of BIPOC students are equal to, and also different from, the Eurocentric cultural and educational approaches. (Ch. 2)

differentiation: Process by which assignments and/or procedures are adapted to fit individual learning styles and student needs. (Ch. 9)

digital accessibility: Work begins with identifying the unique challenges of those with disabilities and the barriers that can exist when interacting with digital materials; e.g., those with hearing differences will need to rely on captions and transcripts to access video and audio material. (Ch. 6)

diplomacy: An engagement of a situation with another person to gather information and assess the status of a concern or problem. (Ch. 11)

direct instruction: Generally refers to instruction that is planned and led by teachers in a face-to-face environment. (Ch. 8)

disability services center: Used in higher education and operating under federal funding to provide accommodations to students with a disability on file; can usually only provide accommodations and remediation of course materials if a student submits a formal request; provides proctoring services for students who need extra time on exams and in-class American Sign Language (ASL) interpreters, and matches students to appropriate **assistive technologies**. (Ch. 6)

discretion: An awareness that a misunderstanding or misinterpretation of comments or actions could be made by another person, resulting in careful monitoring of one's comments or actions. (Ch. 11)

distance education/distance learning: A form of education that takes place outside the set location (brick-and-mortar school). There are many forms of distance education: correspondence, radio, television, and online. (Ch. 1)

distance learning (distance education): Education in which the instructor and student(s) are not in the same physical location and perhaps the same time zone. (Ch. 7)

diversity: Diversity involves the recognition of the visible and invisible physical and social characteristics that make an individual or group of individuals different from one another, and by doing so, celebrating that difference as a source of strength for the community at large. (Ch. 3)

drag and drop: A commonly used assessment method that requires students to click on words, pictures, etc., and move them to an appropriate, corresponding area on the screen. (Ch. 8)

duty to warn: The responsibility of professionals to report when someone is in danger of being harmed; while this may sound similar to mandated reporting, the distinction is that a person could be in danger without being identified as in a vulnerable population. (Ch. 11)

electronic messaging: Mechanism used by instructors and students to communicate with each other via electronic means (email, discussion boards, LMS messaging systems, etc.). (Ch. 9)

energy shifts: Purposeful change in an instructor's teaching approach at regular intervals for the purpose of maintaining student engagement. (Ch. 9)

e-pedagogy: Teaching models for online education. (Ch. 2)

epistemological: Related to the branch of philosophy that focuses on knowledge (epistemology) or how people learn what they know. (Ch. 2)

equity: Refers to the enactment of specific policies and practices that ensure equitable access and opportunities for success for everyone. It is important to differentiate equity from equality; in order to be equitable, we cannot treat everyone the same. To be equitable, we must treat individuals according to their needs and provide multiple opportunities for success. (Ch. 3)

Eurocentric: A belief that European principles and practices are central and superior to others. (Ch. 2)

extension: Process by which assignments and/or procedures are adapted to accommodate students who have mastered current learning objectives. (Ch. 9)

face-to-face meeting: Includes virtual, synchronous meetings or **in-person** meetings where students and teachers are visible in real time but not necessarily in the same geographical location. (Ch. 10)

fidelity: Those who have a position of service to others follow a practice of truthfulness and honesty with others. (Ch. 11)

flipped classroom: Teaching strategy whereby the instructor provides an online video lecture that students watch outside the classroom (as homework), freeing class time for active learning strategies (small group and hands-on activities). (Ch. 9)

flipped course: Also referred to as a **lightly blended course or lightly hybrid course**; 15%–39% of course content is presented through a synchronous or asynchronous online format, which includes materials, assignments, grading, and meetings. (Ch. 10)

folx: Per Robertson (2018), folx is a nonbinary word used to refer to people who exist outside of the gender binary. Robertson emphasized that *x* is used to "bring in more identities to the conversations, such as womxn, latinx, and alumx" (p. 49), e.g. (Ch. 3)

grading procedures: The rubrics which correspond to each assignment providing a clear guide to the evaluation process and provide the instructor an objective means by which to grade students, as well as an explanation to students about how quickly feedback and grades will be returned on assignments. (Ch. 7)

guided didactic conversation theory: Students are motivated to learn when there is a friendly relationship between teacher and students; the most influential factor in student motivation. (Ch. 4)

guided notes: Teacher-prepared notes that are typically in the form of an incomplete outline that requires students to write/type the missing information while listening to a lecture, watching a video, or reading a passage. (Ch. 8)

habitus: The construct through which an individual incorporates their cultural variables to formulate a structure that may enhance or restrict their future success. (Ch. 4)

heterocentric: A belief that centers heterosexuality and views other forms of sexuality as deficient. (Ch. 2)

heutagogy: The study of self-determined learning. (Ch. 2)

higher-order thinking: Taxonomical organization of thinking (based on Bloom's taxonomy) that requires students to create and evaluate content. (Ch. 9)

idealized influence: Consideration of how a leader compels the best from faculty and staff. (Ch. 12)

identifying student needs: Process by which an instructor evaluates student urgency and need for a particular item (e.g., technology). (Ch. 9)

inclusion: Refers to the enactment of specific policies and practices that ensure equitable access and opportunities for success for everyone. It is important to differentiate equity from equality; in order to be equitable, we cannot treat everyone the same. To be equitable, we must treat individuals according to their needs and provide multiple opportunities for success. (Ch. 3)

individualized consideration: How a leader tends to follower needs. (Ch. 12)

individualized education plan (IEP): Widely supported and encouraged for many students, giving them extra support and creative strategies to succeed in school and are part of the Individuals with Disability Education Act (IDEA) of 1997. (Ch. 6)

in-person learning: Teacher and student are present in real time in the same geographical location. (Ch. 10)

inspirational motivation: Reflects the energy invested in setting and pursuing a vision. (Ch. 12)

institutional IT department (or institutional information technology department): The department tasked with the coordination and management of daily functions of the information systems of a university or institution, including internet, class platforms, computers, phones, and audio-visual equipment. (Ch. 7)

instructionism remediation: Noninteractive, teacher prescribed remediation plan for the student. (Ch. 4)

intellectual stimulation: The leader is key in stimulating innovation, creating an environment that fosters critical questions, and fostering creativity in solutions. (Ch. 12)

internalization: Learning something apart from one's own thoughts. (Ch. 4)

international standard book number (ISBN): Allows the students to locate the correct source quickly and reduces misunderstanding of editions or versions of materials. (Ch. 7)

internet and software requirements: Specifications determined by administration or instructors with regards to working and dependable internet and reliable email software with attachments receiving/sending enabled, as well as specific software requirements for course work. (Ch. 7)

intersectional pedagogy: A theoretical framework for teaching, rooted in feminist theory, that provides educators with strategies to examine social structures and processes that create inequity and strives to promote a pathway to equity through social justice efforts and the decolonization of education. (Ch. 2)

intersectionality: Rooted in intersectional theory and based on the premise that the major systems of oppression interlock to create advantage, privilege, disadvantage, and oppression based on one's unique social location. (Ch. 2)

justice: Assures everyone of equal access; based on what a person does need or seek, everyone is given access to an equal degree. (Ch. 11)

leader behaviors: The behaviors of a leader that contribute to the success of their endeavor. (Ch. 12)

leader traits: The traits of a leader that contribute to success of their endeavor. (Ch. 12)

learning management system (LMS): Technology designed and used to assist both instructors in providing information to students and students in learning the material. Also known as **online learning environments,** equal to a physical classroom in needs of organization and administration by instructors. (Ch. 5)

liberatory pedagogy: A theoretical framework for teaching with an emphasis on reflecting upon and changing the social world and involving the development and emergence of critical consciousness. (Ch. 2)

manipulatives: Physical items that are used by students to enhance understanding of a lesson (usually catering to a tactile learning style). (Ch. 9)

massive open online course (MOOC): 100% of course content is made available online to participants; may or may not be registered with the institution hosting the course; free of charges or tuition to the participants; typically no course credit is available to participants. (Ch. 10)

method of instruction: An introduction to the delivery of the course providing insight into how, when, and where the course will be provided. (Ch. 7)

microaggressions: Intentional or unintentional derogatory or harmful slights/insults that target a person or group (Sue et al., 2007). (Ch. 3)

mission statement: A motivational statement connects the instructor and learner through a shared mission in learning, skill development, and ethical practice in their field of study. (Ch. 7)

modality: A mode or method of instruction. In the case of online education, this may be a synchronous, asynchronous, or hybrid model of instruction. (Ch. 1)

multiculturalism: Often considered "a wide range of multiple groups without grading, comparing, or ranking them as better or worse than one another and without denying the very distinct and complementary or even contradictory perspectives that each group brings with it" (Pedersen, 1991, p. 4). (Ch. 7)

multiple minority: an individual who has multiple components of their identity that further marginalizes them (for example, a student can be African American, lesbian, female, and living with disabilities). (Ch. 3)

netiquette (or internet etiquette): Considerations of professional background choices, whether live or virtual; sharing screen time; time management during discussions; and maintaining professional vocabulary, facial expressions, and behaviors in online classes. (Ch. 7)

nonmaleficence: People should not be harmed; if harm is the likely result of an action, then that action should not be done. (Ch. 11)

Nth name selection: Process of randomly selecting a student name at a predetermined Nth interval. (Ch. 9)

online education: A form of distance education that utilizes the internet, computers, and other related media. (Ch. 1)

online learning: 80% to 100% of course content is presented through a synchronous or asynchronous online format and may include face-to-face or synchronous learning opportunities. (Ch. 10)

ontological: Related to the branch of philosophy that focuses on the nature of reality (ontology). (Ch. 2)

optical character recognition (OCR): Technology designed to scan images of text and convert to digital text that is then ready to be read aloud by a screen reader or used in other digital spaces; most often performed on a PDF document to make it more accessible. (Ch. 6)

para teachers: Members of the community trained to help students with remedial needs. (Ch. 4)

pedagogy: The theory and practice of teaching. (Ch. 2 & Ch. 4)

platforms: For the administration of online courses; they provide fundamental purposes including a means for students to receive information from the instructor including assignments and grades and to provide interactions between the student and their instructor and peers, as well as a means for students to complete forms of evaluation including quizzes and examination. (Ch. 7)

policies and procedures: Guidelines provided by administrators and instructors to guide various aspects of behaviors and issues management within a course. (Ch. 4 & Ch. 7)

polling: Process of seeking feedback from students by providing options whereby they can express agreement or disagreement by voting (usually by raising hands or clicking a "checkmark" in a learning management system). (Ch. 9)

positionality: Awareness that one's perspectives and beliefs are influenced and affected by one's social location and world views. (Ch. 2)

proactive approach to digital accessibility: For example, captioning videos you create for your class, whereas a reactive approach is waiting for a student to ask for a captioned video; important because it helps us to meet the diverse needs of our students even when they may not disclose a disability; also minimizes the need for retroactive, rushed fixes. (Ch. 6)

problematic behavior: Less than desired behavior in the classroom that might require remediation. (Ch. 4)

professional code of ethics: The guide set forth by a licensing, accrediting, or professional association to help guide ethical decision-making by professionals in its membership. (Ch. 7)

professionalism: Fundamentally appropriate language for professional students in class, emails, discussion boards, or assignments. (Ch. 7)

quick response (QR) codes: A type of matrix barcode that can be inserted into assignments or lecture materials for the purpose of allowing students to electronically access websites and other online information. (Ch. 9)

random selection method: Any method that allows for the randomized selection of students for the purpose of answering questions or performing a task in class. (Ch. 9)

remediation: Tactics and strategies designed for improving students' performance. (Ch. 4)

required textbooks: Textbook(s) for the course; necessary information includes the authors names, book title, edition if applicable, and publisher. (Ch. 7)

safe space: A virtual or in-person space, facilitated and governed by the instructor, where participants collaborate to establish ground rules and a sense of community, allowing participants to be seen, heard, and challenged with respect, despite differences, especially those pertaining to multicultural diversity and intersectionality. (Ch. 10)

safe zone workshops: Promote equity in online learning environments; an LGBTQ ally training initiative. (Ch. 3)

screen reader: Software application that assists those with visual impairments to use a computer. (Ch. 6)

screensharing: The process of allowing remote viewing access to one's computer screen or electronic documents (usually used by an instructor in a synchronous online class session). (Ch. 9)

semester: The academic schedule, usually comprising 16 weeks, during which postsecondary courses are held. (Ch. 7)

social constructivism: Knowledge building within a social context. (Ch. 4)

social justice: "The scholarship and professional action designed to change societal values, structures, policies, and practices, such that disadvantaged or marginalized groups gain increased access to these tools of self-determination" (Goodman et al., 2004, p. 795). (Ch. 7)

social location: One's unique combination of social categories such as gender, race, ethnicity, ability, class, and sexuality. (Ch. 2)

social sharing: Sharing of information via social media. (Ch. 4)

speech-to-text: Functions crucial to allow users with mobility and vision differences to dictate text; may be used in word processing systems, course learning management systems (LMS), or even on a phone to dictate a text message. (Ch. 6)

student response group: Collaborative grouping of students in an online setting for the purpose of student engagement and idea sharing. (Ch. 9)

student services office or student success office: The institutional office or department responsible to coordinate responses to student issues in performance, including evaluating and approving necessary accommodations, to ensure student success. (Ch. 7)

student success: The goal of all educators regardless of instructional format achieved by meeting the student's needs consistently within an environment that supports learning and growth; is the result of engagement and effective classroom management, structure, effective communication, and creating a sense of community combined with effective assessment and feedback. (Ch. 4)

submission of assignments: Explanation of the expected means of submitting assignments and the location of assignment links within the course platform for submitting assignments on time. (Ch. 7)

syllabus: Information provided by instructors regarding the course expectations of student responsibilities and behaviors, and assessment of student learning in a course. (Ch. 4 & Ch. 7)

synchronous class: Instructor and students meeting together on an online platform at the same time, sharing information and discussion in live time. (Ch. 4 & Ch. 7)

synchronous learning: A form of learning that takes place in real time with both student and instructor present in the online classroom at the same time. One example of synchronous learning would be a live video classes with students. (Ch. 1); Learning that occurs with the teacher and student being present in the same space, in real time; however, not necessarily in the same geographical location. (Ch. 10)

technocentrism: The subtle tendency to associate interactivity, convenience, and engagement through the application of technology with improved education. (Ch. 2)

think, pair, share: Strategy whereby students are asked a question, given time to "think" about the question, "paired" with at least one other student to discuss the question, and asked to "share" responses to the question that were generated within the collaborative pairing. (Ch. 9)

GLOSSARY

thirdspace: "A socially constructed space built from the multiple perceptions, meanings, values, and ideologies of students and instructors" (Carruthers & Friend, 2014). (Ch. 2)

traditional course: Course that includes synchronous meetings on a consistent day and time throughout the course of a semester where the majority of the curriculum is taught orally, with the instructor and learners in the same space in real time, and where less than 14% of content is available in an online format. (Ch. 10)

transformational leadership: The four key concepts that guide the leader: individualized consideration, idealized influence, inspirational motivation, and intellectual stimulation. (Ch. 12)

trauma-informed pedagogy: A theoretical framework for teaching that incorporates an understanding of trauma's impact on the brain, emotional, behavior, thoughts, and learning. (Ch. 2)

universal design for learning (UDL): The process of making learning effective and usable for all; can extend beyond accessibility to address learner preferences, styles, and methods of instruction that meet students' needs; where accessibility is considered when integrating technology into the learning environment, universal design involves the usability of that technology and extends to how the technology is integrated into the learning plan, along with the other elements of the course. (Ch. 6)

user-centric design scaffolding: A design thinking mentality whereby instructors begin by asking themselves questions in order to determine key elements of the student experience. (Ch. 5)

vendor resources: Guides provided by the company that builds the LMS used; provides information on functions and uses; may include community spaces for questions, comments, and/or suggestions. (Ch. 5)

virtual learning: Also known as an online format; a space or a community on the World Wide Web or internet; includes asynchronous and synchronous content available on the internet, typically on a course management system. (Ch. 10)

voice command: Functions use the same underlying technology as speech-to-text functions, allowing users with mobility and vision differences to control their device using their voice. (Ch. 6)

wait time: Purposeful amount of time the instructor waits between asking a question and selecting a student to answer the question. (Ch. 9)

warm demander: An educator who demonstrates personal warmth toward their students while also setting high standards for educational achievement. (Ch. 2)

Wigmore test: A legal procedure related to privileged communication. Specifically, the Wigmore test is used to determine if the release of confidential information is of sufficient benefit to a court as to outweigh the potential risk to the person. (Ch. 11)

writing style: A set of expectations regarding formatting, citations and references standardized for a field of study. (Ch. 7)

zone of proximal development: Area between what a student can learn on their own and with the help of someone else. (Ch. 4)

INDEX

A

Abenavoli, R. M., 35
academic honesty and ethical considerations, 115–116
access barrier, 95, 97, 103–104, 106
accessibility accommodations, 95, 98, 100
accommodations statement and procedures, 116
accountability of students, 65–66
Accreditation Commission Council on Occupational Education (COE), 113
Accrediting Commission of Career Schools and Colleges (ACCSC), 113
Accrediting Council for Continuing Education and Training (ACCET), 113
Accrediting Council for Independent Colleges and Schools (ACICS), 113
ADA guidelines. *See* Americans with Disabilities Act (ADA)
ADDIE model, 84–85
ADDRESSING model, 53, 55
administration of online programs, 215–224
Adult Learning Service, 4
age, and multicultural aspects of online teaching, 50
Akyildiz, S. T., 20, 22
Ali, D., 186
Alim, H. S., 31
Allen, I. E., 183–184
alt text, 102, 104–105
Alward, E., 190
Amazon Alexa, 101
American Counseling Association (ACA), 115
    Code of Ethics, 206–207, 210
American Federation of Teachers, 13
American Psychological Association (APA), 113, 115, 245

Americans with Disabilities Act (ADA) guidelines, 97, 205
Americans with Disability Act, 205
Anderson, S. K., 201
andragogy, 20–21
androcentric colonial practice, 24
answer bias, 173
anti-Black racism, 27
"Ask the Class," 36
assessment, 161–162
    and student success, 73–75
    completing online, 74–75
    drag and drop, 162
    essays and open-ended responses, 161
    importance of, 73
    in postsecondary education, 74–75
    in primary school, 74
    in secondary school, 74
    online teaching and learning in secondary education, 176–177
    polling, 162, 176–177
    quizzes, 161
assignment links, 115
assignments
    and rubrics, 117
    for visual presentations, 96
    submission of, 115
assisting students with technology, 157, 168–169
assistive technology, 97–98, 100–101
    keyboard, 101
    optical character recognition (OCR), 101
    screen readers, 101
    speech-to-text functions, 101
    voice command functions, 101
Association for Computing Machinery (ACM), 115
Association of Advanced Rabbinical and Talmudic Schools (AARTS), 113
asynchronous assignments, 184

asynchronous classes, 62, 112, 114, 191
asynchronous learning, 4, 184–185
asynchronous written discussions, 186
attendance/participation, 114–115
audio and visual media learning, 182–183
Aust, R., 69–70
authentic leadership, 217
autonomous-supportive teaching style, 169
autonomy, 200

B

Back, S., 21
backwards design, 84–85
Baker, K. Q., 183
balancing time, in remote environment, 13
"banking" concept of education, 29
banking model, 29
Barber, W., 73
Baron, A., 48
behavioral engagement, 188–189
bell hooks, 29
beneficence, 200
Bernard, C., 31
Bernstein, R. S., 49
Bertram, B., 199
best practices, 35
biterm, 112
Bitmoji classroom, 159
Black and Indigenous People of Color (BIPOC), 25, 30–33
Blackboard, 69, 86, 101, 116
Blackboard Collaborate, 159
Black feminists pedagogy, 28–29
Blakely, C. H., 221
Blanchard, A. L., 183
blended learning environment, 4
blended or hybrid courses, 184
Boettcher, J. V., 184–186
Boitshwarelo, B., 73

237

Bonilla-Silva, E., 32
Boston Gazette, 85, 182
boundaries in online education, 210–212
Box, 115
brave spaces, 26, 186, 191
Bring Your Own Device (BYOD), 155
British Broadcasting Company, 182–183
Buckley Amendment, 202
building community, 36–37
Burgstahler, S., 98
Busia, A. P. A., 30
Butler, L. D., 33

C

Canvas, 86, 101, 116
captions, 102, 105
Carello, J., 33
Caruthers, L., 26
Caughlin, D. E., 109, 111
caution, 211
Chatterjee, R., 183
Chick, N., 36, 38
Chromebooks, 156, 169
chunking work, 163
classroom management
  and student success, 62–64
  online, in postsecondary education, 64
  online, in primary school, 63–64
  online, in secondary school, 64
classroom structure, 64–67
  accountability of students, 65–66
  communicating expectations, 65
  importance of, 66
  providing online, 66–67
  rules and policies, 65
  student success through, 64–67
class size, 8–9
Clayton-Pedersen, A. R., 49
Clery Act, 203
clinical programs, special consideration for, 223
code-switching, 31
cognitive differences, 96
cognitive engagement, 188
collaborative engagement, 189
colonialism, 24, 48
colonization, 24
color-blind ideology, 32
communication, 67–69, 160
  creating recordings, 160
  in online learning, 186–187
  in postsecondary education, 68–69
  in primary school, 68
  in secondary school, 68
  learner feedback, 175
  limiting length of recordings, 160
  making videos personable, 160
  online teaching and learning in secondary education, 174–176
  privileged, 203–204
  screensharing best practices, 176
  visuals, 175
communication differences, 97
community, 69–70
  building in postsecondary education, 72–73
  building in primary school, 71
  building in secondary school, 71–72
  building online, 70–71
confidentiality
  of clients, 113
  of students in class, 114–117
connectedness, 69–73
  in postsecondary education, 72–73
  in primary school, 71
  in secondary school, 71–72
Conrad, R. M., 184–186
conscientiousness, 216
constructivist remediation, 75
content dump setups, 89
context of technology and online learning, 167–168
copyright, 115
copyright statements, 115
Corey, C., 201
Corey, G., 201
Corey, M. S., 201
Correia, A. P., 183
correspondence learning, utilizing postal service, 182
correspondence school model, 4
Council for Accreditation of Counseling and Related Educational Programs (CACREP), 113
Counsel for the Accreditation of Education Preparation (CAEP), 113
course description, 111
course length, 112
course objectives, 113
course pages, 101–102
course policies and procedures, 190
course requirements, 114
course schedule, 116–117
COVID-19 global pandemic, 6, 20, 156, 168, 181, 215, 224
creating
  online classroom, 189–191
  recordings, 160
  virtual classroom, 159
Crenshaw, Kimberle, 55
critical consciousness, 26–28
critical cross-cultural education, 53–55
critical pedagogy, 25–26
critical theories, 25
cultural assumptions, 70
cultural competence, 31
culturally responsive classroom management, 70
culturally responsive pedagogy, 30
  cultural competence, 31
  high academic expectations, 30–31
culturally sustaining pedagogy, 31–32
custom resources, 87
cybersymbiosis, 192
Cyrus, K., 55

D

Dailymotion, 169
Dalton, S. S., 36
Davis, C. K., 183
Dawson, S., 183
decoloniality, 24
decolonialization, 24–25
decolonization, 24
deficit approaches, 30
DeRue, D. S., 216
difference pedagogies, 30
differentiation, 177
differentiation and extension strategies
  higher-order thinking questions, 177–178
  online teaching and learning in secondary education, 177–179
  online videos for remediation and extension, 178–179
  quick response (QR) codes, 179
digital accessibility, 95, 97–98, 100, 104, 106
  best practices, 101–106
  challenges in, 95–97
  cognitive differences in, 96

communication differences in, 97
in higher education institutions, 97
in K–12 education, 98
mobility differences in, 96
proactive approach to, 97–98
universal design for learning (UDL) and, 98–101
vision differences in, 96
Digital Learning Compass: Distance Education Enrollment Report (Allen & Seaman), 183
diplomacy, 211
direct instruction, 162
disability services center, 97
disability status, 50
discretion, 211
distance education
defined, 110, 181
evolution of, 181–185
Distance Education Accrediting Commission (DEAC), 113
distance learning. *See also* distance education
defined, 4, 110
history of, 4–5
transition to, 12
diversity, equity, and inclusion (DEI), 47
background, 47–48
in online learning, 48–49
documents, 101–103
PDFs, 102
presentations, 103
spreadsheets, 103
drag and drop, 162
Dropbox, 115, 158
duty to warn, 205
Dykman, C. A., 183

E

Edison, Thomas, 182
Edmentum, 156, 161
educator(s)
self-care, 35
self-involvement in teaching strategies, 38
trauma-informed, 33–34
Edutube, 178
Eisel v. Board of Education of Montgomery County, 204
electronic messaging, 175
Emmer, E. T., 63
emotional engagement, 189

energy shifts, 169–170
example, 170
e-pedagogy, 22–23
epistemological position, 19
essays and open-ended responses, 161
ethical considerations, 115–116
ethical decision-making model, 201–206
Clery Act, 203
Family Educational Rights and Privacy Act (FERPA), 202
federal regulations, 202
Health Care Portability and Accountability Act (HIPAA), 202–203
Health Information Technology for Economic and Clinical Health Act (HITECH), 203
mandated reporting/duty to warn, 204–205
preventing violations of HIPAA/HITECH, 205–206
privileged communication, 203–204
Title IX Act, 203
ethics
autonomy, 200
beneficence, 200
fidelity, 200–201
justice, 200
nonmaleficence, 200
principles of, 200–201
ethnicity, 50–51
Eurocentric colonial practice, 24
evaluation of online programs, 220–221
Evertson, C. M., 63
evolution
of distance education, 181–185
of online learning, 181–185
extension, 177

F

Facebook, 167
face-to-face courses, 184
face-to-face learning sessions, 184
face-to-face meetings, 184
faculty and staff
connection, 219–220
training and engagement, 219
Falk, L. K., 111
Fallot, R. D., 33
Family Educational Rights and Privacy Act (FERPA), 86, 202

Federal Communications Commission, 182
Federal Educational Rights and Privacy Act (FERPA), 222–223
Federal Radio Commission, 182
feminist pedagogy, 28–29
FERPA. *See* Family Educational Rights and Privacy Act (FERPA)
fidelity, 200–201
"firstspace," 26
Five Keys to High-Quality Classroom Assessments, 161
flipped classroom, 174
benefits of, 174
challenges of, 174
flipped courses, 184
folx, 48
Fox, O. H., 52
Fredericksen, E. E., 219
Freire, P., 29
Friend, J., 26
Fuentes, M. A., 50

G

Gardner, Howard, 163
gatekeeping, 206–209
decision-making capacity, 207–209
Gaytan, J., 183
gender
and multicultural aspects of online teaching, 53
and Title IX Act, 203
generational influencers, and multicultural aspects of online teaching, 50
George, Bill, 217
Glance, D. G., 185
Glassner, A., 21
Goldberg, A. E., 52
Goodrich, K. M., 77
Google, 156
Google Assistant, 101
Google Classroom, 157, 179
Google Drive, 115, 158
Google Forms, 161, 164
Goralski, M. A., 111
grading procedures, 117
Grammarly, 115
graphics, 96
guided didactic conversation theory, 70
guided notes, 159–160

H

habitus, 61
Hammond, H. G., 219
Harper, William Rainey, 4
Harris, M., 33
Hassel, H., 36
Health Care Portability and Accountability Act (HIPAA), 202–203, 222–223
  preventing violations of, 205–206
Health Information Technology for Economic and Clinical Health Act (HITECH Act), 203, 205–206
  preventing violations of, 205–206
Heberle, A. E., 27
Herlihy, B., 201
heterocentric colonial practice, 24
heterosexism, 27, 52–53
heutagogy, 21–22
high academic expectations, 30–31
higher-order thinking, 177
higher-order thinking questions, 177–178
history of online learning in primary education, 156
Holland, T. P., 201
Holt, D. M., 183
home office
  intangible factors for, 11
  locating right place, 11
  setting up, 10
hooks, b., 186
Houston, S., 77
hybrid learning, 69, 184
hyperlinks, 102, 104

I

Ice, P., 72
idealized influence, 217
identifying student needs, 168
IEPs. *See* individualized education plans (IEPs)
inclusive pedagogical frameworks, 23–32
  Black feminists pedagogy, 28–29
  critical pedagogy, 25–26
  culturally responsive pedagogy, 30–31
  decolonialization, 24–25
  feminist pedagogy, 28–29
  intersectional pedagogy, 28–29
  liberatory pedagogy, 29
individualized consideration, 217
individualized education plans (IEPs), 98
informal chatroom, 191
information security, 222–223
in-person learning, 187
inspirational motivation, 217
Instagram, 167
Institutional IT departments, 116
instructionism remediation, 75
Integrated Postsecondary Education Data System (IPEDS), 215–216
intellectual stimulation, 217
internalization, 76
International Accreditation Counsel for Business Education (IACBE), 113
International Standard Book Number (ISBN), 111
Internet
  and software requirements, 110, 116
  online learning through use of, 183–184
internet etiquette. *See* netiquette
intersectionality, 28
  importance of, 55–56
intersectional pedagogy, 28–29

J

James, S. M., 30
Jim Crow, 32
Johnson, N., 219
justice, 200

K

Kahoot, 161
Kerr, R., 51
keyboard, 101
Khan Academy, 156, 178
Kilpatrick, A. C., 201
Kitchener, K. S., 200–201
Kleinfeld, J., 30
Knowles, M., 20–21, 37
Kurubacak, G., 51

L

LaBianca, J., 72
Ladson-Billings, G., 30–31
language, and multicultural aspects of online teaching, 51–52
leader behaviors, 216
leadership, 216–217
  authentic, 217
  transformational, 217
leader traits, 216
learner feedback, 175
  electronic messaging, 175
  learning signals, 175
learning management systems (LMSs), 85–87, 175–176. *See also* online learning environments
  communication in, 175
  custom resources, 87
  in accessibility best practices, 101–102
  in recruiting practices, 218
  using technology in school's, 169
  vendor resources, 87
learning signals, 175
learning stations via breakout rooms, 159
learning styles, 163
learning targets, 157
legal and ethical issues, 199–213
  boundaries in online education, 210–212
  ethical decision-making model, 201–206
  gatekeeping, 206–209
  moral distress, 201
  National Council for State Authorization Reciprocity Agreements (NC-SARA), 212
  principles of ethics, 200–201
  social media, 212
  syllabus, 209
  vicarious liability, 209–210
Legon, R., 184
lesbian, gay, bisexual, transgender, queer, and other sexually marginalized groups (LGBTQ+), 52–53
liability, vicarious, 209–210
liberatory pedagogy, 29
lightly blended courses, 184
lightly hybrid courses, 184
Li, N., 50
lived experience and classroom content, 37–38
LMSs. *See* learning management systems (LMSs)
Lui, C., 71

M

Major, C. H., 221
managing
  materials, 158
  time, 157–158
mandated reporting/duty to warn, 204–205
manipulatives, 175
Martin, D., 13
Martin, M., 13
Marzano, R. J., 159, 162
Mason, R., 221
massive open online courses (MOOCs), 184–185
materials, managing, 158
Maykut, C., 21
McEwen, B. C., 183
McLaughlin, T., 73
McNeal, K., 48
Mehall, S., 36
Meltzer, Lynn, 158
mental health, 13–15
method of instruction, 109, 112
microaggressions, 32, 51
Microsoft OneDrive, 115
Microsoft Teams, 176
mission statement, 111
mobility differences, 96
modality, 9
Moodle, 101
moral distress, 201
Morin, Jack, 211
Mosley, Della, 27
Moyer, D. M., 183
multicultural aspects of online teaching
  age and generational influencers, 50
  disability status, 50
  ethnicity (including race), 50–51
  gender, 53
  identifying, 49–53
  language, 51–52
  religion and spirituality, 50
  sexual orientation, 52–53
  socioeconomic status, 52
multiculturalism, 117
multiple minority, 55
Musil, C. M., 49

N

National Center for Education Statistics, 167, 181
National Committee on Education by Radio, 182
National Committee on Science Education Standards and Assessment, 36
National Council for State Authorization Reciprocity Agreements (NC-SARA), 212
National Education Association, 62
National Society for Professional Engineers (NSPE), 115
"net-centric" learning approach, 22
netiquette, 114
Nickols, M., 22–23
Ni, S., 69–70
Noddings, N., 185
nonmaleficence, 200
nonnormative, 52
Norman, Jeremy, 156
Nth name selection, 172

O

Occupational Safety and Health Association (OSHA), 113
OCR. *See* optical character recognition (OCR)
O'Keefe, L., 56
online classroom
  course policies and procedures, 190
  creating, 189–191
  informal chatroom, 191
  structure, 66–67
  university/college resources, 191
  weekly announcement hub, 190
  weekly module folders, 190–191
online courses, 184–185
  description, 111
  design, 83–92
  historical overview, 84–86
  length, 112
  nature of, 112
  objectives, 113
  requirements, 114
  schedule, 116–117
  using school's system, 86–87
online education, 3–4, 7
  boundaries in, 210–212
  legal and ethical issues in, 199–213
  mastering technology for, 11
  preparation for, 12
online engagement framework, 187–189
  behavioral engagement, 188–189
  cognitive engagement, 188
  collaborative engagement, 189
  emotional engagement, 189
  social engagement, 187–188
online learning, 48–49, 181
  communication in, 186–187
  context of, 167–168
  correspondence learning utilizing postal service, 182
  definitions, 184–185
  diversity, equity, and inclusion in, 48–49
  evolution of, 181–185
  history of, in primary education, 156
  online engagement framework, 187–189
  relationship, connection, and communication in, 185–189
  through use of Internet, 183–184
  understanding, 84–85
  universal design for, 56
  utilizing radio and television, 182–183
online learning environments. *See also* learning management systems (LMSs)
  adding course content, 90
  communication in, 185–186
  creating, 190
  development of, 85–86
  good and bad practices, 88–90
  importance in recruiting practices, 218
  in student assessment, 161
  student engagement in, 187
  types of documents, 90–92
  user-centric design scaffolding, 88–90
  vs. storage closets, 87–92
online learning in higher education
  mastering technology in, 192
online pedagogical frameworks
  e-pedagogy, 22–23
  heutagogy, 21–22
online post-secondary education
  creating online classroom, 189–191
  evolution of distance education and online learning, 181–185
  overview, 181
  relationship, connection, and communication in online learning, 185–189
  technology in higher education, 192
online programs
  administration of, 215–224

clinical programs, 223
evaluation, 220–221
faculty and staff, 218–221
faculty and staff connection, 219–220
faculty and staff training and engagement, 219
information security, 222–223
leadership matters, 216–217
legal and ethical considerations, 222–223
recruiting and retention, 218
student engagement and support services, 221–222
student safety and crisis management, 223
online teaching
and e-pedagogy, 23
cost of, 10–11
professional fulfillment, 6–8
pros and cons of, 7
relationships, 9–10
virtual classroom, 7–8
work life, 5–6
online videos for remediation and extension, 178–179
ontological position, 19
optical character recognition (OCR), 101
othermothers, 30–31

P

Palmer, S. R., 183
para teachers, 76
Paris, D., 31
Parsons, P., 222
Pauldi, 205
PDF document, 102
pedagogy, 69
critical, 25–26
culturally responsive, 30
culturally sustaining, 31–32
defined, 19–20
effective teaching strategies across, 35–38
feminist, 28–29
intersectional, 28–29
liberatory, 29
traditional, 20
trauma-informed. *See* trauma-informed pedagogy
personal time, balancing work in, 13
Phelps, Y., 190
PHI. *See* protected health information (PHI)

Phillips, A., 48
Phillips, Caleb, 182
Pitman, Sir Isaac, 85, 182
platforms, 116
Plato, 224
policies and procedures, 62, 115, 190
Poll Everywhere website, 177–179
polling, 162, 176–177
Porche, M. V., 33
Portugal, L. M., 218
positionality, 23
positive reinforcement, 77
postal service, 182
postsecondary education
assessment in, 74–75
communication in, 68–69
community building in, 72–73
connectedness in, 72–73
online classroom management in, 64
presentations, 103
primary education, 155–165
assessment, 161–162
assisting students with technology, 157
communication, 160
history of online learning in, 156
online teaching and learning in, 155–165
remediation, 162–164
student engagement, 158–160
tutorials and instructional videos, 157–158
primary school
assessment in, 74
communication in, 68
community building in, 71
connectedness in, 71
online classroom management, 63–64
remediation in, 76
principles of ethics, 200–201
privileged communication, 203–204
proactive approach to digital accessibility, 97–98
problematic behaviors, 75–77
professional code of ethics, 115
professional fulfillment, 6–8
professionalism, 114–115
professional relationships, 10
protected health information (PHI), 113, 203, 206
Public Broadcasting Act, 182

Q

quick response (QR) codes, 179
Quizlet, 161
quizzes, 161

R

"racial battle fatigue," 33. *See also* racial trauma
racial trauma, 33
racism, 27, 32
Radio Act of 1912, 182
Radio Act of 1927, 182
radio and television
audio and visual media learning utilizing, 182–183
random selection, 171–173
challenges with, 172–173
process for, 172
ReadWriteThink, 169, 178
recordings
creating, 160
limiting length of, 160
recruiting and retention, 218
red flag, 51
Redmond, P., 187
relationships
online teaching, 9–10
professional, 10
student, 9–10
religion
and multicultural aspects of online teaching, 50
and spirituality, 50
remediation, 162–164
and student success, 75–78
chunking work, 163
constructivist, 75
defined, 75
direct instruction, 162
in primary school, 76
in secondary school, 76–77
instructionism, 75
learning styles, 163
self-assessment, 163–164
Remley, T. P., 201
remote environment
balancing time in, 13
balancing work in, 13
mental health in, 13–15
wellness in, 13–15
Renn, K. A., 53
required textbooks, 111–112
Roache, D., 219
Roberts, J. J., 110
Robertson, L., 73

Robertson, Q. M., 48
Rodriguez, A. J., 49
Rosen, J., 212
rubrics
   assignments and, 117
   example of, 117–120
   grading, 33, 117

S

SafeAssign, 115
safe spaces, 25–26, 186
safe zone workshops, 52
Salmon, G., 221
SARA Policy Manual, 212
scavenger hunts, 159
Schooling During the COVID-19 Pandemic, 215
Schwartz, H., 185
screen readers, 96, 101–104
screensharing, 176
Seaman, J., 183–184
secondary education, 167–180
   assessment, 176–177
   assisting students with technology, 168–169
   communication, 174–176
   context of technology and online learning, 167–168
   differentiation and extension, 177–179
   online teaching and learning in, 167–180
   student engagement, 169–174
secondary school
   assessment in, 74
   communication in, 68
   community building in, 71–72
   connectedness in, 71–72
   online classroom management in, 64
   remediation in, 76–77
"secondspace," 26
self-assessment, 163–164
self-determined learning, 20
semester, 65, 112
Sener, John, 192
Serdyukov, P., 22–23
sexism, 28, 37
sexual orientation, 52–53
Shainwald, E., 48
Shelton, K., 222
Sheppard, G., 204
Shin, R. Q., 77
Skype, 176
Smith, Frederick, 182
social constructivism, 72
social engagement, 187–188
social justice, 117
social location, 23
social media, 212
social sharing, 71
socioeconomic status, 52
speech-to-text functions, 101
spirituality
   and multicultural aspects of online teaching, 50
   and religion, 50
spreadsheets, 103
Stanny, C., 110
State Authorization Reciprocity Agreements (SARA), 212
Staying the Course: Online Education in the United States (Allen & Seaman), 183
storage closets, *vs.* online learning environments, 87–92
structure. *See* classroom structure
student-centered approaches, 38
student engagement, 158–160
   2-minute response, 173
   creating a virtual classroom, 159
   energy shifts, 169–170
   flipped classroom, 174
   guided notes, 159–160
   learning stations via breakout rooms, 159
   online teaching and learning in secondary education, 169–174
   random selection, 171–173
   scavenger hunts, 159
   student response groups, 170–171
student relationships, 9–10
student response groups, 170–171
student safety and crisis management, 223
student services office, 116
student success, 61–78
   and classroom management, 62–64
   as goal of educators, 61
   overview, 61
   through structure, 64–67
student success office, 116
Sue, D., 201
Sue, D. W., 201
Survey Monkey, 177–179
syllabus, 62, 209
   contact information for instructor in, 112
   course description in, 111
   course objectives, 113
   defined, 62, 109
   developing online, 109–164
   fundamental components of, 111
   importance of, 110–117
   importance to instructor, 110
   importance to student, 111
   method of instruction in, 112
   mission statement in, 111
   multicultural/ethical considerations regarding, 117
   required textbooks in, 111–112
   social justice considerations regarding, 117
   use of, 110–117
synchronous class, 50, 62, 112, 114, 187, 191
synchronous learning, 4, 184

T

Tarasoff v. Regents of the University of California, 205
teacher-centered educators, 38
teaching strategies
   building community, 36–37
   centering students, 38
   co-creating knowledge, 38
   connecting lived experience and classroom content, 37–38
   effective, across pedagogies, 35–38
   self-involvement of the educator, 38
Teaching to Transgress (hooks), 186
technocentrism, 22
technology
   assisting students with, 157, 168–169
   clear learning targets, 157
   context of, 167–168
   identification, 168
   training, 169
"The Hallway," 36
think, pair, share activity, 173
thirdspace, 26
TikTok, 167
time, managing, 157–158
Title IX Act, 203
Torrisi-Steele, G., 25
traditional courses, 183–184
traditional pedagogy, 20
training, 169
Trammell, B. A., 110
transactional distance, 70
transformational leadership, 217
trauma-informed educators, 33–34
trauma-informed pedagogy

educator self-care, 35
in practice, 33–34
trauma's impact on brain, 32–33
tutorials and instructional videos, 157–158
   managing materials, 158
   managing time, 157–158
   virtual classroom environment, 158
2-minute response strategy, 173

U

UDL. *See* universal design for learning (UDL)
UNESCO, 215
United States Census Bureau, 215
universal design for learning (UDL), 56, 98
   assistive technology, 100–101
   digital accessibility and, 98–101
   multiple means of engagement, 100
   multiple means of expression, 99
   multiple means of representation, 99
university/college resources, 191
University of Iowa, 182
University of Phoenix, 183
University of Wisconsin–Extension, 182
U.S. Bureau of Labor Statistics, 10
user-centric design scaffolding, 88–90

V

vendor resources, 87
verbal immediacy, 71
Vesely, P., 72
vicarious liability, 209–210
Vimeo, 169
virtual classroom, 192
   creating, 159
   delivery method, 8
   intangible factors for, 11
   large class size, 8–9
   locating right place, 11
   small class size, 8
virtual leadership competencies, 190
virtual learning, 182
virtual teams, 190
vision differences, 96
visuals, 175
voice command functions, 101

W

wait time, 173
Wang, V. C. X., 25
warm demander, 30
websites, 96, 102–104
weekly announcement hub, 190
weekly module folders, 190–191
Welfel, E., 202, 204
wellness, 13–15
Wheeler, A., 199
Wigmore test, 204
work life, 5–6
World Wide Web, 156, 183
writing style, 115

X

Xu, Y., 77

Y

Yan, Z., 73
YouTube, 167, 169

Z

Zembylas, M., 53
zone of proximal development, 76
Zoom, 116, 157, 176, 222

ABOUT THE EDITORS

Tricia M. Mikolon

Tricia M. Mikolon, Ph.D., CRC, LPC, BC-TMH earned her Ph.D. in counselor education and supervision from Regent University. Her master's degree is in rehabilitation counseling from the University of Scranton, and her Bachelor of Science degree is in psychology from Elizabethtown College. She is a Certified Rehabilitation Counselor and holds an LPC in Pennsylvania and is a Board Certified Telebehavioral Health Provider. Dr. Mikolon's interests include correctional fatigue, the impact of self-definition and coping skills on holistic recovery, and the use of art therapy techniques in counseling. She is employed in the Counseling Department at the University of the Cumberlands as an assistant professor and has been on numerous dissertation committees. Additionally, she retired from the Pennsylvania Department of Corrections as a psychological services specialist after 20 years. While there, she served on the Critical Incident Stress Management Team (CISM) and provided instruction to staff on various training topics including mental health issues, suicide prevention, reinforcing positive behaviors, and cognitive behavioral interventions on both the student and instructor training levels. She has authored works on rehabilitation counseling and corrections fatigue and has presented on the topics of corrections fatigue, motivational interviewing, and co-occurring disorders. She is an active member of Chi Sigma Iota, the American Counseling Association, The Fraternal Order of Police (Pennsylvania), and Psi Chi.

Tammy Hatfield

Tammy Hatfield, Psy.D., HSP earned a Doctor of Psychology degree in clinical psychology from an American Psychological Association (APA) accredited program at Spalding University in Louisville, Kentucky, a Master of Science degree in clinical psychology from Murray State University, and a Bachelor of Arts degree in psychology from the University of Kentucky. She is a licensed psychologist with the health service provider designation in the state of Kentucky. Currently, Dr. Hatfield is a professor who teaches online in the School of Social and Behavioral Sciences at University of the Cumberlands. Dr. Hatfield's areas of expertise and interest include online teaching, intersectional feminist pedagogy, critical theories, socially just pedagogies, social justice, prevention of violence against women and children, individual and cultural diversity, identity development, advocacy, gender studies, body image, psychological assessment, first generation students, and Appalachian culture. Dr. Hatfield currently serves as the president of the Kentucky Psychological Foundation, and as an ambassador for the Kentucky Psychological Association. She is a past president of the Kentucky Mental Health Counselor's Association and a former vice president of the Kentucky Counseling Association. She is a member of the American Counseling Association, the Association for Counselor Education and Supervision, the Association for Multicultural Counseling and Development, the Kentucky Psychological Association, and the Kentucky Counseling Association.

ABOUT THE CONTRIBUTORS

Portia Allie-Turco (Chapter 2)

Portia Allie-Turco, LMHC, NCC, is a doctoral student in the School of Social and Behavioral Sciences at University of the Cumberlands. Her professional experience includes the roles of licensed mental health counselor, counseling clinic director, college lecturer, chief diversity officer, and clinical consultant. Her research and clinical focus is on healing generational, historical, and racial trauma.

Adrienne Baggs (Chapter 10)

Dr. Adrienne Baggs completed her PhD at the University of Florida while specializing in multicultural health, heath disparities, and spiritual issues counseling. She is currently an associate professor of Counselor Education and Supervision at the University of Cumberlands where she regularly serves as a subject matter expert in advanced educational research and mindfulness-based approaches in counseling and conducts research on mindfulness. She has extensive clinical experience in a variety of settings including schools, prisons, substance abuse recovery centers, college and university counseling centers, and private practice.

Melissa Brennan (Chapter 2)

Melissa Brennan, MA, LPC, is currently completing her PhD in Counselor Education and Supervision at University of the Cumberlands. Her areas of interest include school counseling, social justice, gender studies, diversity and equality, child and adolescent counseling, and online teaching and counseling.

Marina Bunch (Chapter 12)

Marina Bunch, MA, LMHC, is a licensed mental health counselor and qualified supervisor in the state of Florida. She is also a PhD candidate at the University of the Cumberlands' Counselor Education and Supervision program. Her research interests include leadership development through a life-span lens and attachment-related psychopathology. Professionally, Marina specializes in infant and early childhood mental health and has presented on various related topics. Marina currently holds the position of chief operating officer at a private nonprofit organization in Sarasota, Florida.

Jason Creekmore (Chapter 8)

Jason Creekmore, EdD earned his doctorate in educational leadership in 2012 and also hold several teaching and administrative certifications. His areas of research include student motivation, program evaluation, and principal leadership styles. He has served seven years as a middle school teacher, five years as a middle school principal, and eight years as a college professor, the last four of which serving as associate dean. He also enjoys serving as a Council for the Accreditation of Educator Preparation reviewer for teacher preparation programs across the nation.

Tiffany Darby (Chapter 3)

Dr. Tiffany Darby earned a PhD in Counseling and Human Development Services from Kent State University. She is an associate professor serving as the director of Doctoral Field Experiences at the University of the Cumberlands and the owner of an online counseling private practice, Darby Counseling & Consulting, LLC. Dr. Darby is an independently licensed counselor in Ohio, Pennsylvania, and Kentucky; a clinical supervisor; and a qualitative researcher interested in culturally responsive practices, supervision, and online counseling.

Shannon Deaton (Chapter 9)

Dr. Shannon Deaton, EdD, is dean in the School of Education at University of the Cumberlands. He co-authored a book on education in 2015 titled *The Active Learning Classroom*, and he has published numerous other scholarly articles in the areas of assessment, educational technology, and leadership. Shannon lives with his wife and three daughters in Corbin, Kentucky.

Alcia Freeman (Chapter 3)

Dr. Alcia Freeman, PhD, NCC, began her career as a counselor educator in 2018. She is a licensed professional counselor in the state of Michigan and a nationally certified counselor. She has focused her career on promoting the mental health and academic advancement of underserved populations.

Megan Fogel (Chapter 6)

Megan Fogel, MLT, is an instructional designer at the Ohio State University helping to develop online courses for the university's fully online degree programs. After completing a bachelor of arts degree from Ohio State, she received her master of learning technologies degree through one of the aforementioned Ohio State Online programs. She teaches an undergraduate learning strategies course in an online format through the Dennis Learning Center at Ohio State. She has spent recent years researching digital accessibility and universal design for learning, delivering workshops on the topic, and helping to build more accessible online courses.

Sarah Johansson (Chapter 2)

Sarah Johansson, MEd, earned her master's degree in school counseling from Loyola University in Maryland and is a currently completing her PhD in counselor education and supervision at the University of the Cumberlands. She has worked as a K–12 school counselor for over a decade where she has focused on student advocacy, specifically related to LGBTQ+, poverty, equity, and inclusion.

Tara Kroger (Chapter 5)

Tara Koger, MA, has held a variety of roles at Ohio State University, beginning as an instructor in education and human ecology and moving into an instructional design role within the Office of Distance Education and eLearning. She launched and managed one of the largest faculty iPad professional development programs to support the university's adoption of a one-to-one student device program across six campuses.

Matthew Lyons (Chapter 12)

Dr. Matthew Lyons is a professor and dean of the School of Social and Behavioral Sciences at the University of the Cumberlands. He earned his PhD in counselor education at the Ohio University. Dr. Lyons previously held faculty and leadership positions at Central Michigan University, the University of New Orleans, and Palmer Theological Seminary. His research interests include leadership and human spirituality.

Laura Moore (Chapter 10)

Laura Moore, MEd, NBCC, LPC, earned a Bachelor of Arts degree in psychology from Transylvania University and a Master of Education degree in counseling and human services, with a specialization in mental health counseling, from Lindsey Wilson College. She is currently pursuing a PhD in counselor education and supervision at the University of the Cumberlands. She is licensed by the Kentucky Board of Licensed Professional Counselors to practice counseling independently in the state of Kentucky. She has met the professional counseling standards of the National Board of Certified Counselors since April 4, 2011.

Brooke Nelson Murphy (Chapter 7)

Brooke Nelson Murphy, MS, LPC, NCC, CCTP, graduated from Athens State University with a Bachelor of Science degree in biology and chemistry and from Troy University with a Master of Science degree in counseling and psychology, and is currently a doctoral student pursuing her PhD in counselor education and supervision. She is a licensed professional counselor in the state of Alabama, works in a private practice setting, and previously worked as an adjunct professor in the Pharmacy Technician Program at Virginia College. Her recent research interests focus on trauma sensitivity training and education.

Kristin Page (Chapter 1)

Kristin Page, PhD, LMHC, NCC, has her PhD in counselor education from the University of Florida and is an associate professor and director of the master's programs at the University of the Cumberlands. Her areas of current research include best practices in online education, recidivism and mentally ill offenders, the language of substance use, and the impact of trauma on first responders. She regularly teaches online in the master's in counseling program.

Gary Patton (Chapter 11)

Gary L. Patton, PhD, LPC, earned a doctorate in counselor education and supervision at Ohio University. As a licensed professional counselor, he served on a hospital ethics committee for 26 years and currently serves as an investigator for the West Virginia Board of Examiners in Counseling. He teaches ethics in the doctoral program of the Department of Counseling at the University of the Cumberlands.

Debra Perez (Chapter 4)

Debra M. Perez, MA, LPCC, BCTP-II, SCPG, received her master's degree in professional counseling from New Mexico Highlands University. She is board certified in telebehavioral health and holds a special certification in problem gambling treatment and aromatherapy. As a counselor, she serves rural New Mexico, providing counseling online, while also teaching counselor education as an adjunct professor. She has authored numerous book chapters and articles, as well as acted as editor on a textbook. She is currently a doctoral candidate at the University of the Cumberlands.

Tera Rumbaugh Crawford (Chapter 1)

Tera Rumbaugh Crawford graduated from the University of Louisville's education bachelor's program and CACREP-accredited counseling master's program. She is currently pursuing her PhD in counselor education and supervision at the University of the Cumberlands. Her research interests include school counseling, mental health practices in schools, and childhood trauma. Tera has taught elementary students in-person for seven years, elementary students online for one year, and masters students online as a teaching assistant.

Diedre Wade (Chapter 4)

Diedre Wade, MA, LPCC-S, LPCC-S, is a licensed professional clinical counselor supervisor in Kentucky and a licensed mental health counselor in Florida. She graduated from Liberty University with a master's in professional counseling in 2012. Diedre has experience working in drug court, inpatient behavioral health, and residential treatment, all while working in her private practice. She is a counselor education and supervision PhD student at the University of the Cumberlands.

CPSIA information can be obtained
at www.ICGtesting.com
Printed in the USA
LVHW051455020323
740783LV00009B/1067

9 781793 524973